# THE DISCIPLINE OF POPULAR GOVERNMENT:

## *Lord Salisbury's Domestic Statecraft, 1881—1902*

# THE DISCIPLINE OF POPULAR GOVERNMENT:

*Lord Salisbury's Domestic Statecraft,*
*1881—1902*

## PETER MARSH

*Associate Professor of History, Syracuse University*

**THE HARVESTER PRESS, SUSSEX**
**HUMANITIES PRESS, NEW JERSEY**

First published in 1978 by
THE HARVESTER PRESS LIMITED
*Publisher: John Spiers*
2 Stanford Terrace, Hassocks, Sussex

**British Library Cataloguing in Publication Data**

Marsh, Peter
    The discipline of popular government.
    1. Salisbury, Robert Arthur Gascoyne-Cecil,
    *Marquess of*
    I. Title
    941.081'092'4          DA564.S2

    ISBN 0-85527-980-X

Humanities Press Inc.
ISBN 0-391-00874-9

Photosetting by Thomson Press (India) Ltd., New Delhi
Printed in England by
Redwood Burn Ltd., Trowbridge and Esher

# ACKNOWLEDGEMENTS

In the course of this study, I have received cooperation, help, counsel and kindness from a host of sources. I wish to acknowledge the gracious permission of Her Majesty Queen Elizabeth II to quote from and cite the papers of Queen Victoria and King Edward VII in the Royal Archives, and of the present Lord Salisbury for similar permission with regard to my use of his great-grandfather's papers. I appreciate the warm welcome which Ms. Jane Langton and her colleagues in the Round Tower of Windsor Castle have always extended to me, and also the kindness of Lord and Lady Antrim and Dr. T. S. Wragg. I am grateful for permission from the National Trust at Hughenden Manor, Lord Cairns, the University of Birmingham, Lord Chilston and the Kent County Council, the National Union of Conservative Associations, the Trustees of the Chatsworth Settlement, Lord St. Aldwyn and the Gloucestershire Record Office, Lady Onslow, the Duke of Rutland, the Directors of the Goodwood Estate Company Limited and the West Sussex County Archivist and Record Office, Lord Hambleden, Mr. P. Gwynne James and the Hereford and Worcester County Record Office, Lord Londonderry, Lord Balfour, Lord Harrowby, and Lord Scarsdale, to quote from and cite papers in their possession. Mr. G. D. M. Block, Ms. Susan Brown, Professor D. W. R. Bahlman, Ms. Christine Woodland, Professor Stephen J. Tonsor, and a succession of graduate assistants at Syracuse University, particularly Ms. Judith Loyman, have helped me in a variety of ways. Mr. J. F. A. Mason and the staff at the library of Christ Church, Oxford, the Inter-library Loan staff at the Syracuse University Libraries, and the archivists at Hatfield House have given me patient help and kindness over a succession of years. Dean H. J. Hanham, Dr. Gerard Evans, Professor Donald Akenson, Mr. Mark Dean, Professor John Vincent, Dr. Maurice Cowling, Professor Michael Hurst, Dr. David Brooks, Professor Richard Soloway, Professor Emmet Larkin, Dr. Barbara Malament, and Professor Richard Rempel have read and given me invaluable advice on successive chapters of this study; of course, they bear no responsibility for its final shape. Finally, my thanks are due to the American Council of Learned Societies, the American Philosophical Society, the Senate Research Committee and the Appleby-Mosher Fund of Syracuse University, the Master and Fellows of Emmanuel College, Cambridge, and especially to the Earhart Foundation, without whose generous support I could not have carried this study through.

PETER MARSH
*Syracuse, New York*

The Duchess of Devonshire to Margot Asquith: 'We have both married angels; when Hartington dies he will go straight to Heaven'—pointing her first finger high above her head—'and when Mr. Asquith dies he will go straight there, too: not so Lord Salisbury', pointing her finger with a ⌐ diving movement to the floor.

MARGOT ASQUITH, Autobiography, I, 141

# CONTENTS

TO STEPHEN

who pointed out to me that the biggest
nerve in the body is in the backbone

# CHAPTER 1

# *DEFIANCE*

And what you want, to bring Conservatism in touch with the people, if you will allow me to say so with all deference, is simply this: not that you will flatter & knuckle down to them but go before them, in the strength of your own principles and advocate those principles, & so bring yourselves face to face with the people.

*a delegate from West Bradford to the 1886 Annual Conference of the National Union of Conservative Associations.*

When Disraeli died on 19 April 1881, the Conservative party had little but the memory of an inimitable man to guide it. Twelve months before, it had been subjected to a devastating electoral defeat. The spirit in its shattered ranks was stirred soon afterward by the pluck of its physically decaying leader, by the revelation over the Bradlaugh affair of the instability of the Liberal majority, and by the floundering of Gladstone's Government over Ireland. But the defeat of 1880 had been so unexpected, at least in its magnitude, that bewilderment and loss of confidence could not be quickly dispelled. Had the victory of 1874 been a lucky accident? Was the natural condition of the Conservative party to be in a minority, as it had been for the generation before that? Was Disraeli's vision of it as a popular party a chimera?

Conservatives found these doubts all the more sobering because Britain was acquiring a popular electorate. The Conservatives themselves had given the vote in 1867 to all male householders in borough constituencies, and the Liberals intended to make male household suffrage universal before the term of the new Parliament expired. Household suffrage would fall substantially short of universal suffrage. Still, if it was not quite yet democracy, it was certainly popular government. Of the three general elections since the Reform Act of 1867, the Conservatives had lost two; and extension of household suffrage to the counties was commonly expected to make their electoral task still harder.

Belying general expectations, the electorate created by that extension proceeded, with two short-lived interruptions, to install predominantly Conservative Governments for twenty years. Except for the last three years during which the phenomenon disintegrated, these Governments were led by a prime minister, the third Marquis of Salisbury, whose views and character only made the phenomenon more remarkable.

Lord Salisbury was more of a diehard than any Conservative leader since his godfather, the Duke of Wellington. The particular object of his hostility and of his fears was popular government. He had made his political debut as a scathing critic of Disraeli's efforts to accommodate his party to the coming of democracy. He was an aristocrat as much by intellect as by birth, and he disparaged the demagogic arts. Of febrile psychological makeup, socially ill at ease outside his family, a man who retired often nightly to his country house and was happiest when alone behind thick double doors locked and bolted, he was an unlikely manager of men. A man of unshakable religious conviction and stern moral probity, hostile to social collectivism, he was out of sympathy with most of the cultural and philosophical currents reshaping English thought at the end of the nineteenth century.

Yet he led the Conservatives to their longest tenure of power since the fall of Wellington. He won more elections more decisively than any other nineteenth-century prime minister since the Great Reform Act.[1] He held the office of prime minister longer than any other man of any party has done since 1827.[2] He proved himself a master without superior in the arts of Cabinet management. He oversaw the creation of a machinery of party organization which subsequent Conservatives learned to regard as a model. Moreover, for all his arch-Conservatism, it was Salisbury who formed and consolidated an alliance with dissident Liberals, the ardently sought but elusive objective of his predecessors and rivals, which enabled Conservatives to replace Liberals as the normal majority party.

It is a historical commonplace that during Salisbury's leadership of the Conservative party the general direction of British politics, mildly Liberal since 1830, turned toward the Conservatives. But historians have either underestimated or completely ignored Salisbury's contribution to the change. Obviously a shift of such a nature, in the lay of the political land, could not be brought about by one man. Some historians have kept their eyes on the social and electoral soil to the neglect of the generals who marched their troops over it. Others have been mesmerized by Disraeli, the glory of whose exploits grew only greater after his death. But as for Salisbury, historians have been deceived by the inconspicuous character of his leadership, by his aloofness and by the aura of honour which surrounded him. They have been distracted, as contemporaries were, by his more glamorous colleagues, Lord Randolph Churchill and Joseph Chamberlain, and also by his own absorption with and mastery of foreign affairs. With a few outstanding exceptions,[3] historians have failed to see in Salisbury an astute and often devastatingly skilful general in domestic party warfare. The tactical mastery which he displayed in dropping Churchill from the Cabinet in 1886 has won repeated but reluctant admiration as a singular episode rather than as a heightened illustration of Salisbury's usual capacity. Those few who have appreciated that capacity have tended to convey too shallow an impression of his purposes.

This book will explore the intentions of Lord Salisbury in securing for himself the leadership of a party with which he had been repeatedly disillusioned and of a country whose newly popular constitution he profoundly distrusted. It will analyse his resolution of the essentially moral tension in the relationship between leader and followers which his uneasiness about the Conservative party and his distrust of popular government exacerbated. It will examine the nature of his leadership including the agents and bases of power upon which he relied. It will describe the stages through which his pursuit of his purposes went, stages which were defined by the limiting forces to which he had to accommodate himself. Finally, it will assess his accomplishment. It is a study in domestic politics. Foreign affairs, to which Salisbury devoted so much of his time and talent, will be a strictly subordinate concern, discussed only for their bearing upon his power at home, whether in the Cabinet, in Parliament, or in the country. Similarly, the recesses of Salisbury's very private personality will be discussed only as they bear upon his domestic statecraft. By temperament, by philosophy, and by his rank which kept him out of the House of Commons, Salisbury was both inclined and obliged to exercise his leadership to an unusual extent indirectly, through and in concert with his colleagues and lieutenants and the party's organizational machinery. He will therefore often be offstage in the following account. It is a story of discipline: of how Lord Salisbury attempted to curb the impulses of popular government, and of how, in the process, it also disciplined him.

## i. The Change of Command

Nothing in Salisbury's career prior to the death of Disraeli had proven the younger man's capacity for party leadership. There was, on the contrary, much in that career to indicate that he would have considerable difficulty in leading the Conservative party as now educated by Disraeli, and in leading it to power.

The two most famous rebellions in the annals of the Conservative party had been Disraeli's against Sir Robert Peel in 1846 over the Corn Laws, and Salisbury's against Disraeli over the Reform Bill of 1867. Disraeli demonstrated how rebellion could be used to mark oneself out as a future leader. He not only voiced the opposition which many inarticulate Conservative backbenchers felt toward Peel's proposal to repeal the Corn Laws. He mobilized the voting power of Peel's Conservative critics and drove him from office. Salisbury's personal acceptability as a rebel leader in 1867 was much greater than that of Disraeli, a blatant adventurer, in 1846. But Salisbury refused to play the part. Though he carried Lord Carnarvon and General Peel with him in resigning from the Cabinet, he did not attempt to organize the forces in the Conservative party which were suspicious of where Disraeli was leading them. Nor did Salisbury concert forces with the potential Adullamite and Whig opponents of the Bill in the Liberal party. The only immediate result of his resignation from the Cabinet was to render the Bill still more radical. When, following Salisbury's example, Conservative opponents of a sizeable expansion of the electorate withdrew their support from the Ministry, Disraeli felt obliged to bid for support from advanced Liberals in the House of Commons by accepting amendments which widened the Bill's scope.[4]

Tactically, then, Salisbury's resignation was unwise, the action of an inexperienced Parliamentarian. More to the point, his reluctance to organize a rebellion seemed to indicate that he was not of the stuff from which leaders are made. His stature was enhanced by his conduct in 1867, but as a man of principle 'too honest ... for his party and his time,'[5] not as a practical alternative or successor to Disraeli. He deepened the impression that he lacked political vigour when his father died in 1868 and he faced the prospect of removal from the centre of political battle to the House of Lords. His departure from the Commons was viewed with dismay not only by diehard Tories but by some Whigs including Lord Grey who shared his revulsion over 1867.[6] The power to refuse an inherited title had never been tested, he was urged to try, and he considered doing so.[7] But he decided against it. He was, he explained, 'so disgusted with the course the Tories had pursued in respect to Dizzy's Reform Bill that I did not think it worth the trouble to stay in the House of Commons'.[8]

By philosophy as well as by temperament, Salisbury was an unlikely leader for the Conservatives to adopt because until the mid-1870s he rejected, and he never wholeheartedly adopted, the strategy which Disraeli taught the party to accept. It was a strategy derived from faith in the power for good of social relations transcending class bounds, particularly between the natural governing classes vaguely defined and the working class. From the Young England movement in the 1840s through sporadic collaborations with Cobden and Bright in the 1850s to the 1867 Reform Bill, this Disraelian strategy had expressed itself in willingness to adopt selected Liberal or Radical measures.

To Salisbury it was deeply repugnant. As a boy in the heyday of Peel, he had asked what the differences were between Conservative and

Liberal; and when told, he promptly responded that he was "an *illiberal* Tory."[9] For twenty years after his entry into Parliament in 1853 as M.P. for the family borough of Stamford, Salisbury was the Jeremiah of the high Tories, inveighing against the the conduct of Disraeli as he danced along the banks of the mainstream of British politics toward democracy. What offended Salisbury even more than the patent democratizing implications of the second Reform Act was Disraeli's success in drawing the Conservative party on to support such a measure. It was a seduction, dextrously brought about, willingly submitted to. It was the logical consummation of forty years of surrendering at the behest of the party's leaders what the party believed in: Roman Catholic disabilities in 1829, the Corn Laws in 1846, tariff protection again in 1852, Jewish disabilities in 1859, and now the sharply restricted franchise.

Though he never ceased to regret the large step taken by the second Reform Act toward democracy, Salisbury began in the mid-1870s to demonstrate fresh determination to defend the interests he had at heart as well as possible under the new circumstances. He led the Conservative diehards in the Commons from a distance, urging them for example to abstain on the Irish University Bill of 1873[10] for fear that otherwise Gladstone's Ministry might be replaced by a minority Conservative Government like that of 1867 which would try once again to hold onto office by currying the favour of one Liberal faction or other. His efforts on this occasion were not successful. Gladstone was defeated; but, to Salisbury's relief, Disraeli refused to form a Government, preferring to force Gladstone's tired and now tarnished Ministry to drag out its days a little longer.

The restraint which Disraeli displayed in 1873 relieved Salisbury, and made him more willing than he would otherwise have been to accept office under Disraeli after the Conservative victory in the general election of 1874. The two men continued to view each other warily, but with a determination to work together as long as that was at all possible. They took care to avoid rupture over the Public Worship Regulation Bill of 1874 though they disagreed on it.[11] When their difference became acute in 1877 over the Eastern Question, Salisbury repelled the thought of resignation. Lord Carnarvon, who had resigned with him in 1867 and shared some of his feelings on foreign policy now, suggested the possibility; but Salisbury retorted that resignation was 'a card which could not be played twice by the same persons.'[12] Unlike Carnarvon who remained a maverick in the Conservative party, Salisbury had begun to appreciate the counter-productivity of such behaviour. He was also discovering the dividends of loyalty, particularly the influence it earned within the Cabinet.

Eventually it was the Eastern Question that drew Salisbury and Disraeli together. Salisbury came to the conclusion that the mainsprings of Disraeli's thought about foreign policy—insistence on the national interest, and concern about British prestige—were sound. Disraeli's notions for applying these principles could be 'featherheaded' as Salisbury continued to remark.[13] Still, he found Disraeli open-minded and capable of shrewd judgement; and it became Salisbury's function to examine and to reject or clarify and apply Disraeli's promptings. For his part, Disraeli found in Salisbury a natural craftsman in the conduct of foreign relations, a colleague who mastered every subject he took up, a powerful debater, above all a man of courage. Had he at last found a Minister who embodied his youthful ideal of the aristocratic ruler, self-possessed, with great talents, devoted to the service of his country? In the last two years of the Ministry after Salisbury was transferred from the India to the Foreign Office, the two men moved into a close relationship, the younger man admiring the old prime minister's spirit and knowledge of the ways of the world, the old man relying on his Foreign Secretary's powers of intellect and application to work and enjoying his steel as a disputant.

The Ministry came to its shattering end in the general election of 1880. The Liberals renewed their triumph of 1868, piling up a majority of 112 over the Conservatives alone and of 50 over the possible combined opposition of Conservatives and Irish Nationalists. What accounted for the defeat? Salisbury's attempts to answer this question in correspondence with his Chief indicated that he had acquired a sound sense about elections. He put his finger on the depression in agriculture and trade,[14] and went on to question the capacity of the current crew of party organizers, whose sanguine predictions had misled the Cabinet into calling a general election sooner than necessary. These comments could have been made by any knowledgeable Conservative who was reluctant to admit that the electorate were dissatisfied with the performance of the Conservative Government. Salisbury felt no such reluctance, even about his own performance as Foreign Secretary. He believed that the electorate had condemned his foreign policy, and was not surprised by the reaction.[15] He was himself uneasy about the showy character of his course of action over the Middle East in 1878, which he defended as unfortunately necessary in order to put Britain on a clearcut path after two years of indecision by his predecessor.

On second thought, Salisbury found some consolation in the election results. The size of the Liberal majority might indicate a shift of grim proportions in a Radical direction in the desires of the electorate, fulfilling his forebodings in 1867.[16] On the other hand, Gladstone would have his work cut out for him controlling so many M.P.s, some of them impatient for results because of the greatness of their victory, all of them less likely to subordinate their personal inclinations to the party whips when the chances of the Government falling from power seemed remote.

Salisbury also hoped that the lurch to the left would stiffen Conservatives' willingness for resistance: as he commented to Disraeli, 'many of our friends want frightening.'[17]

What saved Conservatives from complete demoralization as they surveyed the wreckage was the indomitable spirit of their Chief. Disraeli roused the thinned ranks of his supporters at the opening of the new Parliament by promising, however well he had earned repose, to continue to lead them in battle. Some thought that his physical strength would not be equal to more than sporadic personal appearances, leaving day-to-day management to his lieutenants in Lords and Commons. He soon dispelled this expectation. It was Salisbury, exhausted from two years at the Foreign Office, who was out of commission. The old leader shamed younger peers by the tenacity with which he defied the long, hot summer of 1880 and threaded a way for the Conservative majority in the House of Lords through the complexities of the legislation the new Government sent up, rejecting the Irish Compensation for Arrears Bill, amending the Burials Bill, and letting the Hares and Rabbits Bill through despite the anguish of sporting landlords. Sir Stafford Northcote's mild leadership of the party in the Commons soon provoked ardent spirits to appeal over his head to Disraeli. The leadership of the party continued to be vested totally in him.

Yet he and the rest of the party recognized that he would not live to form another Government, that the party must look for a new leader. Ambiguous to the end, Disraeli encouraged the hopes of Salisbury and Northcote. He gave Northcote heart by reiterating to him Northcote's own strategy for handling the Whigs, 'making them seem to take the initiative and supporting them rather than taking it ourselves and putting them in the distasteful position of having to desert their own party and join the Tories.' He even talked to Northcote about who should be dropped from the Cabinet 'when you form a Ministry.'[18] Yet Northcote was well aware that this did not amount to clear endorsement. He may have sensed that Disraeli talked to him as a subordinate but to Salisbury as a partner. He probably had wind of Disraeli's encouragement of the 'Fourth party', the quartet of young M.P.s led by Lord Randolph Churchill who were impatient with the restraining hand Northcote gave the party in the Commons.

As for Salisbury, Disraeli spoke to him of the pleasure with which he looked forward to Salisbury's becoming leader in the House of Lords,[19] and he left the impression that leadership of the entire party would follow. But, as with Northcote, Disraeli never went beyond broad hints. For the agreement between Disraeli and Salisbury on matters of policy was limited to foreign and imperial affairs: or, as Arthur Balfour put it, 'to the last they resembled each other (so far as I could see) in little except courage, patriotism, and wit.'[20] On domestic affairs, particularly on the strategy to be followed when, as in 1867 and now, the party found itself in a minority, the two men had not achieved a meeting of minds. The repetition with which, after the election, Salisbury urged upon Disraeli the need for stiff tactics in opposing the Government revealed his uneasiness about Disraeli's tendencies, an uneasiness which Disraeli undoubtedly recognized and reciprocated.

The initiative in the House of Lords for selecting Disraeli's successor came, with becoming discretion, from the second tier of leaders. Lord Cranbrook, Secretary of State for War and then India in the late Ministry, raised the question with Salisbury in October of 1880.[21] Cranbrook had no love for Northcote, who had been chosen instead of him to lead the Commons when Disraeli went to the Lords;[22] he was an orator who appreciated Salisbury's trenchancy of speech; and, like Salisbury, he was a spirited Conservative and a high churchman. Salisbury's response to Cranbrook was restrained but encouraging.[23]

Cranbrook immediately wrote to the Duke of Richmond, the highest-ranking peer in the party, having served as leader in the Lords during Gladstone's first Ministry. According to traditional etiquette, Richmond would have to waive his claims before Salisbury could succeed to the leadership of the upper House; but Cranbrook understood that Richmond would feel no reluctance in doing so. Richmond responded promptly and favourably though without conspicuous enthusiasm.[24] He also conveyed the information about Salisbury's willingness to Lord Cairns, Lord Chancellor under Disraeli and Richmond's closest political friend. Richmond and Cairns had already discussed the question, and, after each had established that the other waived his claim, they agreed that Salisbury was the man.[25]

In the House of Commons, the initiative for a Salisbury succession came from quite a different quarter. The departure of Disraeli and Cranbrook to the Lords in 1876 had left the front bench in the Commons to able but cautious respectabilities. They were accustomed to the rococo colour of Disraeli, having learned that it masked an essentially moderate politician. They felt no comparable security about Salisbury; and those who were undecided between Salisbury and Northcote on their merits were inclined toward the latter by the practical desirability of a leader who sat in the House of Commons. It was from the Fourth party that a campaign to secure Salisbury as Disraeli's successor was launched. In the autumn of 1880, Sir John Gorst, precariously combining Fourth party loyalties with direction of the Conservative national organization, conveyed his suspicions of Northcote's wish for an alliance with Whigs to Salisbury, and applauded a speech he had given at Taunton.[26] Lord Randolph Churchill canvassed on Salisbury's behalf among the regular Conservative rank and file in the Commons.[27] Arthur Balfour, nephew of Salisbury and intent to forward his claims, was the first to voice the Fourth party's criticism of Northcote in public.[28] Balfour kept his Fourth party *confrères* and his uncle in touch with each other. Salisbury cautiously encouraged the alliance, and accepted Churchill's invitation to deliver one of his first public addresses since the general election, in Churchill's constituency of Woodstock.

The weeks of increasing enfeeblement which preceded Disraeli's death did not resolve the party's mind on the succession. As soon as Disraeli died, Salisbury acquired outspoken support beyond the ranks of the Fourth party, most prominently from one of the leading metropolitan Conservative newspapers, the *Standard*.[29] But opposition to him became outspoken also. Frederick Greenwood, editor of the Conservative *St. James's Gazette*, opposed the selection of Salisbury as leader even of the Lords for fear that he would destroy all hope of cooperation with Whigs and moderate Liberals against the Radicals.[30] Opposition to Northcote from other quarters was at least as strong. The party moved quickly toward a compromise, whereby Salisbury would lead in the Lords, Northcote would lead in the Commons, and for the party as a whole the two would provide joint leadership.

It was an unhappy if inevitable solution. It would certainly deprive the party of clear leadership, and might exacerbate its divisions. The most recent precedent for a dual leadership, the Liberals' experience after Gladstone retired in 1875, when Granville led in the Lords and Hartington in the Commons, was not encouraging. The compromise did not go unchallenged. The selection of Salisbury as leader in the Lords went smoothly enough; though even in the Conservative peers' assembly there was silent opposition, and Cranbrook was surprised to discover in conversation with Richmond as they walked toward the meeting that Richmond was disappointed about but resigned to the selection of Salisbury instead of himself.[31] There was no need for a meeting of the Conservatives in the House of Commons since Northcote was already leader there; and no assembly of the combined Parliamentary party was planned. The challenge to the settlement came from Salisbury's supporters, first in the Council of the National Union of Conservative Associations, then from the *Standard*.[32] Salisbury did not encourage the challenges, for they only irritated his critics and bred sympathy for his rival. The decision as to who would become prime minister and hence leader of the party when it succeeded in toppling the Liberals was left to time.

## ii. The Outlook of the New Leader

The new leader in the House of Lords was a delicately wrought piece of psychological sculpture. Physically he had already begun to assume the massiveness which, added to over six feet of height, a thick beard, high forehead and meditative eyes, would enhance the impression he later conveyed of imperturbable gravity. The impression was deceptive, like his lineage. Everyone remembered his illustrious forefathers in whom the great Elizabeth and James I had placed their confidence, but forgot the light weathercocks of the following century and a half.[33] It was not until the seventh Earl and first Marquis of Salisbury joined William Pitt's Ministry in 1783 that the family reasserted its political respectability and launched its modern tradition of Toryism; and the influence of the first two Marquises rested largely on their social position.

As a young man, the third Marquis of Salisbury was disabled by neuroses strong enough to bring his undergraduate career at Oxford to a hurried conclusion and to send him round the world on a rehabilitating cruise. A dark streak of depression had run through successive generations of Cecils. The third Marquis endured an acutely unhappy childhood after the death of his mother when he was nine. Whatever the roots of his neuroses, they were brought under control by a profound religious faith hostile to the speculations which his otherwise restless intellect could raise, and by a radiantly happy, upper middle class marriage. What he called his 'nerve storms' grew gradually less frequent and intense, his periods of depression shorter and more shallow. He began to use his wit quietly to woo as well as publicly to deride.

Still, a sense of living in a beleaguered enclave, of having to keep the forces of hostile barbarism at bay, pervaded his mature outlook. What he said of science could have been applied to his view of civilization:

> We live in a small bright oasis of knowledge surrounded on all sides by a vast unexplored region of impenetrable mystery.[34]

In dealing with people outside his intimate family circle, he was always on guard. The root of his politics was fear. The threatening aspect of the world as Salisbury saw it made him a fighter. Though he had no faith that things would improve, though he was contemptuous of optimism, he could not rest in in-action. Not quite despairing, he fought; when he lost, he would be plunged into gloom, only to rise and fight again.

The structure of Salisbury's political thought as he took up the Conservative leadership in the Lords was of a piece with his psychological makeup.[35] Its object was to stiffen the defences of the civilized order where alone he felt secure, an order based on the ownership of property, particularly landed property, an order conducted by men of education and elevated by the Established Church. The object was unoriginal. But he pursued it with a sternly emotionless, analytical and empirical style of argument remarkable in a Tory. The physical science which Salisbury found most attractive was chemistry, because it offered little play to "scientific imagination."[36] In a similar spirit, his political argument was divest of the appeals to traditional sentiments, real or imaginary, which had characterized Tory rhetoric since Bolingbroke. Gone any trace of Burkean romanticism. Similarly he put aside Disraeli's evocative language about the bonds of attachment which should exist between the natural aristocracy and the people. Instead, he appealed to hard self-interest, which he broadened for popular consumption by stressing the dependence of labour upon capital. His unadorned language made his meaning disconcertingly clear.

The power of Salisbury's argument was not so much to woo as to deter. Its thrust was critical rather than constructive. The order which he cherished did not need to be built. What he wished to do was retard the encroachment of Liberal and Radical reforms upon that order, and for that purpose he exposed their practical implications and workings. Liberalism was a creed of vision, sometimes of modest construction, more far-reaching when developed by utilitarians, glorious in the idealistic phase voiced by Gladstone in his Midlothian campaigns. Salisbury undertook to dissect the Liberal vision. He did so in his first years as leader in the Lords through a series of public speaking campaigns, by attempting to draw into productive association some of the reflective Conservative talent in the country, and, with less circumspection but most fully, in an article which he hoped would remain anonymous in the *Quarterly Review*.

The article, entitled 'Disintegration,' was a detailed critique of the workings of popular government. Salisbury's object in writing it was not to reverse the trend toward ever more popular government. That, he recognized, was impossible. 'It is as useless,' he wrote, 'to repine at this process, as to repine because we are growing order.'[37] The movement had taken hold of the whole western world. In England the dam impeding its advance had been broken in 1867. Until then, his chief objective had been to maintain the dam. But once it was gone, it could not be replaced. Salisbury's acceptance of the irrevocability of the second Reform Act reduced his objective from the avoidance of popular government to the disciplining of it.

He wished to look popular government fully in the face, particularly at its deceptive and dangerous features, in order to arouse the forces in the country capable of offsetting the dangers. Accordingly, he began his article for the *Quarterly Review* by casting a cold eye on the process by which the popular will was supposed to be made effective through Parliament. The popular will, in his estimation, was as unstable as the desert sands, all the more so now that the Ballot Act had freed the voter from the responsibility of accounting for his choice on election day. The picture taken of the popular will at election time bore no necessary resemblance to its configuration later in the life of a Parliament. Furthermore, as long as M.P.s were elected constituency by con-

stituency rather than in strict proportion to their party's share of the
popular vote in the country as a whole, a modest swing of opinion in
marginal seats could produce a majority in the Commons for one side
quite out of keeping with its real electoral strength. The returns in the
general election of 1880 were commonly interpreted to imply a
devastating repudiation of Conservative policies and a mandate to the
Liberals. Salisbury repeatedly pointed out that, if two thousand voters
in the constituencies where the contest was closest had cast their ballots
for Conservatives instead of Liberals, the Liberals would not have
emerged with a majority in the House of Commons.[38]

When one looked from the electoral to the Parliamentary arena,
things were no better. The transmission of public opinion through
Parliament was distorted often beyond recognition by 'the peculiar play
of parties within its walls,'[39] by jockeying for personal advantage within
parties and in debate, and ultimately by the desire to gain and retain
office. In short, the notion of government *by* the people was illusory.

> The 'people,' as an acting, deciding, accessible authority, are a myth. Except on
> rare emergencies, when they are excited by some tempest of passion, or some
> exceptional emergency, the 'people' do not speak at all. You have put an
> utterance into their mouths by certain conventional arrangements, under which
> assumptions are made which, though convenient, are purely fictitious: as for
> instance, that those present at the process of voting represent the absent; that a
> majority, however small, represents the whole; that a man's mind is a perfect
> reflex of the minds of fifty thousand of his fellow-citizens on all subjects because he
> was chosen, as the best of two or three candidates, in respect to a particular crisis
> and a particular set of subjects, by a bare majority of those who took the trouble to
> vote on a particular day.[40]

Government by an unfettered House of Commons in the name of the
people was worse than a distorted illusion; it was socially
disintegrating—hence the title of the article. Now that the House of
Commons was becoming a thoroughly popular assembly, it accentuated
antagonisms between class and class. The most desirable feature of
government in Salisbury's estimation was that it be dispassionate,
removed, whether by inherited position, education, or economic
security, from the perpetual clash of interests and classes. The task of a
governor was to arbitrate between popular forces rather than to lead one
portion of them to impose its will on the others. As long as the
government of Britain had been in the hands of kings, or of kings and
aristocrats, or of a propertied and educated electorate, it could function
properly, for, being in a small minority, these could not but know that
government was in their hands as a trust. But once the numerous
beneficiaries of the trust took it into their own hands, the task of
dispassionate governance became very much more difficult. It was that
problem to which Salisbury wanted Britain to address itself. Ways must

be found to keep any one class, however numerous, from imposing its desires upon the country. Ways must be found to enable 'the generality of the nation' to express its 'cool and deliberate judgement.'[41]

In order to neutralize the electoral dominance of the labouring masses, Salisbury tried to arouse the defensive instincts of the threatened interests: 'Churchmen, landowners, publicans, manufacturers, house-owners, railway share-holders, fundholders.'[42] Only his express desire for dispassionate government saved his appeal from blatantly exacer-bating the very warfare between classes that he feared. What he aimed for was such an even match between the forces of property and the forces of labour that the deciding power would be vested in referees. But the match would not be even, for the referees and the spokesmen of property would often be one and the same. Salisbury had wished to retain the pre-1867 electorate because he believed that property bred a sense of responsibility, that economic security bred judicious detachment, and that education fostered stability of judgement. He wished still to keep executive power in hands of the same sort.

Since the old electorate could not be restored, the other restraining agencies still available within the political system would have to be used more vigorously. The need was particularly acute in Britain because its governing mechanisms had been designed at a time when the need was to protect the majority who did not possess political power against the small minority who did. In his early years Salisbury had held up the United States as a horrifying illustration of democratic barbarism; but now that Britain too had popular government, he confessed his envy for the devices of the American constitution which diffused and muted the force of a popular wave of sentiment. The British body politic contained only two institutions which might be put to similar use: the House of Lords and the Conservative party. But for many years they had been exercised bashfully.

If some Conservatives had doubts about the wisdom of choosing Salisbury as their leader, Salisbury had doubts about the wisdom of relying upon the Conservative party as an instrument for his purposes. For it had become Disraeli's eager mistress. Salisbury was not at all sure in the early 1880s that the British two-party system, which had become rigid only in response to the duel between Disraeli and Gladstone, would persist once both men had died. He wondered whether the country would move from two ideologically amorphous parties into several more strongly defined groups on the French model:[43] and that prospect held some attractions for him. The Conservative party confronted Salisbury with a problem with which he would wrestle, in one form or other, throughout his career: how to reconcile party unity with resolute defence of established interests. The Conservative party could provide its leader with a large body of support famous for its loyalty. But its willingness to surrender its dearly held interests was equally famous. Peel had tried, and Disraeli had contrived, to cultivate that willingness. To Salisbury it was a curse. His first and great commandment for the Conservative party was to be resolute.

But what he was concerned about was a matter of posture and style more than of principle. Salisbury's behaviour disguised this distinction. His stiff tactics made him appear to be a man of inflexible principle. Nevertheless, in domestic politics as in foreign, the policies which he adopted were dictated by consideration of tactics more than of principle. Dogmatic principles, he believed, were, like idealism, out of place in politics;[44] more important than the policies was the way one proceeded to implement them. The object of his endeavours was stability, to be produced by well considered and firm resistance to radical change.

Firmness of this sort was even more important than the attainment of office. It was on this point that Salisbury took issue with Disraeli. Disraeli had put the pursuit of power first, much to the detriment of resolute government. To Salisbury such a course, indistinguishable from the Whig policy of 'buying off the barbarians,' only demoralized the forces of resistance to ill-considered change. Furthermore, Disraeli's strategy presupposed that the Liberal and Conservative parties were in dispute over the middle ground in the field of political battle, the possession of which would bring victory. Salisbury insisted that the middle ground had been deserted by the Radicalized Liberal party. Again and again he sought to make the point that the party of Gladstone bore no relation except in name to the party of Grey and Palmerston,[45] that the natural home for those who were loyal to the tradition of Grey and Palmerston was the Conservative party. Even the Whig policy of appeasing popular discontent was no longer applicable, he argued, because the current discontents were, for the most part, either aroused by hope that the Liberal habit of concession would persist, or otherwise contrived. 'Some time ago in London,' he told an Edinburgh audience,

> there was a man brought up for the crime of arson, and he was found to discover this curious industry. It was the custom of the police to give every man half-a-crown who should be the first to inform them of any fire that might occur. The practice of this man was first to set fire to a building and then to rush off to the police and earn half-a-crown by informing them of the fire. Now, this is precisely the position of the Radical party ... .[46]

The Radicalization of the Liberal party under Gladstone gave an advantage to Conservatives: it made them the only appropriate spokesmen for the broad mass of natural, small 'c' conservatives. Salisbury insisted that that body of opinion predominated in the country and was being stirred out of its normal lethargy by the successive Radical innovations. But even if that were not quite the case, even if anachronistic party loyalties and diffidence among the conservatively inclined majority held it back from electing Conservative governments, the Conservative party should act resolutely. Through vigilant opposition in the House of Commons, through firm resistance by the Conservative majority in the House of Lords, through well-attended demonstrations out of doors, through by-election victories, the Conservative party could neutralize the pressures on a Liberal government from its left wing and at the very least slow down the pace of Radical change.

Now that the reign of public opinion had begun, politicians, even when possessed of a large majority in the House of Commons, knew that they must give account of themselves to their new masters, not just at election time but day by day before the jury of the press and the increasingly frequent large public meetings. Gladstone with his Midlothian campaigns and Chamberlain with his National Liberal Federation had raised this new authority high. Very well, they should be met at their own game, and if not beaten, then paralysed. A Liberal Ministry was such a feeble thing, with its ear to the ground, so easily intimidated. To fight for less than complete victory was not futile and need not be dispiriting. Salisbury was exhilarated by the strategy he outlined, and he sought to infuse his party with the same spirit.

His political philosophy worried many Conservatives, at least in its fully developed form in 'Disintegration.' The *Standard*, for example, was alarmed by the article's thorough-going critique of popular government and its reluctance to rely on 'the instincts and traditions of the great mass of the nation.'[47] Disraeli's teaching had sunk deep in his party.

But Salisbury's views were less out of keeping with the state of political thought in Britain than the politicians and the newspaper pundits knew. Among the intellectual community, less concerned than they about the fortunes of party warfare and more concerned about the nature and assumptions of the body politic, Salisbury was not alone. A swing from left to right was taking place among the British intelligentsia, uneasy about the implications of the second Reform Act for the quality of government, not at all reassured by Gladstone's public-speaking campaigns and the huge majority of 1880, grudgingly impressed by Disraeli's insistence on strength in the Imperial Government. Disraeli was too fanciful and too much enmired in day-to-day politics for their sober and refined tastes. Salisbury also was muddied with these activities; and there were too many traditional and material ingredients in his Conservatism to make them feel at home. Most of them found their eventual way to the right through Liberal Unionism. Yet at last the Conservatives had a leader whom the intellectual community could respect if not directly follow. And with some of their own writings Salisbury was in close accord.

Two of them, Sir Henry Maine and Sir James Fitzjames Stephen, had been associated with him, first in mid-century as regular writers for the *Saturday Review*, more recently in the business of governing India. Maine was on the India council in London during Salisbury's term as Secretary of State for India from 1874 to 1878. The contacts of Salisbury with Stephen, who succeeded Maine from 1869 to 1872 as legal member of the council in India itself, were less direct and frequent. The apprehension of all three men about the course of English politics in the late 1860s and the 1870s was focused by their common experience of India. Britain maintained tranquillity and order there over a vast population of one hundred and fifty millions, partly through a small army, partly by firm, consistent, self-assured rule.

Of the three men, Salisbury was the most moderate. Stephen's experience in India led him, in *Liberty, Equality, Fraternity*, published in 1873, to emphasize the importance of physical power to a government's authority. The knowledge of India which Salisbury acquired as Secretary of State impressed him, not so much with the importance of armed force, but with the power which a reputation for reliable determination could give to civilian government. He was as close to Gladstone as he was to Stephen in believing that the character of a government was as important as the force at its disposal.

There was, however, a double standard by which a politician could be censured for arguing a case which might win applause for a theorist. Salisbury's article, 'Disintegration,' and the articles of Sir Henry Maine which formed the basis for his book, *Popular Government*, were published at about the same time; and the two authors had discussed their ideas with each other beforehand.[48] *Popular Government* shared some important conclusions with 'Disintegration': the social importance of private property and inviolable contracts, the weakness of restraints upon popular government in Britain compared to the United States, and the impossibility for all practical purposes of finding out the will of the people. Maine claimed that his book was the fruit of objective observation and scientific analysis of political society, the same kind of observation which had distinguished his great earlier works, *Ancient Law* (1861) and *Village Communities* (1871). In fact *Popular Government* was a lightly substantiated, partisan polemic.[49] It was less sophisticated than Salisbury's article, reflected scantier, less careful observation, and was more extreme in tone and conclusions. Yet 'Disintegration' was greeted with a flutter of nervous disapproval, while *The Times* hailed Maine's work as one of the most important contributions to the philosophy of politics in a long time.[50]

Lord Acton noted Maine's *Popular Government* as symptomatic of a swing towards illiberal views in Britain.[51] But though the Liberal faith was on the wane, the conventions of Liberal thought still served as the canons of acceptable behaviour for politicians. Lord Hartington and

Lord Rosebery among the Liberals might feel little more love for democracy than did Salisbury; but, without too great a strain on their consciences, they could in public express a watery sympathy with popular government, while, in the privacy of high party councils and high office, they attempted to restrain it. To Salisbury such conduct appeared ineffectual. And he warmly supported the initiative of Alfred Austin, his spokesman among the editorial writers of the *Standard*, in founding a new society, appropriately named the Cecil Club, and a new journal, the *National Review*, to bring together and provide an outlet for Conservative men of letters and reflective Conservative politicians.[52] What Salisbury wanted to cultivate was an unabashed but intelligent expression of Conservative thought; and he was disappointed by the 'lack of ardour' in the *National Review*'s first number.[53]

However useful in the long run, attempts to modify the country's political cast of mind had no more than subordinate importance to Salisbury as he took up the leadership of the Conservative party in the House of Lords. 'Disintegration' was the last article he wrote for the *Quarterly Review*, and brought his journalistic career substantially to a close. For the rest of his life, he would express and forward his purposes through public speech, private correspondence, and political manoeuvre.

## iii. Desertion

The spirited quality of Salisbury's Conservatism brought him perilously close to failure in his first year and a half as leader in the Lords. The task which he faced at the outset of his leadership provided a searching test of his abilities. For he had to pursue three goals simultaneously. He had to make his titular command over the Conservative peerage effective. He intended, in the process of doing so, to have the House of Lords make more vigorous use of its constitutional powers than it had done over the previous generation. And throughout these years in opposition, he was engaged in unspoken but pervasive competition, mainly but not exclusively with Northcote and then Churchill, for the leadership of the Parliamentary and national party as a whole. Northcote and Salisbury could not conduct a conclusive competition with each other until they were secure in their own Houses: Salisbury was mainly concerned for a while with his position in and policy for the House of Lords. But the skill with which he led the Lords would be watched attentively in the Commons.

For the Conservatives possessed a commanding majority among the Lords, and therefore looked to the upper House as one of their most promising weapons. Whenever there were sizeable defections from Liberal voting strength in the Commons on pieces of legislation sponsored by the Government, the Conservative peers could pass appropriate amendments or even reject the legislation outright, arguing in their defence that the voting in the lower House weakened any claim that the measure was covered by the mandate which the Government had received from the electorate. And if the Government should run into serious difficulties and its popular support showed signs of disappearing, the Lords could precipitate an election. These tactics, to be successful, would have to be conducted with skill and a fine judgment of the issues and occasions on which to defy the Government, finesse such as Disraeli had displayed in the summer of 1880. The tactics also required good management of the party in each House and close coordination between them so that action taken in one place would not prove embarrassing in the other.

Salisbury encountered almost as much unruliness among Conservative peers as Northcote found in the Commons, but of the opposite sort. The amiable moderates who dominated the Conservative front bench in the Commons were powerfully represented on the front bench in the Lords by the Duke of Richmond and Earl Cairns. Cairns was an Ulsterman whom many considered to be the most brilliant lawyer of his day; and he was in touch with Northcote. Richmond was a bland eminence dubbed by the Prince of Wales 'the farmer's friend' because of his desire to give his tenants leases so liberal that, if imitated by other landowners, they would eliminate the need for reforming legislative intervention.[54] The two men shared feelings of resentment at being passed over for the leadership in favour of Salisbury. They were ready to move into any breach which Salisbury's truculence might create, and to replace him if he fell.

The peers as a group were a passive lot. They felt no need to distinguish themselves with the aggressive debating skills admired in the Commons, and they were fearful of provoking retaliation from the enlarged electorate. None was more apprehensive than the Irish peers who, though hit hard by the agricultural depression, received regular, grim reminders of what the wrath of an unappeased tenantry could bring. Salisbury knew, however, or at least he hoped, that the patience of the aristocracy was not boundless. In any case, he set himself the task of stiffening their spines. He gratified the peers by belittling the pretensions of the House of Commons. He invested the phrase 'the other place' with conspicuous disdain; and he rarely ever sat in the Peers' Gallery of the Commons to witness its debates.[55]

There was a risk in using the House of Lords to defy the Government over anything but a very unpopular measure such as no Government was likely to demand: the Liberals might raise a cry of 'the peers versus the people,' and call a general election. Their appeal would probably succeed unless the public could be brought to appreciate the wisdom of fairly regular assertion by the Lords of their constitutional powers, more frequent than the country and the Lords themselves had grown accustomed to since the 1830s. Salisbury set out to make the House of Lords more active and aggressive than it had been for half a century. He proposed, in effect, to tilt the balance of the constitution back in favour of the upper House. His attempt was as disturbing an initiative in one direction as the activities of Joseph Chamberlain and his Radical allies were in the other.

Repeatedly in his public speeches Salisbury sought to cultivate the requisite public support, particularly by stressing the point that defiance of the Commons was not tantamount to defiance of the people. The duty of the House of Lords, he said, was to reflect 'the permanent and enduring wishes of the nation as opposed to the casual impulse which some passing victory at the polls may in some circumstances have given to the decisions of the other House.'[56] One substitute for checking of the Commons by the Lords would be frequent, triennial or even annual elections, a substitute which Salisbury presented as obviously un-attractive: but he pointed out that the Lords could bring about something comparable by refusing to do the Commons' bidding and thus forcing an election.[57] He admitted that the Lords' reflection of public opinion, though more reliable than the Commons', had its own distortion, a Conservative one; but he argued that this distortion was a passing phenomenon, produced by the Radicalism of Gladstone's Government, and that, in any case, it was a distortion which erred only on the side of safety.[58]

The particular subject which confronted Salisbury upon his election as leader in the Lords was the Irish Land Bill that Gladstone had introduced two weeks before Disraeli died. Many considerations seemed to make the Bill a tantalizing opportunity for the Lords to stand up to the Commons. The subject of relations between landlord and tenant, with which the Bill dealt, was one which virtually every peer knew first hand, if not in Ireland, then on the larger island. The Government could not claim to have an electoral mandate on the Irish question for, by their own admission, it was a question which Liberal leaders had brushed aside in the general election. And already the Government had suffered a loss of support from their followers and a fall at the hands of the House of Lords over a closely related measure, the Irish Compensation for Disturbance Bill of 1880.

The Lords' rejection of that Bill produced a chain of consequences, however, which forced Salisbury to realize that the Land Bill of 1881 could not be subjected to the same treatment. To begin with, unrest among the Irish tenantry, whom the rejected Bill was supposed to appease, had intensified, producing the first prominent boycott. Salisbury hoped that the landlords would stand up to intimidation, freely evicting tenants who did not pay their rent: for, as he explained to Disraeli, this would 'bring about a collision, & force the Government either to act or to confess its incapacity.'[59] Instead, the landlords showed signs of surrendering to their tenants. The Ulster Conservatives caved in, concluding that it would be better to receive reduced rents than no rents at all. Then the commission appointed by Disraeli before his defeat to enquire into the agricultural depression, and chaired by the Duke of Richmond, brought in a report conceding the need for some sort of tribunal between landlords and tenants in Ireland to adjust rents. Finally, before introducing the Land Bill, Gladstone offset potential Whig and Conservative criticism by putting through a Crimes Bill which vested the Irish executive with powers, sweeping even by Salisbury's standards,[60] to repress lawless agrarian agitation.

The Land Bill itself was a masterpiece of ambiguity. The one clear thing about it was that it would create a machinery of commissioners and sub-commissioners to revise Irish rents, subject to the barest minimum of review. The Bill was not at all clear about the spirit in which this machinery would work. After the Ulster Conservatives caved in, Salisbury calculated that Gladstone's best course would be to 'take advantage of the split in our ranks & produce a moderate Whig Bill.'[61] Salisbury had much to learn before his tactical skill would rival Gladstone's. The Bill which Gladstone brought in was Radical in its potentialities but blandly Whig in its packaging. It offered no handle to its opponents.

Salisbury was left to flounder. His instincts told him to attack; but he knew that he could not drive an attack to its logical conclusion. He tried, therefore, to combine the language of defiance with the tactics of compromise. Failure was probable. He was saved from it only by Gladstone's desire for a generally acceptable Act rather than for a fight.

Salisbury greeted the Bill with an article in the *Quarterly Review* which attempted to strip away its disguise. 'Loot,' he declared, 'pure loot, is the sacred cause for which the [Irish] Land League has summoned the malcontents to its standard':[62] and Gladstone's Bill, in a bid for Irish support, offered them the loot they sought. The Bill was confiscatory: by including a scale of compensation for disturbance in the assessment of fair rent, it would simply transfer some of the landlords' property to the tenants. Its machinery would operate despotically. In practice the Bill would be counter-productive, for it would discourage capital investment in Irish agriculture, and, by establishing joint ownership of the land, would set landlord against tenant in internecine conflict. But Salisbury did not go on to conclude that the Bill must be rejected. Instead he advocated 'full and prompt compensation ... for tenant's improvements, on the one hand, and an efficient machinery ... for the recovery of rents on the other':[63] in essence a measure to facilitate the operation of natural economic forces.

After the Bill passed through the Commons, the Conservative leaders in the two Houses agreed[64] upon a course to pursue in the Lords which reflected similar ambivalence. They decided to accept the Bill at its second reading, and then to amend it in committee. The body of the speech[65] in which Salisbury presented this advice to the House of Lords would have been more appropriate for the opposite course. Adding depth to the confusion, the amendments which the Conservative leaders induced the Lords to insert cut to the very heart of the Bill. Still, the Lords' acquiescence in the second reading was interpreted as an admission of the Bill's necessity, and encouraged a belief that, after the Bill returned to the lower House, the Lords would accept 'any decent offer of compromise'[66] from the Government.

Salisbury roughly disappointed this expectation. Far-reaching though the Lords' amendments were, Gladstone treated them respectfully in the Commons, rejecting few outright. Northcote was pleasantly impressed, and counselled his partner to respond with new proposals rather than insist on his original amendments.[67] But when the Conservative leaders' council assembled next day, Salisbury 'was not disposed at all to yield all points.'[68] The council was unable to reach specific agreement before the Lords met to deal with the Commons' changes. On the floor of the House of Lords, though still in consultation with Cairns and Edward Gibson as the leading Irish Conservative M.P., Salisbury insisted even on amendments originally proposed by dissident Whigs who were now willing to close with the Government.

In doing so, he threw aside the strategy, which Northcote meant to pursue in the Commons and Disraeli had followed in the Lords, of making full use of Liberal divisions. Wringing its hands, the *Standard*, which in April had hoped that Salisbury would be given the leadership of the entire Parliamentary party, admitted that he was bearing out all his enemies' predictions.[69] The Conservative leaders' council split. Gibson, an ally of Northcote, insisted that 'The loss of the Bill would by almost every rational man in Ireland be regarded as unmixed calamity.'[70] Lord Carnarvon added his voice in favour of backing down. Salisbury gave way, and agreed that Gibson should try to devise an acceptable compromise with the Government.

Salisbury did so with reservations, which deepened as soon as the council disbanded, and were not alleviated by the terms of the settlement which Gibson secured. Salisbury swallowed it. But when the council turned from accepting the settlement to a general discussion about the proper way for the House of Lords to function, he showed himself to be an unrepentant hardliner. Someone argued that the Lords' ability to stand up to the Government was lessened by Gladstone's impulsive and excitable nature: 'in some ways he must be regarded as a kind of lunatic.' Salisbury shot back, 'If it is such an advantage to the government to be able to use that argument, we should have a lunatic too. I offer myself for the position.'[71] There was personal ambition as well as concern about the House of Lords wrapped up in that remark.

Tempers over the Irish question, far from improving in the immediate wake of the Land Act's passage, worsened. The commissioners appointed under the Act, and more particularly the auxiliary commissioners, began to reduce Irish rents much more steeply than the Government had expected and had led the Opposition to expect. Conservatives feeling deceived, and Irish landlords feeling robbed, were in no mood for further concessions. On the other hand, the reception of the Act in Ireland by tenant farmers and Nationalists was disturbing though not totally discouraging. Charles Stewart Parnell, the Irish leader, adopted an attitude so belligerent and provocative that the Government had him thrown into prison. Subsequently, as he predicted, disorder spread uncontrollably and grew more ugly; but many tenants, particularly in Ulster, made full use of the Act.

Having vindicated its authority against Parnell, the Government was determined to give the Act full and unimpeded opportunity to have the effect they desired. If rents were being cut more than expected, that only proved to the Government that rack-renting was more extensive than had been appreciated. The Government refused any cooperation with an enquiry launched by the House of Lords, and then sought to extend the application of the Act to tenants who were behind on their rent by helping them pay off their arrears. But the Arrears Bill of 1882 looked suspiciously like part of the price which the Government paid to win the cooperation of Parnell. Such a Bill was Parnell's foremost demand in the dealings into which he entered through an intermediary with the government. The discussions led to his release from Kilmainham Gaol; and less than two weeks later, Gladstone introduced the Bill. Inevitably, it was denounced as part of a discreditable 'Kilmainham treaty.'

The Bill quickly shaped up as a measure upon which the House of Lords could not merely defy but bring down the Government. Conservative disapproval of it was universal—even Richmond censured it as a reward for delinquency[72]—and deepened as it went through the Commons. It was unpopular among a variety of the Government's supporters in the Commons, and the majorities by which it passed through Committee were small. Even Irish Nationalists were unenthusiastic, regarding the eventual Bill as insufficiently generous. The public, maddened by a succession of spectacular crimes which reached a terrible climax in the assassination of the new Irish Secretary, Lord Frederick Cavendish, on his first evening in Dublin, were most unlikely to look with favour upon Liberals in the event of an early election.

Nevertheless Salisbury, after his experience with the Land Bill, had his doubts about the wisdom of adopting a hard line. It would be less discreditable to enter debate on the Bill avowing a willingness to compromise than to shilly-shally in the Lords again, taking up a firm position one day only to abandon it the next. That was the kind of behaviour which people had come to expect of the Conservative party and the House of Lords; and Salisbury's object was to disabuse men of these expectations. He continued to inveigh against the Government's philosophy of concession, but in general terms. He hesitated to condemn the Arrears Bill out of hand; and in an effort to make sure of his ground, he took pains to ascertain the opinion of the party in the Commons as well as in the Lords.[73]

He was edged into a posture of outright opposition to the Bill by strong pressure in both Houses. The party was, however, divided, not over the Bill itself, but over the extent to which they should press their opposition. Salisbury, the Commons leadership, and the bulk of the party in the Commons were willing to bring on a general election by defying the Government over the Bill; but a minority including Richmond were not.[74] To satisfy both sections was impossible, yet the attempt was made. A compromise was agreed upon, whereby the Lords would give the Arrears Bill a second reading but then push for two amendments. One would make each application under the Bill dependent on the landlord's consent; the other included the saleable worth of tenant right in estimating a tenant's ability to pay his arrears. Salisbury had some difficulty in inducing the meeting of Conservative peers convened for consideration of the Bill to hold back from rejection of the second reading. He won the dissidents over by pledging himself to stand by the amendments, come what may.[75]

These tactics repeated the error of 1881. By giving the Bill a second reading, the Lords accepted its principle, only to pass amendments, particularly the first one, which would vitiate it in practice. Furthermore, the process of amendment and counter-amendment in the two Houses confused the issue, and took time during which uncertainty could grow among the rank and file.

Perhaps in order to save the Bill,[76] Gladstone had already succumbed to pressure within his Cabinet for a naval bombardment of Alexandria. This action was the climax of an attempt, conducted fitfully until now, to consolidate British interests and power in Egypt which were challenged in an uprising led by Arabi Pasha. Initially the bombardment weakened the Government: John Bright resigned from the Cabinet. And the situation in Egypt deteriorated before it got better: Alexandria was pillaged by angry Egyptians. But as British forces went on to restore order and impose their will in Egypt, public opinion at home swung in favour of the Government. The critical character of affairs in Egypt also made an immediate change of government undesirable. Conservatives' desire for an immediate election evaporated. Gladstone drove his advantage home. He rejected the Lords' first amendment, and intimated that if the Lords insisted upon it, Parliament would be dissolved. At the same time he offered a substantial accommodation on the second.

Northcote was slow to catch the change in sentiment on the Conservative benches behind him. Not so Lord George Hamilton, Salisbury's Under-Secretary at the India Office from 1874 to '8, who warned his former chief, even before Gladstone made his offer, that Conservative M.P.s now recoiled from the prospect of a general election.[77] John Gorst, in his capacity as Principal Agent of the party, substantiated their reaction by reporting to Salisbury and Northcote in some detail that the party could hope to do no better in a general election now than they had done in 1880.[78] When Gladstone took his stand, Conservative support for the amendments to which Northcote continued to adhere fell off dangerously; and the Bill went back to the House of Lords in the shape that Gladstone specified.

Peers who owned land in Ireland joined the chorus for concession. They would fare somewhat better with the amendments accepted by Gladstone: the prospect of another poor harvest had reduced their will to fight: and some feared for their lives if the Bill were not enacted. The Queen, anxious to avert a collision between the two Houses, communicated her wishes to a leading Irish Conservative, the Duke of Abercorn.[79] Cairns and Richmond gave the chorus a lead. Cairns took the initiative, informing Richmond and Salisbury among others that he could not adhere to the policy adopted by the caucus;[80] and then conspicuously he withdrew from London to the North. Richmond took over. When the Conservative peers met[81] to decide how to deal with the Commons' amendments, he intervened early in their proceedings to present the case of concession.

Salisbury had pledged his word at the previous meeting, and he would not back down. He began the meeting, which was held in his London residence, with a brief but unequivocal statement of the reasons for adhering to their original position. He did not plead for support. He did not remind the meeting of the pressure for a hard line which those present had put upon him formerly. He simply reaffirmed his promise to stand by the amendments. However the others might behave, he would not set another example of bowing to the Government and its majority in the Commons. Then he watched as Richmond and Waterford counselled capitulation. His most loyal lieutenants responded by suggesting that it would be better to close ranks with the capitulators than to reveal the party's split ranks to the public when, because of the split, the Bill was sure to pass. Once the direction the discussion was taking became quite clear, Salisbury called for a division, those favouring his policy to move to one side of the room, those against to the other. Not more than one in three went with him.

That afternoon in the Lords, when the Commons' amendments came on for discussion, Salisbury bluntly admitted the split,[82] which was now common knowledge. He stated briefly that he himself would stand by the original amendments but that, in view of the obvious result, he would not bother the Lords by calling for a division. Richmond, equally candid, presented the case of the Conservative majority. On the voice vote Salisbury, together with Cranbrook, spoke out his 'not content'; and the Bill passed. 'I saw,' Cranbrook recorded in his diary, 'that the iron entered his soul.'[83]

## iv. Rival Manoeuvres

None of the Conservative leaders came out of the affair well. Northcote had maintained the hard-line strategy as long as the Bill remained in his House, a fact to which Salisbury had been careful to draw attention.[84] The Conservative defectors on the final vote in the Commons and an overwhelming majority of the Conservative peers had rejected the judgment and the leadership of their respective captains on this particular issue; and some of the dissidents intended the mutiny to go farther. Still, it did not enhance the reputation of the rebel leaders. W. H. Smith, First Lord of the Admiralty under Disraeli and a moderate who had not wanted a confrontation with the Government over Irish arrears, still despised the faint hearts in both Houses who made no attempt to hide their desire to run rather than fight.[85] Cairns' leaving town looked weak. Richmond gave offence by voicing his opposition to Salisbury's policy publicly in the Lords.

The arrears crisis made the dual leadership of the Conservative party, inherently an unstable arrangement, still shakier. Salisbury's and Northcote's handling of the crisis encouraged further challenges to their authority within their own Houses, without doing anything to alleviate the inevitable rivalry between the two men. That rivalry was conducted subtly but nonetheless intensely over foreign as well as domestic affairs.

Providentially from Salisbury's point of view, foreign and imperial affairs darkened the horizon throughout Gladstone's second Ministry. Unavenged military defeats followed one upon another, from Majuba Hill in 1881 to Khartoum at the beginning of 1885. They produced two reactions, both critical of the Government. English national sentiment was outraged, and responded by picking up the banner of Empire from the fallen hand of Disraeli. This reaction, dubbed 'jingoism' by its enemies, was countered by a reassertion among Manchester School

Radicals of the principles which Gladstone had proclaimed in his Midlothian campaigns. These men opposed imperial activities which extended Britain's liabilities and exposed the country to draining financial outlays as well as military setbacks. The Cabinet was divided, some of its members retaining the imperial instincts of Lord Palmerston, others actuated by the precepts of Cobden or Midlothian. And the conduct of affairs overseas was vested in three men—Lord Granville at the Foreign Office, Lord Derby at the Colonial Office, and Gladstone—who were inattentive or indecisive administrators or were otherwise preoccupied. The Government rocked from crisis to crisis which they had not foreseen and hence had not defused.

Foreign policy was Salisbury's strong suit. After serving five years of apprenticeship at the India Office, he had made a spectacular debut as Foreign Secretary in 1878, laying the groundwork for the Congress of Berlin. Abroad and at home, he won more respect as a diplomat in two brief years at the Foreign Office than any Foreign Secretary since Palmerston. His comments on the performance of his successor at the Foreign Office carried much more than the weight of a party leader, much more than Northcote's. The contrast in competency between Salisbury and Lord Granville or, for that matter in this field, Gladstone served as a steady reminder of the advantage that a Conservative Government could bring.

Salisbury sorely needed this distinction. For he could not derive strength for his claim to the leadership from any domestic constituency. He was not 'the farmer's friend,' and he had no special ties to the City, to trade or industry. He did not represent any particular region within the Kingdom. He had no personal ties with suburban Conservatism. He was not the special darling of the Established Church. He stood alone, not sharing even the cultural reflexes of Victorian England. As Lord David Cecil has recently recalled:[86]

> my grandfather was not a Victorian as the term is generally understood. His tone, his point of view, were those of an earlier age. Like his literary style, they recalled the eighteenth century . . . [which] judged good sense to be a better guide to conduct than fine feeling, and combined a firm Christian faith and morality with a down-to-earth unillusioned view of human nature and human prospects.

What he offered his party was personal talents, not representative reflexes or associations. The eminent position he had acquired in diplomacy served as a pedestal for the display of those talents.

The message which Salisbury preached, to rapt Conservative attention, on foreign policy was intimately related to the message which he wished to instill upon the party in every regard. Contemporaries, like later historians, noticed the moderation of his comments on foreign in contrast to domestic policy; and no doubt it served his purposes in the early 1880s to play the judicious statesman on the former and the rabid partisan on the latter. Yet there was a large common denominator to his commentary on affairs abroad and at home: insistence not so much upon which policy to pursue but on the steadfastness with which one pursued it. Salisbury had more sympathy with the imperialist reaction than with its opposite, but he saw merit in both. For both were concerned with the relationship between Britain's responsibilities and its strength. He differed from little Englanders in putting the accent on strength; he differed much more from pure Gladstonians in minimizing the value of cultivating the good will of peoples such as the Afghans. And these differences, pungently expressed, warmed the hearts of imperialists. But there was a pacific strand in the Conservative party, stretching back through the Peelites to Bolingbroke, as well as the newer, stronger imperialist strand. Salisbury threaded his way between the two camps of critics by concentrating his own criticism upon the shifts and changes of the Government as it responded to the flux of events over which it seemed to have no control: this was his text in a steady succession of blistering attacks. He adhered to it not only when the Government suffered reverses but also over the bombardment of Alexandria despite its popularity at home and the proof it appeared to furnish of the effectiveness of a Disraelian approach. Salisbury met the objections of both little Englanders and imperialists by arguing that, if from the beginning of the troubles in Egypt the British Government had adhered to a clear policy and assembled a force obviously capable of enforcing it, the bombardment with its subsequent loss of English as well as Egyptian life and property would not have been necessary.[87]

He responded with a similar combination of biting style and moderate substance to another divisive issue of the early '80s, fair trade. In this case the need to act cautiously was more obvious since the division was entirely within the Conservative party. The depression in trade and agriculture which had brought Disraeli to defeat in 1880 showed no signs of letting up; and because it was aggravated by the erection of tariff walls on the Continent and across the Atlantic, it revived the demand in England for similar tariff protection. A National Fair Trade League was launched in the summer of 1881. This very issue had split the Conservative party and alienated the public thirty-five years before, and Conservatives had spent a generation in the wilderness as a result. There, on the Conservative front bench in the Commons, was Lord John Manners, a veteran of the Corn Law controversy eager to do battle for tariffs again. Below the gangway, the young Randolph Churchill, anxious to exploit any source of Conservative discontent, toyed with the flag of fair trade: and eighty Conservatives voted for a motion in favour of countervailing duties on bounty-supported foreign sugar.[88] Fair traders were victorious or influential in a few by-elections. And they were ardent Tories, drawn by the party's protectionist past or by the lack of any political alternative.

On the other hand, there was some adamantine opposition to fair trade within the party, voiced in Salisbury's ear by Lord Cranbrook.[89] Most Conservatives, like the public at large, remained unconvinced that unilateral free trade was a weakness to Britain and were nervous of any innovations which might raise the price of food. If the depression lingered and deepened, it might make the country willing to change its mind. But for the incumbent leaders of the Conservative party to embrace fair trade without good reason for believing that the public was ripe for such a change would be suicidal.

Northcote was willing to sit on platforms with fair traders and to issue opaque pronouncements. Salisbury responded to the agitation more incisively.[90] Privately he cautioned protectionist colleagues such as Lord John Manners about the divisive potentialities of the issue.[91] Publicly he declared himself in favour of free trade; and he repeated the argument which Disraeli had made in 1879, when the current agitation had begun, that tariff retaliation was not practicable because of the skein of most-favoured-nation treaty obligations which Britain had wrapped round itself. At the same time he argued repeatedly that a policy of threatening retaliatory tariffs in order, for example, to curb the foreign practice of subsidizing some exports with bounties, was entirely true to the spirit of free trade. He scoffed at the Government for weakening its negotiating position by doctrinaire refusal to mention even the possibility of retaliation. His line of argument, trenchantly expressed as always, conveyed to fair traders a feeling that Salisbury was more sympathetic to their cause than Northcote.[92] When the depression showed no signs of easing, Salisbury raised his bid to the fair traders by proposing an expert enquiry into the causes of the depression and the proposals for relief, and by speaking favourably of preferential tariffs with the colonies.[93]

Meeting the desires of the ardent with cautious policies in this fashion might once have satisfied Richmond and Cairns; but no longer. They made trouble again in 1883. Salisbury had no immediate hopes of producing a confrontation with the Government to bring on a general election. The Lords' bluff had been called; and Gilbert and Sullivan were amusing London audiences with a verse from their new musical comedy, *Iolanthe*:

> And while the House of Peers withholds
>    Its legislative hand,
> And noble statesmen do not itch
>    To interfere with matters which
> They do not understand,
> As bright will shine Great Britain's rays
> As in King George's glorious days!

Ireland was quietening down. Egypt for the moment was firmly in hand. And when Parliament reconvened in February, the Government introduced an unexciting programme of legislation.

Salisbury attempted to probe a weak point in the Government's armour, and at the same time to secure the cooperation of Richmond in his role as agriculturalist, by asking him to bring in a Bill to impose severe regulation on imports of foreign cattle. Imports were blamed for the epidemic of foot and mouth disease which was ravaging England, but the Government did not want regulation which would interfere with freedom of trade. Richmond, however, replied that action now would be precipitate.[94]

Then the two men clashed publicly over amendments to the Government's Agricultural Holdings Bills for England and Scotland. Richmond, with considerable landlord support, believed that the Bills, while not seriously damaging the property rights of landowners, were popular among working farmers. He did not want the House of Lords to insist upon amendments unacceptable to the Government, which could then drop the Bills and attach the odium for their loss to Conservatives.[95] Salisbury's estimate of the Bills' significance was a good deal lower. He thought that, if properly amended, they would do little harm or good, but that they might give tenant farmers a salutary, sobering experience of legislative interference in the relations between landlord and tenant. The Government accepted two of the three amendments which the Conservative peers were most concerned about, including the one which Salisbury deemed the most important; but they refused the third. Salisbury pressed on, until a defection led by Richmond forced him to give way.[96]

This quarrel between the two men was not as serious as the one over the Arrears Bill since the Government would have responded to intransigence by dropping the Agricultural Holdings Bills rather than by calling an election. And this time it was Richmond alone who came out poorly. His statement in the House of Lords that loss of the Bills would be 'repugnant to the feelings of the whole of the tenant farmers of the country'[97] drew cries of protest from Tory benches. Salisbury was also able to make a stand for the rights of the House of Lords without dividing his supporters when he threw out two minor pieces of Government legislation[98] on the ground that they had been sent up from the Commons much too late for the upper House to consider them adequately.

Still, in his first three sessions as leader, he had employed defiant tactics unsuccessfully. By the autumn of 1883 the opposition of Richmond and Cairns to his leadership was their all but settled policy; and a small council of prominent Conservative peers was held at Eridge Park, the country house of Lord Abergavenny, to consider the leadership in the upper House.[99] Of the three who attended, only Cairns was an avowed dissident. The host was a neutral concerned only for the welfare of the party, and Cranbrook, the third, was a staunch supporter of Salisbury. But the conference in itself was ample indication that Salisbury's leadership was in jeopardy.

## NOTES

1. Gladstone was his nearest competitor. If the election of 1885 is considered a stand-off, both men won three general elections: Gladstone in 1868, 1880 and 1892, Salisbury in 1886, 1895 and 1900. No party won a majority in 1886 and 1892, but the Conservative achievement in 1886 was greater by every measure than the Liberal achievement in 1892.
2. Only Walpole, Pitt and Liverpool have held office longer.
3. See James P. Cornford's articles in *Victorian Studies*, VII, 1(September 1863), pp. 35–66; in Erick Allardt and Yujo Litturen, ed., *Cleavages, Ideologies and Party Systems* (Helsinki, 1964); and in Robert Robson, ed., *Ideas and Institutions of Victorian Britain* (London, 1967): Andrew Jones, *The Politics of Reform, 1884* (Cambridge, 1972): and A. B. Cooke and J. R. Vincent, *The Governing Passion* (Brighton, 1974). Some historians of the Empire and of foreign policy, preeminently Ronald Robinson and John Gallagher, have appreciated Salisbury's domestic talents without exploring them.
4. Maurice Cowling, *1867: Disraeli, Gladstone and Revolution* (London, 1967), p. 310.
5. Caption to the 'Ape' cartoon of Salisbury in *Vanity Fair*, 10 July 1869.
6. Lady Gwendolen Cecil, *Life of Robert Marquis of Salisbury*, I (London, 1921), p. 293.
7. Before reaching this conclusion, he decided how he would go about staying in the Commons. As he told his son-in-law twenty-five years later: 'There was some difficulty in finding the register of my father's marriage. I should have forbidden my solicitors to search for it, at that time: & if when I took my seat, any one had tried to move the writ, I should have pointed out to them that they had no evidence whatever that my father's marriage was valid: & they had no evidence that the two brother's [sic] older than me who were supposed to have died, had really done so. No existing machinery in the House could have ascertained either of these facts. They might have created the machinery by stature; but they had it not. They would have found it very difficult to exclude me on the mere suspicion that I had a right to take up a peerage. In the then state of feeling I doubt if they would have done so. But matters are changed now.' Salisbury to Lord Wolmer, 7 February 1893, the second Earl of Selborne papers.
8. *Ibid.*
9. Note by 'Etonensis' in the Balfour papers, B. L. Add. MSS. 49855.
10. Julia Cartwright, ed., *The Journals of Lady Knightley of Fawsley, 1856–1884* (London, 1916), p. 239.
11. Peter T. Marsh, *The Victorian Church in Decline* (London, 1969), p. 191.
12. Arthur Hardinge, *The Life of Herbert Howard Molyneux Herbert, Fourth Earl of Carnarvon* (London, 1925), II, p. 357.
13. Lady Gwendolen Cecil, *Life of Salisbury*, I, p. 216.
14. Salisbury to Disraeli, 7 April 1880, Beaconsfield papers.
15. Lady Gwendolen Cecil, *Biographical Studies of the Life and Political Character of Robert Third Marquis of Salisbury* (London, n.d.), p. 31.
16. Salisbury to Balfour, 10 April 1880, in A. J. Balfour, *Chapters of Autobiography*, ed. Mrs. Edgar Dugdale (London, 1930), pp. 127–8.
17. Salisbury to Disraeli, 10 April 1880. Beaconsfield papers.

18. Northcote's diary, 12 July 1880, typed copy, Iddesleigh papers.
19. G. E. Buckle, *The Life of Benjamin Disraeli, Earl of Beaconsfield* (New York, 1920), VI, p. 595.
20. A. J. Balfour, *op. cit.*, p. 108.
21. A. E. Gathorne-Hardy, *Gathorne Hardy, First Earl of Cranbrook* (London, 1910), II, p. 149.
22. Cranbrook was then Gathorne Hardy. He demanded and received elevation to the House of Lords as consolation.
23. Cranbrook's diary, 25 October 1880, Cranbrook papers.
24. A. E. Gathorne-Hardy, *op. cit.*, II, p. 153.
25. Richmond to Cairns, 27 October 1880, Cairns papers; Cairns to Richmond, 29 October 1880, Goodwood MSS.
26. Gorst to Salisbury, 20 September and 1 November 1880, Salisbury papers.
27. Churchill to Chaplin, 30 October 1880, in the Marchioness of Londonderry, *Henry Chaplin* (London, 1926), p. 162.
28. Harold E. Gorst, *The Fourth Party* (London, 1906), p. 117.
29. *The Standard*, 5 May 1881. See also H. St. J. Raikes, *The Life and Letters of Henry Cecil Raikes* (London, 1898), pp. 162–3.
30. J. W. Robertson Scott, *The Story of the Pall Mall Gazette* (London, 1950), pp. 364 and 366.
31. A. E. Gathorne-Hardy, *op. cit.*, II, pp. 162–3.
32. H. S. Northcote to Sir Stafford Northcote, 30 April 1881, Iddesleigh papers; *The Standard*, 7 May 1881.
33. See Ewan Butler, *The Cecils* (London, 1964), and Lord David Cecil, *The Cecils of Hatfield House* (Boston, 1973).
34. Salisbury, *Evolution, a Retrospect* (London, 2nd ed., 1894), p. 15.
35. The following discussion draws heavily upon Paul Smith's introductory essay to his edition of Salisbury's *Quarterly Review* articles [Paul Smith, ed., *Lord Salisbury on Politics* (Cambridge, 1972), pp. 1–109] and to a lesser extent on Michael Pinto-Duschinsky's *The Political Thought of Lord Salisbury, 1854–68* (London, 1967). Paul Smith's essay is a masterly analysis of Salisbury's thought until he became leader, but attempts only briefly to reconcile the theorizing pundit of the 1850s and '60s with the statesman of the 1880s and '90s. Michael Pinto-Duschinsky's study is based largely on Salisbury's writings for the *Saturday Review*.
36. Salisbury on the Chemical Society's Jubilee, *The Times*, 26 February 1891, 6c.
37. 'Disintegration,' *Quarterly Review*, CLVI, 312 (October 1883), p. 570.
38. Salisbury, 'Ministerial embarrassments,' *Quarterly Review*, CLI, 302 (April 1881), 541; Salisbury to the South Essex Registration Association, *The Times*, 25 May 1882, 11c; Salisbury at Dorchester, *The Times*, 17 January 1884, 10c.
39. 'Disintegration,' p. 566.
40. 'Disintegration,' *Quarterly Review*, CLVI, 312 (October 1883), 571. Cf. Salisbury to Canon MacColl, 27 August 1884, Malcolm MacColl, *Memoirs and Correspondence*, ed. G. W. E. Russell (London, 1914), p. 279: 'That impersonation of "the people" as a thing you can love or hate—or be the "foe" of—belongs to the dialect of the French Revolution. It means nothing.'
41. 'Disintegration', p. 566.
42. *Ibid.*, p. 565.
43. Salisbury to T. H. S. Escott, 1 November 1882, Escott papers.
44. Lady Gwendolen Cecil, *Biographical Studies*, p. 52.
45. Salisbury at Bristol, *The Times*, 14 November 1881, 7e; and at Edinburgh, *The Times*, 25 November 1882, 5d–f.
46. *Ibid.*
47. Editorial, 20 October 1883.

48. See Paul Smith, ed., *Lord Salisbury on Politics* (Cambridge, 1972), 348n.
49. George Feaver, *From Status to Contract: A biography of Sir Henry Maine, 1822–1888* (London, 1969), pp. 223–227.
50. *The Times,* 22 October 1885, 13a.
51. Herbert Paul, ed., *Letters of Lord Acton to Mary Gladstone* (New York, 1904), p. 332.
52. Austin to Salisbury, 28 August 1881, 8 November 1882, and resolutions enclosed with the letter of 27 October 1882, Salisbury papers; Salisbury to Austin, 29 October 1882, Austin papers
53. Austin to Salisbury, 23 February 1883, Salisbury papers.
54. Sir Ernest Clarke, *Charles Henry Gordon-Lennox, Sixth Duke of Richmond and Gordon* (London, 1904), pp. 6–7 and 11; Richmond to Cairns, 20 December 1882, 10 February and 3 March 1883, Cairns papers.
55. The only recorded occasions of his sitting there were to hear Forster's resignation speech in 1882 and a statement by Balfour in 1899 on the state of public business. During Gladstone's fourth Ministry, he attempted to keep in touch with the course of debate in the Commons by posting a secretary in the gallery. H. W. Lucy, *A Diary of Two Parliaments*, II: The Gladstone Parliament, 1880–1885 (London, 1886), p. 235; *Hansard*, 4th ser., LXXII, 1473 (19 June 1899); Salisbury to the Speaker of the House of Commons, 10 March 1893, copy, Salisbury papers, typed drafts.
56. Salisbury at Newcastle, *The Times*, 12 October 1881, 7a.
57. Salisbury at Liverpool, *The Times*, 14 April 1882, 6b.
58. Salisbury at Watford, *The Times*, 7 December 1883, 7a.
59. Salisbury to Disraeli, 1 December 1880, Beaconsfield papers.
60. Lady Gwendolen Cecil, *Life of Salisbury*, III, p. 43.
61. Salisbury to Disraeli, 20 December 1881, Beaconsfield papers.
62. 'Ministerial embarrassments,' *Quarterly Review*, CLI, 302 (April 1881), p. 536.
63. *Ibid.*, p. 566.
64. For an inside record of this and subsequent discussions, see A. B. Cooke and A. P. W. Malcolmson, comp., *The Ashbourne Papers, 1869–1913* (Belfast, 1974), pp. 11–18.
65. *Hansard*, 3rd ser., CCLXIV, 254–270 (1 August 1881).
66. *The Standard's* editorial, 9 August 1881.
67. Northcote to Salisbury, 11 August 1881, Salisbury papers.
68. A. B. Cooke and A. P. W. Malcolmson, comp., *The Ashbourne Papers, 1869–1913* (Belfast, 1974), p. 11.
69. Editorial, 13 August 1881.
70. A. B. Cooke and A. P. W. Malcolmson, *op. cit.*, p. 13.
71. *Ibid.*, p. 17.
72. Richmond to Cairns, 6 June 1882, Cairns papers.
73. Salisbury to Henry Manners, 8 July 1882, copy, Salisbury papers.
74. Salisbury to Cairns, 21 July 1882, copy, Salisbury papers, and note by Balfour on 'The House of Lords and the Arrears Bill. —July—August 1882,' Balfour papers, B. L. Add. MSS. 49962.
75. Salisbury to Cairns, 21 July 1882, copy, and to Lady John Manners, 24 July 1882, copy, Salisbury papers.
76. Ronald Robinson and John Gallagher, *Africa and the Victorians* (London, 1961), 111–2.
77. Hamilton to Salisbury, 4 August 1882, Salisbury papers.
78. Gorst to Salisbury, 8 August 1882, Salisbury papers. Gorst to Northcote, same date, Iddesleigh papers.
79. G. E. Buckle, ed., *The Letters of Queen Victoria*, 2nd ser., III (London, 1928), pp. 323 and 326.

80. Cairns to Richmond, 6 August 1882, Goodwood MSS.
81. Described by Salisbury to his wife, 10 August 1882, in Lady Gwendolen Cecil, *Life of Salisbury*, III, 54; by Cranbrook in his diary, 11 August 1882, in A. E. Gathorne-Hardy, *op. cit.*, II, 181–2; and by Richmond to Cairns, 13 August 1882, Cairns papers.
82. *Hansard*, 3rd ser., CCLXXIII, 1335 (10 August 1882).
83. A. E. Gathorne-Hardy, *op. cit.*, II, 182.
84. Lord John Manners to Northcote, 5 August 1882, Iddesleigh papers.
85. Smith to his wife, 9 August 1882, in Viscount Chilston, *W. H. Smith* (London, 1965), p. 175.
86. Lord David Cecil, *The Cecils of Hatfield House* (Boston, 1973), p. 241.
87. Salisbury at Hatfield, *The Times*, 8 August 1882, 6a–b.
88. B. H. Brown, *The Tariff Reform Movement in Great Britain, 1881–1895* (New York, 1943), p. 59.
89. Cranbrook to Salisbury, 20 September 1881, copy, Salisbury papers.
90. *Hansard*, 3rd ser., CCLXIII, 220–225 (7 July 1881); CCLXVI, 20 (7 February 1882); CCLXXX, 12–13 (8 June 1883); Salisbury at Newcastle, *The Times*, 13 October 1881, 7d.
91. Salisbury to Lady John Manners, 22 September 1881, Rutland papers.
92. Charles Whibley, *Lord John Manners and His Friends* (Edinburgh, 1925), II, pp. 273–275.
93. Salisbury to R. Winn, 4 September 1884, copy, Salisbury papers; Salisbury at Dumfries, *The Times*, 22 October 1884, 6d; Salisbury at Welshpool, *The Times*, 23 April 1885, 7f.
94. Salisbury to Richmond, 27 and 31 March and 7 April 1883, Goodwood MSS.
95. Richmond to Cairns, 29 August 1883, Cairns papers.
96. Salisbury to Lord John Manners, 23 August 1884 [3], copy, Salisbury papers; *Hansard*, 3rd ser., CCLXXXIII, 1825–7 (24 August 1883).
97. *Hansard*, 3rd ser., CCLXXXIII, 1621 (22 August 1883).
98. Bills on Irish Parliamentary Registration and Scotch Local Government.
99. Cairns to Richmond, 29 October 1883, Goodwood MSS.

CHAPTER 2

# ELECTORAL AND TORY DEMOCRACY

> Parliamentary reform is the gage of battle, and
> the Party which carries it will have power for a
> quarter of a century.
>
> *Lord Randolph Churchill to the Annual Conference of
> the National Union of Conservative Associations,
> 2 October 1883*

Just over a year after the Eridge Park conference, Lord Salisbury
emerged not merely as the unrivalled leader in the House of Lords, but
as the just short of formally recognized leader of the full Parliamentary
party. And in the process of doing so, he impressed his strategy of
Conservatism upon his House and party.

The Government's performance overseas, particularly in the Sudan,
demoralized Liberals and angered Conservatives, who therefore
displayed a new eagerness to drive the Ministry out. But the critical
debate of 1884, though inter-woven with the controversy over the
Sudan, was conducted on a domestic issue. The Government's chief
proposal for the new session of Parliament was a Franchise Bill to extend
the borough household suffrage of 1867 to the counties. It drew a
response from Salisbury which showed him to have developed a new
tactical finesse and flexibility. After being embarrassed by his colleagues
in the Lords and outmanoeuvred by Gladstone for three sessions, he had
become Gladstone's tactical match. He also demonstrated an
appreciation of the relative strength of the various factions or schools
within the party, and an ability to bring them together in effective
combat.

But the same year witnessed another fight, with Lord Randolph
Churchill over the National Union of Conservative Associations and the
organization of the party. In as serious a way as the fight over
Parliamentary reform, this one raised questions about the leadership of
the party and about its character and composition. In the conflict with
Churchill Salisbury was able to secure no more than a treaty or truce.
Which it was would depend on the willingness and ability of the two men
to work together. Salisbury eliminated one rival only to see another rise
up. For a further two years he was obliged to participate in another dual

leadership. Churchill could not hope immediately to grasp the first place, if only because he had never held even minor public office. But he posed a much more serious threat to Salisbury than Northcote had done. With Northcote the dual leadership was nothing worse than awkward, since Northcote was easily outshone and undermined. There was no outshining Churchill. In addition, much more sharply than Northcote, Salisbury and Churchill entertained different conceptions of the function of the Conservative party now that British politics were extensively popularized. Whether these styles and conceptions were compatible only time would tell.

## i. The Third Reform Bill

In the first phase of his political career, during the 1850s and '60s, Salisbury had been obsessed with the dangers of electoral reform; and condemnation of Disraeli's conduct over the Reform Bill of 1867 never ceased to be a central tenet of his domestic creed. Yet in 1884 he played out a variant of 1867.[1] He did not meet the third Reform Bill with a direct negative, but handled it as a matter of tactics. Eventually he cooperated in the Bill's passage in order to make sure that the Conservative party's interests were not sacrificed in the redistribution of seats.

The cardinal differences between the second and third Reform Bills from Salisbury's standpoint were two fold. In the first place, like most of his contemporaries, Salisbury saw the 1867 Act as the watershed between restricted and popular government. It had created a predominantly working class electorate. The momentum toward a fully popular electorate thereafter was ineluctable. Because the 1867 Act had enfranchised householders only in boroughs and not in counties, a subsequent measure to make good the omission was logical. All that was left to decide was the timing and framing of the extension. In the second place, whereas in 1867 Disraeli's behaviour gave the Conservative party a reputation for concession, Salisbury's conduct in 1884 restored to the party a reputation for firmness. Since on the substance or principle of Parliamentary reform the game was already lost, style was of the first importance.

From the moment the Liberals won the general election of 1880 it was clear that a third Reform Bill would be forthcoming; it had been promised by almost all Liberal candidates. Conservatives were immediately on guard. Some feared that extension of household suffrage to the counties would weaken landlord influence in what traditionally had been the base of Conservative electoral strength. Others were more concerned about the need for a redistribution of seats in keeping with the geographical distribution of an enlarged electorate. Redistribution was of critical importance. It was highly susceptible to partisan manipulation; and it was unpopular among M.P.s of both parties, who had secured themselves in existing constituencies. It therefore provided Conservatives with a golden opportunity to trip up the Government, whether it brought in a combined measure or tried to deal with the franchise and redistribution separately. Disraeli looked forward to combat with Gladstone on this familiar ground in 1881.[2] But on the justifiable assumption that another general election would be expected as soon as a new Reform Bill was enacted, Gladstone did not propose to take action for several years.

Salisbury was at one with Disraeli in approaching the issue purely as a matter of tactics and party interest. He neither welcomed nor greatly feared extension of household suffrage to the counties. As another Radical change to the detriment of territorial influence, he disliked it. But he did not expect the new county electors to depart from the Conservative traditions of rural England even if they owed their enfranchisement to a Liberal Government:[3] the urban voters enfranchised in 1867 had not proven grateful to Disraeli in the general election of 1868. Salisbury had also come to recognize more explicitly than Disraeli the 'Villa Toryism'[4] of suburban householders, a good many of whom lived in county rather than borough constituencies.

Still, on balance, Salisbury preferred retention of the existing electorate to the uncertain consequences of a new one. Many of the counties were populated now by industrial, commercial or mining centres, and the impact which enfranchisement of their householders would have on the Conservative party was worrying. Salisbury's primary object in seeking a confrontation between Lords and Commons in 1881 and '82 had been to precipitate a general election before Gladstone introduced his Reform Bill.[5] That way the Conservatives could capitalize on the Government's disappointing performance generally and on the unpopularity of its Irish and imperial policy, undeflected by the probably popular issue of Reform. If the Conservatives won, they could delay action or fashion a measure to suit themselves. If they lost but increased their strength in the House of Commons, they would be better able, in cooperation with Whigs, to reduce a Liberal Government's action on this and other matters to modest proportions. The disappointment of these hopes found Salisbury in a gloomy mood at the beginning of 1884, sure that Gladstone was about to bring in a Franchise Bill unaccompanied by redistribution, equally sure that a general election called on an extended franchise without redistribution would ruin the Conservative party for a generation, and doubtful about the Lords' willingness to insist upon a combined measure.[6] The Government's Franchise Bill was promptly introduced.

It did not deflect Salisbury until June from an intention to provoke a general election on other grounds. For public attention was divided between the Bill and the Government's folly of follies overseas: the despatch of General Gordon to evacuate British contingents in the Sudan, particularly at Khartoum, beleaguered by the forces of the Mahdi. Gordon, though well acquainted with the Sudan from his days as a crusader against the slave trade, was by temperament an astonishingly poor choice to direct an evacuation.[7] Once in Khartoum his combative instincts found their way through his imprecise instructions, and he decided to hold his ground. Englishmen watched with deepening unease as the Mahdi's men closed round him while the Government, reluctant to despatch another mission to rescue the rescuers, delayed action. Gordon was the latest in a succession of military commanders whom the Government had allowed to go into the Sudan, only to be cut to pieces.

Salisbury hoped that his situation would become so acute that the Government would fall before Conservatives were faced with the need to decide on the Franchise Bill. The party in the Commons, with his encouragement, slowed up the Bill's progress until June. But, distracted by internal divisions and poorly led by Northcote, it could delay the Bill no longer. Though the Government continued to procrastinate about Gordon, the Franchise Bill proceeded to the Lords. Salisbury was obliged to pick up the gage of electoral reform.

Now that the matter could not be avoided, he focused attention on redistribution. He did so partly for tactical reasons, but also because it was redistribution that worried him most. Franchise extension was acceptable if unwelcome; redistribution involved questions of vital moment. All of the devices or principles pertinent to redistribution which he raised for consideration in the next few months—single-member constituencies, separation of rural and urban populations and of middle and working class districts within urban areas, proportional representation, cumulative voting[8]— had a common denominator: they were means to secure a fair representation of minorities.[9]

Salisbury assumed that the Conservatives were normally a minority party. That did not disconcert him. On the contrary, he thought it infinitely better for the party to forward the minority interests it represented with conscious determination than for it to sacrifice those interests in a bid for majority support.[10] Looking at the problem from another angle, he had suggested that,

> A Liberal Government in office, too weak for violent legislation, is, perhaps, the condition of things most favourable to the maintenance of the Constitution—for the professional advocates of change find themselves by the force of circumstances retained to defend inaction... .[11]

His concern with redistribution was to ensure that the Conservative minority was represented in proportion to its numerical strength. '...by a free country,' he told an audience in Kingston-on-Thames,

I mean a country where people are allowed, so long as they do not hurt their neighbours, to do as they like. I do not mean a country where six men may make five men do exactly as they like.[12]

Fair redistribution of seats meant five Conservative M.P.s, or thereabouts, for every six Liberals.

He was also anxious that constituency boundaries be drawn as much as possible to keep separate the interests and classes which the two parties represented. It was all very well for Radicals to talk about 'the people' as an undifferentiated mass. What Salisbury saw instead were classes and interests with differing concerns and desires which, if fairly represented, could be adjusted but many of which, if heaped together, would be lost. They would be lost either if the franchise were extended without redistribution, or if redistribution was fashioned by Liberals in their own interests. Despite his recognition of 'Villa Toryism,' Salisbury feared that household suffrage in the existing counties would tilt the balance toward the Liberals in what had been safe Conservative seats.[13] A similar result could be achieved by a Liberal redistribution scheme in which the Whig electors of small boroughs would be dumped into hitherto Conservative county constituencies, while large cities like Birmingham continued to be treated as unified multi-member constituencies so that Conservatively inclined middle-class suburbanites could be swamped by Radical working men. Salisbury did not share Disraeli's vision of working-class 'angels in marble.'

Apart from the substance of the issue, there were other subjects which he kept in mind in shaping his tactics: his rivalry with Northcote, the role of the House of Lords, the cohesion of the party, and popular reaction. It all made for a very complicated problem.

Taught by previous experience, Salisbury did not rush to an answer. He undertook a series of speeches in the spring and early summer in different parts of the country both to sound out and to prepare the public. By mid-June he had made up his mind.[14] His decision was to resist the Franchise Bill at the second reading in the Lords, not point blank but with a reasoned amendment refusing to pass the Bill without an accompanying measure for redistribution. The manoeuvre was the work of a matured tactician. Amendment in committee after second reading was unworkable, as the experience of the Arrears Bill had proved. Point blank opposition would be embarrassing and internally divisive: only a small minority in the Commons had taken issue with the principle of franchise extension. The issue of redistribution, on the other hand, raised popularly intelligible questions of principle which the Government's Franchise Bill sought to avoid.

Furthermore—and this was of central importance to Salisbury—the Government might well dissolve Parliament through unwillingness or sheer inability to combine redistribution with franchise extension. Quite apart from the intrinsic difficulty of securing the consent of the House of Commons to the details of a scheme of redistribution, the Government's hold over its majority in the Commons was weakening. The Cabinet was notoriously divided. The Parnellites were moving into total opposition. The Irish Coercion Act would be up for renewal in 1885, a subject certain to weaken the Government in each of these regards. Conservatives were, in addition, more than suspicious that the Government had no intention of enacting a redistribution Bill before dissolving Parliament. Conservatives calculated that a general election on an extended franchise without redistribution would ruin them, many thought for a generation.[15] Why should Liberals resist the temptation?

Salisbury still wanted a dissolution with the existing electorate and constituencies. Insistence on redistribution was a means to that end.[16] Though the Conservative party was not well united, and though its constituency organization was in turmoil,[17] Liberals were demoralized and the public alienated over the Government's overseas policy. Even now that the issue of Parliamentary reform had been raised, most Conservatives were confident of emerging from an election strengthened if not victorious. But if the Government attempted to call his bluff by bringing in a scheme of redistribution, Salisbury would be reluctantly content. Not just any scheme of redistribution would do. Salisbury would use his command over the House of Lords to prevent enactment of the Franchise Bill until a redistribution tolerable to the Opposition had been accepted. He would settle for that.

His tactics placed Gladstone in an awkward position, as they were intended to do. All but one of the possible responses of the Government to rejection of the Franchise Bill by the Lords had to be ruled out. To seek a fresh mandate from the electorate by dissolving Parliament would concede what Salisbury wanted. So would resignation. The Queen could be asked to create enough Liberal peers to override the Lords' veto; but traditionally such a request was a last resort, and the Queen was almost certain to refuse it until another general election was held. The only course open to the Government was the one it had followed with uniform success previously when the House of Lords proved difficult: to break down the peers' resistance by working on their fear of public opinion. This could be done quietly through approaches to neutrals and timid Conservatives in the upper House. If that failed, Liberals could beat the drum at public meetings out of doors.

Gladstone brought his formidable skills of persuasion to bear upon uncertain Whigs, the bench of bishops, and non-partisan peers such as the poet laureate, Lord Tennyson. 146 lords voted against the Conservatives' motion, reducing their majority to 59. On the other hand, the Conservative ranks held firm. The pair of Tory lords, Cairns and Richmond, who had served Gladstone so well in the past, failed him now. At the beginning of the year Salisbury had at last won Richmond's consent to introduce a Bill to prevent further epidemics of disease among cattle by regulating their import;[18] and the move proved to be a complete success. Because it elicited substantial support among Liberal landlords in the Commons, the Government reluctantly brought in a limited measure. It was too limited to satisfy either House, and the Government was forced to back down again by stiffening it. Relations between Salisbury and Richmond were, as a result, in good repair. More important, Richmond shared Salisbury's forebodings about the result of an election on an extended franchise without redistribution.[19]

Accordingly, though Richmond sent up familiar signals of uneasiness about Salisbury's intransigence when the Franchise Bill reached the Lords, this time they were faint. It was Cairns who moved the official Conservative amendment to the second reading; and Richmond promptly seconded him. Cairns served as the intermediary with Lord Granville for a last minute exploration by the Government of the possibility of compromise; but he abided by Salisbury's response which brought the negotiation to an end.

Salisbury's tactics commanded decisively widespread support within the Parliamentary party in both Houses, consolidated at several meetings. Almost all Conservatives in Parliament were concerned about redistribution. Salisbury had his own ideas about which of the redistributory devices he suggested for protection of the minority were more likely to be acceptable and effective. His ideas were closer to those of the party's progressive wing, who favoured single-member constituencies and extensive disfranchisement, than to those who favoured the more traditional techniques for minority protection such as three-member constituencies, though he saw some use for these techniques too. When the time came to settle on the main lines of redistribution, Gladstone was taken back by the lack of commitment to tradition which Salisbury displayed. But to declare himself at this early stage would have been to alienate support, all of which he needed if the Government was to be forced to climb down. Furthermore, some of his staunchest supporters were diehard opponents of the Franchise Bill whether or not it was accompanied by redistribution. He therefore held a balance in his language between calls for a dissolution and calls for redistribution. The only dissidents were a handful of Tory Democrats around Lord Randolph Churchill; and, though unhappy at the prospect of a general election fought over Parliamentary reform, they were preoccupied, first with the fight over the National Union, later with consolidating the position of respectability within the party which that fight gained for them.

A second attempt was made to soften the Lords' stance, through a compromise motion by Lord Wemyss to proceed with the Franchise Bill but at the same time ensure that Parliament was reconvened in the autumn to deal with redistribution. The compromise seduced very few. Any possibility that it would be accepted was eliminated by uncharacteristic clumsiness on Gladstone's part. In a speech to the Liberal Parliamentary party, he broke confidence by revealing the negotiation between Cairns and Granville which had preceded the Lords' first vote, and thus ruined the chance for early resumption of negotiations with Cairns or his ilk. Gladstone further undermined would-be compromisers by indicating that the Government would not push a redistribution scheme forward until the Franchise Bill had been enacted. And he put the Lords' backs up by threatening their House with "most grave" consequences if they persisted in rejecting the Bill.

As soon as the attempt to avoid collision between the Lords and Commons failed, the Government decided to put everything else aside, to reconvene Parliament in the autumn for the sole purpose of passing the Franchise Bill, and in the meantime to take to the platform, telling the public of their efforts for Parliamentary reform which the Conservative party and the House of Lords were frustrating. Public response was genuine and extensive. Nearly 1,300 meetings voicing Liberal opinion were held, many of them without prodding from party leaders, whatever Conservatives might claim to the contrary; and the figures for total attendance reached into the millions.

Conservatives, however, blunted the force of the agitation by convening meetings of their own. Not that there were as many Conservative meetings: they were outnumbered by Liberal meetings seven to one. And the Conservative meetings were less spontaneous, usually arranged by central initiative. Yet they were better attended—the main Conservative rallies were as large as the main Liberal ones—and they were more enthusiastic than Liberals had expected. This effort enabled Conservatives to play a numbers game, a game which of course they lost, but one which allowed them to raise doubts about the massiveness of public support for the Liberal position and hence to insist that it need not be regarded as overwhelming by the House of Lords.

After wondering whether he should display his contempt for the Liberal agitation by spending the summer in France,[20] Salisbury rose to the challenge of platform combat. The issue was not one he preferred, and he did his best to keep General Gordon in the public's mind. Yet he was not sorry that the constitutional function of the House of Lords was to the fore in the controversy. If the upper House was successfully to play the part he desired for it, the public had to be brought to understand and respect it for doing so. As he told a Glasgow audience,

If the House of Lords is to stand, as I believe it will, it will stand because the British people believe that it is the best arrangement that can obtain, not because they have forgotten its existence.[21]

In the present instance the House of Lords was making classical use of its power. It was preventing the party currently dominant in the House of Commons from enacting a measure which, in the estimation of its opponents, would perpetuate its power. Furthermore, the House of Lords was not setting itself up in defiance of the people. On the contrary, it was urging that the people be consulted in the fullest available way, through a general election. And redistribution was as much a matter of principle in reforming the electorate as franchise extension.

He undertook a speaking tour through Scotland right after Gladstone's tour in Midlothian, with the explicit intent, not so much of drawing forth public opinion, as of educating it.[22] Conservatism was not, in his estimation, the creed of stupid men. The capacity to govern was produced in part by education; and since ultimate power was now vested in the public, one of the responsibilities of public leaders was to teach the public the principles of good government. Salisbury welcomed as evidence of the relationship between Conservatism and fresh reflection the fact, as he claimed, that in Scotland it was the young men who were inclined to the Conservative side whereas the old remained wedded to their traditional Liberalism.[23]

His style of oratory was in keeping with this intent. It was lean, with little literary or rhetorical embellishment, though lightened by cynical wit. His speeches were well considered but never written out beforehand; he delivered them slowly, keeping the line of thought clear. Though rarely as rousing as Gladstone's, Churchill's or Chamberlain's, they carried conviction; they read well, and lifted him into the ranks of the best half dozen speakers of his day. He had been serving an apprenticeship in platform oratory since the last election. He and Northcote had taken to the platform soon after the change of Government and had returned to it regularly, as Disraeli had seldom done. Still, Salisbury disliked the appearance of pandering to the public. He took pleasure in foiling attempts to make him adopt Gladstone's habit of impromptu speeches at railway stops. He reserved himself for well planned rallies.

The target of the Liberal agitation and of the Conservative counter-agitation was the potentially dissident Conservative peerage. If Liberal efforts could crumple the spines of thirty Tory lords, the Bill could get through the upper House before redistribution was tackled. For practical purposes, the thirty boiled down to two. If Richmond and Cairns decided to give way, their prestige would do the trick. On the substance of the controversy, on the need for redistribution to accompany the franchise, the two stood uncharacteristically firm. Where they differed from Salisbury was in his desire to force a dissolution or at least to hold up the Franchise Bill until he could get an acceptable redistribution scheme.[24] As long as redistribution accompanied the franchise, Richmond and Cairns were willing to leave the details of redistribution to the House of Commons with its Liberal majority. The pressure which brought them to this conclusion came from the Queen rather than from the public, though the public agitation heightened her determination to break the Parliamentary impasse. What saved Salisbury from an unacceptable compromise of this sort was its rejection by Gladstone,[25] who still saw hope for his Franchise Bill by itself.

The hope was unrealistic. The details of redistribution were brought to the fore in everyone's mind by two publications. Salisbury brought out an article in the *National Review*[26] in which he dealt with electoral statistics in some detail and canvassed several possibilities for re-distribution. Two weeks later, the scheme for redistribution which a Cabinet committee under the chairmanship of Sir Charles Dilke had been considering was leaked to the *Standard*. Parliament reconvened toward the end of October; and for another month Gladstone and Salisbury kept their troops in fixed positions. But secret probes were launched to discover how far the leaders or their important supporters were prepared to yield.

It was Gladstone who made the bid for compromise which eventually broke the impasse; it was Salisbury who held out longest. To that extent Salisbury was the victor. But the balance of victory and defeat in the eventual settlement was more complicated than that, and came close to a draw. Gladstone offered privately through Northcote, and then publicly in the House of Commons, to enter into friendly communication with the Opposition on redistribution, to introduce a Redistribution Bill, and to make its passage a vital question to the Government, if the Opposition would give adequate assurances that the Franchise Bill would be passed without delay. To sweeten the offer, he added that, if it were taken up quickly, the Franchise Bill would not take effect until 1 January 1886. Salisbury rejected the proposal when offered privately and was disposed to do so again when offered publicly, for he believed that under its terms the Lords would still be required to pass the Franchise Bill *before* Gladstone would negotiate about redistribution.

He accepted the offer as a result of two developments. Through his nephew Arthur Balfour he learned that negotiations on redistribution could precede enactment of the Franchise Bill. At the same time, prompted by the Queen, Richmond and Cairns insisted that Salisbury accept the offer. It is impossible to determine which of these two events decided Salisbury. Gladstone's offer as clarified through Balfour brought Salisbury's second choice of an agreed scheme of redistribution within reach. On the other hand Salisbury made no attempt to conceal his disappointment that the deadlock had been broken and a dissolution postponed;[27] but this confession may have been calculated to appease the diehards whose disappointment was more acute than his own. Part of Salisbury's tactical power was that he kept his motives a mystery.

The risk in agreeing to negotiations on redistribution was that, if Gladstone insisted on unacceptable provisions, the Lords might not resume the fight. Salisbury therefore entered the negotiations[28] determined that, if at all possible, they should succeed. And he got a settlement which he could accept. He would have liked direct minority representation in the larger cities by means of three-member constituencies; but he found that, while the Liberal negotiators were strongly opposed, Conservatives in these cities were not sufficiently united on the point to force the issue.[29] He therefore decided on indirect minority representation by division of the country into single-member constituencies: and that was done for all but the City of London, the Universities, and twenty-three middle sized cities. Revealing his sympathy with the position of the advanced men in the party, he pushed the level at which small boroughs lost separate representation up from 10,000 to 15,000[30] and the level at which the next size of boroughs with double representation lost one of their members up from 40,000 to 50,000. The agreement, called 'the Arlington Street Compact' after Salisbury's London residence where it was concluded, also provided that the drawing of electoral boundaries was to be entrusted to boundary commissioners with specified instructions. In dividing boroughs, they were to pay attention to the pursuits of the population; in dividing counties, they were to keep populous and rural areas separate as far as possible and convenient. The Franchise Bill was to be enacted immediately; and the Government staked its life on the agreed redistribution provisions. In addition, the Compact preserved the University seats. The negotiations came close to failure on this point. Salisbury insisted upon it, not only as a source of Conservative support, but as a symbol, however small, that the principles underlying the redistribution were not wholly democratic.[31]

Apart from dotting the i's and crossing the t's of the agreement, the remaining task was to win consent to the Compact from the party. Salisbury did not expect and did not encounter serious resistance. The response of the Parliamentary party when Northcote and he presented the agreement to them was one of sobered acquiescence. There was no feasible alternative. With the exception of a few diehards, the leaders had received ready consent when they asked for authority to enter into the negotiations in the first place; and it was difficult to demand better results without being privy to the negotiations which had, understandably, been conducted behind closed doors. Some consultation with the rank and file had gone on while the settlement was being worked out. But, apart from the matter of three-member constituencies, Salisbury had paid attention to it only when it suited his purposes. Once the Compact was concluded and the leaders who had negotiated it threw their strength behind it, the rank and file and even the second tier of leaders were powerless to resume the fight unless they could arrange a mutiny on both sides of the House of Commons. And Conservative critics of the agreement were divided. Traditionalists regretted the loss of multi-member constituencies because of an accurate foreboding that smaller constituencies would give rise to candidates of a lower social class.[32] Advanced men regretted that the Compact did not go farther in disfranchising small boroughs and did not provide for single-member constituencies universally.

The chief Conservative casualty of the whole affair was Sir Stafford Northcote. His leadership in the House of Commons had been under attack from the Fourth party ever since the change of Government in 1880; and his performance, unlike Salisbury's, had shown no improvement. As Conservatives' anger at the conduct of the Government mounted, so did their impatience with Northcote. His inadequacies were shown up by the brilliant contrast of Churchill, though when Churchill launched direct attacks on Northcote, they rebounded in displays of support for the leader. Even loyal lieutenants of Northcote recognized dispiriting weaknesses in him. He had served Disraeli adequately as manager of government business in the House of Commons when failing health forced the old Chief to accept a peerage. But Northcote never acquired the authority of leader for himself, because he lacked the gifts for opposition.

Rarely had a Government stumbled more often or had such bad luck as Gladstone's second Ministry—in Ireland, in southern Africa, in Egypt and the Sudan, and with continuing economic depression at home. Again and again the knife for execution was placed in Northcote's hands; and as often he fumbled with it. His speeches on the platform ranged from dull to duller, though they commanded respect as was amply demonstrated later after his sudden death. By 1882, when he rose to speak in the House of Commons the quiet buzz of private conversation continued.[33] He conducted the Opposition in a responsible spirit; but Liberals took it for weakness, and directed their fire at Salisbury even though he could not be there to receive it.[34]

The general strategy which Northcote followed—to conform Conservative policy to that of dissident Whigs, and to support the Government when attacked by its Radical wing, in order eventually to achieve a Conservative-Whig alliance—might have been a sound one. But it was fatally weakened by Northcote's manner. Seemingly overawed by Gladstone, whom he had once served as private secretary and whom until 1880 he continued to address as 'my right honourable friend,' Northcote struck neutral observers as 'monotonously conciliatory.'[35] High-spirited Tories, in Henry Cecil Raikes' memorable phrase, saw 'the hands of perplexity travelling up and down the sleeves of irresolution.' In the spring of 1884 Edward Hamilton noted that, 'One can never dine in Tory company... without hearing Sir S. Northcote slighted.'[36]

Yet he was in possession of the party leadership in the Commons; and it was known that the Queen had indicated an intention of selecting him as prime minister should the Liberal Government fall.[37] Salisbury was determined to edge him out of contention for the supreme leadership of the party, though without hurting him any more than necessary. Their careers had been linked since 1858 when they were returned together as Members for the borough of Stamford. They had acted with courtly if superficial deference in the dual leadership since 1881, taking pains to avoid the appearance of disunity. They played by the rules of gentlemen. Still, a divided leadership could never be better than awkward.

Salisbury shaped his tactics throughout the reform controversy to the double end of defeating the Liberals and superceding his rival. Northcote was somewhat more disposed than Salisbury to take issue directly with extension of the franchise.[38] Northcote was even more interested, after a successful speaking tour through Ireland during the autumn of 1883, in focusing the Tory attack on the Irish features of electoral reform, particularly the over-representation of Ireland as a whole and the under-representation of Belfast. Salisbury, for all his intransigence over Ireland otherwise, did not want to focus the attack over reform there, partly because Northcote was now identified with that angle, partly because the Conservatives would need Parnellite votes in the Commons if the Government was to be defeated over the Sudan. Northcote's hesitant, consultative approach[39] enabled Salisbury to make sure that the decisive confrontation over reform was left to the House of Lords, his ground. Sir Charles Dilke, a shrewd Radical, was asked in August what the game of the Lords was, and replied:

> It is not the 'game of the Lords':—it is the game of Salisbury. He has made himself undisputed leader of his party.[40]

Northcote botched his work in the Commons, at one point allowing the Franchise Bill to receive a unanimously favourable vote. In October, before Parliament reconvened, he was left out, to his dismay,[41] from a conference in Scotland between Salisbury and the potentially dissident peers, Richmond and Cairns. When negotiations with the Government were finally decided upon, Northcote could not be excluded—though Salisbury did take care to keep the group of negotiators small in order to exclude Richmond and Cairns, and restricted to privy councillors in order to exclude Churchill. Salisbury, Gladstone and Dilke then plunged into discussion at a dizzy pace, with disarming informality—no tables to write on, and maps strewn all over the floor—and with a mental agility that reduced the slower participants, Northcote and Hartington, to fluttering ineffectuality.[42] Once the principles of the Compact were established, the details were left entirely to Salisbury and Dilke.

The course of the Redistribution Bill through the House of Commons confirmed Salisbury's ascendancy. For it was up to Northcote to vote with the Government whenever Covservative M.P.s, often egged on by Churchill, challenged the agreement; and on occasion Northcote found himself with humiliatingly little support. When the situation threatened to get out of hand, it was Salisbury who laid down the law to the Conservative Parliamentary party, though to little effect. Otherwise he was removed from embarrassment by his seat in the Lords. Everyone but Northcote, and even Northcote in moments of discouragement,[43] recognized now that Salisbury was the man who, if the task of government fell to Conservatives within at least the next year or two, would be called upon to take charge.

The other clear dividend of the reform conflict from Salisbury's point of view was its demonstration of the Lords' ability on a major issue to defy a Liberal Government in possession of a large majority in the Commons, and to force it to compromise. This was a dividend which distinguished the passage of the Reform Acts of 1884/5 from those of 1832 and 1867. As for the actual provisions of enfranchisement and redistribution, their implications for the future of the two British parties were unclear and lay in the lap of the electoral gods. It turned out that Salisbury had done his work well, but that fact does not prove prescience on his part. His concern to secure fair representation for the minority proved excessive, for in alliance with the Liberal Unionists the Conservatives were soon to become the majority party. And it was redistribution rather than the Franchise Act which placed the working class, in whom Salisbury had little confidence, for the first time in a position to dominate the election in a majority of constituencies. On the other hand, his insistence that constituency boundaries be drawn to coincide as far as possible with occupational and therefore class lines served the interests of the Conservative party as he conceived of it.

## ii. Lord Randolph Churchill and the National Union

The outcome of the other conflict in which Salisbury was engaged in 1884 was much more ambiguous. At the Annual Conference of the National Union of Conservative Associations in the previous October,

Lord Randolph Churchill and John Gorst engineered the passage of a resolution calling for a 'legitimate share' of influence for the National Union within the party's organization. They planned to implement the resolution through the election of a slate of candidates to the Council of the National Union containing a majority of men who would cooperate with them. Though the results of the election were mixed, they led to the appointment of an organization committee controlled for the moment by Churchill's supporters and charged with responsibility to implement the resolution. Churchill forced his way into the chair of this committee over the head of the chairman of the Council, Lord Percy, and then approached Salisbury of behalf of the committee with a request for consultation. What developed was a bid to wrest control of the party machinery from its current managers and ultimately to assume direction of the party.

The challenge to Salisbury was not immediate. Churchill deliberately approached Salisbury alone rather than the dual leadership. From the beginning of his guerrilla warfare against Northcote in 1880, Churchill had hoped to see Salisbury installed as leader of the whole party. In the wake of the fiasco over the Arrears Bill, Churchill revealed his own ambitions for the leadership. But since an immediate seizure of the leadership for himself was not practicable, he continued to regard Salisbury as an acceptable alternative, at least for the time being.

Salisbury had been willing to speak from the same platform as Churchill at Woodstock, Churchill's constituency, in November 1880, and to speak to Disraeli in explanation of Churchill's attacks on Northcote.[44] Like Disraeli, Salisbury could not help having a little sympathy with a young man making a mark through rebellion as he himself had done. But he was embarrassed by Churchill's attempts to vault him into the leadership over Northcote, for they invariably backfired. Furthermore, laurels bestowed by Churchill could be taken away by the same hand. And in most matters of policy the reflexes of Salisbury and Churchill were antithetical. Salisbury responded to Churchill's overture on behalf of the new organization committee of the National Union by proposing to include Northcote in the conference, though he kept the correspondence in his own hands.

Lord Randolph Churchill posed a potentially deadly threat to Salisbury, much more serious than did Northcote. Both in Parliament and on the public platform Churchill was dazzling. As a man of opposition in the Commons, he was everything that Northcote was not. Quick and as dextrous in manoeuvre as Gladstone, he darted around the Grand Old Man with incessant punches delivered from unexpected angles or with great force. Friend and foe swarmed into the chamber to enjoy the fight. Out of doors the language of his assaults upon the Ministry was unmeasured, rambunctious yet 'set off by an artificial pomp of style.'[45] Though his appeals were often, on any analysis, crude demagogy directed against persons even more than policies, they were nonetheless incisive.

Churchill had all the makings for successful leadership bar one, which was not immediately apparent but which Salisbury possessed to perfection: staying power, or the art of biding one's time. He could not put up with slower natures even among loyal followers. Though he was the most scintillating of companions and surrounded by admiring associates, the path of his advance was to be strewn with the wounded bodies of those he turned on. He had another liability. However much principle there may have been in his creed of Tory Democracy, he did not possess moral weight. His dexterity as a fighter conveyed a contrary impression of unalloyed opportunism. But that was not obviously fatal. The 1880s were a decade of moral uncertainty. Gravity was still valued, but so was brilliance. W. H. Smith, 'Old Morality,' was to follow Churchill as leader in the House of Commons and to succeed where Churchill had failed. But Churchill succeeded where Northcote failed. Ultimate victory was to lie with two men who combined moral weight and brilliance: Salisbury and Gladstone. But in 1884 that was far from clear.

Salisbury did not respond to Churchill's challenge in 1884 either with the tactical skill he was deploying against Gladstone over the Reform Bill or with the determination which the incompatibility between their brands of Conservatism, so apparent in retrospect, would lead one to expect. It had taken Salisbury three years to develop the finesse necessary for successful confrontation between the two parties. It would take him another three to master the skills of intra-party conflict. Furthermore, Salisbury and Churchill had enough in common to disguise the degree of their incompatibility. Their apparent similarities were largely matters of temperament. Both were men of spirit frustrated by timidity, appreciative of talent, and undeterred from adopting bold counsels by the conventional wisdom of moderate men. They admired each other's skill in discomfiting Liberals. And in Northcote they had a common rival, though their different styles in dealing with Northcote made cooperation against him difficult.

Their conceptions of Conservatism seemed to be poles apart. The reincarnation in Churchill of Disraeli's coquetry with Radicals was the very strategy which Salisbury's pursuit of the leadership was intended to defeat. Churchill denounced the future to which Salisbury was urging the Conservative party to reconcile itself, of 'a long period of endless opposition, perhaps occasionally chequered by little glimpses of office with a minority.'[46] In its place Churchill held out the tantalizing prospect of becoming a triumphant majority. While in the anonymous pages of the *Quarterly Review* Salisbury analysed the pitfalls of popular government, Churchill told a cheering crowd of Conservatives at Birmingham to

> Trust the people. You, who are ambitious, and rightly ambitious, of being the guardians of the British Constitution, trust the people and they will follow you and join you in defence of that Constitution against any and every foe.
>
> I have no fear of democracy. I do not fear for minorities; I do not care for those checks and securities which Mr. Goschen [and, though he did not say so, Lord Salisbury] seems to think of such importance. Modern checks and securities are not worth a brass farthing.[47]

Churchill was more than willing to pay the price in policy which the prospect he painted would cost. The creed of Tory Democracy as he preached and practised it was almost indistinguishable from Liberalism, the outlook which he presumed to be natural to the majority of Englishmen. Apart from his flirtation with fair trade against the rigidities of official Liberalism, Churchill pursued a policy of out-Liberalling Gladstone's Ministry. As his son later put it: 'To split the Government majority by raising some issue on which conscientious Radicals would be forced to vote against their leaders, or, failing that, by some question on which the Minister concerned would be likely to utter illiberal sentiments, and bound to justify a policy or a system which the Liberal party detested, was his perpetual and almost instinctive endeavour.'[48] He argued that the Employers Liability Bill of 1880 did not go far enough, that the Government's Irish policy was wrongly dependent on coercion, that its errors in South Africa and Egypt stemmed from inadequate sympathy for Boer and Egyptian nationalism; and on budgetary matters he called for still further reduction of the estimates. His aim was not to secure a fusion with the Radicals, but to upstage them, to capture for the Conservative party the platform of 'peace, retrenchment, and reform' which had served Liberals for more than a generation so well.

To give the platform a Conservative colour, he held up for popular veneration the institutions of Crown, Church and Lords. However, beyond acts of obeisance, he offered nothing to guard or strengthen them.[49] He also tried to throw the mantle of Disraeli over his programme; and in the press it was described as an elaboration of the fallen leader's teaching. But Tory Democracy was highly selective Disraelianism. Churchill was critical of Disraeli's legacy in foreign policy, particularly of the commitment to Constantinople and the Turk. In private he found still more to censure about Disraeli, and admired mainly his fighting spirit and rebelliousness.[50]

Two creeds of Conservatism more dissimilar than Salisbury's and Churchill's would be hard to conceive. But in learning to work with Disraeli, Salisbury had discovered that successful collaboration in party politics did not require identity or even easy compatibility of creeds. It required only an ability and willingness to work out practical agreements on practical problems, however philosophically irreconcilable the creeds might be that led each collaborator to the agreed conclusion. That recognition could be applied even to a Joseph Chamberlain, as events were to show. All Salisbury required was an ability to work together. That requirement Churchill could not meet; but three years would pass before that was clear. In the meantime, if political considerations so required, nothing in Tory Democracy would prevent Salisbury from working with Churchill. And they had their points of agreement on policy. Like Churchill, Salisbury did not share the common Conservative fondness for Turkey. Both men were in varying degrees ambivalent about the expansion of empire. Both, though unflinching in their determination to maintain British ascendency in India, detested the 'damned nigger' attitude common among British residents there.[51]

Moreover, 1884 found Salisbury engaged in an initiative in social reform which struck some Conservatives (and the labour leader Henry Broadhurst) as nothing short of socialism. He had recently published an article in the *National Review* on 'Labourers' and artisans' dwellings.'[52] It brought the subject of slum housing to the forefront of political discussion. There were tactical reasons for raising the subject. Like regulation of the import of cattle, it was a subject which Gladstone had recently brushed aside. It might divert attention from the impending struggle over Parliamentary reform. It might upstage Churchill. And the moment was ripe for action. Just before Salisbury's article was published, public imagination was caught by an anonymous pamphlet, *The Bitter Cry of Outcast London*, which vividly described conditions in the slums and the vice they bred.

Policy considerations of a higher level were also involved. Raising the subject of slum housing helped to point up the limitations of Liberalism and the material benefits of Conservative government. Overcrowding in the slums was, as Salisbury saw it, a wry commentary on 'improving' Liberalism. The problem had been greatly exacerbated by civic works such as the Thames embankment, new streets, viaducts, and public buildings, for which room had been made by demolishing slums without rehousing the dispossessed. The building of Farringdon Street alone had caused the displacement of 40,000.[53] As one medical officer commented, 'All improvements recoiled on the poor.'[54] Salisbury also argued repeatedly that Radicals' preoccupation with constitutional and purely political reform diverted attention from what the state could be doing for men's material wellbeing. He wanted to buttress the Conservative party's reputation for social concern and thus to dissipate 'the absurd delusion that the dislike of democracy entertained by the Tory party means indifference to the welfare of the poor.'[55]

There was more than political calculation to Salisbury's initiative.

His article came out so soon after *The Bitter Cry* that it may have been independently conceived. In any case he had been drawing attention to the subject in his speeches as leader since 1881. It had been included in his first election address back in 1853, and was treated in some of his writing for the *Saturday Review* in the 1850s and '60s.[56] The state, in his estimation, needed to concern itself about the housing of poor urban artisans, not just because civic improvements were partially responsible for their plight, but also in order to make up for the weakness in cities of the sense of social obligation which induced rural landowners like himself to build cottages for agricultural labourers.[57] He responded to the subject paternalistically; but his understanding of the urban housing problem was still remarkable. By concentrating on overcrowding rather than sanitation, he plunged to its heart as no politician had done before.[58]

Still, his response to slum housing was anomalous. Though in each of his subsequent Ministries, important housing legislation would be passed, that was the sum-total of his personal contribution to social welfare during his many years of power. His analysis of urban housing left little to be desired by the standards of his day; but he did not apply the same kind of analysis, nor did he invest the same intensity of concern, in the many other areas of social need. He was afraid of counter-productive consequences if the owners of land or capital were interfered with, afraid also of alienating his right wing and thus forfeiting their active support at election time. It was significant that in 1882, between speeches on urban housing, Salisbury delivered an address as chairman of the Railway Officers and Servants Association in which he appealed for public subscription to its pension fund;[59] pensions for railway workers, he argued, were the responsibility of the public rather than the companies since the public in this case was the real employer.

Salisbury followed his *National Review* article with a successful motion in the House of Lords for appointment of a royal commission on urban working class housing. As the Commission got under way, Dilke, who was its chairman, was taken aback by the searching nature and extent of the enquiry which Salisbury wanted undertaken.[60] But Salisbury began to draw back when Chamberlain, in a series of speeches which came to be known as the 'Unauthorized Programme,' embedded discussion of working class housing in an assault upon the owners of land.[61] The eventual Act, passed in the summer of 1885 during Salisbury's 'Caretaker' Ministry, was not an insignificant measure. Following the lines of the Commission's report, it empowered London's Metropolitan Board of Works to build and let working-class housing.[62] Yet neither the report nor the Act were as ambitious as Salisbury's earlier prodding could have produced.

To return to Churchill: his Tory Democracy, though first fully launched over the Employers Liability Act of 1880, was much more concerned with political than social advance, and, for tactical reasons, he did not take a prominent part in support of Salisbury on urban housing. Still, Salisbury's initiative opened up a field for potential cooperation between the two men on the domestic front where they were otherwise most sharply divided. All this was, however, to look ahead. Collaboration was possible, but only, so far as Salisbury was concerned, if forced upon him.

By resorting to the National Union of Conservative Associations, Churchill seized upon a sphere where Salisbury was vulnerable: Churchill appealed to the middle and working class Conservatives of the cities who had organized and manned local associations, only to be ignored by the party's central management. Salisbury did not grip the imagination of the party at large as Churchill did.[63] However bold his attacks on the Government or his aspirations for the party and the House of Lords, his public manner was always august. Churchill was impudent. He enjoyed crumpling tin gods, jeering at worthies, throwing stones at giants; and popular audiences loved it. Furthermore, though Salisbury saw the potential of "Villa Toryism" and, even before Churchill, sensed the importance of mobilizing opinion through constituency associations,[64] he had yet to recognize the necessity of less exclusive party management. He was part and parcel of the upper class party establishment whose neglect of local party stalwarts was resented. His comments on slum housing also indicated that he did not fully appreciate the social and civic responsibility of which his Villa Tories were proving themselves capable.

Since the defeat of 1880, party policy had been framed by consultations among the members of the late Cabinet, while the task of rebuilding the party's organization had been vested in a 'Central Committee' manned by some of the same men and their appointed officers. The network of constituency associations was assiduously extended. But when the delegates from associations federated in the National Union met for their Annual Conference, their deliberations were ignored. They knew that it was in the larger towns, where the National Union was most vigorous, that conservatives had done fairly well in 1880 as compared with the aristocratically dominated counties. They recalled that borough results had produced the margin of victory in 1874. They saw that Chamberlain's National Liberal Federation, a more tightly organized and more vigorous version of the National Union, was given much of the credit for the Liberal victory in 1880, and that it had gone on to impress its wishes on the Government. They believed, quite rightly, that the interests and desires they represented— urban rather than rural, and more reformist than their rural counter- parts—had gone largely unheeded, whether the party was in power or out. They were loyal to the party, commonly because they were strong supporters of the Established Church, but not to the party leaders.

Tory Democracy was designed to appeal to borough Conservatives of the middle and working classes; and the one forum where they could ventilate their grievances was the National Union. Churchill was led to it by his ally John Gorst, one of the National Union's founders and the guardian of its interests while he served as Principal Agent of the party from 1870 to 1877 and again after 1880. There had been rumblings of discontent at the Union's Annual Conferences since 1876. The Conference of 1880 had proved particularly hard to manage.[65] The only way that the loyalist leadership at the 1883 Conference could cope with Churchill's resolution was to adopt it themselves in hopes of diffusing the rebellious force behind it. Churchill found eager support from a large minority in the subsequent organization committee and ready acquiescence from a working majority.

Salisbury blundered repeatedly in his treatment of the overtures which Churchill induced the committee to make. Initially wishing to avoid a collision, Salisbury disregarded the warnings of Northcote and Edward Stanhope[66] and sent Churchill an imprecise outline of work which the National Union might properly undertake. Churchill wildly exaggerated the letter's implications. He treated it as a *magna carta* empowering the National Union to take over much of the work of party management outside Parliament and to bring constituency pressure to bear upon the shaping of party policy. When Salisbury clarified his meaning and reaffirmed the primacy of the Central Committee, Churchill responded defiantly. Lord Percy as chairman of the National Union's Council then attempted to oust Churchill from the chair of the organization committee. The bid failed; Percy resigned his chairmanship of the Council; and Churchill was elected in his place. But Salisbury continued to deal with the National Union through Percy. Compounding the insult, he had George Bartley, Gorst's recent replacement as Principal Agent, serve notice that if the National Union continued to pursue its separate way, it would have to find new office accommodation outside party headquarters. At this point both sides drew back. Northcote, Gorst and Sir Michael Hicks Beach explored the possibilities of compromise, while Churchill awaited Salisbury's reply to a somewhat modified statement of the organization committee's ambitions for the National Union.

Salisbury sent Churchill a response which was temperately worded but unyielding. The role Salisbury offered the National Union was primarily one of responsibility for propaganda and for the proliferation of local associations. It also envisaged local election work—watching registration, providing volunteer canvassers, and conveying voters to the polls—but this was to be handled in concert with the Central Committee. The powers of the Central Committee were to remain undiminished, while, in order to ensure harmony between the two institutions, Salisbury proposed that the Parliamentary whips, who worked with the Central Committee, should also sit *ex officio* on the Council of the National Union with a further right to be present at meetings of all sub-committees. In return, two members of the National Union Council would be invited to join the Central Committee.

Churchill exploded. Hurriedly convening a meeting of his supporters on the organization committee, he secured agreement to a reply which he had drafted. It declared the refusal of the National Union to 'continue to be a sham, useless, and hardly even an ornamental portion' of the party's organization; announced a determination to emulate the Birmingham caucus of Chamberlain; described Salisbury's proposal about the whips as 'extravagant and despotic;' and concluded with an unspecified but unmistakable threat:

> It may be that the powerful and secret influences which have hitherto been unsuccessfully at work on the Council, with the knowledge and consent of your Lordship & Sir Stafford Northcote may at last be effectual in reducing the National Union to its former make-believe and impotent condition: in that case we shall know what steps to take to clear ourselves of all responsibility for the failure of an attempt to avert the misfortunes and reverses which will, we are certain, under the present effete system of wire-pulling and secret organization, overtake & attend the Conservative party at a General Election.[67]

'This', Northcote remarked to Salisbury, 'is not encouraging.'[68]

Churchill's unmeasured attack violated the canons of party loyalty which Conservatives held in particularly high esteem. Once again both sides drew back, and the pursuit of a mutually acceptable compromise was resumed. One of the peacemakers was Lord Abergavenny, a veteran party organizer and fund-raiser. Though one of the most powerful of the unseen men of influence against whom Churchill inveighed, Abergavenny was himself a bit of a rebel, interested in broadening party institutions. He was currently engaged in establishing a less expensive, less exclusive version of the Carlton Club, named the Constitutional. And he was unimpressed by the performance of the Central Committee, particularly of its most active member, Edward Stanhope. The Central Committee was merely the current, expanded form of the long-standing organizational executive of Principal Agent and whips. Abergavenny discovered that Churchill would agree to a return to the smaller traditional body and, if that were granted, to the inclusion of whips on the Council of the National Union. He relayed the news to Salisbury. Salisbury was not wedded to the Central Committee; he recognized that the traditional form of organizational executive would not derogate from the party leaders' authority. Nonetheless, that authority would be diminished if the change was made at Churchill's behest; and he turned this solution down.

Still, accommodation was on its way, when the negotiations were

accidentally disrupted. One member of the National Union's organization committee, J. S. Maclean, a supporter of Churchill's aspirations
for the National Union but of Salisbury's leadership, unaware of the
peace discussions which were going on, brought before the committee a
motion for a conference with the Central Committee. Salisbury did not,
as was later claimed,[69] break off the discussions to await the vote on
Maclean's motion. Churchill, however, treated it as a motion of want of
confidence in himself; and when it was carried, he resigned from the
Council chairmanship.

For a moment it looked as though his bid for power through the
National Union had failed. But the acceptance of Maclean's motion
proved instead to be a blow to Salisbury. For Churchill's resignation
elicited demonstrations of the popular support which he possessed and
Salisbury did not. A deputation of the chairman of eight constituency
associations in large cities met in London and conferred with Churchill.
Then they waited upon Salisbury to express their sympathy with
Churchill's objectives, and sent a memorandum to the National Union's
Council urging it to restore Churchill to the chair. A delegation of
undergraduates from Cambridge hung round Churchill's house all one
day to assure him of their support. Uneasiness about the row spread so
far that the Carlton Club acted to withhold its funds from the party.
There was fear that the Junior Carlton would follow suit, and that
private subscriptions would fall off as well.

Northcote took fright, alarmed by the combination of this trouble and
the difficulties which Churchill and his small band of allies in the House
of Commons were making over the Franchise Bill. Churchill had
abandoned his early opposition to the Bill and was voting against the
official Conservative attempts to impede its passage. Northcote conjured
up a spectre of the party split into two warring camps in a general
election fought over the issue of Reform. In the interests of peace, he
urged postponement of the National Union conference scheduled by the
loyalists for July.[70] Salisbury, however, was confident that he could
carry the bulk of the party with him on the Franchise Bill. He
cooperated with the loyalists of the National Union in their preparation
for a showdown. They were able, despite Churchill's re-election as
Council chairman, to summon the National Union conference for July
and to convene it in Sheffield where the local association was known to
be friendly. They also arranged a dinner for all delegates, except known
Churchill supporters, at which Salisbury would speak on the eve of the
conference.

The rebels were equally active. Under Gorst's tutelage, they worked
in the member associations for election of amenable delegates. Once the
delegates arrived, they found themselves caught up in a war of
hospitality between the two sides. The moment of decision would come

with the elections for a new Council. Each side circulated a slate of candidates. The voting was preceded by distribution of the correspondence between the organization committee and the party leaders, and by an open discussion. From the chair, Churchill called for election of a Council which would put his movement in undisputed control. The loyalists called for a Council representative of all sections but with 'a predominance of those whom experience shows bear true allegiance to the leaders of the party.'[71]

The results of the balloting appeared to give Churchill what he sought. He himself led the poll. Of the remaining thirty-five places, twenty-one went to men on his slate. A night of elation in the rebel camp was followed, however, by a sober morning. Cautioned by the loyalists' lack of discouragement, they took a more careful look at the results. The rebel slate had included some neutrals. Nineteen from the loyalists' slate had been elected, as were three men on neither slate. If Churchill had a majority, it was small and unreliable. The election results were in fact humbling to both sides, though more so to the loyalists than to the rebels. Publication of Churchill's intemperate letters had not shocked the delegates into line with the party leadership. In the discussion preceding the vote, however, uncommitted delegates expressed impatience with continuation of the dispute. Half a year of campaigning by Churchill produced a Council as mixed as the one he had begun with. If the election proved to Salisbury that the alternative to accommodation with Churchill was a deadlocked party machine, it did not give Churchill control.

One of Churchill's lieutenants, Sir Henry Drummond Wolff, stayed on briefly in Sheffield, long enough to conclude that an overture to Salisbury would be wise. A career diplomat and a happy companion for whom politics was more a game than a serious pursuit, Drummond Wolff sought out Churchill at the London residence of Lord Wimborne. The challenge which the House of Lords had just laid down to the Government over the Franchise Bill lent urgency to the situation. Drummond Wolff secured Churchill's somewhat reluctant consent for an approach to Salisbury, and then went next door to Salisbury's house. Salisbury was ready to work out an agreement. 'A temporary retreat on account of the peculiar circumstances of the moment would be wisest,' he told Balfour: 'It need involve no admission of defeat; nor compromise any future action.'[72] He arranged to meet Churchill later that day at a garden party at Marlborough House which both would be attending.

There, with the same swiftness which characterized his negotiations with Gladstone and Dilke on redistribution, Salisbury and Churchill reached an agreement. In part it followed the lines of the compromise to which the two sides had all but agreed before the disruption over Maclean's motion. The Central Committee would be replaced by the traditional executive of whips and Principal Agent, which would retain supreme power as the party leaders' deputies in matters of organization. A modest increase of party funds would be allotted to the National Union, but the Principal Agent would be appointed as its treasurer. Questions of personal ambition as well as party organization were at stake. To settle these, it was decided that Churchill would abandon his candidacy for the chairmanship of the newly elected National Union Council in favour of Sir Michael Hicks Beach. Hicks Beach was acceptable to the old guard as a former Cabinet Minister, yet had recently entered into friendly relations with Churchill. In a similar spirit, vice-chairmanships would be given to Gorst, a junior whip Akers-Douglas, and Balfour. And Churchill would be lifted—though, as it turned out, only part way—into the inner councils of the party leadership.

The casualties of the agreement were few. Gorst was deeply concerned about the development of the National Union, the powers of which would now continue to be circumscribed; and he strongly suspected that his personal interests had been sacrificed by Churchill to Salisbury. Though the suspicion was unfounded, Gorst became a perennial sour rebel, embarrassing subsequent Salisbury Ministries by reiterating the Tory Democratic creed while holding a succession of secondary offices. On the other side, Lord Percy felt betrayed by Salisbury's failure to insist on full victory for the loyalists after their months of battle on his behalf against Churchill, whom they now must regard as a leader. Beyond Gorst and Percy, there were no hard feelings. Salisbury took steps to retain, and Churchill to acquire, the goodwill of Stanhope. The concordat was celebrated quickly with a dinner given by Salisbury to the newly elected Council, and a month later by a public demonstration in Manchester at which Salisbury, Churchill and Hicks Beach delivered speeches.

There was another, lesser clause to the agreement. Drummond Wolff and Churchill had founded the Primrose League, an organization named after Disraeli's supposedly favourite flower, designed to mould 'into a compact body the more active and energetic partisans of the newer and more democratic school of Conservatism,'[73] and to attract a mass membership with a Masonic style of ritual and titles. Neither its expected credo nor its florid character was to Salisbury's taste. He had therefore given it only cool approval. That approval was now made official, and the League ceased to be distinctively Tory Democratic.

Institutionally the agreement with Churchill was a victory for Salisbury. The executive of the party organization remained under the party leaders' full control; and in its lean, revised form it was expected to function more efficiently than the cumbersome Central Committee. As for the National Union, its cooperation was now assured. If it proved more vigorous than before in extending local associations and in propaganda, that was all to the good. The Primrose League would serve as a powerful supplement.

At the level of personal ambition, the victory was Churchill's. Though he had not supplanted Salisbury, he had accomplished all he expected. His goal was inclusion in the councils of the party leaders. That he had achieved, and more. For the publicity of the dispute, and hence of its settlement, underscored the fact that he was one rival with whom Salisbury had to come to terms. Northcote's lessening influence was underscored by his absence when the agreement was concluded and from the subsequent celebration in Manchester. Churchill was now close to replacing Northcote in a new dual leadership—though Salisbury managed to check the ambitions of both men over Parliamentary reform.

### iii. The Formation of the Caretaker Ministry

Ever since becoming leader in the Lords, Salisbury had hoped to precipitate the fall of Gladstone's Government. The prospects for doing so brightened in the early months of 1885. The survival of the Government hinged, as it had from the beginning of the reform controversy, on the survival of General Gordon in Khartoum. A rescue mission had at last been launched in October of 1884. It reached Khartoum at the end of January, only to find that, two days before, the city had fallen and Gordon with it. When the news reached London, the moral authority of the Government vanished.

The possibility of replacing the Liberals in office under current circumstances had powerful attractions for Salisbury.[74] It would almost certainly lead to his appointment as prime minister and hence would formalize his ascendancy over the party as a whole. It would enable him to demonstrate his ability to put Britain's overseas relations in order. There was, however, a perplexing snag. Unless he could call for an immediate general election, his Government would have to work without the cordial support of a majority in the House of Commons. But Parliament was hard at work restructuring the electorate in keeping with Arlington Street Compact; and it was commonly assumed that a general election should not be held until late in the year, the soonest that the new electors could be registered and the new constituencies established. Though Salisbury continued until March to contemplate the possibility of a dissolution on the old franchise,[75] he knew that it would be difficult to justify.

The older men in the party, mindful of the embarrassments in which earlier minority Ministries had placed them, were very reluctant to experiment with another. Others might yearn for victory or be hungry for office. But no one had denounced the corrupting propensities of minority Conservative Governments more vigorously than Salisbury. Furthermore, the establishment of one now would allow the failings of the Liberal Government to recede from the public mind, while the Conservatives acquired a record of their own which they would have to defend.

The anger aroused by the death of General Gordon put these doubts temporarily at a discount. Few Conservatives disagreed with Salisbury's decision that 'it is the duty of the opposition to do all it can to turn out the Government, however disagreeable, & injurious to us as a party, such a result might be.'[76] But the attack in the Commons was pressed by Northcote with a weakly worded censure motion supported by a feeble speech. Churchill was away in India. The Government survived with a majority of fourteen.

Soon after Churchill returned, Gladstone improved his reputation by reacting vigorously to Russian encroachment on the western approaches to India. In doing so, he sharpened the Conservative dilemma about whether to drive him out. Some of the diehards drew back. But Salisbury's contempt for the fitfulness of Gladstone's foreign policy was profound. He felt no more inclined to sit by impassively when Gladstone asked for a vote of £11 millions to meet the danger of war in Afghanistan than he had when Alexandria was bombarded. Taking the reaction of the old regulars of the party into account, he did not wish to plunge for the Government's jugular vein himself. But if others wished to press the attack, he was ready to accept the consequences.

Churchill forced the pace. Gladstone had begun his speech to the Commons proposing the vote of credit tamely enough, and Churchill left the chamber. But Gladstone then launched into a general attack on his Conservative predecessors' handling of foreign policy. Northcote did nothing, allowing the motion to pass without protest. Furious, Churchill wrote to Salisbury, proposing that a group of ardent spirits in the Commons concert efforts to attack the Government from now on with relentless vigour. He did not propose to restrict the group to his personal allies but, in the spirit of the National Union agreement, to place Sir Michael Hicks Beach at its head and to include men not usually congenial to himself.[77]

If Churchill acted upon the proposal with anything like his normal resourcefulness, it was likely to bring the Government down. Knowing this, Salisbury gave the enterprise his blessing, stipulating only that Churchill and his 'Janizaries' should design their attacks in the form of assistance to Northcote.[78] Salisbury kept in touch with the insurgents' deliberations, whether personally or through Balfour. It was at Balfour's house that a motion designed to bring Irish Nationalists and Conservatives into the same voting lobby against the Government on the budget was designed. The motion took issue with the increased duty on beer and spirits, to which the Irish—and some Liberals—objected, and with the increased burden on land, to which Tories objected.

'Nothing could be more intolerable than a ministerial crisis just now', Salisbury wrote to Lady John Manners the day before the Commons was to debate the motion, '—& nothing would be harder on the Tories. To have to govern six months with a hostile but dying Parliament, is the very worst thing that can happen to us.'[79] His words were less than candid, for he knew about the motion and its potentialities. The 'Janizaries' were not confident of victory. But in the Liberal camp, compounding the rank and file's demoralization, the Cabinet was on the verge of breaking up. Probably with the connivance of their leaders, seventy-six Liberals were absent when the vote was taken. The Government was beaten by a majority of twelve, and they resigned.

After initial elation, doubts spread to all sections of the Conservative party as they waited for the Queen, who was at Balmoral, to receive the resignation of the Government and commission the formation of a successor. Nevertheless, a preponderance of opinion in the party favoured replacing the Liberals. So did Salisbury, despite his balanced presentation of the pros and cons when he met with close colleagues to consider the situation. When the Queen's commission—and with it recognition that he was leader of his party—came to him, he proceeded to Balmoral; and her impression when he met her was that he was 'much pleased.'[80] Though he asked her to enquire whether Gladstone's tender of resignation was his fixed determination, he did not push the matter, as Disraeli had done in 1873, to the point of refusing to form a Ministry. His request was intended to underscore the Queen's mandate to him; and he used the mandate to allay the doubts of potential colleagues and diehard backbenchers about the wisdom of taking office.[81]

The task of composing the Ministry threatened to be more difficult for Salisbury than the decision to take office. Northcote was bitterly disappointed that the Queen had commissioned Salisbury to form a Government without so much as a word of explanation to himself, in spite of her earlier assurances. Salisbury acted quickly to assuage his disappointment. Proposing to take the Foreign Office himself, he suggested that Northcote become First Lord of the Treasury, the office associated with the premiership for more than a century, and that Northcote should also take the powers of patronage customarily associated with the office. Northcote's response was less than cordial. When Salisbury proposed Balfour for the Local Government Board because 'when we come to Local Government Legislation, I must have some one there with whom I can be in close relations,' Northcote took it as an 'indication of the intention to grasp at everything.'[82]

Salisbury assumed, to begin with, that Northcote would retain the leadership in the Commons in spite of the discontent he had provoked. Not having had first hand experience of Northcote's inadequacy in that role, Salisbury, like his fellow peer Cranbrook,[83] was not aware of the full magnitude of the discontent. But by the time he reached Balmoral he knew that not only Churchill but Hicks Beach, W. H. Smith, Lord John Manners, and even Edward Gibson who had until recently been an ally Northcote,[84] regarded his continuation in the leadership as unacceptable. Northcote had provided Salisbury with an escape by raising the possibility of his elevation to the Lords. An honourable accommodation was still possible.

Churchill, however, pursued a line of conduct designed to discredit Salisbury as well as Northcote. By letting his refusal to serve under Northcote's leadership in the Commons become common knowledge, he humiliated Northcote. At the same time, he managed to bring out some indecision in Salisbury about forming a Ministry. First, though the diehards' fear of a minority Ministry focused upon the influence which Churchill might exert, he contrived to join forces with them in a vote on some remaining details of the Redistribution Bill. Thirty-four Tory M.P.s voted with him, a worrying demonstration of Conservative opposition to taking office.

Salisbury was engaged in negotiations through the Queen with Gladstone about guarantees for minimal cooperation from the Liberal majority in the Commons. He used the negotiations to open up the possibility of refusing to form a Ministry. Churchill, who agreed to participate in the Conservative leaders' council, promptly swung round. He argued the case for taking office, and leaked out word of Salisbury's hesitation. But Salisbury was just as quick. He used an assurance from the Queen about Gladstone's intentions as sufficient justification for accepting office: and the deed was done.

The task of composing the Ministry then proceeded well. Churchill had overplayed his hand; and though Northcote was removed from the House of Commons, Salisbury rejected Churchill's other demand, for the exclusion of Sir Richard Cross from the Cabinet. Cross had been one of the most productive Home Secretaries of the century, and though over-fondness for the bottle had since debilitated him,[85] Salisbury would not throw him over. Churchill acquiesced meekly. Northcote was mollified with an earldom in addition to the First Lordship and the share of patronage which Salisbury had originally offered him.

Public knowledge of Churchill's ultimatum about Northcote made the composition of the Ministry, when finally announced, look like a rebel triumph. Hicks Beach, who had voted with the mutineers on the Redistribution Bill, was installed as leader in the Commons. Yet, as close observers noted, the distribution of offices still favoured the regulars, even more indeed than their intrinsic capacities warranted. Disraeli's former colleagues, disparaged by Churchill as 'the old gang,' were fully represented. His only allies in the Cabinet were sympathetic regulars, Hicks Beach and Hamilton; and Hamilton had been repelled by Churchill's recent behaviour.[86] Salisbury gave Churchill the India. Office for the same reason that Disraeli had given it to Salisbury years before. Checked by the Viceroy in India and the India Council at home, Churchill's scope for making trouble at least in his own department would be limited.[87]

The composition of the Caretaker Ministry was, in fact, a sound reflection of the composition of the Parliamentary party. Though Churchill was the sole Tory Democrat in the Cabinet, the vibrations surrounding his appointment made him count for much more than one. In any case, Tory Democrats were not numerous in the Parliamentary party. Through Churchill their influence in the Cabinet would be fully proportionate to their number. By including Churchill on a reduced version of Churchill's terms, Salisbury avoided Gladstone's error in forming the Cabinet of 1880 when he gave the large group of new Radicals no more than one representative, Joseph Chamberlain, and placed him in the lowest office.[88] Salisbury's Cabinet was slightly more aristocratic than Gladstone's;[89] but, however unenterprising, that was not as inappropriate in the Conservative context as in the Liberal. The personal rivalries within the party were also surprisingly well composed. Fate had assisted Salisbury in this regard with the death of Lord Cairns earlier in the year. Richmond, made President of the Board of Trade and then Secretary for Scotland, lacked his indispensable ally. The flaw in the Cabinet was on a matter of policy, the policy implied by Lord Carnarvon's appointment as Lord Lieutenant of Ireland.

## NOTES

1. The following discussion draws heavily upon Andrew Jones' perceptive study, *The Politics of Reform, 1884* (Cambridge, 1972). There is also a valuable doctoral dissertation by W. A. Hayes, 'The background and passage of the Third Reform Act', University of Toronto, 1972.
2. Balfour to Salisbury, 8 April 1880, Salisbury papers.
3. Malcolm MacColl, *Memoirs and Correspondence*, ed. G. W. E. Russell (London, 1914), pp. 104–105; Salisbury at Birmingham, *The Times*, 30 March 1883, 10d.
4. Salisbury to Northcote, 25 June 1882, copy, Salisbury papers.
5. Salisbury to the Queen, 16 August 1882, in G. E. Buckle, ed., *The Letters of Queen Victoria*, 2nd ser., III, pp. 327–9; Salisbury to Lord John Manners, 30 January 1883, Rutland MSS.
6. Salisbury to Lord John Manners, 21 November 1883, Rutland MSS.; Lady Frances Balfour to Gerald Balfour, January 1884, in Lady Frances Balfour, *Ne Obliviscaris* (London, [1930]), I, p. 422.
7. Salisbury described him as 'a man whose life has not been spent in retreating, but in advancing and in striking hard blows against the enemy.' *Hansard*, 3rd ser., CCLXXXIV, 20–21 (5 February 1884).

8. *Hansard*, 3rd ser., CCXC, 1369 (17 July 1884); Salisbury, 'The value of redistribution,' *National Review*, IV, 20 (October 1884), p. 157.

9. Churchill thought of single-member constituencies as a form, indeed as the only workable form, of minority representation. Andrew Jones, *op. cit.*, p. 215.

10. Cf.Salisbury to the Rev. C. R. Conybeare, 19 September 1881, copy, Salisbury papers: 'If it were possible to maintain a party under such conditions, I should be disposed to wish that the Conservatives should remain permanently a very strong opposition. That is undoubtedly the condition of things under which the wearing away of the Constitution is most nearly suspended.'

11. Salisbury, 'Disintegration,' p. 560.

12. *The Times*, 14 June 1883, 7b.

13. *Hansard*, 3rd ser., CCXC, 458 (8 July 1884).

14. Balfour to Austin, 22 June 1884, Austin papers.

15. Salisbury to MacColl, 11 July 1884, in Malcolm MacColl, *op. cit.*, p. 93.

16. 'My earnest hope is that no arrangement will be come to of which the effect will be that redistribution will be handled by the present Parliament.' Salisbury to Cairns, 4 July 1884, copy, Salisbury papers.

17. *Infra.* pp. 47–59.

18. *Supra*, p. 29; Salisbury to Richmond, 11, 18 and 22 January 1884, Goodwood MSS.; *Hansard*, 3rd ser., CCLXXXIV, 37 (5 February 1884); D. W. R. Bahlman, ed., *The Diary of Sir Edward Hamilton* (Oxford, 1972), II, 553, 599 and 606; *Hansard*, 3rd ser., CCLXXXVIII, 146–147 (13 May 1884).

19. Richmond to Cairns, 16 September 1884, Cairns papers.

20. Arthur Hardinge, *The Life of Henry Howard Molyneux Herbert, Fourth Earl of Carnarvon, 1831–1890* (London, 1925), III, pp. 102–3.

21. *The Times*, 2 October 1884, 7c.

22. See particularly his speech at Dumfries, *The Times*, 22 October 1884, 6a and d.

23. Salisbury in Edinburgh, *The Times*, 24 November 1882.

24. C. C. Weston, 'The royal mediation in 1884,' *English Historical Review*, LXXXII, 323 (April 1967), p. 303.

25. Salisbury to Richmond, 16 October 1884, Goodwood MSS.; Cairns to Salisbury, 28 October 1884, Salisbury papers; Salisbury to Richmond, 2 November 1884, Salisbury papers: Drafts.

26. 'The value of redistribution: A note on electoral statistics,' *National Review*, IV, 20 (October 1884), pp. 145–162. Though bearing an October date, the issue of the *National Review* was published on 25 September.

27. Salisbury to Cranbrook, 18 November 1884, copy, Salisbury papers; G. E. Buckle, ed., *The Letters of Queen Victoria*, 2nd ser., III, p. 582.

28. For a close examination of them, See Mary E. J. Chadwick, 'The role of redistribution in the making of the third Reform Act,' *Historical Journal*, XIX, 3 (September 1976), 665 ff.

29. See e.g. Salisbury to H. McNiel of the Manchester Conservative Club, 26 November 1884, and to Balfour, 30 November 1884, Salisbury papers: Drafts.

30. The Cabinet was ready to raise the figure to 20,000. Salisbury contented himself with 15,000.

31. *Hansard*, 3rd ser., CCXCVIII, 1372 (8 June 1885).

32. E. g. Edward Stanhope to Northcote, 21 November 1884, with Northcote's letters to Salisbury, Salisbury papers.

33. R. R. James, *Lord Randolph Churchill* (New York, 1959), pp. 112–113.

34. *The Times* editorial, 6 December 1883, 9a. Cf. Lord Bryce, *Studies in Contemporary Biography* (London, 1904), p. 223.

35. H. W. Lucy, *Memories of Eight Parliaments* (New York, 1908), p. 205.

36. D. W. R. Bahlman, ed., *The Diary of Sir Edward Walter Hamilton* (Oxford, 1972), II, p. 590. 'At the same time,' Hamilton continued, 'they admit he is indispensable to them.'

37. The Queen to Northcote, 15 May 1881, G. E. Buckle, ed., *The Letters of Queen Victoria*, 2nd ser., III, p. 219; and 'A Tory' [Churchill] to the ed., *The Times*, 29 March 1883, 9f.

38. Northcote to Lord John Manners, 22 November 1883, copy, Salisbury papers. Cf. Northcote to Sir John Hay, 3 December 1883, copy, Salisbury papers.

39. Northcote to Salisbury, 23 April 1884, Salisbury papers.

40. Dilke to Grant Duff, 15 August 1884, quoted in W. A. Hayes, 'The background and passage of the third Reform Act,' University of Toronto Ph.D. dissertation, 1972, p. 272.

41. Sir Edward Clarke, *The Story of My Life* (London, 1918), pp. 224–5.

42. Gladstone noted how 'Lord Salisbury took the whole matter out of the hands of Northcote, who sat by him on sofa like a chicken protected by the wings of the mother hen.' Autobiographical memoranda, 1897, quoted in Andrew Jones, *op. cit.*, p. 82.

43. Northcote to Salisbury, 9 January 1885, Salisbury papers.

44. Salisbury to Beaconsfield, 1 December 1880, Beaconsfield papers.

45. Lord Rosebery, *Lord Randolph Churchill* (London, 1906), p. 91.

46. Churchill's words, quoted in R. R. James, *Lord Randolph Churchill*, p. 114

47. *Ibid.*, p. 147.

48. Winston S. Churchill, *Lord Randolph Churchill* (London, 1906), I, p. 230.

49. The Church of England, as he conceived of and defended it, was 'essentially the Church of religious liberty.' Speech at Birmingham, 16 April 1884, in W. S. Churchill, *Lord Randolph Churchill* (London, 1906), I, p. 298.

50. Winston S. Churchill, *op. cit.*, II, pp. 140–143; Lord Rosebery, *Lord Randolph Churchill*, p. 100. He later told his constituents at Paddington that 'Sir Robert Peel even more than Lord Beaconsfield adopted all the principles and ideas of what people call Tory Democracy.' Quoted in W. J. Wilkinson, *Tory Democracy*, Studies in History, Economics and Public Law, Columbia University, CXV, 2 (New York, 1925), pp. 21–22.

51. R. R. James, *Lord Randolph Churchill*, p. 160; *infra*, p. 277.

52. *National Review* (November 1883), pp. 301–16.

53. A. S. Wohl, 'The housing of the working classes in London, 1815–1914' in S. D. Chapman, ed., *The History of Working-Class Housing* (Totowa, New Jersey, 1971), p. 19; Salisbury, *op. cit.*, p. 306.

54. Quoted in A. S. Wohl, *op. cit.*, p. 20.

55. Salisbury to Austin, 25 November 1883, Austin papers.

56. Paul Smith, *Disraelian Conservatism and Social Reform* (London, 1967), *passim*; Paul Smith, ed., *Lord Salisbury on Politics*, pp. 49, 52 and 314; Michael Pinto-Duschinsky, *The Political Thought of Lord Salisbury*, p. 44; Salisbury at Newcastle, *The Times*, 13 October 1881, 7d; at Birmingham, *The Times*, 30 March 1883, 10c; at Bermondsey, *The Times*, 31 May 1883, 6b.

57. Neil Kunze, 'Lord Salisbury's ideas on housing reform, 1883–1885,' *Canadian Journal of History*, VIII, 3 (December 1973), pp. 250–2.

58. This point is put forward and substantiated by A. S. Wohl in an article entitled 'The Bitter Cry of Outcast London' in the *International Review of Social History*, XIII, pt. 2 (1968), 189–245 and in an edition of Andrew Mearns' 1883 pamphlet together with some of the ensuing article literature: A. S. Wohl, ed., *The Bitter Cry of Outcast London* (New York, 1970), p. 34.

59. *The Times*, 9 March 1882, 5f.

60. Dilke papers, B. L. Add. MSS. 43876. ff. 4–8.
61. Stephen Gwynn and G. M. Tuckwell, *The Life of the Rt. Hon. Sir Charles W. Dilke* (London, 1917), II, pp. 18, 104 and 126; Salisbury to Dilke, 28 January 1885, Dilke papers.
62. For a fuller description, see Enid Gauldie, *Cruel Habitations* (London, 1974), p. 290.
63. 'Arthur will not acknowledge what is obvious, that Salisbury has not got the confidence of the Conservatives at large, and that outside Parliament they hold back from his lead. It cannot be because they think him rash, for Randolph who is undoubtedly believed in, and followed by the mass of the Conservatives, particularly the younger Tories, is rash to madness.' Lady Frances Balfour to Gerald Balfour, 7 April 1884, in Lady Frances Balfour, *Ne Obliviscaris*, I, p. 427. Cf. Sir Edward Clarke, *The Story of My Life* (London, 1918), p. 191.
64. *Infra*, pp. 184ff.
65. Lord Percy to Salisbury, 2 letters of October 1880, Salisbury papers. For other informative discussions of Lord Randolph's fight for the National Union and of the problems underlying the fight, see H. E. Gorst, *The Fourth Party* (London, 1906); F. H. Herrick, 'Lord Randolph Churchill and the popular organization of the Conservative party' *Pacific Historical Review*, XV, 2 (June 1946), pp. 178–191; H. J. Hanham, *Elections and Party Management: Politics in the time of Gladstone and Disraeli* (London, 1959); R. T. McKenzie, *British Political Parties* (London, 1963); James Cornford, 'The transformation of Conservatism in the late nineteenth century,' *Victorian Studies*, VII, 1 (September 1963), pp. 33–66; and E. J. Feuchtwanger, *Disraeli, Democracy and the Tory Party: Conservative leadership and organization after the second Reform bill* (Oxford, 1968).
66. Stanhope to Balfour, 12 January 1884, Balfour papers (Whittinghame); Northcote to Salisbury, 24 February 1884, Salisbury papers.
67. Churchill to Salisbury, 3 April 1884, Salisbury papers.
68. Northcote to Salisbury, 4 April 1884, Salisbury papers.
69. Winston S. Churchill, *Lord Randolph Churchill*, I, p. 325.
70. He claimed that Salisbury agreed with him: but the claim was immediately disputed, and Salisbury's subsequent behaviour did not bear it out. Northcote to Wortley, 21 June 1884, copy, and Percy to Balfour, 22 June 1884, Balfour papers (Whittinghame).
71. Percy's speech, National Union Annual Conference Minutes, 13 July 1884.
72. Quoted in Kenneth Young, *Arthur James Balfour* (London, 1963), p. 87.
73. *The Reminiscences of Lady Dorothy Nevill* (London, 1906), p. 286.
74. I am deeply indebted in this section, in the following chapter, and in the first two sections of chapter IV, to the provocative work of A. B. Cooke and J. R. Vincent, *The Governing Passion: Cabinet government and party politics in Britain, 1885–86* (Brighton, 1974).
75. Salisbury to Austin, 5 March 1885, Austin papers.
76. Salisbury to Austin, 19 February 1885, Austin papers.
77. The men he mentioned by name were Raikes, Chaplin, Dyke, and Gibson. Churchill to Salisbury, 18 April 1885, Salisbury papers.
78. Salisbury to Churchill, 28 April 1885, copy, Salisbury papers.
79. Letter of 7 June 1885, copy, Salisbury papers.
80. G. E. Buckle, ed., *The Letters of Queen Victoria*, 2nd ser., III, p. 660.
81. A. E. Gathorne-Hardy, *Gathorne Hardy, First Earl of Cranbrook* (London, 1910), II, p. 220; Charles Whibley, *Lord John Manners and His Friends* (Edinburgh, 1925), II, pp. 308–9; R. R. James, *Lord Randolph Churchill*, p. 181.
82. Northcote's diary, 11 June 1885, copy, Iddesleigh papers.
83. A. E. Gathorne-Hardy, *Gathorne Hardy, First Earl of Cranbrook*, II, p. 216.

84. A. B. Cooke and A. P. W. Malcolmson, comp., *The Ashbourne Papers, 1869–1913* (Belfast, 1974), pp. xiv–xv.
85. D. W. R. Bahlman, ed., *The Diary of Sir Edward Walter Hamilton*, II, p. 582.
86. Hamilton to Salisbury, 15 June 1885, Salisbury papers.
87. Northcote's diary, 16 June 1885, Iddesleigh papers.
88. Cf. John Morley, *Life of Gladstone*, II, p. 630.
89. There were eight commoners among the fifteen members of Gladstone's 1880 Cabinet including the heir to a duchy, Hartington. There were six commoners among the sixteen members of Salisbury's Cabinet. Two of the peers, Iddesleigh and Halsbury, were elevated to the Lords when the Cabinet was created. Two of the commoners, Churchill and Hamilton, were sons of dukes, and a third, Stanley, was the heir to an earldom.

# CHAPTER 3

## THE POINT OF INTERSECTION

Steersman, be not precipitate in thine act
Of steering, for the river here, my friends,
Parts in two channels moving to one end.
This goes straight forward to the cataract;
That streams about the bend:
But though the Cataract seem the nearer way,
Whate-er the crowd on either bank may say,
Take thou "the bend"; 'twill save thee many a day.

*Tennyson, 'Compromise' (November 1884)*

It was to be over Ireland that Lord Salisbury discovered a point where his desires, the interests of his party, and the prejudices of his country came together powerfully. He used the Irish question to consolidate his primacy over the party, to stiffen its reflexes, to forge an alliance (to be dealt with in the next chapter) with the Unionist defectors from the Liberal party, to get rid of Churchill, and hence to establish himself in office for almost fourteen years until he chose to lay the burden down.[1]

But the discovery did not come quickly. Salisbury felt his way during his first year and a half as official leader of the Conservative party, sometimes preoccupied elsewhere, sometimes fumbling, veiled, ambiguous even when he sounded bold, profoundly cautious, looking to his right and left. Though the outcome was dazzling, the path to it was often dark.

### i. Ireland

Ireland was an ill-omened subject for all British statesmen, and particularly for Conservatives. Essentially English and traditionally Anglican, the Conservative party did not have the strong ties with the Celtic fringe and religious minorities which made Liberals amenable to Irish pressures. Ireland thus provided the most searching test of the Conservatives' capacity to govern. No one had found a way to reconcile the needs and desires of Ireland with some of the strongest prejudices and principles of Tories. Attempts to satisfy the former uninhibited by the latter had shattered the careers of the younger Pitt and Peel. But refusal to give fresh thought to Irish discontent or to respond to changes in its intensity would amount to a confession of inadequacy.

Charles Stewart Parnell was engaged throughout the first half of the 1880s in building what amounted to an autonomous Irish state, bringing out the nationalism in and fusing together the tenant farmers and shopkeepers hit by an acute depression in agriculture, the Irish Parliamentary party, and the Roman Catholic Church.[2] Lord Salisbury never fully appreciated the solidity of Parnell's achievement. Salisbury was quick to recognize the shift of power in Ireland away from the official executive to Parnell and the Land League,[3] and soon afterward admitted also that Parnell's popular base was massive.[4] But he refused to admit that Irish alienation from rule by Westminster had become a permanent, irreducible fact which the United Kingdom must accommodate.

Instead, he placed what was happening to Ireland with what was happening to the Empire and at home, as part of the process of 'disintegration, the kindling of the animosity of classes . . . and the social revolution'[5] which Radical government brought about by pandering to popular agitations. The rot, as he saw it, went back a century, to 1782, when the Whig Ministry of Lord Rockingham granted Ireland an independent legislature, 'Grattan's Parliament.' Since that time

> The internal history of Ireland has been a continuous tempest of agitation, broken by occasional flashes of insurrection. The legislation of the period has been a continuous stream of concession.[6]

Gladstone's policy followed a similar pattern:

> every successive instalment of concession was wrung from them by agitation on the other side, so that even the grace and value of their vicarious generosity, whatever it may be, is absolutely lost.[7]

This persistent refrain gave Salisbury's commentary on Irish policy an appearance of stiffness; and certainly all attempts at violent intimidation put his back up. But this reflex was compatible with considerable flexibility in dealing with 'the Irish difficulty.' The Irish question, he told an audience in 1882, was like 'an old chronic malady that a man has, which he knows very likely he may never get rid of, but which, by judicious and careful treatment, he may make comparatively harmless, which he may prevent from bursting forth in dangerous paraxysms.'[8] What the Irish patient needed was firm, foresighted, equitable treatment: just enough power in the hands of the authorities to keep crime and conspiracy close to the level normal in any country, just enough reform to ease genuine grievances without disturbing vested interests.

The fitfulness of the Liberals' Irish policy was closely related to and as unhealthy as their willingness to grant concessions under duress. Salisbury objected to the extreme oscillations in Gladstone's treatment of Ireland, from neglect to coercion as well as concession. The Land Act

of 1881 revolutionized relations between tenant and owner; the
accompanying Crimes Act shocked Salisbury by its violation of
customary rights, though because of the then acute disorder in Ireland
he had not attempted to impede its passage. He therefore felt great
sympathy with the contempt which Parnellites had acquired for the
Liberal Government; and he was ready to experiment in the government of Ireland with greater friendliness on the part of the executive and
with practical reforms, particularly with the proposal to help Irish
tenants buy out their landlords.

The combination of Land League terror with the 1881 Land Act had
all but eliminated the Anglo-Irish landlord as an effective bulwark of
British influence. Landlords were afraid to stand up to agrarian
intimidation, and the 1881 Act had reduced them to co-owners with
their tenants. Parnellites were not satisfied, and wanted to turn the
tenants into full owners. Salisbury agreed, for the soundest of
Conservative reasons. The only landlord interest still worth protecting
was their economic investment; and, coming on top of agricultural
depression, the sharp lowering of rents under the Land Act made many
landlords willing, even anxious, to sell if a decent price could be settled
on. By enacting a measure to facilitate land purchase, Parliament would
give rise to a class of peasant proprietors with an interest in stable
government, and would also reduce the incidence of friction between
landlord and tenant. There was an added, partisan advantage. Though
some Liberals led by John Bright had long favoured land purchase,
Gladstone was lukewarm about it, in part because the loan by the
government of the purchase price to the tenant—an essential feature of
all such schemes—did not sit easily with his devotion to governmental
economy.[9] A scheme of land purchase sponsored by the Conservatives
would draw attention to a critical limitation in the Liberal leader.

Salisbury's willingness to experiment with medicines to cure the
malady of Ireland was, however, limited not only by his hostile reaction
to violent demand but also by his insistence that party leaders must be
loyal to their rank and file. He invested this insistence with moral force.
Furthermore, as he interpreted the precept, its effect was to deepen the
Conservative party's conservatism. For he applied it much more often to
the slowest than to the most progressive adherents of the party.

The past century of Tory and Conservative party history seemed to
Salisbury to prove his point. The conservative forces which gathered
round Pitt in the 1790s and gave Britain stable government for another
thirty years had been demoralized and scattered by Peel when, in 1829
and again in 1846, he enacted the very measures which his followers had
placed him in office to oppose. Morally, Peel's behaviour was inexcus-
able: 'No amount of public gain,' Salisbury had written, 'will even
extenuate a course of conduct which involved a "betrayal of party

attachments." [10] What made things worse, there had been no public gain. On the contrary, by shattering his party Peel had brought about the passage of two measures, the 1832 Reform Act and the 1846 repeal of the Corn Laws, in a more extreme, more hastily considered, less balanced form than would have been the case if they had been 'carried through under the ordeal of a legitimate party conflict.'[11] Salisbury drew two conclusions from this analysis: first, that if he did not keep the Conservative party together, the pace of reform would accelerate; and secondly, that the group of Conservatives to whom the party leaders should always remember to pay heed were old-fashioned Tories of the sort Peel had offended.

Still, Salisbury did not interpret this last lesson rigidly. A similar censure to the one which he applied to Peel could have been applied to Pitt and the rupture of Pitt's following in 1801 over his commitment to Catholic emancipation. Salisbury, however, exonerated Pitt.[12] Pitt was Salisbury's historical hero, the man who trounced Fox and North when they abandoned their respective parties' principles in 1783,[13] the Olympian administrator, England's leader in the war against Revolutionary France, the architect of Castlereagh's foreign policy. The image of Pitt, victor in the last great convulsion of parties in 1783-4, never left Salisbury's mind in the crisis of 1885-6. The impact of the image was ambiguous. It hallowed the Union with Ireland in Salisbury's eyes, for the Act of Union was 'Mr. Pitt's work:'[14] but the memory of Pitt also broadened Salisbury's sense of the traditions of the party, and presented him with a model of flexibility which he could appreciate.

In the first half of 1885—and indeed until December—Irish affairs were not at the forefront of most minds in Westminster. It was not in order to take Ireland in hand that Salisbury approved of Churchill's plans to bring about the fall of Gladstone's Ministry. Salisbury wanted primarily to capitalize upon the Liberals' shocking management of foreign affairs. Ireland was a subordinate concern.

Still, there was a preliminary question about Ireland which Salisbury had to answer before Churchill and Hicks Beach could launch an all-out assault upon the Government. The Crimes Act of 1881 was due to expire at the end of the 1885 session of Parliament. Could it be allowed to lapse? Only a majority Liberal Government could renew it, if indeed any Government could: for, in addition to Parnellite M.P.s, a large number of Radicals and a much smaller number of Conservatives were opposed to renewal. A minority Conservative Ministry could not overcome such opposition. Knowing that he could not renew the Act, was Salisbury willing to defeat and replace Gladstone in office? No considerations of foreign policy would excuse replacement of the Liberal Government if the prospective Conservative prime minister was unable to satisfy himself beforehand that Ireland could be governed without coercion. Apart from the question of administrative practicality, there were conflicting partisan considerations. A decision not to renew the Act would probably secure enough Parnellite support for the Conservatives in the Commons to bring the Government down. On the other hand, the implications of such a voting alliance with Parnellites would alarm the stiff regular Tories.

Sir Michael Hicks Beach and Churchill raised this question with Salisbury and Edward Gibson, as the party's leading Irishman, before pressing their attack on the Liberal budget. On the administrative question, Gibson's answer was clear: he assured his interrogators that conditions in Ireland at the moment justified an attempt to govern without the Act. But the final decision had to come from Salisbury, not only as the probable Conservative prime minister, but as 'the only man who could persuade'[15] the Conservative party to allow the Act to lapse, with all that that implied. Gibson's report did not set Salisbury's mind quite at ease. But once the Queen commissioned the Conservatives to form a Government, they could check the facts on which they based their preliminary conclusion. Moreover, if the situation in Ireland deteriorated quickly before the end of the session, the Act could be kept in force until the general election by recessing rather than proroguing Parliament up to the moment of its official dissolution. These considerations were enough to secure Salisbury's consent.

The decision was conveyed to the political world as soon as Gladstone informed the Commons that his Government intended to renew some provisions of the Crimes Act. Churchill saw Parnell, who wanted to know his views on coercion should the Conservatives gain power. Churchill asserted that he would not be part of any Cabinet which under present circumstances, renewed the Act. 'In that case,' Parnell responded, 'you will have the Irish vote at the elections.' Churchill, in an unusually cautious speech to the St. Stephen's Club, also intimated to the public that a Conservative Government might not think the Act's renewal necessary. Salisbury deliberately refrained[16] from discouraging or encouraging the Parnellite hope to which Churchill's words gave rise. Thirty-nine Parnellites voted with the Conservatives on Hicks Beach's subsequent amendment to the budget; and jubilant shouts from the Irish benches of 'No coercion' greeted the announcement of the Liberal Government's fall.

By agreeing to risk the expiry of the Crimes Act and, as a corollary, by accepting a voting alliance with the Parnellites, Salisbury strained the loyalty of stiff Conservative regulars severely. And though some of them demonstrated their uneasiness by joining Churchill's mutiny on the Redistribution Bill,[17] Salisbury continued to put a strain on their loyalty with regard to Ireland until the general election was over. For the political outlook was extraordinarily cloudy. The Franchise Act had created a new and therefore unpredictable electorate. The complete redrawing of the electoral map added to the uncertainty. Salisbury's primacy over the Conservative party was also new and insecure. At seventy-six years of age, Gladstone might retire at any moment. There were several rival candidates for the Liberal succession, and each would give the party a different character. The political complexion of Ireland seemed much clearer than the British one: but there was room for uncertainty about Ireland too, because the Franchise Act, which would double the British electorate, would treble the Irish one. Until these clouds of uncertainty began to lift, Salisbury was less interested in stiff resolve than in flexibility, though subject always to the imperative of party unity.

The Conservative party allowed him a large amount of room for manoeuvre, for it was of several minds on the subject of Anglo-Irish relations. By and large the rank and file in and out of Parliament were chauvinistically Protestant and English, without sympathy for the Catholic, Nationalist majority of Irishmen. But among Conservatives who lived in Ireland or knew it first hand, or who had begun to think about it in a broad context, this reaction was modified. Among the Orange Conservatives of Ulster, it was stiffened. Otherwise among the informed or reflective minority, it was for the most part softened, and in a few cases was transformed into sympathy for Home Rule. There was, in fact, a minor tradition or school of Conservative support for Home Rule associated with Isaac Butt, Parnell's predecessor in the leadership of the Irish Parliamentary party. That school had almost vanished: but there were other, non-Irish considerations at work among Conservatives which fostered a willingness to think freshly about Ireland. In the Conservative party's fight to uphold the interests of denominational education, the Roman Catholics of Ireland were cordial allies. And in quite a different sphere, the proven compatibility of growing independence with imperial loyalties in Canada and Australia suggested that a solution for the tensions in Anglo-Irish relations might be found in some form of colonial or federal government.

This counter-current in Conservative opinion was pressed upon Salisbury by three men: Churchill, Hicks Beach, and the Earl of Carnarvon. Churchill had come to know Ireland, and had acquired some sympathy for its aspirations and sufferings, from his days assisting his father, the Duke of Marlborough, who in the late 1870s had been the Lord Lieutenant of Ireland. Back at Westminster, Churchill cultivated friendly relations with at least one Nationalist, Biggar. Cooperation with Parnellites formed part of Churchill's strategy of attack on Gladstone's Ministry. The Fourth party and the Parnellites supported each other to get enough votes for motions of adjournment; and

Churchill's support for Parnellite complaints about coercion was outspoken. As the pulse of politics quickened in 1884, so did his courtship of the Irish in Parliament.

Hicks Beach was more restrained and discreet. But he had been in charge of the administration of Ireland in the mid-'70s, when he too displayed mildly reformist tendencies; and he came away with sensitivities akin to Churchill's. Paternal in his relations with his own Gloucestershire tenants even though that placed him in embarrassing financial straits, Hicks Beach had no sympathy with those Anglo-Irish landlords, often absentees, who would resort without a pang to eviction rather than adjust rents to falling prices.

The ability of Churchill and Hicks Beach to sway the councils of the party was out of all proportion to their popular support among Conservatives. This disproportionate influence accrued to them from their personal talent, enhanced by the lack of talent on the rest of the front bench in the Commons, a lack made still worse at the formation of the Caretaker Ministry when Gibson insisted on going to the upper House as Lord Ashbourne and Northcote was driven there by Churchill.

The power of Churchill was also a measure of the party's lack of self-assurance and its uncertainty about the public. Conservatives who knew what they wanted, and believed that the public wanted it too, were few and far between. Old-fashioned Tories knew what they venerated and what they feared; but they could not assure themselves that the massive popular electorate, living and working in new ways weakly fettered by traditional restraints, was likely to agree with them. Modernity diluted the creed of most other Conservatives, and they wandered uncertainly between their personal predilections and what they guessed were the predilections of the public. They were therefore impressed by Churchill's confident reading of the public mind, and doubly impressed by the popular response he evoked.

Lord Carnarvon, the other prominent Conservative to urge a fresh approach to Ireland upon Salisbury, had twice been Colonial Secretary, and he approached Anglo-Irish relations from an imperial point of view. He had presided over the enactment of Canadian confederation in 1867, and had tried a decade later to apply the Canadian model to south Africa. It was to Canadian and also Australian experience that he harked back with regard to Ireland. He was struck by the life-story of two colonial statesmen, Darcy McGee in Canada and Charles Gavan Duffy in Australia, both of whom began as rebellious Irishmen but developed into responsible cooperators with Britain once they emigrated to partially self-governing colonies. The implications of this experience for Ireland seemed clear to Carnarvon: trust Ireland with internal self-government, subject of course to ample guarantees for imperial supremacy, and the rumbling rebellion would come to a halt.

Salisbury broached the subject of Ireland with Carnarvon late in 1884; and in the following February and March, at the time of Parliament's debate on the death of General Gordon, the two men discussed it again in considerable depth. Salisbury could not satisfy himself about the conditions upon which the success of Carnarvon's solution depended. In the first place, Salisbury did not trust the Irish. The dictates of morality on the Irish question, as he felt them, had to do with the relationship between political leaders and their followers rather than between the English and Irish peoples. Trust, which he regarded as of critical importance between party leaders and followers, he did not expect, let alone rely upon, between the Imperial government at Westminster and a popularly elected Irish legislature in Dublin. Even in England he did not trust an untutored popular electorate: and if the Irish were not cursed with a double dose of orginal sin, neither were they blessed with a double dose of wisdom or virtue. The classes and interests in Ireland which might be relied upon to cultivate good relations with Britain—the landlords, and the industrialists and working men of Protestant Ulster—were the very classes and interests which feared and would be endangered by Home Rule. The popularly elected spokesmen for Ireland at Westminster displayed little enthusiasm for preserving British sovereignty. If these men, the probable leaders of an Irish legislature, could not be trusted personally, constitutional guarantees of imperial supremacy could not be trusted either. History, argued Salisbury, provided no example of constitutional devices successfully withstanding passionate popular demand.[18]

Unyielding though this reponse to Carnarvon was, it was not couched in such a way as to bring the discussion to a close. In later talks with Carnarvon, during the first weeks of the Caretaker Ministry, and again on the eve of the general election, Salisbury ruled out Home Rule, in other words an elected legislature in Dublin for all of Ireland, as an option for the Conservative party at least so long as he was its leader. But he did not attempt to stop, or even vigorously to discourage, those in the party who wished to wrestle with the possibility of reconciling the Irish desire for Home Rule and effective preservation of imperial supremacy. He pledged himself publicly with regard to Ireland to stand by the traditions of his party. But he said nothing to clarify what those traditions were. On the contrary, by agreeing to see whether Ireland could be governed without coercion, and by framing his public remarks on Ireland to avoid alienating any section of the party, he allowed the traditions of the party to become more than usually opaque.

The groping, uncertain character of Salisbury's Irish policy was aggravated by his conciliar approach to Cabinet government. On top of the burdens of the premiership, he took the demanding post of Foreign Secretary, a combination virtually without precedent. He took the business of the Foreign Office almost entirely into his own hands, delegating little but routine tasks to its permanent staff; and he did not tend to consult the Cabinet about international affairs unless pressed to do so. He expected his colleagues to run their assigned departments with similar independence. Furthermore, he regarded other members of the Cabinet as representative of segments of the party whose wishes had to be respected. His enforced absence as a peer from the critically important theatre of the Commons accentuated his sense of need to conciliate his lieutenants there. He was acutely aware that his drawing power outside Parliament as a public figure and speaker, unless seconded by a collective effort among his colleagues, would be no match for Gladstone's. Unless Conservatives worked together, they could not tie the giant down. Salisbury therefore saw his function as prime minister as one of helping to reconcile internal disagreements and working out formulae which all could accept.

This style of executive leadership could work to his satisfaction only if the ministers in charge of politically sensitive departments and the leaders in the Commons shared or were ready to defer to his own inclinations. But, at least until his leadership of the party was firmly established, his range of choice for leader in the Commons would be restricted to the very few who were commanding in debate; and, by nature, men with such talent tended to have wills of their own. His choice for politically sensitive departments was not similarly restricted.

His choice of Carnarvon to take charge of the administration of Ireland as Lord Lieutenant was as unnecessary as it was mistaken. Salisbury knew that Carnarvon's assessment of what was possible for Ireland, and his own, were very different. Admittedly, if Ireland was to be governed without coercion, its administration had to be placed in the hands of someone creditable as a peacemaker. Carnarvon met that requirement. But so did some others. Salisbury selected Carnarvon because they had long known each other and had agreed more often than they disagreed, because they moved in similar circles, because they were aristocrats, men of learning, and high churchmen. The selection was an early indication of Salisbury's aristocratic bias and penchant for friends or relative in composing Cabinets. He would have done better to select someone like W. H. Smith, First Lord of the Admiralty in Disraeli's Cabinet and the man Salisbury chose to replace Carnarvon in the following January, a steady bourgeois who had been the first frontbench Conservative to propose land purchase for Irish tenants yet was always anxious to seek out and defer to the will of his colleagues.

## ii. The Conduct of the Caretaker Ministry

The ambivalence and the diffusion of responsibility in the new Government were suggested by the unusual character of its initial statements to Parliament. Salisbury announced the Ministry's intentions to the House of Lords on all matters except Ireland: Ireland he left to Carnarvon. Carnarvon then outlined the principles of his Irish policy in words which many who heard him could not believe Salisbury would have chosen.[19] Carnarvon recognized the reality of Irish nationalism; and he spoke of trust, the very thing that Salisbury had told him he could not give to Ireland:

> trust [said Carnarvon] begets trust, and it is, after all, the only foundation upon which we can hope to build up amity and concord between the two nations.[20]

He concluded his remarks with a statement which could easily be interpreted as envisaging an imperial form of Home Rule:

> And just as I have seen in English Colonies across the sea a combination of English, Irish, and Scotch settlers bound together in loyal obedience to the law and the Crown, and contributing to the general prosperity of the country, so I cannot conceive that there is any irreconcilable bar here in their native home and in England to the unity and the amity of the two nations.[21]

Just before these statements were made, the Cabinet agreed on its Irish legislation for the remainder of the session. The Parnellite whip had offered his Conservative counterpart Irish Nationalist support in Parliament in return for enactment of two small measures, one of which the Cabinet accepted: a Labourers Bill to improve the conditions of poor farm workers.[22] Closer to its heart, the Cabinet also approved of a land purchase scheme which came to be known as the Ashbourne Act after its sponsor, Edward Gibson, now Lord Ashbourne.

Even before this programme was launched, there were uneasy rumblings in the Conservative ranks, fearful that at least one member of the Cabinet had entered into an agreement with Parnell, like the infamous 'Kilmainham treaty' of 1882. The finger of suspicion pointed to Churchill.[23] A week after Carnarvon's statement, these fears surfaced over the Maamtrasna murders. Three Irishmen had been executed and five sentenced to penal servitude for the particularly horrible slaughter of an Irish family in 1882 in a wild corner of the West of Ireland, Maamtrasna, Co. Galway. Subsequently doubts about the verdict, and charges that the prosecution had intimidated a witness to secure the execution of a man they knew to be innocent, had arisen. Lord Spencer, the Liberal Lord Lieutenant who was applying the Crimes Act sternly, had reviewed the case and decided that justice had been done. The Parnellites denounced his decision in an attempt to discredit his administration. The issue was debated in 1884 in Parliament. Most Conservatives had supported Spencer; but a few, including Churchill and Gorst, now Solicitor General, had taken the other side. Parnell moved for a further review of the case by the new Ministry.

The Cabinet, Churchill alone dissenting, decided to reject Parnell's motion. Hicks Beach, however, had second thoughts; and, with the power which his position as leader in the Commons gave him, he informed Carnarvon, who was away in Ireland, that he could not agree. Reluctantly and tentatively Carnarvon gave way. But he wrote off in vigorous protest to Salisbury: 'It is, as you will see, of *vital* importance involving personal and collective honour . . . the whole administration of law and justice may be shaken if we seem lightly to reopen the acts of our predecessors, and a corresponding blow given to confidence in Government.'[24] Salisbury's feelings on such an issue were identical to Carnarvon's; and he wrote to Hicks Beach immediately, asking him to consult the Cabinet before responding to Parnell's motion. Time may have precluded a Cabinet meeting, for the motion was to be debated next day; but Salisbury was able to discuss the motion with Hicks Beach before the debate.

In spite of Salisbury's efforts, Hicks Beach's conduct of the debate was a disaster. He kept his own remarks to the Commons brief and formal, stating simply that the Irish administration should and would receive any request for judicial review as a matter of course. His restraint did not disguise the magnitude of the concession; and from the Liberal front bench Sir William Harcourt denounced it, to cheers from Conservative backbenchers. Hicks Beach compounded his error by excluding hard-liners from his selection of subsequent Ministerial speakers. Harcourt was followed by Churchill and, still worse, by Gorst who laced his speech with a reference to the 'reactionary Ulster Members'[25] opposing Hicks Beach's course.[26]

The damage to the party internally was not irreparable, though the debate left a thickened sediment of suspicion about the Ministry's Irish connections, and Salisbury had to fend off accusations of a 'Maamtrasna treaty.'[27] To counteract the impression which the Maamtrasna debate had left, Salisbury and Hicks Beach took early opportunities to speak highly of Lord Spencer; and Gorst was officially rebuked by the Cabinet. Though confused about the line their leaders wished to follow on Ireland, the party—except for its Ulster contingent—settled down. But the debate quickened rank and file dislike of concessions to Ireland, and consequently reduced the ability of the Ministry to demonstrate its sympathy with Irish needs. Carnarvon had to abandon plans he had made to respond generously to Irish financial needs and to support Irish Catholic educational institutions.

The suspicions of a 'Maamtrasna treaty' did not alert Salisbury to the insuperable risks of a meeting between any of his colleagues and Parnell. It was a measure of Salisbury's preoccupation elsewhere that he gave Carnarvon permission to meet privately with Parnell. Their meeting, which took place secretly in an empty house, was the one episode in the life of the Caretaker Ministry upon which Salisbury later looked back with acute embarrassment. Carnarvon's purpose in arranging the interview was strictly limited beforehand by himself and by Salisbury to probing the intentions and minimum demands of Ireland's uncrowned king. Carnarvon rejected any thought of bargaining with him. Parnell was, however, certain to attempt a similar probe of Carnarvon's intentions. And Carnarvon's initial statement to the Lords should have indicated to Salisbury that Carnarvon was unlikely to respond to Parnell's enquiries in such a way as to rule out Home Rule. Salisbury urged Carnarvon to take Lord Ashbourne along to the meeting as a third party to guard against later misinterpretations of what passed there. Carnarvon did not do so because 'he felt bound to show his complete confidence in Mr. Parnell, and in no way to imply even the smallest suspicion or *arrière-pensée*.'[28] Carnarvon's confidence was belied, and Salisbury's fear was borne out, in the following June when Parnell, now anxious to discredit the Conservatives, told the public that Carnarvon had promised him a generous measure of Home Rule if, with Irish support, the Conservatives emerged successfully from the general election.

Long before Parnell's disclosure, Salisbury was embarrassed by the interview. As soon as it took place, Carnarvon reported to him at Hatfield; and though disconcerted to learn that Ashbourne had not been present, Salisbury conveyed to Carnarvon approval of his conduct. Yet he refused to allow either the Cabinet or the Queen to be informed about the interview. Even after Parnell revealed it to the public, Salisbury was reluctant to permit Carnarvon to give Parliament a contradictory account. When he finally gave way to Carnarvon's insistence on a public explanation, he urged Carnarvon to keep it formal and brief, advice which Carnarvon did not follow. Still, by agreement, Carnarvon said nothing of Salisbury's approval of the meeting. That information, though suspected, was not admitted till the general election of 1886 was well over. The meeting of Carnarvon and Parnell tarnished Salisbury's image as one who had never, even remotely, flirted with the idea of granting Ireland Home Rule, an image which was vital to his reputation.

The Cabinet met, for the first time since the disbanding of Parliament, on 6 October 1885, one day before Salisbury was to deliver the party's election manifesto in a speech at Newport. The subject which the Cabinet dwelt upon was Ireland. Carnarvon reported on the current situation. The expiry of the Crimes Act had not, as some feared, been followed by a general deterioration of law and order. In fact, the number of violent crimes had decreased. Boycotting, on the other hand, had continued to spread. Salisbury worried about English reaction to it. But the Crimes Act was ineffective for dealing with boycotting. The individual actions of boycotters were rarely illegal. It was their coordination and intent that subverted constituted authority; and law was an inherently poor instrument for dealing with intentions.

The conclusion which Carnarvon drew from the boycotting and other manifestations of Irish unrest was that they should be dealt with by coming to terms with what he held to be their ultimate goal, namely Home Rule. He presented this conclusion to the Cabinet tentatively, and did not press for a decision. He met with no support. Cranbrook, Northcote now Earl of Iddesleigh, and even Hicks Beach argued that Carnarvon's conclusion was impossible for the Conservative party. For the moment, in other words until the general election was over, the Cabinet tacitly agreed to disagree.

Salisbury did not object to this result. How to repress boycotting was a genuine problem. To force the Cabinet to a decision and thus provoke resignations on the eve of a general election would be suicidal. And he saw no reason to throw Parnell into the arms of the Liberals 'whose blunders have almost created the National League...ruined the landlords, exasperated the tenants, and made the government of Ireland almost impossible.'[29] Still, the Cabinet's indecision accentuated the delicacy of his immediate task at Newport.

His speech, as he described it afterward to Churchill, was an 'egg-dance.'[30] Salisbury intended it to draw all sections of the Conservative party together, to quicken their determination to defend the interests which they held in common, and to divide the Liberals. He presented a package of domestic reforms designed to meet the concerns of advanced Conservatives but carefully limited to minimize the offence to loyal vested interests.

The Newport manifesto in fact reflected to perfection the strategy which Salisbury intended to follow in his domestic policy, a strategy which he explained to Churchill a year later in national rather than partisan terms:

> We have so to conduct our legislation that we shall give some satisfaction to both classes and masses. This is specially difficult with the classes—because all legislation is rather unwelcome to them, as tending to disturb a state of things with which they are satisfied. It is evident, therefore, that we must work at less speed, & at a lower temperature, than our opponents. Our bills must be tentative and cautious; not sweeping & dramatic. But I believe that with patience, feeling our way as we go, we may get the one element to concede, & the other to forbear.[31]

Accordingly, at Newport Salisbury expressed his support for popularly elected local government, arguing for it not as a democratizing measure, but because it could counteract governmental centralization. He advocated cheaper legal costs for transferring land titles, a reform advocated by Radical assailants of the landed interest; but Salisbury reassured landowners by reminding them how oppressive they too had found these costs. He expressed doubt that legislation to foster the creation of small allotments of land for working-class gardens would prove successful, since it conflicted with economic forces tending toward concentration of land ownership and toward the conversion of arable land into pasture: but he argued that the good of all concerned would be served if the clergy and charities owning land were enabled to sell it more easily, and he pointed out that the land they possessed was often peculiarly well situated for garden allotments. Local option to close public houses he was prepared to support, but only on Sundays.

There was one set of issues on which Salisbury could speak with resounding decisiveness: the maintenance of religious education and of the Established Churches.[32] Here was a cause on which he could rally support and split his opponents. Support for the Established Church was one of the cardinal, distinguishing tenets of English Conservatives' creed, while Scottish Conservatives sympathized either with their own Established Church or with the Church of England. Support for denominational education appealed deeply to the Irish Catholic clergy. On the other hand, this set of issues divided Liberals painfully not just from the Catholic Irish but from each other. In the spring of 1885, on a motion to disestablish the Church of Scotland, 28 Scottish Liberals had abstained, 7 had voted no, and 27 had voted yes.

Gladstone attempted with initial success in his election manifesto to play down the controversy by hedging his remarks. Joseph Chamberlain, however, in his anxiety to consolidate his Nonconformist base, resurrected and extended the controversy. The Liberation Society claimed the support of more than two-thirds of the Liberal candidates in its campaign for disestablishment. But nineteen prominent Liberals led by Lord Selborne, Lord Chancellor in the late Government, issued a manifesto urging churchmen not to vote for anyone committed to disestablishment. Salisbury exploited this disagreement and, without alienating the Irish, delighted Conservatives by making defence of the Established Churches the centrepiece of his campaign.

On Ireland his remarks at Newport were tilted toward the hardliners. Because of the sharp antagonism between the Irish majority and minority, he cast doubt on the wisdom of extending the creation of small elective local authorities to Ireland. He declared that he had 'never seen any plan or any suggestion which gives me at present the slightest ground for anticipating that it is in [the direction of imperial federation] that we shall find any substantial solution of the difficulties of the problem.'[33] Still, his remarks were equivocal. He did not dispel the possibility that, if small local authorities were unacceptable for Ireland, larger authorities for Ireland's four historic provinces might meet the objection, a possibility which he had discussed with one of his colleagues in June.[34] And Liberal analysts seized upon the phrase 'at present' in his statement about the application of imperial federation to Ireland as a significant loophole.

Loopholes gaped still more conspicuously in his comments on Ireland several weeks later at the Guildhall. Though he promised to protect the Irish minority who had 'fallen into unpopularity and danger' because they had stood by England, he accompanied his mention of the minority with the phrase, 'if such exist.'[35] He went on to emphasize that, subject to maintenance of the integrity of the Empire and protection of the hypothetical minority,

> the policy which every English Government, and I am sure the present, would pursue would be to do everything possible to give prosperity, contentment, and happiness to the Irish people.

The room for manoeuvre which these speeches gave him deceived Gladstone and beguiled Parnell. Shortly after his Guildhall speech, Salisbury repeated to Carnarvon his inability to contemplate Home Rule. But the speech left Gladstone with a contrary impression. Parnell's reaction was of more immediate moment. The guarded public statements of Salisbury and Churchill, following upon Carnarvon's secret interview with him, led the Irish leader to believe that Conservatives would be willing to bid high for his support if that was necessary in order to stay in power after the general election. Whether in order to bring about that result, or in order to keep the Liberal majority so small that they would want Irish support in order to replace the Conservatives, Parnell issued a statement shortly before balloting was to begin, advising Irishmen in England and Scotland to vote against the Liberals.

Apart from Ireland, the performance of the Caretaker Ministry enhanced the reputation of the Conservative party. The Ministry had wound up the business of Parliament with productive discretion. The main legislative initiative of the Ministry, the Ashbourne Act, was carried with bipartisan support. So too were the other measures which the Government took over from its predecessor: the Artisans' Dwellings Act, for which Salisbury and Dilke were jointly responsible, and a Bill to create the post of Secretary of State for Scotland. In an essentially partisan gesture, the Ministry appointed a royal commission to inquire into the depression in trade and industry. The bland title of the commission did not disguise its intent, which was to give advocates of protective tariffs an opportunity they desired to present their case. Liberals denounced the commission, and all prominent Liberals who were asked to serve on it refused. But they could not prevent its appointment, which rested entirely with the executive authority. Appointment of the commission enabled the Government to satisfy 'fair traders' without committing itself to their cause.

The outstanding achievement of the Ministry was its demonstration, through Lord Salisbury, of how the foreign affairs of a great nation ought to be conducted—and for Salisbury this demonstration was the chief object of the whole enterprise. He rehabilitated England in Europe's eyes, lent lustre to his party, and enhanced his personal authority. The change was not in policy but in conduct. Salisbury was not at all enamoured of the policies which Gladstone and Granville had initiated. But, as he explained to the House of Lords, 'There is really no alternative before us but steadily buckling to with a view of amending all the evils, or a considerable number of the evils which exist, by a cautious and circumspect policy.'[36] He picked up the threads, particularly in Afghanistan and Egypt, where Granville had left them, and wove them with an assurance and persistent attention to detail which contrasted sharply with Granville's lackadaisical performance. However uncomfortable the comparison made them, Liberals had to confess their admiration for Salisbury's management. For the threads were theirs. Granville could not secure the agreement which Gladstone wished to reach with Russia over the borders of Afghanistan: Salisbury succeeded. Trouble, again with Russia, erupted in the Balkans where the Bulgarians, divided by the Treaty of Berlin into two states, sought a unified state under Prince Alexander. Because its predominant sentiment now would be self-reliant nationalism rather than grateful subservience to Russia, the Russians opposed unification, which they had wanted in 1878. Reversing his position for the same reason, Salisbury, who had engineered the division of 1878, now supported unification. In doing so, he satisfied the Liberals who championed Balkan nationalism and the Conservatives who distrusted Russia. And he gratified the pride of all Englishmen by leading the great powers of Europe in securing the unification.

Welcome though this performance was after five years of unhappy Liberal administration, it allowed public memory of those years to grow dim, and gave Liberals time to freshen their appeal. Chamberlain spread his wares before the public, a package of proposals designed primarily to appeal to the newly enfranchised agricultural labourers at the expense of their landlords. Salisbury took up the challenge eagerly, believing that Chamberlain's 'Unauthorized Programme' would frighten many moderate Liberals into casting Conservative votes. But Chamberlain's arrows hit the target at which they were aimed.

The election broke previously established patterns of voting behaviour. The first results to be announced were for borough constituencies. Hitherto considered bastions of Liberal strength, they returned Conservatives in droves. The county constituencies turned the results around. Son after son of landed magnate, whether he ran as Whig or Tory, was rejected by the newly enfranchised electors. The county losses neutralized the Conservatives' borough victories. Even with Irish support, the impact of which was disputed, Conservatives registered a total net gain, in comparison with 1880, of a paltry 10 seats. They won 86 seats fewer than the Liberals.

That was exactly the number of successful Parnellites, all of them pledged to Home Rule and under iron discipline. By sweeping the Irish constituencies outside Ulster, the Parnellites inaugurated a new phase in Anglo-Irish relations. Home Rule, hitherto dismissed in England as a bogey or no more than a distant possibility, moved suddenly to the centre of debate. At the same time, by securing a number of seats equal to the difference between the Conservative and Liberal totals, Parnell and his men intensified the unstable quality which British politics had possessed since the death of General Gordon. Even with full Parnellite support, the Conservatives in the new House of Commons would barely match the Liberals. A Liberal Government facing Parnellite as well as Conservative opposition would be similarly paralysed.

## iii. The Interregnum (December 1885-January 1886)·

The acutely frustrating balance in the newly elected Parliament between the two British parties made both willing to modify their strategies of war with each other. At the same time, the new power with which Parnellites could press the Irish demand for Home Rule forced the British body politic to consider radical modification of the relationship between the two islands, whether in the direction of concession or of repression. The conjunction of these two sets of concerns provided Lord Salisbury with a rare opportunity to modify the reflexes of his party and the political complexion of the country. With little advance warning, the weeks between the final returns from the general election at the beginning of December and the fall of the Caretaker Ministry late in January brought him to the crisis of his career. Eventually he resolved it with decisive success; but during the moment of crisis, unremitting caution and occasional error brought him close to failure.

One course of action which the election results seemed to bring within the realm of possibility was for the two British parties to hammer out an agreement on Irish policy, perhaps on the model of the Arlington Street Compact. That was the solution to which, among Liberals, Gladstone, and among Conservatives, Carnarvon were inclined. The Caretaker Ministry had given ample indication of the room for manoeuvre on Ireland which Conservatives possessed. If some national forum for discussion of Anglo-Irish relations could be devised, and if the demand for immediate decision could be held at bay while those discussions proceeded, they might serve to bring much if not all of the party's rank and file to accept some scheme for limited autonomy: and Ireland would then have to accept what it was offered. That was what Carnarvon proposed: appointment of a joint commission of the two Houses of Parliament to enquire into the relations between Ireland and the rest of the United Kingdom.

Gladstone harked back to the crises of 1829, 1846 and 1867, when solutions to urgent national problems had been devised by Tory or Conservative Ministries and were enacted, in face of some resistance among their usual followers, by support from the Whig or Liberal Opposition. He did not dwell upon the fact that each of those moments of Tory heroism were followed by long stretches of Whig or Liberal government. Gladstone offered Salisbury his support in the present crisis if the Government would introduce a measure to satisfy Irish aspirations.

Salisbury had no use for consensus Conservatism. In the past, he had held the models of 1829, 1846 and 1867 up to reprobation. His object in domestic politics was to overcome the consequences of Conservatives' behaviour in those years. Furthermore, quite apart from this philosophical predisposition, the practical case against compliance with the proposals of Carnarvon and of Gladstone was very strong.

Both proposals assumed that there was opportunity for calm, non-partisan deliberation. But no such opportunity existed, initially because the results of the general election had produced feverish uncertainty about the possession of office. The Conservatives had all but lost, the Liberals all but won the election. Yet many Liberals, just emerging from bitter electoral contests against Parnellite opposition, were in no mood for the collaboration with the Irish which was needed to hold office securely. Gladstone tried to give himself quiet room for inter-party negotiations. He approached Salisbury privately through Balfour, and warded off pressure, whether from his colleagues and party supporters or from the Irish, by veiling his intentions. But uncertainty about his inclinations only intensified the unsettlement in every camp. Many of Gladstone's contemporaries, supporters as well as enemies, recognized his general appetite for power, and therefore put a cynical construction on his behaviour in December.

Gladstone saw his offer to Salisbury as an altruistic, self-subordinating act in the interests of the country. The effect of this assumption of righteousness upon Salisbury was to turn his cynicism to disgust. His account to Churchill of the offer dripped with contempt: 'Gladstone has written Arthur a marvellous letter saying that he thinks 'it will be a public calamity if this great subject should fall into the lines of party conflict.' — & saying he desires the question should be settled by the present Government. His hypocrisy makes me sick.'[37] Gladstone was asking Salisbury to pursue a course of action which would split the Conservative party, to shoulder a responsibility which would minimize Liberal divisions, and all without assurance that Gladstone would enable the

Government to remain in office after the measure was enacted.

All doubts about the wisdom of rejecting Gladstone's overture were dispelled by the 'Hawarden kite,' a news leak by Herbert Gladstone that his father favoured Home Rule. Gladstone seemed prepared to play on both sides of the street; and the Cabinet spurned his offer with evasive disdain.

Apart from Carnarvon who was absent in Ireland, the Cabinet's rejection of the offer, and hence of the pattern of 1829, '46 and '67, was unanimous. It was a pattern more often praised than blamed. Most members of the Caretaker Cabinet had supported the Reform Bill of 1867, some as members of the Derby-Disraeli Cabinet. The Bill was the central action in the career of Disraeli, whose person and legacy most Conservatives claimed to revere. Nevertheless, by 1885 the pattern had remarkably few advocates. Iddesleigh, who had been a leading Secretary of State in 1867, now described the model as 'gradual surrender of position after position at the bidding of our opponents.'[38] Churchill, the embodiment of Tory Democracy, insisted that, 'The Disraeli epoch of constant metamorphoses of principle and party has passed away. Radical work must be done by Radical artists; thus less mischief will arise.'[39] Salisbury could not have put it better.

This unanimous reaction wiped the party's behavioural slate clean. But the Cabinet did not go on immediately to replace the old design with a new one: for they disagreed about the pattern they wished to establish. Salisbury had long possessed a clear conception of the pattern he desired, one of defiance rather than consensus. Toward the end of December, he discerned a groundswell of hostility to Irish demands, particularly within but not restricted to the Conservative party. He became increasingly convinced that Britain had lost patience with the Irish and yearned for determined government. This surge of opinion was exactly of the sort he had been waiting for. Ireland might give him the issue he needed to maximize and stiffen the forces of natural conservatism in England. He promptly jettisoned his pre-election interest in doing 'everything possible to give prosperity, contentment, and happiness to the Irish people.' He now wanted to stand up against Irish nationalism.

The adoption of a hard line on Ireland would, however, be counterproductive if it split the Cabinet and hence the party. Unity of the party was a prerequisite for Salisbury's purposes. Firmness in the party's defence of the interests which it represented was his objective; but it could be pursued no more quickly than the party as a whole would run.

These considerations ordered Salisbury's priorities in January. He wanted to take a resolute stand against the Irish National League and in defence of the Union. Although the new Parliament had not yet met, he felt sure that it looked for and would welcome such a stand. But he would not press the pace any faster than the Cabinet were willing to go. Such caution might be wise if unheroic. It was, however, compounded to the verge of discredit, first in December by his reluctance to tender the Ministry's resignation, then in January by his diffident management of the Cabinet.

The politics of the interregnum were a poker game between an old master, Gladstone, and a new challenger, Salisbury. Each man kept his cards close to his chest. Salisbury strongly suspected that he held winning cards and that Gladstone's were weak. His hunch was correct, but he played his cards so poorly that he lost the first hand.

The most direct way to win the hand would have been for the Ministry to resign, thus forcing Gladstone to declare his hand. Important voices in the Cabinet urged that course: Carnarvon even before the Cabinet rejected his proposals on Ireland; Churchill, Hicks Beach and Smith immediately afterward; and Balfour in the light of Gladstone's overture. Carnarvon's argument, though related to his fear that the Cabinet would not agree with him on Irish policy, was particularly cogent:

> If we resign, [the Liberals] either must form a govt, in which case their dissensions will tear them to pieces and perhaps place them at our control, or they must refuse to make a govt which again would place us in a far stronger position.[40]

Salisbury rejected resignation. Though he had several reasons for doing so, they were not compelling. An urgent appeal from the Queen[41] to remain in office did not add anything to the balance of considerations except sentiment. Salisbury disliked, as one more manifestation of popular sovereignty, the practice initiated by Disraeli in 1868 of resigning after an adverse general election without waiting for the new Parliament to meet: but a philosophical aversion of this sort need not have taken precedence over tactical advantage. He was beguiled by Liberal dissensions into believing that they might enable the Caretaker Ministry to survive for a little while without indicating its intentions. He did not want to do anything which might assist Gladstone by clarifying the situation. As he put it to Churchill, 'The fact, that Gladstone is mad to take office, will force him into some line of conduct which will be discreditable to him, and disastrous, if we do not prematurely gratify his hunger.'[42]

Herbert Gladstone's intimation of his father's intentions through the 'Hawarden kite' opened a new tactical phase. The Hawarden kite had the effect of revealing just enough of the Grand Old Man's intentions to put his opponents off guard without depriving him of vital support. He refused to confirm or deny the accuracy of the disclosure, and he took great pains to avoid being further drawn, even by former Cabinet colleagues, let alone publicly. The right tactical response for the

Government in this situation would have been to declare enough of a contrasting policy to force Gladstone into the open. But the Cabinet, interpreting the Hawarden kite in the light of Gladstone's overture through Balfour, were more certain than the rest of Parliament or the public at large that Gladstone was intent upon Home Rule. The Cabinet therefore failed to appreciate the necessity of forcing Gladstone to state his intentions clearly. The Ministers also were divided between a majority, who favoured a firm stand against the Irish nationalist agitation, and an influential minority, led by Hicks Beach and, less reliably, Churchill, who continued to hope that the Irish question could be held in suspension by a mixture of concessions, firmness, and distraction of Parliament's attention elsewhere.

The Ministry resorted to a policy of inconclusive compromise. Salisbury acquiesced, in the first place because he could not be sure that the party as a whole would follow the strong course he preferred, in the second because, as he reckoned it, no amount of strength in policy would compensate for a split in the party. As he put it to Churchill,

> my dominant feeling is . . . that we should be a united Cabinet—if possible with a united party. I have been throughout ready to postpone my individual opinion to this primary consideration. We have no right to the luxury of divided councils in a crisis such as this.[43]

However justifiable in principle, in practice Salisbury's dedication to the unity of the Cabinet bred weakness and confusion. Though fed up with Carnarvon, he put off accepting Carnarvon's proffered resignation and, until the press got word of the resignation, contemplated transferring Carnarvon to another post in the Cabinet. Still true to the assumption that each Minister possessed the initiative within his own department, Salisbury even cooperated with Carnarvon in composing the initial draft of the passage on Ireland in the Queen's speech for the opening of Parliament. The draft which they submitted to the Cabinet allowed for continued cooperation with the Irish, and therefore confused the Cabinet about the prime minister's wishes. Soon afterward, his line stiffened, and he became almost desperately anxious to meet Parliament with an unequivocal statement of the Government's determination to uphold the union with Ireland by fortifying its criminal law. Even so, when Churchill and Hicks Beach remained unconvinced though willing to defer to his authority, he did not press the point. He settled for a hesitant statement in which the Government said that it would uphold the Union with Ireland and indicated that some stiffening of Irish criminal law would probably prove necessary.

It was in the Cabinet that the power at Salisbury's disposal was the greatest. The situation went from bad to worse once Parliament met; for in Parliament Salisbury's disabilities as a peer, and the power of Hicks Beach and Churchill as leaders in the Commons, came into play. The first few days of the new Parliament were among the most frustrating in Salisbury's entire career as leader. Despite all Churchill's sensitivity to nuances of feeling in the previous House of Commons, Salisbury had read the mood of the new House better than he. After weeks of wondering, M.P.s on both sides were disappointed at the indecisiveness of the Government's statement on Ireland. This disappointed reception made an opportunity for Gladstone's magnetism to impress itself on his uncertain following. If a Conservative Government felt unable vigorously to reassert the authority of the Union, then perhaps Gladstone's alternative, however distasteful it might be, was inevitable. Gladstone, for his part, played his hand well. The Government had done nothing to oblige him to reveal his intentions in any detail. He kept his cards to his chest, and as 'an old Parliamentary hand' advised his followers to do the same.

Salisbury watched helplessly from the House of Lords as his lieutenants in the Commons threw his few remaining cards away. He wanted the debate on the Queen's speech to be sustained to give W. H. Smith, who had taken over control of the Irish administration from Carnarvon, time to provide evidence to justify prompt introduction of a coercion Bill. Whether deliberately or not, Churchill foiled Salisbury. Churchill cut short the debate on an amendment criticizing the recent annexation of Burma by rising to reply immediately after Gladstone had spoken. Liberal and Irish forces then gathered to defeat the Government on an amendment by Jesse Collings criticizing the absence in the Queen's speech of proposals for allotments and small holdings of land for agricultural labourers. Salisbury hoped to forestall this amendment with a friendly counter-amendment, and he secured the Speaker's agreement to notice the mover of the friendly amendment first. Hicks Beach, however, entrusted the counter-amendment to an inexperienced backbencher who, through nervousness, failed to rise at the appropriate moment; and Collings gained the floor.[44]

By now Churchill and Hicks Beach were convinced of the superiority of a repressive Irish policy to any cautiously balanced alternative. Just before the debate on Collings' amendment began, the Government attempted to bring the question of Ireland to the fore and force Gladstone into the open. Hicks Beach announced the intention of the Government, if it survived Collings' motion, to introduce a coercion Bill as a matter of urgency and to follow it later with a land Bill extending the policy initiated by the Ashbourne Act. The annoucement came too late. It was patently the last gasp of a dying Government, made without the substantiating report from Smith which the Government had previously said it must await. There was no need for Gladstone to respond. The immediate order of business gave Collings the floor.

His amendment brought the Government further embarrassment. It had to be opposed since it was an amendment to the address; but its substance was not incompatible with the Government's programme. Bills had been promised in the Queen's speech (in line with the Newport manifesto) to facilitate the sale of glebe lands and to make the transfer of land easier and cheaper. Heedless of these promises, Henry Chaplin, spokesman for the squires on the Conservative benches, proceeded to blast Collings' proposals. Balfour, as President of the Local Government Board, had to get up and attempt to repair the damage. Edward Hamilton expressed a common reaction when he commented, 'The Govt. have certainly played their last cards with consummate clumsiness.'[45]

## iv. Gladstone's Third Ministry

Though the circumstances of Salisbury's fall from office were humiliating, his experience for the first time as leader of the entire Parliamentary and national party in opposition was sweet. Freedom from office eased the restrictions which the leaders in the Commons could place upon him. He was now better able to give Conservative policy toward Ireland the complexion which he had desired since the turn of the year, a complexion which the jockeying for advantage among the contenders for power in both parties rendered still more desirable.

After waiting during the months of February and March while Gladstone prepared his proposals, the House of Commons was presented with a Home Rule Bill more thorough-going than the Government's apprehensive supporters and impatient opponents had anticipated. It proposed to give Ireland an autonomous legislature, and an executive responsible to that legislature with power over all but a list of subjects—chiefly involving the Crown, war and peace, the armed forces, overseas relations, regulation of trade, coinage and legal tender—which were reserved for the imperial Parliament at Westminster. Ireland's representatives in both Houses at Westminster were to be withdrawn, a provision on which Gladstone later proved willing to compromise. The landed and Protestant minorities were to be protected by a generous land purchase Bill, by a prohibition against the establishment or endowment of any religion, and by the creation within the unicameral Irish legislature of two 'orders,' the upper one consisting of peers and men elected on a propertied franchise, each order possessing a suspensive veto over the initiatives of the other. The Bill drove everything else from Parliament's mind until the Commons reached a decision upon it early in June.

Both before and after the Bill's introduction, Salisbury by and large left the Parliamentary campaign to an eager Churchill. For the Parliamentary campaign was an entirely House of Commons affair. There was an excellent chance of defeating the Bill in the Commons, and only if the Bill survived through the Commons would the Lords be called upon to act. Even if the Bill reached the Lords, no one doubted that the Lords would throw it out, in all probability precipitating a general election. Salisbury devoted his attention to the general election which, one way or another, would likely take place within the next few months, and to the public platform. It was through an intermittent succession of speeches at public functions from mid-February until the end of June that he shaped the Conservative stance on Ireland to his liking.

He had not spoken directly to the public since the general election; and therefore he began the new succession of speeches by reducing the ambiguity of his pre-election statements. Before the election he had promised that the Conservative Government would remain true to the party's traditions on Ireland, but he had not explained what these traditions were. Now he defined them to mean preservation of Pitt's Act of Union. Before the election he had insisted upon protection of the Irish loyalist minority—'if such exist.' Now he elevated that requirement into the most insistent dictate of honour:

> abandoning to your enemies those whom you have called upon to defend you and who have risked their all on your behalf . . . is an infamy below which it is impossible to go.[46]

And he identified the minority as "landowners, educated men, bankers, merchants, students,"[47] groups and interests dear to a Conservative whether they were in Ireland or the rest of the United Kingdom. The class implications of this argument were apparent well before the first of May when Gladstone presented the debate over Home Rule as one between the classes and the masses.[48]

The force of this new clarity in Salisbury's speeches was lessened by persistent suspicion that the Conservatives might still resort to some form of Home Rule if that proved tactically advantageous. The suspicion was not restricted to Liberals nor, among Conservatives, to uninformed backbenchers. During the transfer of power early in February, when Salisbury met Gladstone to inform him about the state of Britain's foreign relations, W. H. Smith wondered whether they might also discuss an accommodation on Ireland. Suspicions were quickened hours before the Commons' decisive vote on the Home Rule Bill when, without identifying the Minister involved, Parnell revealed his secret conversation of the previous August with Carnarvon. To counteract these suspicions, Salisbury made his opposition to Home Rule publicly, unequivocally and repeatedly clear.

This display of determination was also intended to satisfy the popular desire for firmness toward Ireland, thus harnessing that desire to the general purposes of Conservative government as Salisbury envisaged it. He appealed to that desire in what proved to be the most famous speech of his entire career, his address to the National Union of Conservative Associations on 15 May in St. James's Hall. The speech was studded with the 'blazing indiscretions' for which he was famous: he coupled the Irish, as incapable of self-government, with Hottentots, and suggested, as an alternative to expensive land purchase schemes, that Irishmen solve their economic woes by emigrating to Manitoba. These comments were exclamation marks to emphasize his central appeal, to English exasperation with Ireland:

> My alternative policy is that Parliament should enable the Government of England to govern Ireland. (Loud cheers.) Apply that recipe honestly, consistently, and resolutely for 20 years, and at the end of that time you will find that Ireland will be fit to accept any gifts in the way of local government or repeal of coercion laws that you may wish to give her. (Cheers.) What she wants is government—government that does not flinch, that does not vary—government that she cannot hope to beat down by agitations at Westminster—government that does not alter in its resolutions or its temperature by the party changes which take place at Westminster.[49]

He gave further resonance to this appeal by sounding the tocsin of empire. With an eye to the next general election, he told the National Union that it was up to them to determine whether the House of Commons' probable rejection of the Home Rule Bill

> shall only be a halt in the gradual process of disintegration and decay, or whether it shall be the first step in a new and bolder Imperial policy . . . .[50]

Three weeks later the House of Commons did indeed reject the Bill, by an unexpectedly large margin of thirty votes. Gladstone, impatient for a popular mandate to settle Anglo-Irish relations amicably as his last accomplishment before he retired, appealed to the arbitrament of a general election. Salisbury travelled north to Leeds, where he struck the imperial note again:

> we come to the bar of that great tribunal, the people of England, pleading the cause of the English Empire . . . .[51]

Yet, despite the ringing quality of these pronouncements, Salisbury retained as much room for manoeuvre on Ireland as he had given himself during the Caretaker Ministry. The chief difference between his speeches in 1885 as prime minister and his speeches during 1886 as leader of the Opposition was that his rejection of Home Rule, private and personal then, was public and official now. The difference in his public posture was a matter of impression and emphasis. Consideration of Parliamentary tactics and party unity still induced him to avoid binding commitments beyond rejection of Home Rule. His fierce speeches were occasionally interspersed with mild ones, gestures of defiance with gestures of passive endurance. He assured the Merchant Taylors, for example, that, even if the Irish malady could not be cured, 'we have proved in the past that we can get on with it and yet carry on our empire to a vast pitch of prosperity.'[52] The government of England could go on, as it had in the past, applying such remedies to Ireland as it thought wise, 'hoping that they may succeed, but in the confidence that if they do not succeed it is not within the power of Irish disaffection to mar the career of a great nation.'

The Conservative alternative to Home Rule was left unspecified. It might be 'manacles and Manitoba', as John Morley epitomized Salisbury's prescription to the National Union. But that prescription was a gesture, not pledge. On Manitoba, Salisbury hastily backtracked, explaining that he had meant only to point out the intolerable burden which Gladstone's land purchase Bill would impose upon the tax-payer.[53] He also denied prescribing coercion for twenty years: and in any case such a policy was impracticable, since it would require bipartisan support in order to survive over a length of time which would see at least three general elections. The latitude which Conservatives retained in Irish policy was still so wide that Captain Colomb, the Conservative candidate in Bow and Bromley, placarded his con-stituency with the slogan, 'Vote for Colomb and no Coercion.'[54] Others such as Churchill's client, Henry Matthews, running in Birmingham, promised equal treatment for Ireland with the rest of the Kingdom.

The electorate upheld the House of Commons' decision to reject Home Rule. 395 opponents of Home Rule were elected, giving them a majority of 120 over the combined forces of Gladstonians and Parnellites. 316 of the anti-Home Rule forces were Conservative, only 20 short of a majority on their own and therefore assured of power so long as the Liberal Unionists did not vote against them. The tally of elected Members was, however, more lopsided than the total electoral vote. Gladstonians still outpolled Conservatives by 1,241,000 to 1,038,000,[55] though the large number of uncontested Conservative victories dis-guised their potential vote total. Many of the Conservative and Liberal Unionist victories were in rural constituencies, where agricultural labourers who had voted Liberal seven months earlier stayed home, whether from disappointment at the lack of action to redeem the promises of Collings and Chamberlain, or from hostility toward Ireland, or simply because the election coincided with the hay harvest. But these agricultural voters had not defected to the other side; they might still be won back by the Liberals. Moreover, the victory was limited to England and Ulster. Three-fifths of the Members elected from Scotland and

five-sixths from Wales supported Gladstone. The verdict of the electorate was precarious, if for the moment clear.

### v. The Formation of Salisbury's Second Ministry

As soon as the Queen asked Salisbury to form a Government, he
reverted to the pattern of 1885: the leadership which he gave during
the opening months of his second Ministry was almost as muffled as in
his first. He did not immediately treat the election as mandating a
display of resolution in the government of Ireland. Home Rule was out.
But all other decisions about how to rule Ireland (most of which had used
the election to reaffirm its commitment to Home Rule) were put off.
Before appointing his Cabinet, Salisbury convened a meeting of the
Conservatives in Parliament to present them with two immediate
alternatives: either to convene the new Parliament now simply in order
to wind up necessary financial business unfinished by the last, and
postpone fresh policy initiatives until the new year; or to convene a full
session of Parliament in October. He made his preference for the first
alternative clear, and the meeting readily agreed. He wanted time:
time, after the excitements of the last eight months, for the civil service in
Ireland and for the country generally to settle down; time for the Irish
Nationalists to respond to the electoral setback, perhaps by encouraging
a revival of agrarian unrest, which would justify the Government in
introducing a coercion Bill; time to feel his way. The main actions of the
new Government with regard to Ireland were exploratory. Royal
commissions were appointed to enquire into the need for a revision of the
1881 Land Act, and into the feasibility of various public works to
stimulate the Irish economy.

In constituting his Cabinet, Salisbury attempted to learn from the
Caretaker Ministry's embarrassments over Ireland by making two
structural changes, neither of which proved successful. There was strong
feeling in the Parliamentary party that Salisbury's preoccupation with
foreign affairs had been partially responsible for those embarrassments.
Reluctantly, Salisbury abandoned the Foreign Office to Lord
Iddesleigh. He himself became First Lord of the Treasury, the
customary post for prime ministers; and for the one and only time in his
career, he had his official residence at 10 Downing Street. At the same
time he created a Cabinet committee on Ireland in which he included
himself, to keep the Irish administration under steady surveillance.
Theoretically these provisions should have corrected critical weaknesses
in his former Ministry. Instead they created new problems without
solving the old. Iddesleigh's conduct of foreign affairs was not as quick or
vigilant as Salisbury's, and gave rise to Cabinet controversy in a field
where a high level of concord previously had prevailed. The appoint-

ment of Hicks Beach as Chief Secretary for Ireland neutralized many of
the advantages which the Cabinet committee should have provided.

If Salisbury's arrangements were to work well, he needed close accord
with the man placed at the head of the Irish administration, a need
heavily underscored by his experience with Carnarvon. But he did not
yet feel independently strong enough to make such a selection. His
enforced absence from the House of Commons, the poverty of the front
bench there apart from Churchill and Hicks Beach, the skill and
authority which these two men displayed, and Churchill's popularity
outside, forced them back upon him. Salisbury felt obliged to divide
between Churchill and Hicks Beach the Cabinet posts which all three
men regarded as critically important: the leadership in the Commons,
and the Irish Secretaryship. Hicks Beach was chosen for Ireland by a
process of elimination. He had not been a success as leader in the
Commons, stiff as he was and apt to respond to backbench enquiries
either with chilling hauteur or with a torrent of billingsgate.[56]
Moreover, though he had a mind of his own, he was in the last analysis a
party man, and would be less likely than Churchill to disregard advice
from his colleagues: a vital consideration in view of a Chief Secretary's
long sojourns in Dublin.

Hicks Beach exacted his toll in terms of policy. He insisted upon the
appointment as Lord Lieutenant of a lightweight, Lord Londonderry,
whose inclinations were akin to Churchill's. It may have been at Hicks
Beach's as well as Chamberlain's bidding that the royal commission on
Irish land was appointed. Salisbury publicly displayed uneasiness about
the appointment, discounting the implication that the settlement of
1881 needed revision, minimizing the severity of the agricultural
depression in Ireland, and arguing that, even if the need for rent
reduction was proved, the burden should not fall on the landowners but
should be alleviated by the state through provision of further facilities for
tenant purchase of their holdings. The prejudice which these remarks
displayed in favour of the landlords upset Hicks Beach. But this and
similar ensuing divisions in the Ministry were bridged by efforts, first of
Churchill, then of Hicks Beach, to harmonize each other's relations with
Salisbury, efforts toward internal accommodation which were seconded by Hamilton and Smith. The Government continued on its
temporizing course, with differing hopes, Hicks Beach and Churchill
hoping that coercion would prove unnecessary, Salisbury looking for a
contrary result.

In mid-autumn, the Government's will was cleverly tested by the
Nationalist 'Plan of Campaign.' Organized with only mild and indirect
approval from Parnell—thus limiting the responsibility which the Irish
party in Parliament would have to bear—the Plan called upon tenants
in a few, well selected estates on which the landlord refused to reduce

rents, to offer collectively to him what they deemed a fair rent. If he rejected their offer, they were not to pay him at all, but were instead to pay their rent into a fund for mutual protection. Except as a violation of contract between tenant and landlord, the illegality of the Plan was open to doubt, because it was conducted on a discretely local basis rather than as a patently national conspiracy, and because the changes in Irish land law had recognized the tenant as a dual owner of the property he rented. Yet the Plan demonstrated the power of popular authority superceding the law, and the example set in a handful of estates induced other landlords who were similarly threatened to capitulate. The Plan avoided the strain which widespread anarchy would place on Liberal support of the Nationalist cause, while it demonstrated the unreality of Unionist government. Hicks Beach was ready to take action against the National League which was organizing the tenants, but suggested that Salisbury discuss the matter with Churchill. Churchill counselled patience for fear of provoking violence. Salisbury agreed, but with a different intent. 'I think', he told Hicks Beach, 'you had better let the flames spread because you won't get the parish engine to come out till you have a good conflagration.'[57]

By the year's end, preparations were being made and pressures were mounting for a more decided course of action by the Government. Prosecutions of key organizers of the Plan of Campaign were launched to ascertain the capacity of the existing law to stop it. At the same time, Irish landlords were reacting with anger to Hicks Beach's conspicuous dislike of them and lack of support for their claims; and their English Conservative friends shared their sentiment. These pressures to stand up to the Nationalists were at odds with another widely felt desire, for political tranquillity after two general elections and four changes of Government in eighteen months. But both bodies of opinion responded with the same sense of outrage when, just before Christmas, the Government was threatened with internal disruption.

## vi. Lord Randolph Churchill's Departure

Since first becoming prime minister, Salisbury had sacrificed coherence in policy, particularly on Ireland, to cohesion in the Cabinet. The only resignation thus far from his Cabinets had been Carnarvon's: and the significance of that resignation had been veiled when it occurred by the publication of an exchange of letters between the two men at the time of Carnarvon's appointment in which he had specified that, for reasons of health, he would accept the Lord Lieutenancy only until the general election. Salisbury's willingness to accommodate internal disagreement was not a fleeting phenomenon, to be accounted for wholly by the unsettlement of politics in 1885–6 and by the insecurity of his recently attained position. Before and afterward he displayed rare capacity to work with men personally uncongenial to him, preeminently Disraeli and Chamberlain, and also to enable mutually uncongenial men, such as Chamberlain and Hartington, to work with each other. Repeatedly during his career as prime minister, he allowed himself to be overruled by his Cabinet colleagues in order to avoid disruption. He was always to be diffident in his use of a premier's power to direct the Cabinet's deliberations and mould its conclusions. The instability and insecurity of 1885–6 only accentuated this disposition.

But there were limits to his tolerance. In the sphere of policy, his prohibitions were kept spare so as to allow ample room for accommodation: no sacrifice of vital interests abroad, adjustment to but no acceleration of the popularly demanded pace of reform, and no Home Rule. In conduct, he required from his colleagues the same forbearance which he himself displayed. He was also jealous of any challenges or threats to his leadership, though, with consummate, inconspicuous, and perhaps often unconscious mastery of the arts of *noblesse oblige*, he managed to hide this cardinal fact from all except his rivals: Northcote, Churchill, and more slowly Hartington. If his family and his nephew-successor, Balfour, suspected this truth, they never let on. The rest of the political world came to accept at face value the aura of honour within which Salisbury moved. In the autumn of 1886, Churchill breached or attempted to breach all these limits except for the prohibition of Home Rule; and, by his behaviour, he put the Union with Ireland in jeopardy as well.

Salisbury, in forming his second Ministry, subjected Churchill to an exacting test by gratifying his maximum immediate expectations. As leader in the Commons with a premier in the Lords, Churchill was answerable on all subjects, and as Chancellor of the Exchequer he had financial oversight for all departments. His responsibility was therefore almost equal to the prime minister's and in the public eye he bulked larger. This double assignment had been common under previous premiers in the Lords. Hicks Beach had carried it in the Caretaker Ministry. It could and, so far as the public could see, initially it did have a sobering effect on Churchill. At thirty-seven the youngest leader of the Commons since Pitt, he conducted himself with surprising modesty and patience. His speeches conveyed a new impression 'of responsibility and great constructive power.'[58] But Salisbury knew that Churchill, when under heavy pressure, could become over-excited and swing wildly between depression and rashness. In August of 1885, reacting to Salisbury's part in an attempt by the Queen to install her son, the Duke of Connaught, as military commander at Bombay, Churchill had tendered his resignation as Secretary for India; and even after Churchill got his way, Salisbury had to coax him to calm down.

After the election of 1886, some members of the new Cabinet, still unsure of their party's hold upon the public, urged upon Salisbury the need for sympatheitc reception of Churchill's initiatives. But it was within the Cabinet, suspected by very few outside, that trouble developed. The first indication of serious division arose in September over foreign policy. Bulgaria was again in turmoil. Russia forced Bulgaria's Prince Alexander to abdicate and thus reopened the question of the relationship between Russia and its desired but recalcitrant satellite. With moral support from Austria and Britain, Bulgaria did not succumb to Russian ambitions immediately; and the Cabinet was able to avoid making a decision about material intervention. But the Balkans remained unsettled. And the Cabinet's tentative deliberations revealed a potential split. Churchill, reinforced by Smith, Hamilton and possibly Hicks Beach, opposed intervention against Russia; but the majority would not tolerate anything which might threaten the independence of Constantinople. To Salisbury, the independence of Constantinople was one of those vital British interests which must not be sacrificed. He left the Queen in no doubt that here was an issue over which the Cabinet could break up.[59]

Attention shifted in October to the home front. Churchill initiated the shift with a speech delivered at Dartford, startling not for its style, which was unusually sober, but for its substance. He presented a dense programme of measures covering almost the entire domestic field: local government, allotments, land transfer, railway rates, Parliamentary procedure, tithes, education. Most of the Dartford proposals were, as it turned out, to be acted upon by this Parliament. Still, the manifesto initially struck the public, Liberals and Conservatives alike, as a bald appropriation of the Liberal if not indeed Radical programme, apart from Ireland. Liberals reacted indignantly, jeering at Conservatives for their sheepish willingness, regardless of their natural inclinations, to follow Churchill wherever he led. Conservatives were bemused. Some applauded. Some sulked. There was little explicit Tory counter-attack.

In substance, Churchill's Dartford manifesto did not go much beyond Salisbury's manifesto a year before at Newport, as Churchill soon pointed out; and he claimed to have cleared its contents with Salisbury beforehand.[60] Dartford was disturbing because the reservations, the accent on caution, and the piecemeal character of Newport were replaced by emphasis on the need to quicken the pace of the party's forward march—precisely what Salisbury wished to prevent.

Churchill pressed the Cabinet to keep the pace set at Dartford, by approving generously framed legislation for the coming session of Parliament on allotments and local government. Salisbury sought to reduce the legislation's scope. The Cabinet were inclined to agree with Salisbury. Hicks Beach, for one, more than shared Salisbury's desire to

deny the proposed elective county councils control over the administration of the Poor Law.

In letters to Salisbury, Churchill flayed Hicks Beach, then the whole
party:

> I am afraid it is an idle schoolboy's dream to suppose that Tories can legislate,
> as I did stupidly. . . . I certainly have not the courage & energy to go on struggling
> against cliques as poor Dizzy did all his life.[61]

He was taut with strain. Preparing a budget for the coming year, looking
into the conduct of a number of departments of state invariably to his
dissatisfaction, devising a strategy for the national contest against
Gladstone and Parnell, initiating legislative proposals right across the
domestic front, all with frantic energy, all alone: it was too much.
Fatigue and exasperation distorted his tactical sense, though not his
judgement of what was at stake. Previously his outbursts to Salisbury
had been met with mollifying sympathy. Now he wanted that, and
more: he wanted capitulation.

Salisbury met Churchill's proddings and expostulations quietly,
without a trace of annoyance—so patiently that others in the Cabinet, in
the clubs, and in the country called for more assertion from him. In a
collegial and respectful vein, protecting himself by keeping to abstrac-
tions, he responded to Churchill's letters with a cautionary analysis of
how the vested interests and classes powerful within the party would
react to the attempt to force 'drastic, symmetrical measures' upon them.
His analysis of the method of resistance they would adopt was acute,
because the method was his own:

> I do not mean that the 'classes' will join issue with you on one of the measures that
> hits them hard, & beat you on that. That is not the way they fight. They will select
> some other matter on which they can appeal to prejudice, & on which they think
> the masses will be indifferent: & on that they will upset you.[62]

Refusing to take the warning, Churchill promptly proceeded to dig
himself just such a grave as Salisbury had described. Churchill presented
the Cabinet in December with a bold budget. It disturbed Conservative
sensibilities by proposing, for example, graduated taxation and increased burdens on land. Still, it was a well integrated package; and
when first outlined to the Cabinet, reaction was passive. Subsequently,
when members had time to reflect and approached him with individual
doubts or queries, his petulant response broke their patience. The kindly
W. H. Smith, often in the past a supportive peacemaker, asked for a
printed outline of the budget because illness had kept him from the
meeting at which it was presented. Churchill shot back:

> Really, considering your frightful extravagance at the War Office you might at
> least give me a free hand for 'ways & means'. If the Cabinet want further
> information on the proposed budget I am ready to be cross examined, but I could

not possibly produce the document you demand. I assume for all practical purposes that the Cabinet have consented to the outline of the budget. The permanent officials are now hard at work on elaboration of details & I shall not trouble my head about it any more until a week or ten days before it is presented to Parliament.[63]

Smith threw up his hands in despair, and wrote Salisbury:

It comes to this.—is he to be *the* Government.
  If you are willing that he should be, I shall be delighted, but I could not go on, on such conditions. He is profoundly impressed with the belief that he has gauged the feeling of the Country and that he is right and everybody else is wrong.[64]

The battle was joined with Churchill's ready consent, on the budget's least attractive feature, reduction of the already exiguous army estimates. Smith, as Secretary for War, had incurred the wrath of his military advisers by the merely stop-gap estimates he had submitted to Churchill. Churchill demanded further cuts. Smith refused, insisting that they would jeopardize the country's security. Nor could another friend of Churchill in the Cabinet, Hamilton at the Admiralty, agree to the cuts demanded in his estimates—until he found that a miscalculation by a Liberal predecessor left him with some unexpected revenue. Sabres were rattling loudly among the Continental powers. With the best will in the world, there could be no assurance that Britain would not be sucked in if they went to war. The fortification of coaling stations was the particular item at issue between Smith and Churchill: and what security could coaling stations give the British navy in the event of war if the stations were not equipped to defend themselves against attack?

Churchill interpreted the issue differently. He saw no risk of war if only Iddesleigh would conduct Britain's foreign relations more peaceably. But the main point was economy. Churchill wished dramatically to appropriate the Gladstonian principle of severely pared governmental expenditure. It had served the Liberals well for half a century. He wanted to nail it to the Tory mast. Its popular appeal particularly with regard to the armed forces had, however, faded, dimmed by rising concern for imperial strength. Churchill and Gladstone were almost alone in their aversion to even meagre levels of military expenditure. Eventually the careers of both men came to lonely terminations on this point.

Churchill took his controversy with Smith to the prime minister. Salisbury was not addicted to lavish military expenditure, but neither, he knew, was 'so little imaginative'[65] a War Minister as Smith; and Salisbury was acutely aware of the storm clouds over the Continent. Churchill had delivered himself into the prime minister's hands. Salisbury destroyed him with quiet, cunning thoroughness.

The premier did not suggest a private interview. Instead he stayed at

Hatfield, giving himself time for manoeuvre. Unable to sit in the Commons and, in any case, a man who worked most happily in the solitude of his study, Salisbury had mastered the art of fighting opponents at one remove rather than face to face. He wrote to Churchill, proposing to refer the matter to the Cabinet. Churchill refused, and reinforced his demand for support by offering his resignation. It was not quite an ultimatum. There was still room for negotiation. But a firm ultimatum, if not on the army estimates, then on some other issue, was sure to come sooner or later.

For two days, Salisbury left the offer of resignation unanswered.[66] Hicks Beach was his concern. If Hicks Beach refused to go on without Churchill, the Ministry could not survive. Salisbury therefore sent Hicks Beach a copy of Churchill's letter, together with another letter from himself. Salisbury's letter conveyed the impression that Hamilton as well as Smith was unable to accede to Churchill's demands, and, still more deceptively, disguised the urgency of the situation. Hicks Beach wrote back, disposed to agree with Smith, yet assuming that there would be time later in the month, when Churchill and Hicks Beach were due to meet, for him to bring Churchill round.

That response, together with clearer assurances from others in the Cabinet whom Salisbury sounded, was enough for his purposes. He at last replied to Churchill, who was furious with impatience and had been alerted by Smith to Salisbury's leanings. With expressions of profound regret, Salisbury accepted the proffered resignation.

Churchill quickly replied with a formal letter of resignation meant to be published. In it he amplified his reasons, extending them to the whole drift of the Government's domestic and foreign policy. The letter was handed in a despatch box to Salisbury during a ball at Hatfield which Churchill's mother, the Dowager Duchess of Marlborough, was attending. Salisbury read the letter expressionlessly, returned to its box, and gave his attention back to his guests. Knowing his man, he was sure that the resignation would be announced in the morning papers, without prior notification of the Queen. He allowed Churchill's offence to the Queen to go unmitigated by a wire from himself. He retired to bed, and next morning, to avoid an embarrassing encounter with the Dowager Duchess over breakfast, he sent down word that he was indisposed. She fled from Hatfield, torn between irritation at this social affront and horror at the morning's news.

Churchill had been let go. If his departure was not dismissal, neither was it deliberate resignation. The decisive action was Salisbury's, though for his purposes it was important for that not to appear to be the case. Drummond Wolff, who had made peace between Churchill and Salisbury once before, tried with Churchill's consent to do so again; but Salisbury held him at bay until Churchill withdrew his commission.

Churchill's departure had nothing explicitly to do with Ireland. But the overriding importance which defence of the Union had assumed reduced the need for Salisbury to fear Churchill. The news of Churchill's resignation fell upon a party preoccupied with Ireland; and Ireland provided the context within which the news was interpreted. However indecisive the Irish policy of the Government had been since the general election, preservation of the Union was generally regarded as the Government's *raison d'être*. Churchill's speech at Dartford had not been enough to alter the focus of attention. Accordingly, with few exceptions, Conservatives at large, Tory Democrats and regulars alike, interpreted Churchill's resignation, not in the light of the issues raised in his public letter to Salisbury, but as a betrayal of the supreme, patriotic objective of the party to which during the election campaign they had subordinated all other, even dearly held interests. He carried only one junior minister, Lord Dunraven, with him, and Dunraven did not resign until February. In the estimation of the party at large, Churchill fell like Lucifer.

Apart from the fortification of coaling stations, his removal did not directly solve any problems of policy confronting the Government. Nor did it immediately dissipate the ambiguities in the Government's Irish policy. By disturbing what security of tenure the Government possessed, and by intensifying its need for closer cooperation with the Liberal Unionists, Churchill's departure threatened initially to prolong the period of unsettlement, now more than a year old.

But, fashioned as unobtrusively as possible by Lord Salisbury, the course of events soon belied the danger. By March, with the introduction of a permanent Irish coercion Bill, the character of the reconstructed Ministry was decisively established, and its prospects for survival in Parliament seemed good. Letting Churchill go was one block in an arch of decisions made by Salisbury over the winter of 1886–7 through which he placed his impress upon the Conservative Ministry, the Unionist alliance, and the politics of the ensuing generation. Defence of the Union with Ireland was the keystone of that arch.

**NOTES**

1. The information on which this chapter relies has been much improved, and its line of thought sharpened, by the work of A. B. Cooke and J. R. Vincent. In addition to *The Governing Passion*, see 'Select documents: XXVII, Ireland and party politics, 1885–7: An unpublished Conservative memoir,' *Irish Historical Studies*, XVI, 62 (September 1968), pp. 154–172; 63 (March 1969), pp. 321–338; 64 (September 1969), pp. 446–471: and also *Lord Carlingford's Journal* (Oxford, 1971).
2. For an incisive summary of this process, see Emmet Larkin, 'Church, State, and nation in modern Ireland,' *American Historical Review*, LXXX, 5 (December 1975), pp. 1244–76.
3. Salisbury at Woodstock, *The Times*, 1 December 1880, 10c.
4. 'Disintegration,' *Quarterly Review*, CLVI, 312 (October 1883), pp. 587–8.

5. Salisbury in Liverpool, *The Times*, 13 April 1882.
6. 'Disintegration,' p. 585.
7. Salisbury in Liverpool, *The Times*, 13 April 1882.
8. Salisbury at Liverpool, *The Times*, 14 April 1882, 6c.
9. D. W. R. Bahlman, ed., *The Diary of Sir Edward Walter Hamilton, 1880–1885* (Oxford, 1972), I, p. 86.
10. *Quarterly Review*, CXVII, 234 (April 1865), p. 558.
11. *Ibid.*
12. He defended Pitt's conduct in 1801 as consistent morally with his conduct in 1783: 'He did not think himself at liberty, after he had gained his object [the Act of Union with Ireland], to repudiate the understanding [i.e. the implied provision of Catholic Emancipation] on which the votes that gained it were given. . . . A contrary view of political morality has been so often sanctioned within the last thirty years by distinguished statesmen of all parties, that Pitt's scruples about the subject of breaking implied promises may appear Quixotic. But no one who applies to public affairs the morality of private life, will doubt that Pitt was in the right.' *Quarterly Review*, CXI, 222 (April 1862), p. 522.
13. Salisbury on Pitt, *Quarterly Review*, CXI, 222 (April 1862), pp. 516–561.
14. Speech at the Hotel Métropole, *The Times*, 18 February 1886, 10b.
15. Hicks Beach to Salisbury, 7 May 1885, Salisbury papers.
16. See Salisbury's speech at the Mansion House, *The Times*, 30 July 1885, 6c.
17. *Supra*, p. 62.
18. Salisbury to Carnarvon, 21 March 1885, copy, Salisbury papers.
19. See Lord Rosebery, *Lord Randolph Churchill* (London, 1906), p. 21.
20. *Hansard*, 3rd ser., CCXCVIII, 1661 (6 July 1885).
21. *Ibid.*, 1662.
22. The other was a Bill to reduce sheriffs' expenses in uncontested elections.
23. Churchill much later told Sir Henry James that in the summer of 1885 Parnell had visited him several times at his house: 'we arranged a great many things in connection with the General Election of that year, the most perfect confidence existed between us.' James' diary, 1 March 1891, typed copy, Lord James of Hereford papers. In all probability, this was an exaggerated recollection.
24. 15 July 1885, quoted in Arthur Hardinge, *The Life of Henry Howard Molyneux Herbert, Fourth Earl of Carnarvon 1831–1890* (London, 1925), III, p. 169.
25. *Hansard*, 3rd ser., CCXCIX, 1123 (17 July 1885).
26. Eventually the original judicial verdicts were again upheld.
27. See Salisbury to Edward Hardcastle, 3 August 1885, Duke University Manuscripts.
28. S. H. Jeyes and F. D. How, *The Life of Sir Howard Vincent* (London, 1912), p. 178.
29. Salisbury to Edward Hardcastle, 3 August 1885, Duke University Manuscripts. Salisbury applied these words to the Irish administration of Lord Spencer, whom he described as 'a stupid, narrow-minded, second-rate man.'
30. Salisbury to Churchill, 8 October 1885, Churchill papers.
31. Salisbury to Churchill, 7 November 1886, copy, Salisbury papers.
32. For an excellent discussion of this point, see Alan Simon, 'Church disestablishment as a factor in the general election of 1885,' *Historical Journal*, XVIII, 4 (December 1975), pp. 791–820. See also D. C. Savage, 'Scottish politics, 1885–6,' *Scottish Historical Review*, XL, 130 (October 1961), pp. 118–35.
33. *The Times*, 8 October 1885, 7c.
34. Charles Whibley, *Lord John Manners and His Friends* (Edinburgh, 1925), II, pp. 307–308.
35. *The Times*, 10 November 1885, 6e.
36. *Hansard*, 3rd ser., CCXCVIII, 1657 (6 July 1885).
37. Letter of 24 December 1885, copy, Salisbury papers.

38. Iddesleigh to Lord Harrowby, 9 December 1885, Harrowby papers.
39. Churchill to Lord Chief Justice Morris, 7 December 1885, quoted in W. S. Churchill, *Lord Randolph Churchill*, II, p. 25.
40. Carnarvon to Salisbury, 6 December 1885, copy, Salisbury papers.
41. Letter of 3 December 1885, in G. E. Buckle, ed., *Letters of Queen Victoria*, 2nd ser., III, p. 707.
42. 11 December 1885, quoted in W. S. Churchill, *Lord Randolph Churchill*, II, p. 22.
43. Letter of 16 January 1886, quoted in W. S. Churchill, *op. cit.*, II, pp. 37–38.
44. Lord Lytton to the Rev'd Whitwell Elwin, 6 February 1886, reporting a conversation with Lady Salisbury, Lytton papers, Hertfordshire County Record Office, D/EK/C38. I am grateful to Miss Vivian Breitel for drawing this letter to my attention.
45. Diary, 27 January 1886, B. L. Add. MSS. 48642.
46. Speech at the Opera House, Haymarket, *The Times*, 15 April 1886, 6e.
47. Speech at the Hotel Métropole, *The Times*, 18 February 1886, 10b.
48. Cf. Eric Strauss, *Irish Nationalism and British Democracy* (New York, 1951), pp. 187–8.
49. *The Times*, 17 May 1886, 6e.
50. *Ibid.*
51. *The Times*, 19 June 1886, 12a.
52. *The Times*, 11 May 1886, 12e.
53. Still, he explored the practicality of governmentally facilitated though not subsidized emigration with Sir Alexander Wood of the Great Western Railway. Salisbury to Wood, 20 May 1886, Salisbury papers, Secretary's notebook.
54. P. D. Clayden, *England under the Coalition* (London, 1892), p. 89.
55. The Liberal Unionists' popular vote was 386,000.
56. He may have received and refused an offer to resume the leadership. See Salisbury to Henry Manners, 28 November 1886, copy, Salisbury papers, and Lady Victoria Hicks-Beach, *Life of Sir Michael Hicks-Beach (Earl St. Aldwyn)* (London, 1932), I, pp. 274–5.
    His austerity and his terrible tongue did not soften with age. He subjected the Secretary for War at the turn of the century, as the Secretary later recalled, to'language which would have made his fame on the lower deck of a battleship.' (The Earl of Midleton, *Records & Reactions, 1856–1939* (New York, 1939), p. 125). The only ornament on his dressing table when he died was a hard, black pincushion made thirty years earlier by one of his children.
57. Quoted in L. P. Curtis, Jr., *Coercion and Conciliation in Ireland, 1880–1892* (Princeton, 1963), p. 158.
58. Lord Curzon of Kedleston, *Modern Parliamentary Eloquence* (London, 1913), p. 38.
59. Salisbury to the Queen, 7 September 1885, quoted in Lady Gwendolen Cecil, *Life of Salisbury*, III, p. 319; Salisbury to Cranbrook, 8 September 1886, Cranbrook papers.
60. Shortly after the speech was delivered, Salisbury described the Dartford program as "thorny." Salisbury to Lord Halsbury, 29 October 1886, Halsbury papers.
61. Churchill to Salisbury, 8 November 1886, Salisbury papers.
62. Salisbury to Churchill, 7 November 1886, copy, Salisbury papers.
63. Churchill to Smith, 18 December 1886, quoted in Robert Rhodes James, *Lord Randolph Churchill* (New York, 1960), p. 284.
64. 20 December 1886, Salisbury papers.
65. Salisbury to Churchill, 15 December 1886, copy, Salisbury papers.
66. Every account of Churchill's departure must be heavily indebted to Robert Rhodes James' biography of him (New York, 1960), chapter 10.

# CHAPTER 4

# *THE ALLIANCE*

A rider who has ridden two horses at once for a
longish journey has, no doubt, cause to congra-
tulate himself that he has not had a tumble; and it
is open to him, if he likes, to claim that the result is
due to his skill. But most impartial persons will be
inclined rather to admire the marvellous good
temper and training of the horses.

*Salisbury to Alfred Austin, 24 August 1892*

Just as opposition to Home Rule enabled Salisbury to impose his stamp
upon the Conservative party, so the alliance between Conservatives and
Liberal Unionists provided him with the means to avoid extreme
oscillations in governmental policy and to restore 'that equable
temperature which, for many generations before 1868, was one of the
distinctive features of our legislation.'[1] Neither achievement was
planned. Over both he waited upon events. The character which the
alliance assumed was not what he originally envisioned. But he proved
able to adapt himself to the alliance's unanticipated shape, and to adapt
the new shape to his own purposes. He also became uniquely adept at
appreciating the limits of the alliance's elasticity and the prerequisites of
its internal vigour, particularly on the Conservative side.

In common with all Conservatives, Salisbury had long felt frustrated
by the division of the natural forces of conservatism in Britain between
Whigs and moderate Liberals on the one hand and the Conservative
party on the other. He predicted that the challenge of democracy would,
in the long run, sort out support for the two parties along natural lines.
Now that the privileges which shored up the supremacy of the
aristocracy and the Established Church had been largely if not entirely
abolished, he perceived that the middle classes would gravitate, were
indeed already gravitating, into the camp of the politically contented.
But he expected the process to be slow while the old generation,
reluctant to abandon their accustomed loyalties, died off.

His design for appealing to natural conservatives who supported the
Liberal party was accordingly patient. Churchill's strategy, like
Disraeli's in 1867, was to broaden the Conservative party's support by
bidding against even advanced Liberals. But such a course of action

alienated Whigs and moderate Liberals. They could see no reason to
surrender their retarding influence within the Liberal party in order to
collaborate with Conservatives who aped the very policies they feared.
Northcote's alternative strategy of responsible opposition, of anxiety to
look at each issue from the point of view of government before subjecting
it to criticism, did not impress the Whigs it was designed to woo; for it
mirrored their own nervous weakness.

Salisbury's advice to his party was to remain true to itself. Only by
setting an example of resolute defence of property and established
institutions could Conservatives hope to gain the confidence of those
with similar concerns in the party opposite. Salisbury's personal
outspokenness set Whig heads shaking. And he did not spare their
feelings. During the 1885 election campaign he caricatured a suggested
Whig and moderate Liberal Government to be led by Lord Hartington,
Lord Derby and G. J. Goschen as a 'Ministry of all the irresolutions.'

> Can you fancy their inner councils—the Egyptian skeleton and Rip Van Winkle
> trying to make up each other's minds and Lord Derby steadily pouring cold water
> upon both?[2]

Still, Whigs usually knew—or thought they knew—where Salisbury
stood, and he struck them accordingly as somewhat more trustworthy
than Disraeli or Churchill and certainly more commanding than
Northcote.

Salisbury departed from this strategy of uncompromising firmness in
forming the Caretaker Ministry. Under normal circumstances, the
results of this departure would have further delayed the moment of
fusion between Whigs and Conservatives, as Salisbury in his irresponsible days as a journalist would have predicted. The Whigs had been
restive to the point of rebellion during Gladstone's second Ministry. But
the ambivalence of the Caretaker Ministry's Irish administration,
particularly the concession of a fresh Maamtrasna enquiry, revived
Whig suspicions of Conservatives.

However, Whig suspicions of Gladstone's leanings on Ireland grew
even stronger than their disgust with Conservatives, particularly in the
wake of the election of 1885. The election created what seemed to some a
rare opportunity for Conservatives to form a coalition with dissident
Liberals or at least to bargain with them for informal support. Churchill
raised the possibility, with specific reference to G. J. Goschen, just
before the balloting began. Soon afterward he expanded his suggestion
into a wide-ranging programme of reform, building upon Salisbury's
Newport manifesto, and designed to accommodate the anticipated
Liberal renegades.

Salisbury threw cold water on both proposals. Rather than attempt to
precipitate a realignment of parties by wooing disaffected Liberals, he

preferred to wait until the Liberal party split of its own accord. He assumed, until the results of the election were known, that the anticipated Liberal rupture would be deferred until Gladstone's retirement,[3] surely not far off in view of his advanced age. After the election he saw that Gladstone, far from holding the party together, might soon drive it apart. This changed expectation did not alter Salisbury's counsel. He put off replying to Churchill's broadened proposal until Lord Hartington declared publicly that he did not intend to enter into coalition with the Tories. Salisbury then used that statement as proof that the moment for bargaining had not yet arrived,[4] ignoring the possibility of bidding for informal Liberal support. He did not even respond to a message which Hartington sent to Salisbury's secretary through the Duke of Manchester assuring Salisbury of Hartington's decided opposition 'to any thing in the shape of an Irish Parliament, or a Central Board sitting in Dublin.'[5]

Apart from pressing the Cabinet in January for a firm stand on Ireland, Salisbury did nothing to woo Liberal Unionists.[6] Had he done so, he might well have received support on a motion of confidence from a larger number than the ninety-three who eventually voted against Gladstone's Home Rule Bill in June. But, in the absence of a formal parting of ways among the Liberals, this support would have been unreliable, free to gravitate back to Gladstone once Parliament had reached a decision on the Irish question. Until the Liberal dissidents broke with Gladstone, Salisbury could hope for little more from them than a brief extension of the life of the Caretaker Ministry.

After the Ministry's fall, he allowed another month to pass before making any overture to Hartington. His only precaution, in view of the Whigs' contemptuous reaction to the timid statement on Ireland in the Queen's speech at the opening of Parliament, was to let them know privately that he had pressed for a harder line.[7] Otherwise he kept his own counsel. Gladstone's skill in reasserting his command over most of the Parliamentary Liberal party in the opening days of the session made Salisbury wonder again whether its rupture would be delayed until Gladstone retired.[8]

Salisbury's desire for a clear break within the Liberal party reflected his low estimate of the Whigs' and moderate Liberals' spine. Arthur Balfour shared his uncle's assessment of the Whigs, and for that reason welcomed the possibility of alliance over Ireland with the un-questionably determined, though Radical, Joseph Chamberlain. Randolph Churchill, for reasons of his own, agreed. But Salisbury recoiled from the prospect of collaboration with Chamberlain, and found Chamberlain's eventual adhesion to the Unionist cause an unwelcome embarrassment. Chamberlain might be potentially Palmerstonian in imperial affairs,[9] and there was no doubt about his desire for a stronger executive *vis-à-vis* the legislature: on these grounds there was room for working agreement. They did not, however, alleviate his Radicalism, which he had recently elaborated in a sharp, sustained attack upon many of the interests and institutions that Salisbury wished to protect. Chamberlain showed no inclination to play down his Radicalism in the interests of cohesive Unionism.

Salisbury wanted the Conservatives to take their stand, and hence attract the Whigs and moderate Liberals, as a 'party of resistance.'[10] The alliance he envisioned would bring about a polarization of parties along lines of principles and also, though less clearly, of class. He did not desire an ill-assorted combination of factions large enough to create a Parliamentary majority. Yet, from the outset, he was aware that things might not work out as he hoped. He had observed in the previous Parliament a strong tendency, not toward bi-polarization, but rather toward a 'grouping . . . of various cliques of supporters'[11] without much regard for their place in the ideological spectrum.

Realignment was made more difficult by the richness of recent personal invective. Hartington was the hardest hit. Salisbury had followed Chamberlain in calling him Rip van Winkle, and Churchill had compared him to a boa constrictor. Chamberlain had likened Salisbury to the lilies of the field who did not toil yet were arrayed more gloriously than Solomon. Salisbury had likened Chamberlain to Jack Cade. Mutual denunciations among future Unionists were slow to stop. After Churchill fired the spirits of Ulstermen by conjuring up the spectre of armed rebellion, Henry James denounced him as almost a traitor.

There were differences too in life-style and in moral gravity which could prove even harder to reconcile in practice than differences in philosophy. Churchill, and to a lesser extent Balfour, shared Chamberlain's free-wheeling willingness to canvass all possible policies and strategies with little regard for consistency with their previous course of conduct. Salisbury despised such looseness, at least when displayed by his enemies, and much preferred Gladstone's strength of conviction. Salisbury and Hartington were made of sterner stuff than the younger generation of Unionists;[12] but culturally and in personal conduct, the older two were poles apart. Whereas Salisbury's Hatfield was one of the very few country houses in England to which the Prince of Wales could not bring his mistress, Hartington conducted a notorious liaison with the Duchess of Manchester. Years later when Hartington, now a close associate, invited Lord and Lady Salisbury to Chatsworth which he had just inherited, the clash in life-style still proved a strain. Lady Salisbury reported to Balfour:

> The minute we arrived here every one sat down to poker & bezique—before we took our bonnets off! & played till dinner. Afterwards we played till 12 & then

we went to bed. . . . No one . . . has the slightest knowledge of, or interest in [Chatsworth's] great treasures of books pictures &c.

Our intellectual guide is Dr. Grey who has a cold & therefore does not shoot. He had heard of the great book of Claude's sketches & asked to see it. The rest were only interested in the fact that it was worth £25000 as the housekeeper said . . . .

. . .I am glad that your uncle goes tomorrow, or he might be guilty of some act of violence which he would regret.[13]

## i. Reaching a Contract

Serious overtures for an alliance were at last launched at the beginning of March 1885 by Churchill and Salisbury, who was about to leave for a holiday in Monte Carlo. The two men divided the work of negotiation. Churchill issued the public invitation on 3 March and then concerted tactics in the Commons with Hartington and Chamberlain. Salisbury, after his return from Monte Carlo, took over most of the discussion with Hartington and also arranged an electoral compact. The pairing for negotiation of Churchill with Chamberlain and Salisbury with Hartington was natural and worked fairly smoothly. The younger pair were closely akin in substance as well as style except on the score of imperialism, where their conflict was still only latent; and they had been friendly with each other for more than a year. The older pair, despite the difference in life-style, shared an assured, aristocratic code of political conduct and a direct manner of speaking. Their personal ambitions were not brazen like those of Churchill and Chamberlain. Furthermore, whereas the younger two thought in terms of legislative programmes, the older two were adept at recognizing all the problems in fresh initiatives.

On the eve of his departure for Monte Carlo, Salisbury asked Hartington to see him privately.[14] They met at Arlington Street. Both men sought reassurance. Hartington wanted to know whether there was any chance of the Conservatives resorting to Home Rule after entering into a combination to defeat Gladstone on the issue, as Disraeli had done over Parliamentary reform in 1866–7. Salisbury's brief but unhesitating 'no' set Hartington's mind at ease. Hartington's response to Salisbury's inquiry was less satisfactory. Salisbury wanted assurance that Liberal Unionists would not return to Gladstone's fold after combining with Conservatives to defeat Home Rule. Hartington, however, 'declined to do more than express the hope that they might act together in defeating any proposition for a separate Irish Parliament.'[15]

The formation of the alliance was signalled by a great meeting in April at the Opera House in London. Salisbury, Hartington, and others including a Radical, Peter Rylands, spoke from the same platform. The meeting produced immediate trouble which demonstrated the wisdom of Hartington's guarded response to Salisbury. Party feeling on both sides ran high, and made cooperation extremely difficult. Hartington had to silence boos from Conservatives in the audience at the Opera House when he mentioned the name of Gladstone. After the meeting, hostile reaction from Liberal associations in constituencies whose M.P.s were declaring for Unionism was vigorous, particularly among Radicals, and widespread, extending to Hartington's own constituency of Rossendale. Many Whigs and moderate Liberals had encountered difficulty before the last election in retaining the support of Radicals within their local associations. With few exceptions, they now found it wise to refuse further joint meetings with Conservatives. Liberal Unionists of all stripes, moderate as well as Radical, used every opportunity to emphasize their continued adherence to the tenets of Liberalism and their repudiation of Conservatism.

Salisbury found this behaviour irritating.[16] Tales of the anguish of Liberal Unionists as they broke the political associations of a lifetime left him unmoved. He would if necessary, he said, walk down the steps of the Carlton Club for the last time without a pang. His comment was self-deceiving. For he was expecting Whigs to break with their tradition of slow accommodation to the forward thrust of their party, while he himself based his rejection of Home Rule on the necessity of abiding by the traditions of his own party; and he had recently proven himself willing to sacrifice strong personal preferences in order to preserve his party's unity.

Though Salisbury was not as sympathetic to Liberal Unionist susceptibilities as Churchill, his assurances about the Conservative rejection of Home Rule carried a weight which Churchill could not convey. The notorious 'manacles and Manitoba' speech served this purpose. Churchill, recognizing the importance of conducting the fight over Home Rule as between Liberals rather than along previous party lines, had pushed Hartington and Chamberlain to the fore in the Commons; and Liberal Unionists also set the pace in the eventual election campaign. Gladstone reacted to this pattern with surprise,[17] thinking the Whigs naive to allow Conservatives to commit themselves so diffidently and infrequently. It was Whig confidence in Salisbury's repudiation of Home Rule that made Churchill's strategy possible.

Still, the main purpose of Salisbury's 'manacles and Manitoba' speech, as A. B. Cooke and John Vincent have explained,[18] was to prevent the formation of a Palmerstonian, predominantly Liberal Government led by Hartington and thus clear the way for a pre-dominantly Conservative Government led by himself. He delivered the speech one day after Hartington made a bid to rally all but doctrinaire Home Rule Liberals, together with reasonable Conservatives, behind a moderate Ministry such as he might form. Salisbury ruined this initiative by presenting resistance to Home Rule in a way calculated to repel most Liberals; and he went on to tell his Conservative audience that much the greatest responsibility for defence of the Union with Ireland would fall upon them rather than upon their gallant Liberal Unionist allies. These remarks provoked the reaction among Liberals that Salisbury desired. Because Hartington was, for the moment, bound to Lord Salisbury in opposing Gladstone's Bill, the speech burned Hartington's bridge with the main Liberal camp to ashes, and at the same time reasserted Conservative leadership for the Unionist cause.

The formal rupture of the Liberal party that Salisbury sought came about through the electoral compact he arranged. A Liberal division in Parliament might, as so often in the past, heal. A Liberal division fought out in a general election was much less likely to do so. For this reason Salisbury differed from many of his Conservative colleagues in desiring an immediate dissolution of Parliament as soon as the Home Rule Bill was defeated. Fearful that an immediate election would not allow enough time for public opposition to Home Rule to mature,[19] Churchill, Hicks Beach and Iddesleigh favoured replacement of the Gladstone Ministry, whether by a Conservative or a Liberal Unionist Ministry or a coalition. Salisbury was not overconfident of the results of a general election.[20] But he feared that another caretaker Ministry would bring out the divisions with the alliance. A dissolution by Gladstone, on the other hand, would keep Home Rule to the fore:

> It will then be impossible for the three sections of Liberals[21] to coalesce against us: & the moderate men will be compelled to give us (at the election) some friendly guarantees.[22]

There was another advantage: a sound defeat of Home Rule in a general election 'would probably involve Mr. Gladstone's retirement,' which Salisbury thought would greatly enhance the prospects of 'the party of resistance.'[23]

The electoral compact was agreed upon in principle early in April. It consisted of a pledge by the Conservative leadership to do its utmost to prevent Conservatives from running against Liberal M.P.s who voted against the Home Rule Bill, and of a less distinct understanding that the Liberal Unionist leaders would counsel their sympathizers to vote for Conservatives against Home Rule Liberals. The less than equal terms of the compact did not detract from its importance in Salisbury's eyes. It constituted the formal parting of ways between Liberals that he had pressed for.

Paradoxically, Liberal Unionists' willingness to enter into the electoral compact was brought about by the same tide of popular Liberal hostility which induced them to abandon joint platform appearances with Conservatives. However guarded their displays of cooperation with Conservatives, and however emphatic their declarations of continued loyalty to the historic tenets of Liberalism, most Liberal Unionists quickly recognized that their opposition to Gladstone over Home Rule would alienate more than enough of their former Liberal support to defeat them unless it was counter-balanced by Conservative support. Assurances that Conservatives would not field candidates against them were indispensible to keep Liberal would-be opponents of Gladstone's Bill up to the mark.

Implementing the electoral compact was uphill work. Many Conservatives found it hard to support Liberals, some of them Radicals, whom barely seven months before they had fought hard to defeat. The task of implementation fell chiefly to Salisbury and the party managers, Akers-Douglas and Middleton. They despatched endless letters to recalcitrant constituency associations and local leaders in the three weeks between defeat of the Bill and the beginning of balloting. The task was complicated by the necessity of scrupulous respect for local autonomy. 'I should,' Salisbury wrote to one Conservative from Bristol, 'be sorry to give any opinion that interfered in any way with the decisions of the local Conservative Authorities. But if, as I understand, Mr. Fry [the incumbent Liberal Unionist] is opposed by a Gladstonian, I should myself certainly vote for him.'[24] In all but three cases, these efforts to prevent Conservatives from running against Liberals who had voted against the Home Rule Bill were successful,[25] though another sixteen Liberal Unionist M.P.s decided not to seek reelection, in probably as many as eight cases because of local Conservative refusal or reluctance to support them.[26]

The unpopularity of the compact among many Conservatives was increased by the extreme reluctance of most Liberal Unionists to treat them with any cordiality. Gladstonians played upon Conservative resentment. It was only late in the campaign after an appeal from Salisbury, that Hartington called upon his supporters in constituencies where no Liberal Unionist was running to vote Conservative.

Liberal Unionist strength in the new House of Commons was reduced from 94 to 79. Salisbury thought they would have done better if they had done more to bring out Conservative support: but they had to make fine calculations between wooing Conservative voters and offending Liberals. Despite the reduction in their number, the successful Liberal Unionists far more than made up for the losses Conservatives incurred from the swing of the Irish vote in Britain to the Liberal side.

## ii. The Formation of the Second Salisbury Ministry

The election returns of 1886 brought Salisbury within sight of his goal of a government of resistance, only to see the prospect recede. Though the returns spelled victory for the Unionist alliance, the election's implications for the character of the new Ministry were not quite clear, because the character of the alliance was still unsettled. No one could be sure that the period of unstable government, now half way through its second year, had come to an end. The Conservatives were twenty seats short of a majority on their own; and the willingness of both Conservatives and of Liberal Unionists to subordinate old party loyalties to the new alliance diminished as soon as the election was over. Conservatives tended to assume that, but for their self-denying electoral compact, they would have won a majority on their own. Liberal Unionists wondered about the future of the Conservative party when, with all their support, it still could not win a majority.[27] Conservatives wanted to behave as if they had a majority. There was little enthusiasm for sharing the spoils of victory, and almost universal opposition to giving Lord Hartington the premiership. Conservative backbenchers and most of Salisbury's colleagues hoped that he would arrange for a purely Conservative Ministry supported by the Liberal Unionists informally.

He held these Conservative counsellors at bay while he negotiated with Hartington for a coalition. Salisbury offered to serve under Hartington. But he coupled the offer with a stipulation, in effect that the coalition must be predominantly Conservative, from top to bottom. The numerical superiority of the Conservatives, reinforced by their returned self-assurance, would make any Unionist coalition heavily Conservative, but only at bottom. The Liberal Unionists, though small in number, were disproportionately strong in administrative and debating talent. A Ministry which put together the ablest Liberal Unionists together with the ablest Conservatives, preeminently Hicks Beach and Churchill, would be uncongenial and even threatening to Salisbury. Its domestic reflexes would be more progressive than he would like. Its natural leader would be Churchill. Salisbury therefore imposed one condition in his offer to Hartington: he would have to exclude Chamberlain from the Ministry. This condition, in itself, could have no material effect, for Chamberlain had already rejected the notion of serving in a coalition government; the significance of Salisbury's requirement was symbolic.

His offer was genuine. If Hartington could be captured in this way, Salisbury would be the strong man though not the formal leader of the Government; its policy need not be more progressive than the Newport manifesto; and the Liberal Unionists who followed Hartington rather than Chamberlain would be absorbed, in fact if not in name, by the Conservative party.

Hartington's response disappointed Salisbury, not so much because his offer was turned down, as because of the way the decision was explained. It revealed that the parties to the alliance were farther from

fusion than he had hoped and that the division on strategy of the natural
conservative forces in Parliament between Whig and Tory persisted.
Whereas Salisbury wanted to concentrate these forces in one camp,
Hartington reiterated the distinguishing Whig belief that these forces
would be more effective if some were at work within the Liberal party.[28]
To cast his lot with Salisbury would mean for Hartington the abandonment of his hopes either for Liberal reunion or to recreate a moderate
coalition such as Lord Palmerston had led in the previous generation.
Moreover, apart from Hartington's personal ambitions, he was acutely
aware that the hope for Liberal reunion gripped Liberals at all levels on
both sides of the split. Though Lord Granville feared that a Ministry led
by Hartington might attract some men on Gladstone's side,[29] the
Liberal Unionist whip told Hartington that formation of a coalition
Ministry could drive twenty-nine of their men into opposition;[30] and
Chamberlain would feel driven to follow them. There was also doubt
whether Liberal constituencies which had elected Unionists, including
Hartington's own Rossendale, would return them if they accepted office
and hence had to stand for re-election.[31] Liberal Unionists, like
Conservatives, also nursed ambitions of swallowing up their allies.
Henry James, for one, hoped that a purely Conservative Ministry would
be tried, found wanting, and replaced by a predominantly or purely
Liberal Unionist one which could thus absorb the alliance.

By declining Salisbury's offer of a coalition though promising
independent support, Hartington arrested the process, which Salisbury
had fostered since May, of narrowing the Unionist alliance into a party
of resistance. Salisbury exaggerated the significance of the setback. It
revived his doubts about the strength of Whigs' and moderate Liberals'
natural conservatism, renewed his bondage to Churchill, and compounded his uncertainty about how to restrain that dangerous partner.

In his gloom, Salisbury did not foresee the reaction: but his
appointment of Churchill to lead the Commons reopened the possibility
of transforming the alliance into a party of resistance. Churchill's
elevation filled Whig and moderate Liberal Unionists with dismay. 'I
regret it deeply;' Goschen told a friend, 'for it is a premium on the arts by
which he has risen to notoriety. I dare say he will steady down; but as he
imitated Dizzy at a distance, so men of even lower *moral* may imitate
Churchill.'[32] Moderate Liberals saw in Churchill nothing but unprincipled adventurousness. They looked to Salisbury to steady the ship
of state. 'My only *reliance*,' Lord Selborne told Sir Arthur Gordon, '. . . is
upon Lord Salisbury. He has both the moral, and, in many respects, the
intellectual qualities necessary for such a crisis: if he can only keep his
turbulent lieutenant in order.'[33] As interested as Salisbury in restraining
Churchill, they assured themselves that Salisbury would prove liberal
enough to satisfy their requirements.

Salisbury was slow to recognize this potential source of reinforcement. His relations with Hartington became courteous rather than candid. What Salisbury observed, with deepening resentment, was the rapprochement which blossomed between Churchill and Chamberlain. These two exchanged laudatory notes about each other's speeches, and met frequently to agree upon tactics. Chamberlain used Churchill to press his own views within the Cabinet. Churchill used Chamberlain to cajole reluctant Cabinet colleagues into line. The alliance was turning into an engine for accelerated reform.

### iii. The Reconstruction of the Ministry

By generating acute strain within the Cabinet, Churchill and Chamberlain broke through Salisbury's reserve with Hartington. The break came in November over reform of local government. Churchill and Chamberlain were fighting against Salisbury's effort to keep administration of the Poor Law out of the hands of the projected elective authorities, and also against Hicks Beach's effort to give the owners of property weighted representation. Salisbury assumed that the Whig and moderate Liberal Unionists would come down on Chamberlain's side. Still, dissension within the Cabinet became so sharp that he broached the subject with Hartington; and Churchill broached it, in Salisbury's company, with Goschen, long a champion of local government reform. To Salisbury's delighted surprise, both Hartington and Goschen expressed agreement with his position. Hartington went on to suggest dealing first with Irish rather than English local government. Few men would advocate granting control over Poor Relief to Irish agricultural labourers; and exclusion of the Poor Law from the provisions of an Irish local government Bill would serve as a precedent for subsequent English legislation. Churchill was so alarmed by Hartington's proposals that he fell back upon Salisbury's proposal, to deal with English local government first but exclude Poor Law administration, as the lesser of two evils.

The conclusions which Salisbury could draw from this episode were limited. The episode indicated that Hartington was not an ally of Churchill, but did not prove that he was a natural ally for Salisbury. A month later, when Churchill offered to resign, Salisbury could not reckon on a strengthened relationship with Hartington to offset the loss of Churchill. Hartington's leanings on domestic policy were still ambiguous. He would be anxious to keep a Unionist Government of some complexion in office, if only to avoid precipitating another general election, in which, by all accounts, Liberal Unionists would fare badly; but that Unionist Government did not have to be of Salisbury's predominantly Conservative kind. If Hartington set its style, there was still no doubt that it would be centrist.

It was the patent impossibility of working with Churchill, not trust that Liberal Unionists would make good his loss, which induced Salisbury to get rid of him. Though he promptly invited Hartington to form or join a coalition Ministry, Salisbury's decision to let Churchill go was a Conservative and risky gamble rather than a Unionist and safe one. He was gambling that a predominantly or, if need be, a purely Conservative Government could prove viable without Churchill.

Initial response to the news of Churchill's resignation proved the strength of Salisbury's Conservative base. By acting on the assumption that the Government depended on him for its survival, Churchill had wounded the self-esteem of his Cabinet colleagues; and they responded, not just by rallying to Salisbury, but also (with the exception of Hicks Beach) by displaying reluctance when Salisbury proposed to give Hartington opportunity to form a coalition Ministry. Similarly stiffened, back bench opposition to coalition with Liberal Unionists extended beyond the premiership to the leadership of the Commons and even to the inclusion of one or two Liberal Unionist peers in the Cabinet as reinforcement for Goschen when he decided to join. By the time Hartington returned from his vacation in Rome to London and received Salisbury's overture, the prickly disposition of the Conservatives, upon whom Hartington would have to rely for the bulk of his Parliamentary support, was obvious.

Salisbury pressed his offer to Hartington to join or form a Ministry in urgent language. Even so, the terms of the offer were cloudier and, if anything, less attractive than those Hartington had rejected in July. Now that Churchill had gone, the Ministry which Hartington was asked to join was more stolidly Conservative than before. If Hartington chose the alternative of forming a Ministry, he could try to include Churchill. But the anger which Conservatives felt toward Churchill bode ill for the attempt. The fact was that Churchill's departure had done nothing to diminish, and perhaps had increased, the ability of Salisbury and the Conservative party to dominate the Unionist alliance—at least until Parliament met again. In order for Hartington to secure a Ministry of which he would be the effective leader, he would have to reduce the pride which Conservatives took from the general election and which Churchill had stung. Yet to break Conservatives' pride would take the heart out of the Unionist alliance. Hartington offered to form a Government only if the Conservative Ministry confessed its need for him to do so by resigning: he was not dismayed when Salisbury rejected the suggestion as demeaning and unnecessary.[34]

Salisbury was not surprised when Hartington declined his offer; nor was he as disappointed as in July.[35] Hartington reaffirmed his informal, Parliamentary support for Salisbury's Government, a pledge all the more significant because it implied support against the expected attacks of Churchill and perhaps Chamberlain. It reopened the possibility for a narrow, naturally conservative alliance of Salisbury and Hartington, in place of the broad, ideologically amorphous alliance of Salisbury and Churchill with Hartington and Chamberlain. The narrow alliance would, of course, reduce the Government's normal majority in the House of Commons, perhaps to thirty:[36] but that would be workable, at least for a while.

Still, Churchill's departure from the Ministry and Hartington's refusal to join it left one weakness which Salisbury was anxious to remedy: the lack of anyone of obviously first rank on the Government's front bench in the Commons. That gap could be filled, and at the same time Salisbury could cement his alliance with the moderate Liberal Unionists, by giving office to George Goschen. Goschen was an acute debater, capable of such destructive criticism that in the early 1880s Gladstone had sought to silence him with a succession of glittering offices—the Viceroyalty of India, the War Office, and the Speakership of the House of Commons—all of which Goschen had refused.[37] A distinguished record in merchant banking made him an excellent nominee to replace Churchill at the Exchequer. He would agree to consider Salisbury's invitation to join the Government only when Hartington urged him to do so: thus his joining would constitute a degree of formal commitment to the Government from Hartington.

Furthermore, Goschen was the Liberal Unionist most akin to Salisbury in political philosophy, anxious to stand up unequivocally for the rights of property. Indeed, Goschen was stiffer than Salisbury, and had led the opposition to the Artisans' Dwellings Act of 1885. He was Liberal rather than Conservative partly because the Conservatives could prove as soft as Liberals. Conservatives' insistence upon linking the ever modern interests of property with defence of the traditionary institutions of Crown, landowning peerage and Established Church also made him uneasy. He was, nevertheless, the Liberal best liked by such unbending Tory landowners as Sir Rainald Knightly. He was a favourite of Queen Victoria. He was so stalwart a son of the Church of England that eventually he became a Church Commissioner. Salisbury commented to the Queen: 'It certainly does seem absurd that he should shrink from calling himself a Conservative. All his opinions are those of the Conservatives. No Liberal constituency in the kingdom will have him however much he may profess himself a Liberal.[38] Any Conservative constituency would elect him at once, if he called himself a Conservative. Surely his continuing to call himself a Liberal is an unreality.'[39]

However unreal, his Liberal affiliations were strong enough to force him to undergo a kind of conversion to Conservative-led Unionism before he would accept Salisbury's offer. He allowed himself to be convinced that moderate Liberals had not only lost their effectiveness within the Liberal party but were needed by their new associates. They were needed, not to increase Conservatives' willingness to contemplate reform, but on the contrary to help 'purge them of the cant of "Tory Democracy", & enabling Conservatives who are now silent, either from hesitation or timidity, to know their own real minds, & express their own real opinions.'[40] Though he insisted upon continuing to call himself a Liberal Unionist, Goschen intended to stabilize the conservatism of the Conservative party. He was, nonetheless, anxious to give his action in joining an otherwise purely Conservative Government the appearance of coalition rather than conversion. To that end, he pressed for the admission to the Cabinet of two Liberal Unionist peers. Salisbury attempted loyally to satisfy this wish, though it pleased him almost as little as it did the Conservative backbenchers. He was not sorry when the effort failed.[41]

But in another way he tried to protect Goschen against the charge of turncoat. Presenting the reconstructed Ministry to the House of Lords, Salisbury interpreted it as embodying a realignment of the party system rather than as apostasy from old commitments:

> if you look into the history of this country since Parliamentary Government began you will find that Parties range themselves, not according to their opinion on 20 smaller subjects which might occupy a portion of their time, but on some one great issue by which men's minds are turned. First, it was a dynastic issue; later on you had the American War; then you had the French Revolution; then you had the great question of Reform; next, the great question of Protection; now we have the great question of Ireland.[42]

This interpretation was less than candid, as Salisbury came close to admitting when he went on to deny that Goschen and his Conservative colleagues differed in four questions out of five. Through the Ministerial reconstruction precipitated by Churchill's departure, Salisbury had obtained precisely what he wanted: a Government which united the natural conservatives of Britain in an alliance dominated by the Conservative party.

This achievement gave him a confidence, which he had never entertained before, in the ability of the forces of natural conservatism in Britain to stem the tide of Radical reform. He signalled his newfound confidence by reversing his stand on the question of House of Commons procedure. Irish obstruction during Gladstone's second Ministry had made the demand for tightened rules of procedure popular on the Conservative side of the House; but Salisbury had dragged his feet. For he assumed that reforming Governments would continue to be much more common than Conservative ones. To tighten the Commons' procedures would deprive the Conservative minority of one of its few means to retard the pace of reform. Though he began to change his mind after the election of 1886, he continued as late as December to oppose 'excessive restriction' in the rules of the Commons.[43] When Parliament reconvened toward the end of January, however, the first action of the reconstructed Government was to propose and push through a severe toughening of the rules. The strengthened alliance with Goschen and Hartington gave Salisbury enough confidence to risk giving a permanent addition to the power of the majority in the elected branch of the legislature. There was, of course, an immediate object which precipitated this action: legislation for Ireland.

## iv. The Common Cause

Ireland brought the Unionist alliance into being. Opposition to Home Rule was its members' common bond. But in 1887 the Parliamentary fortunes of the Government's Irish legislation accentuated tensions which demonstrated the impossibility of speedy fusion between the parties to the alliance. The linked forces of Liberal Unionism and Conservatism hammered out and enacted a substantial, controversial alternative to Home Rule for Ireland; and the lines of internal debate ran through both allied parties. Nevertheless, the year underscored the distinctiveness of each. Hartington in 1886 had preserved only the forms of traditional Liberalism: Chamberlain in 1887 gave them substance. Salisbury had to abandon his initial aspiration for the alliance, but he adjuted himself to the unwelcome course of events. What at the beginning of the year he hoped would become a homogeneous party of resistance, by the end of the year he knew to be a strenuous but workable alliance between consciously dissimilar parties.

In a sense the combined Unionist forces were a party of resistance until the beginning of 1887. Until then, their purpose was simply to prevent Home Rule. Once the election of 1886 had disposed of the immediate threat, the Government, in entire cooperation with the Liberal Unionist leadership, played for time in which to work out its alternative policy for Ireland. The only substantial indication of dissension among Unionists on Ireland came over Parnell's Tenant Relief Bill, which the Government and Hartington's men voted down while Chamberlain abstained. And this division had as much to do with Chamberlain's emphasis on Liberal Unionist independence as with Irish policy.[44]

With the reassembling of Parliament in January 1887, the time for uncommitted deliberation had passed. The range of available options provided abundant material for dissension. Before the general election Salisbury had argued the case for coercion though without committing himself to it; Hartington had implied that Liberal Unionists would use their power to restrain Conservatives' penchant for coercion;

Chamberlain had suggested a plan of internal self-government for Ireland more restricted than Gladstone's scheme. During the autumn a conviction matured, quietly but firmly, in the minds of most of the allies, leaders and backbenchers alike, that early enactment of a coercion law was inevitable. But there was disagreement about the best terms and the desirable degree of severity. There were calls from both camps for a stiffer measure than Hicks Beach contemplated. There was also uneasiness in both camps about coercion, notably among the lawyers Henry Matthews and Henry James,[45] and more widely among Chamberlain's supporters. These divisions made Cranbrook fear that decisive action might prove impossible.[46] It was Goschen who rejected such doubts most vigorously: 'it is the firm intention of the Cabinet,' he told the Queen,[47] 'to ask what *they* think indispensible for restoring law and order in Ireland. . . . It will no longer do to count heads and to see whether, by modification here and there, the support of certain doubtful Members can be secured.' On balance the alliance, instead of deepening diffidence, stiffened the Conservative inclination toward coercion. Coercion, or firm assertion of law and order, was about to replace simple opposition to Home Rule as the distinguishing policy, if not the common cause, of Unionism.

Coercion was balanced, however, by an agreement in March between Balfour, W. H. Smith and the Liberal Unionist leaders to revise the 1881 Land Act in the tenants' interest. Salisbury accepted the agreement as fair. He expected it to strain prejudices in both camps, but trusted that the balance of concessions would secure consent.

The coercion Bill, stiffened in Cabinet after Hicks Beach's retirement as Irish Secretary[48], met initially with a promising if unenthusiastic response among Liberal Unionist M.P.s. Admittedly four slipped back into Gladstone's ranks.[49] Another handful, including Chamberlain's lieutenant, Jesse Collings, had on earlier occasions pledged themselves so unequivocally against coercion that, though insistent in their loyalty to Unionism, they felt unable in good conscience to do more than abstain on the Bill. The rest committed themselves to its support. After caucussing separately, the Parliamentary supporters of both parties to the alliance met together for the first time, to hear rallying speeches from Salisbury, Smith and Goschen. In the Commons both battalions submitted themselves to the rigid discipline necessary in order to make headway against ceaseless Gladstonian and Parnellite obstruction.

Soon dislike mounted among the Unionist forces toward a clause permitting trials to be moved from Ireland to England. The feeling was particularly strong among Liberal Unionists, but was shared by some Conservatives.[50] Salisbury wanted to retain the clause in the Bill as presented by the Government but to allow the Commons to excise it if they wished.[51] He was forced to withdraw it by pressure from Liberal

Unionists, who were reluctant publicly to inflict even a minor defeat on the Government and to divide their own forces: for Hartington and another fifteen would have voted for the clause.

The seal of permanence which the Bill as a whole set on the disruption of the Liberal party more than compensated Salisbury for this embarrassment. While Liberal Unionists supported the Bill doggedly, Gladstonians, even those who were less than enthusiastic about Home Rule, reacted to it with moral abhorrence. The division was hardened by months of passionate debate on the Bill.

It was the Land Bill that forced Salisbury to recognize the limited compatibility of the partners to the alliance. He had been prepared for some sort of Land Bill from the beginning of the second Ministry. Though he doubted the economic necessity, the Government's appointment of a royal commission on Irish land (under the chairmanship of Lord Cowper) implied the possibility of legislation. In due course, the commission reported that greatly deepened agricultural depression in Ireland necessitated remedial legislation. That report, and the March agreement with the Liberal Unionist leaders to couple Bills for coercion and Irish land, made him willing to introduce in the House of Lords what he regarded as a generous Bill, more generous than the Lords were likely to put up with except in deference to him. To overcome the Lords' feelings of repugnance, he staked the Ministry's life upon the Bill. Goschen and Hartington fully appreciated the difficulties they knew Salisbury had to face in the Lords. In common with most Whigs and moderate Liberals, Hartington had disliked Gladstone's 1881 Act; and Goschen had opposed it. They approved of the terms of the Bill Salisbury now introduced, terms which were somewhat less generous than the Cowper commission had recommended. The Bill aroused protracted debate in the Lords, where some of its features were amended, though not to the extent of changing its general complexion.

Chamberlain, however, warned Balfour from the outset that the Bill's concessions to Irish tenants were a quite inadequate counterpoise to the benefits which landlords could expect under the coercion Bill. Since contractual rents could now be better enforced, it was only just to ensure that the level of rents was reasonable. Chamberlain went farther:

> Unless you cut the ground from under the feet of the agitators and Plan of Campaign, and accomplish by law the protection of tenants against injustice which they endeavour to secure by robbing and outrage, you will have the country against you.[52]

The suggestion of doing by legislation what the Plan of Campaign was attempting by illegal pressure was the reverse of attractive to Conservatives. When the Land Bill reached the Commons in July, Balfour introduced it in unaccommodating terms. Liberal Unionist

M.P.s on the other hand, sore from months of bitter debate with their erstwhile Gladstonian friends over coercion, were in a mood to insist on further concessions as due them because of their 'unparalleled sacrifices.' Meeting in separate conclave, they followed the lead of Chamberlain rather than Hartington. Their demands threatened the Unionist alliance with disaster.

The critical issue was revision of the so-called 'judicial' rents set under the Act of 1881. The Bill provided for revision of other rents but not of those. The 'judicial' rents imposed under the earlier Act were, as Salisbury saw it, the sole and meagre inducement which led the Irish landlords to acquiesce in Gladstone's measure. Backed outspokenly by Goschen as well as Balfour, he rejected the demand that the Government now welch on that bargain. Most Liberal Unionists insisted, however, that these rents had been set before the recently deepened depression and ought therefore to be treated on the same basis as all other rents. Their argument received ominous support from the Ulster tenant farmers' representatives and from Churchill.

For a month, Salisbury refused to surrender. The naturally liberal elements within the Unionist alliance, not only among Liberal Unionists but in his own party, were undermining the alliance as he envisioned it, as an agency to consolidate the naturally conservative elements in Britain. He had to decide whether to defy or contain this threat. Defiance would mean resignation, if a majority in the Commons voted for revision of judicial rents; and resignation would probably pave the way for a Unionist Government of a centrist sort, probably led by Hartington. Containment would mean surrender to the demand for revision of judicial rents, in order to preserve the present style of Unionist Government, led by himself and dominated by the Conservative party. But what really would be saved by concession? If conservative principles had to be sacrificed on this occasion, what hope could there be that Salisbury's retention of the premiership would lend strength to conservative concerns when powerfully challenged in future? Cranbrook shook his head doubtfully.[53]

Salisbury at length gave way, but in such a way as to accentuate rather than disguise the sacrifice. He convened an assembly of the Conservative Parliamentary party, peers as well as M.P.s, and admitted representatives of the press. In the glare of this large and unprecedentedly publicized forum, he made no bones about his dislike of the concessions which the Liberal Unionists demanded. Yet he counselled acceptance of them as the price which must be paid to preserve the Union with Ireland; and he sketched 'the fearful confusion in the affairs of the nation which would ensue' if the assembled rejected their allies' demand. A backbencher noted his response for posterity:

> I trembled, as I listened, for the immediate future of my country, and though I hate this opening of the door to revision as much as anyone, yet I at once made up my mind to agree . . . So far as I can gather, most of the English members, both for counties and for boroughs, will agree, against their convictions, to save the country.[54]

His assessment of his fellows was accurate. Apart from two Irish Unionist protesters and uneasy murmurings from Henry Chaplin, the assembly responded to Salisbury's advice with 'very cordial acquiescence.'[55]

The reshaping of the Land Bill at the hands of the Liberal Unionists distorted the natural balance of the alliance, for Conservative M.P.s, who played only a subordinate part in the process, outnumbered Liberal Unionists by almost five to one. Because Liberal Unionists held the balance of power in the Commons, their power over legislation was disproportionate to their numbers. Conservative numbers received their due, however, through control of the executive. The balance of the alliance was, accordingly, restored by an executive decision, made by Balfour with the concurrence of the Cabinet, to proclaim the Irish National League under the Coercion Act as a dangerous and unlawful association. The decision was reached without the preliminary consultation with Hartington he enjoyed in the framing of legislation. He was notified of the decision after it was reached though before it was publicly announced. He warned that it was 'open to every sort of Parliamentary and political objection.'[56] W. H. Smith echoed his fears, and advocated delay in declaring the National League unlawful, in order to indicate to the public that the Government intended to use its new coercive powers with patient restraint.[57] Salisbury and Balfour, however, had not obtained coercive powers in order to hold them in reserve for fear of disturbing a nervous public.

Hartington accepted their decision as the prerogative of the executive.[58] Chamberlain, on the other hand, protested strongly and publicly; and, for the first time, he voted with Gladstone against the Government. His protests did not disturb Conservative contentment, for he coupled them with reaffirmations of his loyalty to Hartington and the Unionist cause. And he carried only six of his adherents with him into the opposition voting lobby. Another seventeen Liberal Unionists abstained. Forty-seven, including John Bright as well as Hartington, voted with the Government.

Salisbury's acceptance of Liberal Unionist demands on the Land Bill, and Liberal Unionist acceptance of the decision to proclaim the League, gave the alliance an altered but stronger constitution than he had envisioned in January. Its strength was attested by the failure of an attempt in July to devise an alternative Unionist Ministry. During the struggle over judicial rents, Churchill and Chamberlain eagerly canvassed the prospects for a Unionist Ministry based upon a new 'National' party to be composed of moderate Conservatives, all Liberal Unionists and discontented Gladstonians. Such a Government could avoid the obvious difficulties of concerting action between unreconstructed Tories and Radical Unionists. A National or Centre party would possess the degree of internal cohesion which the party of resistance Salisbury desired would require. But whereas the party of resistance would exclude Chamberlain, the National party would exclude Salisbury. Churchill's plan had no place for Salisbury even at the Foreign Office, which he promised to Lord Rosebery.[58a]

Hartington was indispensible to both alternatives. Though pessimistic in July about the prospects of the existing Government, he refused to precipitate its replacement at a moment when the Conservative rank and file would be 'puzzled and perplexed at a crisis they don't in the least anticipate or understand the necessity for.'[59] This hesitation about asserting his personal interests was decisive.

The summer also brought Chamberlain repeated demonstrations of the temperamental impossibility of Churchill as a partner. Salisbury had expected that his acceptance of Churchill's resignation would alienate Chamberlain from the Government and lead him either to forge closer links with Churchill or to drift back toward the main body of the Liberal party. Chamberlain canvassed both options; and the outcome of the Round Table conference aimed at Liberal reunion remained in doubt for some months. Churchill had, however, diminished his prospects for collaboration with Chamberlain from the very beginning of his exile from government by displaying the same petulance and poor judgement which had brought his exile about. His report to Chamberlain of his resignation revealed it as a defeat inflicted by an abler man:

> I own I did not think that I should have failed to persuade Lord.S. to take a broad view of the situation. I had no choice but to go; He had been for weeks prepared for it, & possibly courted the crash . . . I had ceased to be useful.[60]

Then, in a speech to the Commons at the end of January, he had described the Liberal Unionists as 'a useful kind of crutch' and had commented on Chamberlain's 'extraordinary gyrations.'[61] 'Why', Chamberlain exclaimed, "will you insist on being an Ishmael—your hand against every man?"[62] In the summer, Churchill twice threatened to go his own way on the Land Bill rather than concert tactics with Chamberlain and Hartington. Echoing the comments of Conservative Cabinet Ministers in December, Chamberlain asked Churchill: 'what part do you propose to leave to your colleagues except that of passive acquiescence in your decisions?'[63] At the beginning of August, Churchill and Chamberlain quarrelled on the floor of the House of Commons. By the end of the summer, they had reached a friendly agreement to go their separate ways.

Salisbury ended the 1887 session more firmly in possession of the reins of government than at its beginning. But the horses he guided were not of his choosing, and their arrangement was foreign to his experience. They formed a Russian troika, not an English team, Chamberlain straining to the left, the Tory peers and squires to the right, Hartington straight ahead. The arrangement was even more awkward because Salisbury held the reins of the troika from a position astride the rightward horse.

Though strange and unexpected, the arrangement was compatible with his earlier strategy for the Conservative party. By accepting the arrangement, he had to abandon his hope for a principled realignment of the two-party system, with radical reformers in one party and a consolidation of natural conservatives in the other. However, before the break-up of the Liberal party over Home Rule quickened that hope, he had urged upon Conservatives the virtue of functioning as a self-conscious and determined minority with only indirect influence upon executive government. The weakness of that advice was its inability to satisfy the natural appetite for office, an appetite which took hold of Salisbury in 1885. The way in which the Unionist alliance had developed satisfied the appetite for office while goading Conservatives to assert their distinctiveness.

What Salisbury had feared in Disraeli and Churchill was their drive for power at the expense of Conservative principles. The compromises which that entailed were made within the secret conclaves of the party's leaders, who feared that to reach compromises publicly would be to bring derision and discredit upon themselves. In the summer of 1887, when the shape of the Unionist alliance was being forged anew, Salisbury, reversing this customary calculation,[64] proved more willing to make concessions to Chamberlain in full view of the public than he had been to Churchill in the privacy of the Cabinet. Concessions made in public stiffened Conservatives' spines. Paradoxically they were also stiffened by Chamberlain's adherence to the Unionist cause, for, as a presumed tribune of the people, his action assured Conservatives that their cause was a popular one.[65] Both by repulsion and by attraction, Chamberlain gave Conservatives the courage of their convictions.

The formation of a party of resistance had eluded Salisbury, and no longer seemed possible. The only viable alternative to the existing alliance was the one projected by Churchill and Chamberlain; and that would leave Salisbury's kind of Conservativism stranded and weaker than ever. The alliance which was shaped in 1887 reconstituted the mid-nineteenth century following of Lord Palmerston, but with this difference: that whereas Palmerston's Parliamentary support included many Radicals but excluded Tories, the alliance of 1887 embraced the Tories and left out all Radicals but the handful who followed Chamberlain. The closer historical parallel was the following of Mr. Pitt.[66] That was the particular spectrum of support which Salisbury had long wished to see reassembled.

## v. Elaborating the Alliance, 1888-1890

### a. Governmental Policy

The agreement on Irish policy hammered out between the allies in 1887 proved adequate for the rest of the decade. The most grudging acquiescence came from Irish landlords who wondered, when rents were slashed under the new Land Act, whether it was not as bad as the Plan of Campaign. Balfour's draconian use of the Coercion Act raised fewer doubts on the Liberal Unionist side. The Opposition's moves to censure Balfour's administration in 1888 won less than a handful of defectors, and one of them, W. J. Evelyn, M.P. for Deptford, was a Conservative. Attacks on the Government's Irish policy had, in fact, the effect of pulling the Parliamentary forces of the alliance together and thus of offsetting the capacity of questions of English policy to remind them of their differences.

There was a negative side to Parliament's preoccupation with Ireland, summed up in Gladstone's claim that, until Home Rule was conceded, Ireland would 'block the way' to reforms needed in the rest of the British Isles. Reinforced by obstructive debate, this claim served Gladstone in two ways. It kept Ireland at the head of the country's agenda. It also induced Liberals to subordinate other issues which otherwise divided them: disestablishment, temperance, collectivist social legislation, increasing defence estimates, and imperial issues generally. Gladstone's strategy served Salisbury equally well. It drew continual attention to the reason for the Liberal rupture. And the domestic legislation to which Gladstone and Ireland 'blocked the way' could exacerbate tensions within the Unionist alliance at least as much as among Liberals. Salisbury was, therefore, as anxious as Gladstone to keep Ireland in the forefront of debate. When, in the last three years of this Parliament, Liberals showed signs of deviating from Gladstone's order of priorities by raising popular domestic issues, Salisbury warned the public that such tactics were a ruse and spoke more than ever about the threat of Home Rule.

Yet he could not allow the claim that Ireland 'blocked the way' to be proven by failure on the part of his Government to add significant domestic legislation to the statute books. He needed to strike a balance, allowing Gladstone to keep the amount of such legislation down to proportions tolerable to Tories, but not so far as to exasperate reforming Conservatives and Radical Unionists. The Government accordingly spent much of its time pushing domestic legislation for Britain through Parliament in face of Parnellite and Liberal obstruction.

'The next Session of Parliament,' Salisbury announced at the end of 1887, 'must be a British Session of Parliament.'[67] The major measure to be proposed was a long overdue reconstruction of local government. Salisbury's problem was to see that a measure was fashioned which would be democratic enough to satisfy ardent reformers among the Government's following, yet restricted enough to avoid alienating the country gentlemen whose control over local government as magistrates would be ended. It was the same problem that had divided Conservatives in the autumn of 1886. Churchill had eventually agreed to a scheme which met Salisbury's strongest objections by providing that one third of the members of each county council would be coopted from the magistracy by the popularly elected councillors, and that control of the police would be divided between the new county councils and the old magistrates. But Hicks Beach had withheld his consent from the compromise, insisting that the representation of property owners was still inadequate. This disagreement had not been resolved when Churchill resigned.

When the subject came back for decision before the opening of the 1888 session, the alliance helped to solve the problem. Radical Unionists felt obligated to concede to Conservatives what they would never have conceded to less advanced Liberals. Chamberlain put up with the restrictions to which Churchill had agreed. Despite these restrictions, the measure amounted to a sweeping, largely democratic reconstruction of local government. And Chamberlain had the pleasure of a further concession, that the coopted councillors need not be magistrates. The Bill enhanced his prestige, for few men were likely to credit Hartington with its progressive features.

Just as Radical Unionists moderated their demands out of deference to Conservatives, so also the alliance brought crusty Conservatives into line. Before the Bill was introduced, Salisbury issued a clear though general statement of the requirements of the alliance:

> if for the sake of a great public object, of an object transcending all other objects, you are maintaining the Government on the support of that which is not a coalition, but is an alliance, you must not wonder, you must not blame us if to a certain extent . . . the colour of the convictions of the Unionist Liberals joins with the colour of the convictions of the Conservative party in determining the hue of the measures that are presented to Parliament.[68]

Hicks Beach accepted the Bill without demur. Though the squires responded to it without enthusiasm, the only Conservative opposition to disturb the course of the Bill in the Commons came from what Salisbury called his 'left wing.'[69] The critical reaction of the 'right wing' did not become widely articulate until the Bill had reached the statute books. In subsequent sessions, Salisbury took pains to see that measures welcome to traditional Tory interests, particularly the Church, were enacted, and that reforms which might make county members sullen were more cautiously circumscribed.

Defections from the alliance over domestic matters were few, and limited mainly to Radical Unionists. The most notable was W. S. Caine, Chamberlain's whip. Caine's defection tended to bear out the view, congenial to Salisbury, that a policy of inaction was safer than attempting compromises on domestic issues which divided members of the alliance. Caine's Unionism was straightforward. But even dearer to him was the cause of temperance. Successive attempts of the Government, first in connection with the County Councils Bill, then with the budget of 1890, to devise a broadly acceptable compromise on the licensing of outlets for alcoholic beverages brought Caine's Unionism to the breaking point. Though more numerous among Liberal Unionists, temperance advocates were far from unknown among Conservatives. There was a strong temperance movement among the Orangemen of Ulster. Sympathy for the cause was common among urban Conservatives, particularly those from London. Churchill adopted the issue after his departure from office. Most Conservatives, however, felt some sympathy for the drink trade, whether as a vested and friendly interest, or as a happy adjunct to the jovial way of life they preferred to Liberal earnestness. For Salisbury, it was a question of individual liberty. 'Sobriety', he had said, 'is a very good thing and philanthropy is a very good thing, but freedom is better than either.'[70] He looked to the spread of education for a gradual diminution in the frequency of drunkenness.[71] The Government sought to settle the question by coupling reduction of the number of licensed outlets with financial compensation for those whose licenses were not renewed.

At first Parliament welcomed the compromise. The temperance lobby, however, Caine among its leaders, insisted upon local option and no compensation; and it whipped up a formidable popular agitation, which eventually carried all before it. 'The Teetotal world has fairly gone mad', Salisbury commented to Lady John Manners: '. . .I think the inebriate world is the least insane of the two.'[72] The Liberal Unionists were the first to give way before the storm. The Government followed their lead soon afterward. For their proposals were almost as unwelcome to the friends of the drink trade as to its enemies.

The Government's insistence on a second attempt, and Caine's leadership of the opposition to it, were too much for both. Hartington asked Caine to resign from his position as a Unionist whip. Soon afterward, Caine resigned his seat to seek a fresh mandate from his constituents, now as an Independent. He was crushed from two sides, Hartington insisting that a Unionist run against him, the local Liberals insisting on a candidate pledged to Home Rule.[73]

The one domestic initiative from the ranks of the Conservative party that threatened the alliance, fair trade or tariff protection, strained the cohesion of the Conservative party almost as much as it strained the alliance. The general election of 1886 raised the number of Conservative fair traders in the House of Commons to over 60;[74] and their proportion of support among party stalwarts in Conservative constituency associations was much greater. Heartened and hopeful, fair traders nevertheless restrained their zeal for another year, anxious to uphold what they regarded as a prerequisite to all other ways of strengthening England and its empire: the Union with Ireland. The ability of the Government to survive Churchill's defection relaxed this restraint. Early in 1887, fair traders launched a campaign to win approval for their policy through the ascending levels of the party's network of constituency associations. Encountering little opposition, in November they succeeded in carrying a fair trade resolution at the annual conference of the National Union of Conservative Associations. But thorough-going free trade had been a distinguishing doctrine of Liberalism for almost forty years: Liberal Unionists were quick to warn their Conservative allies against any resurrection of the controversy.

Salisbury attempted to neutralize the fair trade agitation by elaborating his earlier response to it,[75] still showing sympathy with the cause, but emphasizing its political impracticability from a variety of angles. He brought his powers of critical analysis to bear upon the proposals of the fair traders, which they had kept vague in order to avoid controversies among themselves. He insisted that they must convert the country before they could expect favourable action from the Government, for, unless protective tariffs enjoyed bipartisan support, they would be unstable, and hence could not produce economic security which was their object. Pressing his case, he touched the Conservative fear of class conflict, and warned that restoration of a protective tariff on corn would introduce 'a state of division among the classes of this country which would differ very little from civil war.'[76] His fear of dissension within the Conservative party deepened his anxiety to hold the fair traders at bay. He estimated that nearly half of his party—'1. The representatives of commercial constituencies: 2. The political economists of whom we have a sprinkling: & 3. Those, mostly young men, who are sensitive to the reproach of belonging to the stupid party, & "putting back the clock" '[77]—were wedded as firmly as the Liberal Unionists to free trade.

In spite of his vigorous and repeated warnings, fair traders stuck to their guns, emboldened by their hold on the affections of the stalwarts who manned the party's constituency organization. Year after year, the

National Union of Conservative Associations passed protectionist resolutions.[78] The most glaring of these acts of defiance came in November of 1891, when the annual conference of the National Union, disregarding advice which Salisbury gave in his opening speech, called for imperial preference by an overwhelming, enthusiastic majority.

Salisbury got the message. A general election could not be many months away, and the party needed to be in good spirits for the fray. From the vantage of the Foreign Office, he had observed tariff walls rising abroad and foreign tariff negotiations in which Britain was being ignored. On the eve of the general election of 1892, in a speech at Hastings to a regional assembly of the National Union, he revealed a personal leaning toward fair trade. Doctrinaire refusal to contemplate tariffs despite the world-wide drift toward protection, he declared,

> may be noble, but it is not business. (Loud cheers.) . . . I would impress upon you that if you intend, in this conflict of commercial treaties, to hold your own, you must be prepared, if need be, to inflict upon the nations which injure you the penalty which is in your hands, that of refusing them access to your markets. (Loud and prolonged cheers and a voice, 'Common sense at last').[79]

He quickly stipulated that, at least initially, tariffs should be confined to luxuries and must exclude raw materials, especially foodstuffs. Nonetheless, a cry of warning went up from Birmingham. Salisbury's transgression was not repeated. And it was overlooked by Liberal Unionists in the ensuing tumult of electioneering. Chamberlain was already secretly toying with the notion of imperial preference.[80] The Conservative leader had done little more at Hastings than hearten one faction of his party with a view to the polls.

There was one field of policy apart from Ireland which drew the alliance together, and in this field Salisbury was the magnet: the field of foreign and imperial affairs. The bearing of the alliance on Salisbury's conduct at the Foreign Office was no more than indirect. The alliance gave his Government a security of tenure which augmented foreign confidence and enhanced his natural inclination to take long views. Otherwise, the domestic political context in which he conducted foreign affairs was not so much partisan as national. He was as much concerned with what Lord Rosebery, Foreign Secretary in Gladstone's third Ministry, and even Gladstone himself had to say as with the comments of his own colleagues and allies. There was much party capital to be made from his performance as Foreign Secretary; but he exploited it sparingly. Occasionally he would remind audiences of the contrast between the current stable success of Britain overseas and the costly humiliations of Gladstone's second Ministry. Yet he expressly exempted Rosebery's brief term as Foreign Secretary in 1886 from this comparison; and he went out of his way to point out the consensus on foreign policy among the leaders on both sides in Parliament—until 1891 when Gladstone advocated speedy evacuation of Egypt. Salisbury insisted that foreign confidence in the commitments which Britain made, and foreign respect for British determination, required a Foreign Office above the fray of conflicting parties. As he told a Glasgow audience on receiving the freedom of their city:

> the proscription of [party conflict] from your external affairs is the condition on which your Empire and your dominant position in the world is to be maintained.[81]

It was this consciously national rather than partisan character of Salisbury's foreign policy, and also his ability to devise sober, practical solutions overseas combining Gladstonian moral sensibilities with Disraelian insistence upon the national interest,[82] that won the admiration of Liberal Unionists. John Bright's admiration for Salisbury's handling of Bulgaria in the autumn of 1885 eased his entry the next year into the Unionist alliance. The sorrow of the Whig Unionist, Lord Northbrook, over the rupture of party loyalties of a life-time, was alleviated 'as time went on by the confidence which, contrary to his expectations, he gradually came to feel in Lord Salisbury's conciliatory statesmanship and his cautious and pacific management of foreign affairs.'[83] Without the bloodshed and sudden expenditures which deprived the second Ministries of Disraeli and Gladstone of their popularity, Salisbury reestablished the prestige of England more firmly than the one and cultivated good relations and peace more successfully than the other. He came, indeed, to embody the calm, assured greatness of England between the Royal Jubilees of 1887 and 1897 as much as Victoria herself. That attainment, as well as the national rather than partisan manner in which it was achieved, made him an immense asset to the Unionist alliance.

### b. Party Organization

In addition to matters of policy, the alliance had to extend its provisions to avoid electoral conflicts and to assuage organizational rivalries. The electoral compact of 1886 did not look beyond the immediate general election. Translation of the compact into guidelines for the selection of candidates for subsequent elections was not difficult, though these guidelines were not completed and promulgated until 1889.[84] Liberal Unionist candidates were to succeed incumbent Liberal Unionists who retired or died; Conservatives were to succeed incumbent Conservatives; for Gladstonian vacancies, the Unionist with the strongest personal appeal was to be selected, regardless of party; where such a choice was not obvious, a candidate was to be chosen from the side with the larger amount of local support; and disputes were to be referred to arbitration by local men of eminence, or by the Parliamentary whips or, in the last resort, by Hartington and Salisbury.

General guidelines could not avert delicate, unsettling decisions, particularly once departures in special circumstances were made from the original compact. This happened almost immediately. Goschen had lost his seat for Edinburgh in the general election. When appointed to the Exchequer seven months later, he had to find another. He failed in his first by-election contest, for a very marginal Liverpool constituency vacated by the death of a Gladstonian who had won it narrowly from the Conservatives. Eventually Goschen gained entry to Parliament, not for a Liberal Unionist, Gladstonian or marginal constituency, but for the overwhelmingly Conservative constituency of St. George's, Hanover Square. Still, departures of this sort from the original compact could be offset elsewhere.

What made such adjustments difficult was the extraordinary importance with which by-elections came to be invested, and by a succession of Unionist setbacks. By-elections were contested with unusual intensity from the beginning of Salisbury's second Ministry, because the electorate and the alignment of parties were new. The Government's resort to coercion in 1887 intensified uncertainty about the electoral will. Gladstonians argued, quite rightly, that the voters at the general election had not known what the Unionist alternative to Home Rule would be. Unionists retorted by denouncing the collaboration between Gladstonians and the organizers of the Plan of Campaign. Collusion with defiance of the law had, they insisted, been unknown in England since the seventeenth century,[85] and constituted a shocking departure from the canons of responsible party behaviour. By-elections, accordingly, were treated as referenda on a bitterly sharpened dispute. Hosts of organizers from both sides poured into each constituency in which a by-election was to be held. Rival leaders, including Gladstone, but never Salisbury, went down to campaign. The fortunes of the two fluctuated: but more often than not, the Unionists suffered defeats or reduced vote totals. Their majority in the Commons dwindled from over 100 toward 70. Liberal Unionists proved especially vulnerable, their electoral support tending to gravitate to one or other of the major parties.

These trends exacerbated argument between Liberal Unionists and Conservatives about the size and significance of their contribution to the common cause, about the proportion of seats to which they were entitled, and about the most productive relationship between their local organizations. Estimating the size of each side's electoral base, difficult under any circumstances, was unusually so in the late 1880s because of abnormalities in the two preceding elections. These abnormalities served, if not to disguise the magnitude of Conservative support, certainly to exaggerate that of Liberal Unionists. Conservatives had no way of demonstrating conclusively the size of their base, for they had not fought either general election entirely on their own. They were strongly disposed to believe that, on the second occasion, they could have won a clear Parliamentary majority by themselves. Some local Conservative associations now wanted to insist on their due, and were scornful of their allies' pretensions. Outside Birmingham, electoral quarrels tended, therefore, to surface as Liberal Unionist complaints about Conservatives going their own way heedless of their allies' sensitivities.

The force of these complaints was weakened by Liberal Unionists' attempts to keep their Parliamentary representation close to the level of 1886, regardless of their patently dimininishing electoral support. Still, Liberal Unionists probably possessed the balance of power among the electorate somewhat as they did in Parliament. As in Parliament over Irish policy, so electorally, they translated this power into claims which provoked Conservatives to resist and prevented fusion. The compromise hammered out between the allies about Ireland in the summer of 1887 had its counterpart in the retention of separate but cooperating electoral machines. And, once again, the leaders whose separate concerns this settlement reconciled were Salisbury and Chamberlain. Hartington lapsed into ineffectuality.

After Goschen's election for St. George's, Hanover Square, Liberal Unionist leaders and organizers tended to assume that, having nowhere else to go, Conservative electors would support Liberal Unionist candidates more readily than Liberal Unionist electors would support Conservatives. They used this deduction as an argument in favour of Liberal Unionist candidacies. Captain Middleton, Principal Agent of the Conservative party and a loyal servant of his Chief, recognized the benefit of mutual concessions. Conservative generosity in one constituency was likely to produce heartier Liberal Unionist support for Conservative candidates in surrounding seats.[86] But he cautioned against applying this maxim widely. Conservatives in constituencies where they were strong were likely to resent the imposition of a Liberal Unionist candidate upon them,[87] and to withhold their active support and even their votes. Middleton, therefore, firmly asserted the general rule that a candidate should be selected from the Unionist side which was stronger in the constituency. Charitable exceptions to this rule could be granted, more even by Conservatives than by Liberal Unionists: but the proportion of Liberal Unionist to Conservative candidacies should be governed roughly by their electoral support nationally: and Middleton looked at Liberal Unionist claims about their electoral strength with scepticism.

Much more involved with Parliamentary and Cabinet business than with constituency affairs, Salisbury responded to local pressures less jealously than Middleton. The spontaneous reflex of Hartington and

Salisbury was to look at these matters from each other's point of view. They assumed the role of revered but Olympian adjudicators, each urging his followers to treat the other's followers generously. Yet, just as in Parliament Salisbury sought to avoid alienating backwoods peers and country gentlemen, so he was constantly conscious of the danger of alienating local party stalwarts. The Liberal Unionist whip, Lord Wolmer, undeterred by having Salisbury for his father-in-law, urged Liberal Unionist claims more aggressively than Hartington. Salisbury responded by cautioning Wolmer against taking Conservative support for granted. 'There is', he insisted,

> just as much susceptibility on our side as on the other—& great tact & circumspection in both wings will be necessary in order to secure Liberal votes without losing Conservative votes.[88]

The issue was joined over the relationship between the two parties' local associations. Liberal Unionists, resenting the frequent arrogance of Conservative associations, pushed for joint, neutral machinery. But Liberal Unionists outside Chamberlain's sphere of influence were, on the whole, ineffective organizers. They did not appreciate that electoral machinery ran on partisan passion, not on neutrality; or they may have feared the partisan passion of Liberals which Liberal Unionists had to diminish in order to survive. Middleton, on the contrary, argued that they 'should rather welcome than otherwise any activity on the part of our organization—Without the Conservative party being properly organized for the contest no Liberal Unionist can secure his seat in any future election.'[89]

The dispute was thrashed out at a meeting in Arlington Street during the autumn of 1890 between Salisbury, Balfour and Middleton on the one hand and, on the other, Hartington, Sir Henry James and Lord Wolmer. Overriding Middleton's apprehensions, the conferees agreed to drop the prefixes of 'Liberal' and 'Conservative' in favour of plain 'Unionist' and to the amalgamation of the two parties' constituency committees. Soon after the meeting, Hartington slowed down implementation of the agreement for fear of offending those of his supporters who were still as much Liberal as Unionist. He confined himself 'for the present to sending confidential letters to such of our members and candidates as seem to stand in need of a reminder to cultivate better relations with their Conservative supporters.'[90] Where applied, the agreement dispirited the Conservative organization without creating an energetic replacement. A Liberal Unionist by-election loss at South Molton a year after the Arlington Street meeting enabled Middleton to challenge the policy. He pointed to the result, in Balfour's words to Wolmer, as proof of the dangers attending the action of certain Liberal Unionists who conceived that their policy was to kill the Conservative Associations and to work almost entirely through Liberal Unionist machinery. The result is that when the time of the election comes it is vain for Middleton to send down (as he did to South Molton) some thirty or forty workers and speakers. They have no organisation of their own through which anything could be effected, and the Tory Party, whose zeal they are intended to stimulate, is found to have lost half its vitality.[91]

The goal of organizational fusion was abandoned.

A variation on this theme was played in Chamberlain's 'Duchy,' which extended from the urban constituencies of Birmingham to the suburban and rural constituencies of the surrounding counties. Within that area Chamberlain was even more insistent upon his separate rights and requirements than Middleton was nationally upon his. Nationally Chamberlain continued to toy with the idea of fusion between the allied parties. But he wanted his own regional base, represented in Parliament by Liberal if not Radical Unionists loyal to him and organized by his machine, supported, nevertheless, by vigorous Conservative associations. He clothed his demand by arguing, like Middleton, that cooperation between distinctive associations would maximize the alliance's electoral following. In pursuit of regional control, Chamberlain, like Conservative associations outside his Duchy, trod on his local allies' corns. Salisbury repeatedly had to bring the weight of his authority to bear upon the recalcitrant Conservatives of Birmingham. He did not stint in meeting Chamberlain's requirements. Yet the Conservative leader was apprehensive about the price which the Duchy's Conservatives were called upon to pay.

Trouble first erupted over Randolph Churchill's interest in succeeding John Bright as Member for Central Birmingham. Churchill's design brought Chamberlain and Salisbury together. Chamberlain feared Churchill as a potential rival within his electoral base. Salisbury feared Churchill nationally; and in harsh words he welcomed Chamberlain's low estimate of Churchill's electoral prospects in Birmingham:

> Apart from all questions of compact, I think that the success of such a programme as Churchill has put forward would reduce political life very far below the level it occupies in any other country—even the United States.[92]

When bitterness persisted among Birmingham Conservatives after the election of Chamberlain's nominee in place of Churchill, Salisbury sought to dispel it as vigorously as Chamberlain requested. Chamberlain repaid him in a speech which not only burned his last bridge with the Gladstonian Liberals, but adopted Salisbury's key word, 'disintegration', as his own: 'our joint efforts', he said, standing beside Salisbury at a banquet in Birmingham, have for ever, as I believe, saved this country from a policy of disintegration which is just as contrary to the democratic instinct of our age as it is to all true Conservative sentiment.[93]

Trouble broke out again, shortly before the general election of 1892, over a by-election for a constituency bordering on Birmingham, East Worcestershire, where Chamberlain proposed to install his son, Austen. The point of controversy was the notorious commitment of both Chamberlains to disestablishment. It was raised in this case partly to cloak local hostility to Joseph's interference. But the point had given Conservative party headquarters a good deal of trouble elsewhere. In the 1886 campaign, Salisbury had tried to dismiss disestablishment as a remote issue, which the House of Lords could dispose of at least until the electorate had been consulted specifically about it.[94] In 1887, the Chief Whip, Akers-Douglas, had identified it as a major stumbling block to full Conservative support for Radical Unionists.[95] Three months before the East Worcestershire trouble arose, Salisbury had sought to induce Chamberlain to softpedal his declarations in favour of disestablishment.[96] It was all very well to argue that the common cause of maintaining the Union with Ireland was strengthened by support from groups divided on less pressing issues. The fact remained that, like temperance for Caine, the Established Church for many Conservatives was dearer than the Union. Even Balfour suggested that Austen Chamberlain compromise by promising not to 'give a vote hostile to the Establishment without giving the Constituency an opportunity of expressing its opinions' beforehand.[97] The Chamberlains refused; the national Conservative leadership induced the local leaders to give way; and Austen was quietly elected. But resentment within the Duchy continued to fester.

While electoral arrangements vexed the alliance, patronage soothed it. Hartington and Chamberlain, though refusing Ministerial office, accepted a number of royal commission chairmanships. At an early, awkward period in the relations between the two men, Salisbury was glad to offer, and Chamberlain to accept, appointment as Chief Commissioner for Britain in negotiations with the United States on fisheries. Salisbury was more than willing to be generous in dispensing honours to Hartington's and Chamberlain's clients, though Hartington (and also Wolmer and Goschen), in true Whig fashion, pressed him heavily. The prime minister had to achieve some balance between Liberal Unionist and Conservative claims; and he was unimpressed by the merits of some of Hartington's nominees. 'The difficulty', he noted about one, 'is not so much his probity as his chastity.'[98] Even when not personally embarrassed by Hartington's selections,[99] Salisbury saw that Hartington was credited with his clients' honours, either by allowing

Hartington to convey the first news, or by associating Hartington's name with the public announcement of the award. Patronage was not entirely from Conservative to Liberal Unionist: Middleton pressed Wolmer about offices at the disposal of Liberal Unionist Lords Lieutenant.[100] But the flow was mainly the other way. When the Ministry came to an end, Hartington testified to Salisbury's generosity.[101]

Salisbury had proved to be a much better senior partner for the alliance than could ever have been anticipated. His strongly toned Conservatism, far from hindering an alliance, won greater confidence from Whig and moderate Liberal Unionists than they would have reposed in any Conservative who bid for the middle ground. Yet, when he found himself unable to secure the kind of alliance he wanted, he reconciled himself to the kind of alliance he could get. Even within an ideologically ambivalent alliance, he could give unreformed, anti-popular Conservatives more influence than they could possess under a Unionist Government of the centre led by Lord Hartington. As Conservative leader and prime minister, he embodied and hence accentuated the leanings which distinguished the two allied parties from each other, even while they cooperated. He did for Conservatives what Chamberlain did for Liberal Unionists: he assured them that, though allied with former foes, they need not throw overboard their old principles. The relationship which grew between their local electoral machines reflected this illogical but effective combination. And, since the Conservatives were much the larger partner, they could expect to give the combined forces of the alliance more of a Conservative than a Liberal character. When, many years later, fusion occurred, the amalgamated party was to be recognizably Conservative. Had Lord Hartington acquired the premiership, the amalgamated party might well have emerged bearing the features of Whiggery or old-fashioned Liberalism.

## NOTES

1. Salisbury, 'The value of redistribution', *National Review*, IV, 20 (October 1884), p. 162.
2. Salisbury to the South London Conservative Associations, *The Times*, 5 November 1885, 8c.
3. Salisbury to Churchill, 30 November 1885, copy, Salisbury papers.
4. Salisbury to Churchill, 9 December 1885, quoted in Lady Gwendolen Cecil, *Life of Salisbury*, III, p. 275.
5. 'but,' the message went on, Hartington 'is of opinion that the country would consider that an injustice would be committed if less powers of Local Government were given to Ireland than to other parts of the United Kingdom. He cannot speak for other members of his party without consulting them; but he believes that Mr. Goschen & Mr. Forster entertain the same opinions.' Manchester to Henry Manners, 23 December 1885, Rutland papers.

6. The label had been invented by Hartington, speaking at the opening of the Ulster Reform Club in November 1885. J. L. Lindsay, 'The Liberal Unionist party until December 1887', University of Edinburgh Ph.D. dissertation, 1955, p. 153.
7. He allowed this information to be conveyed through the Queen: the Queen to Goschen, 31 January 1886, copy, *Letters of Queen Victoria*, 3rd ser., I, p. 33. Cf. Lord Askwith, *Lord James of Hereford* (London, 1930), p. 169.
8. Lord Askwith, *op. cit.*, p. 169.
9. Salisbury in 1883 had noted a comment of Chamberlain that, in view of the interests of Britain, it could not look with indifference upon anarchy in Egypt. *Hansard*, 3rd ser., CCLXXVI, 31 (15 February 1883).
10. Salisbury to the Queen, 15 May 1886, *Letters of Queen Victoria*, 3rd ser., I, p. 128.
11. Salisbury to Churchill, 29 March 1886, copy, Salisbury papers. Cf. *supra*, p. 13.
12. Salisbury was born in 1830, Hartington in 1833. Chamberlain, though invariably classed with the younger men, was just three years younger than Hartington. Balfour was born in 1848, Churchill in 1849.
13. 8 November 1892, Balfour papers (Whittinghame).
14. Salisbury to Goschen, 4 March 1886, copy, Salisbury papers; Lord Askwith, *op. cit.*, p. 171; Lady Gwendolen Cecil, *Life of Salisbury*, III, pp. 295–6.
15. Askwith, *loc. cit.*
16. Lady Salisbury expressed the feeling with characteristic vigour: 'Hartington's speeches here have been very annoying.
    "It was all very well to dissemble his love—
    But why should he kick us downstairs?"
However Sir H. James tells me now their seats are safe they will behave better. They are a very mean lot!' Lady Salisbury to Balfour,? 25 June 1886, Balfour papers (Whittinghame).
17. Edward Hamilton's diary, 22 April 1886, XIV, 99, B. L. Add. MSS. 48643.
18. A. B. Cooke and John Vincent, *The Governing Passion* (Brighton, 1974), pp. 57, 80–82, 89, and *passim*.
19. A fear which Chamberlain shared. Chamberlain to Churchill, 22 June 1886, Churchill papers.
20. Lady Gwendolen Cecil, *Life of Salisbury*, III, p. 298. He became more confident as the spring wore on. *Letters of Queen Victoria*, 3rd ser., I, pp. 128 and 134–135.
21. i.e. Hartington's men, Chamberlain's and Gladstone's.
22. Salisbury to Churchill, 29 March 1886, copy, Salisbury papers.
23. Memorandum by Salisbury for the Queen, 15 May 1886, *Letters of Queen Victoria*, 3rd ser., I, p. 128.
24. Salisbury to G. S. Harvey, 22 June 1886, Salisbury papers, Secretary's notebook.
25. In one of these three, East Hampshire, the incumbent Liberal Unionist candidate was Salisbury's son-in-law, Lord Wolmer. The local Conservatives insisted upon a contest since Wolmer had won in 1885 through the division of the Conservative opposition to him between two candidates. Salisbury intervened to prevent one of his late Ministerial colleagues, Sir Richard Webster, from campaigning against Wolmer. Otherwise Salisbury felt disabled from intervention because of his personal relationship with Wolmer. But Salisbury's daughter, Wolmer's wife, Lady Maud, who had kept out of view in 1885, now campaigned at Wolmer's side. By a small majority he kept the seat.
26. D. C. Savage, 'The general election of 1886 in Great Britain and Ireland', University of London Ph.D. dissertation, no. 21842, 1958, pp. 521–2; J. L. Lindsay, 'The Liberal Unionist party until December 1887', University of Edinburgh Ph.D. dissertation, 1955, p. 217.
27. Col. Hozier, Hartington's chief extra-Parliamentary organizer, commented: 'As

far as I can see, the Conservative party are played out. If with all our help they can get only 316 seats they can never have a majority in the House. Many of them will come over to the moderate Liberals who seem to me the party of the future.' A. R. D. Elliot, *The Life of George Joachim Goschen, First Viscount Goschen, 1831–1907* (London, 1911), II, p. 94.

28. Hartington to Salisbury, 24 July 1886, in Bernard Holland, *The Life of Spencer Compton, Eighth Duke of Devonshire* (London, 1911), II, p. 170.

29. Agatha Ramm, ed., *The Political Correspondence of Mr. Gladstone and Lord Granville, 1876–1886* (Oxford, 1972), II, p. 456.

30. Akers-Douglas to Salisbury, 17 July 1886, Salisbury papers.

31. Salisbury to Hicks Beach, 24 July 1886, copy, Salisbury papers. A form of this problem arose in Chamberlain's 'Duchy' of Birmingham in August, when Henry Matthews, the only Conservative elected for any of the Birmingham constituencies, was appointed Home Secretary. In the general election Chamberlain had supported Matthews against the Gladstonian candidate, Cook. To support Matthews in a by-election, without other local contests to divert attention, would compromise Chamberlain's reputation as a Radical and strain the willingness of Birmingham's Liberals to follow his lead. Churchill, Matthews' patron, forced the point; Chamberlain reluctantly indicated his support by means of a telegram from his brother-in-law; and Matthews was reelected. The result did nothing to remove Chamberlain's nervousness. Churchill to Chamberlain, 7, 9 and 12 August 1886, Chamberlain papers; Chamberlain to Churchill, 8 and 9 August 1886, Churchill papers.

32. Goschen to A. L. Bruce, 22 August 1886, A. R. D. Elliot, *The Life of George Joachim Goschen* (London, 1911), II, p. 97.

33. Letter of 29 July 1886, Roundell Palmer, First Earl of Selborne, *Memorials*, Part II: Personal and political, 1865–1895 (London, 1898), II, pp. 229–230.

34. Salisbury's telegram to Hicks Beach, 31 December 1886, copy, Salisbury papers.

35. Salisbury to the Queen, 26 December 1886, Salisbury papers; the Queen's journal, 28 December 1886, in *The Letters of Queen Victoria*, 3rd ser., I, p. 236; J. L. Lindsay, *op. cit.*, pp. 315–316; Lady Frances Balfour, *Ne Obliviscaris* (London, [1930]), II, p. 74.

36. A. R. D. Elliot, *op. cit.*, II, p. 104.

37. He accepted appointment as special ambassador to the Sultan from 1880 to 1881.

38. In the general election he had been defeated by a Gladstonian at Edinburgh.

39. Letter of 30 December 1886, Royal Archives C38/89.

40. Alfred Austin to Salisbury, 1 January 1887, Salisbury papers.

41. Salisbury to Cranbrook, 7 January 1887, copy, Salisbury papers.

42. *Hansard*, 3rd ser., CCCX, 32 (27 January 1887).

43. Speech to the City Conservative Club, *The Times*, 9 December 1886, 5e.

44. J. L. Garvin, *The Life of Joseph Chamberlain* (London, 1933), II, p. 268.

45. A. W. Fox, *The Earl of Halsbury* (London, 1929), pp. 129–31; Lord Askwith, *op. cit.*, pp. 191–2.

46. Cranbrook's diary, 1 March 1887, Cranbrook papers.

47. Goschen to the Queen, 11 March 1887, *The Letters of Queen Victoria*, 3rd ser., I, p. 284.

48. *Infra*, p. 143.

49. Peter Davis, 'The Liberal Unionist party and the Irish policy of Lord Salisbury's Government, 1886–1892', *Historical Journal*, XVIII, 1 (March 1975), p. 89.

50. B. E. C. Dugdale, *Arthur James Balfour* (London, 1936), I, pp. 134–5.

51. Viscount Chilston, *W. H. Smith* (London, 1965), p. 252.

52. Chamberlain to Balfour, 31 March 1887, in J. L. Garvin, *op. cit.*, II, p. 305.

53. Cranbrook's diary, 16 July 1887, Cranbrook papers.
54. Sir Richard Temple, *Letters and Character Sketches from the House of Commons*, ed. Sir R. C. Temple (London, 1912), p. 404.
55. Salisbury to the Queen, 19 July 1887, P. R. O. CAB 41/20/40.
56. Hartington to Churchill, 21 August 1887, in W. S. Churchill, *Lord Randolph Churchill*, II, pp. 350–351.
57. B. E. C. Dugdale, *Arthur James Balfour*, I, pp. 139–40.
58. Hartington to Churchill, 21 August 1887, in W. S. Churchill, *Lord Randolph Churchill*, II, pp. 349–351. Churchill was surely right in pointing out that, if the Ministers had had private information which proved the necessity for their action, they would have revealed it to Hartington. Churchill to Hartington, 22 August 1887, Devonshire papers. Their action was an expression of executive power as much as of administrative policy.
58ª Robert Rhodes James, *Lord Randolph Churchill*, p. 322
59. Hartington to Chamberlain, 13 July 1887, in J. L. Garvin, *op. cit.*, II, p. 434.
60. Churchill to Chamberlain, 24 December 1886, Chamberlain papers.
61. *Hansard*, 3rd ser., CCCX, 289 and 290 (31 January 1887).
62. Chamberlain to Churchill, 2 February 1887, Churchill papers.
63. Chamberlain to Churchill, 12 July 1887, Churchill papers.
64. The conventional view was expressed succinctly by Edward Hamilton (diary, 19 July 1887, XVII, 103, B. L. Add. MSS. 48646: 'Compromises in Cabinet are inevitable: but concessions out of doors weaken and discredit a Govt.'
65. 'You made a splendid speech last night. It is curious that you have more effect on the Tory party than either Salisbury or myself. Many of them had great doubts about our policy until you spoke.' Churchill to Chamberlain, 27 August 1886, Chamberlain papers.
66. Cf. Lord Selborne to Sir Arthur Gordon, 6 June 1887: 'There seems to be a great and an increasing resemblance between the circumstances of this time and those in which Fox's Jacobinism separated him from such men as Burke, Elliot, and the rest of the anti-Jacobin Liberals of the last years of the eighteenth century. I anticipate the consequences, now as then, may probably be a rather long continuance of Conservative Governments composed of honest and patriotic, though perhaps not very strong men; but with this difference in favour of the present time, that there is no danger now of any reaction toward a merely obstructive Conservatism.' Selborne, *Memorials*, Part II: Personal and political, 1865–1895 (London, 1898), II, p. 272.
67. Speech at Derby, *The Times*, 20 December 1887, 7b.
68. Salisbury at Liverpool, *The Times*, 13 January 1888, 7d.
69. Report of a meeting of the Conservative Parliamentary party, *The Times*, 22 June 1888, 9f. See below p. 162.
70. Speech in Kingston-on-Thames, *The Times*, 14 June 1883, 7b.
71. Not so racing: 'that seems to get *worse* as civilization advances.' Salisbury to Lady John Manners, 20 November 1886, copy, Salisbury papers.
72. Salisbury to Lady John Manners, 12 June 1888, Rutland papers.
73. He returned to Parliament in 1892 as a straight Gladstonian.
74. S. H. Zebel, 'Fair trade', *Journal of Modern History*, XII, 2 (June 1940), p. 173–174.
75. *Supra*, pp. 27–8.
76. Salisbury to a deputation from the hops industry, *The Times*, 3 May 1888, 10d.
77. Salisbury to McDonnell, 20 December 1892, McDonnell papers. Cf. Salisbury's reply to a deputation on behalf of the hops industry, *The Times*, 3 May 1888, 10d.
78. B. H. Brown, *The Tariff Reform Movement in Great Britain, 1881–1895* (New York, 1943), pp. 73–8.

79. *The Times*,19 May 1892, 10b.
80. J. L. Garvin, *op. cit.*, II, pp. 468–9.
81. *The Times*, 21 May 1891, 10c.
82. See Peter T. Marsh, 'Lord Salisbury and the Ottoman Massacres,' *Journal of British Studies*, XI, 2 (May 1972), pp.63–83.
83. Bernard Mallet, *Thomas George Earl of Northbrook* (London, 1908), p. 232.
84. By Salisbury at Bristol, *The Times*, 24 April 1889, 6c.
85. Salisbury's speech, *Hansard*,3rd ser., CCCXXII, 44 (9 February 1888).
86. Middleton to Balfour, 14 August 1889, Middleton's copy book, Chilston papers.
87. Middleton to Salisbury, 9 August 1889, Salisbury papers.
88. Note by Salisbury on the letter from Wolmer to Salisbury of 27 June 1891, Salisbury papers, with Wolmer's letters to Salisbury.
89. Middleton to Akers-Douglas, 9 July 1887, in Viscount Chilston, *Chief Whip* (London, 1961), p. 135, Cf. Salisbury to Akers-Douglas, 19 July 1887, Middleton's copy book, Chilston papers.
90. Hartington to Salisbury, 7 October 1890, Salisbury papers.
91. Balfour to Wolmer, 16 November 1891, Balfour papers, Letter books, B. L. Add. MSS. 49877.
92. Salisbury to Chamberlain, 16 August 1889, Chamberlain papers.
93. *The Times*, 26 November 1891, 10c.
94. Salisbury to the Rev. G. L. Wilson, 15 June 1886, Salisbury papers, Secretary's notebook; Salisbury to Mr. Beck of Barrow, 28 June 1886, *The Times*, 1 July 1886, 9d.
95. Akers-Douglas to Reginald MacLeod, 5 November 1887, Akers-Douglas' political letter books, Chilston papers.
96. Salisbury to Balfour, 25 January 1892, Balfour papers, B. L. Add. MSS. 49690.
97. Balfour to Wolmer, 1 January 1892, Balfour Letter books, B. L. Add. MSS. 49877.
98. Salisbury to Hartington, 10 May 1891, Devonshire papers.
99. 'I am consoled as to — by the reflection that every-body will know it is your doing.' Salisbury to Hartington, 16 May 1891, Devonshire papers.
100. Middleton to Wolmer, 2 February 1889, Middleton's copy book, Chilston papers.
101. Devonshire to Salisbury, 23 June 1892, Salisbury papers.

CHAPTER 5

# THE STRUCTURE, EMPLOYMENT, AND LIMITS OF LORD SALISBURY'S POWER, 1887-1890

> I have never been able to make up my mind
> whether it is better to be devoured piecemeal,
> beginning at once: or to fight for a delay, & then
> to be devoured in a gulp. Both processes come to
> very much the same thing in the end.

*Salisbury to Lord Cross, 20 November 1893*

With the departure of Lord Randolph Churchill, Salisbury became the unchallenged leader of the Conservative party. 'They [the Government] have now only one really able man', Carnarvon commented, '—all the rest are ciphers in popular estimation.'[1] The fortunes of various Cabinet Ministers over the following three months reinforced Salisbury's supremacy. By a twist of fate, Churchill brought his former foe, Sir Stafford Northcote, now Lord Iddesleigh, down with him. Iddesleigh's conduct of the Foreign Office has drawn criticism, and not only from a minority in the Cabinet led by Churchill. Salisbury fretted over Iddesleigh's lack of despatch. The reconstruction of the Government, in particular Goschen's appointment to the Exchequer, gave Salisbury opportunity to make a change. Goschen, who had an intimate knowledge of Egyptian affairs, expressed serious reservations about Iddesleigh.[2] Salisbury wanted to transfer Iddesleigh to another office, but could not act promptly because of his invitations to Liberal Unionist peers to second Goschen within the Cabinet. Word of Salisbury's intentions leaked to the press. Iddesleigh reacted indignantly. He rejected Salisbury's blandishments, and insisted on retiring completely. Salisbury was embarrassed, but perhaps not entirely sorry to see his erstwhile rival go, for Iddesleigh had never fully reconciled himself to Salisbury's leadership. Embarrassment turned, however, to horror when Iddesleigh, entering Salisbury's ante-room at 10 Downing Street for a departing interview, suffered a heart attack and died. Salisbury was appalled: 'As I looked upon the dead body stretched before me, I felt that politics was a cursed profession.'[3] The tragedy's political cost to Salisbury was slight. The public, angry about the fate of an esteemed if unarresting gentleman-politician, blamed Churchill for necessitating the Government's reconstruction rather than Salisbury for mismanaging it.

In March, shortly before the Government's Irish legislation was introduced, Hicks Beach's health gave way, and he had to resign as Irish Secretary. Despite the strains in their relationship, this event brought Salisbury near despair. For two months Hicks Beach, convinced at last of the need to stiffen the Irish criminal code, had been hammering out a coercion Bill in concert with the rest of the Cabinet. His resignation placed that accomplishment in jeopardy. Publicly wringing his hands, Salisbury likened the Irish question to one of those nightmares, which he knew so well as a younger man,

> where a danger or a horror presses upon you which you feel that you ought to be able to dissipate, but something fetters your limbs and paralyzes your energies . . . .[4]

His dismay at Hicks Beach's resignation was, however, fleeting. He quickly replaced him with Arthur Balfour, who, as Scottish Secretary, had not hesitated to employ coercion in dealing with recent tenant disturbances in the west of Scotland. Together with the installation of W. H. Smith as leader in the Commons, this appointment made Salisbury master in his Cabinet.

His ability to put that mastery into practice was, however, open to question. Until the break with Churchill, the self-effacing manner with which Salisbury presided over the Cabinet worried colleagues who had worked under earlier Chiefs. Iddesleigh, surveying the conduct of the Caretaker Cabinet, observed that Salisbury had 'not guided his colleagues, but has thrown questions loosely before us, taken a division, and proposed himself ready to adopt the decision of the Cabinet whatever it might be.'[5] After four months of the second Ministry, Cranbrook bemoaned the lack of improvement. He counselled Salisbury that, 'Interrogated singly each [minister] expresses an opinion but all would be prepared to make concessions without sacrifice of any great principle to combine in the production of the best of which circumstances admit . . . . The position requires your distinct *lead* and your just self assertion.'[6]

Salisbury shied away from the role of *prima donna* by calculation as well as by temperament. He did not want, and he believed himself unable, to play the demagogue or charismatic leader. That was the approach chosen by Churchill and Gladstone. It reflected their knowledge that their parties would not fall naturally into a mould suited to their ambitions but had to be forced by their acquisition of personal popularity. Salisbury, on the other hand, derived much of his strength as a regular Conservative. All he wanted from the country was that its natural conservatism should manifest and express itself. His party in Parliament adhered to him as the marshall of its strength *vis-à-vis* the Liberal Unionists. His best hope of making the party more effectively conservative lay in honouring backbench Conservative prejudices.

His management of the Cabinet reflected similar calculations. Like the Parliamentary party, his Cabinet colleagues were for the most part a dull lot, powerful only collectively. They shied away from Carnarvon's and Churchill's enthusiasms, and closed ranks quickly, with expressions of injured propriety, when the two men's transgressions led to their removal from the party's councils. 'I do not like the notion', wrote Sir Henry Holland, soon to be rewarded with the Colonial Secretaryship, 'that the Conservative party's very existence depends on one man, however able.'[7] Doubtful of their popular support except on the issue of the Union, they had gone along with Churchill because of his seeming grasp of public sentiment, until he mistook it. Then Salisbury gave them the courage of their convictions.

Salisbury too was doubtful, not of his own convictions, but of their acceptability to the now sovereign democracy. That doubt led him to look upon his Cabinet colleagues as more than bulls in a herd. He treated the Cabinet as a council of ambassadors who, whatever their personal talents, came from various regions, classes and interests within the electorate. Churchill was the ablest and most powerful of these ambassadors; and Salisbury had joined in council with him for what, in terms of strain, had been a very long time. When Churchill tried to push beyond this confederate relationship to a unitary one bearing his own impress, Salisbury let him go. But Salisbury's view of the nature and function of the Cabinet council did not change. That view was to give him long years in office, but also curtailed his power.

Salisbury exerted his leadership lightly, by courtesy, wit and capacity for work, rather than by persuasion. Persuasion he dismissed as inappropriate, not only because of his conception of the Cabinet, but also because the processes of thought by which he reached his conclusions were not affected by other men's processes. His was an insulated mind, and so, he presumed, were others'. Still, he impressed his colleagues. Like his children, whom he dealt with in similar fashion, they enjoyed being treated as ambassadors. He gave them more than respect. He treated them with the exquisite courtesy of a passing generation. He was always concerned for their health and about the strain which their work and attendance, particularly in the obstructed Commons, placed upon them. He inquired after their wives and children. To most people conspicuously aloof, he kept his door, whether in London or Hatfield, always open to members of the Cabinet.

Whether they came or merely wrote, he dealt with the problems they referred to him incisively. His powers of intellect escaped no one. And he laced his responses with irrepressible wit. His wit was the one talent he feared. Fatigue only deprived it of restraint, with consequences that could prove embarrassing. In public he held himself in check. But occasionally his sense of the ridiculous pierced through his usual decorum. A complaint which Lord Stanley of Alderly made to the House of Lords about the purchase by the Trustees of the Chantrey Bequest of a nude portrait of St. Elizabeth of Hungary got the better of Salisbury:

> I am wholly unable to enter into the discussion to which the noble Lord invites me, until he can lay down for me some canon as to the course artists should pursue in dealing with the question of clothes or no clothes. Artists take a very different view of the subject from that taken by the majority of mankind, and some of the matters which they represent as wholly innocuous and, indeed, praiseworthy would, if translated into ordinary life, attract the attention of the police. . . .even in the representation of sacred subjects I have observed on the part of artists that a desire to exhibit their knowledge of the human form and their command of flesh tints has overcome the inclination to clothe saintly persons with a sufficiency of garments. . . .There is one topic of consolation, however, which I would suggest to the noble Lord. I have not been myself to the gallery in which this picture is to be placed. But some friends of mine have been there, and they assure me that it is in a place of great seclusion suited to the exhibition of works of this kind. . . .If the picture had been sold to a private owner it would have been exhibited by him in his gallery, and all kind of persons, including maid servants and others, would have seen it every day. . . .[8]

Salisbury's capacity for work was as impressive as his wit. It had to be, if he was to combine the premiership with the Foreign Office; and his unwillingness to delegate much more than clerical responsibility to the permanent staff at the Foreign Office compounded the need. Without freedom as a peer from the protracted demands of a seat in the Commons, Salisbury could not have handled this administrative load. His work load also helped to account for his absence from the Parliamentary lobbies and social gatherings, and for his nightly retreat to Hatfield. Only by secluding himself could he deal with his double office. His colleagues, and opponents too, were awed by his prodigious capacity for work. 'I suspect, if the truth were known', Lord Rosebery wrote of his rival many years later, 'it would be found that he was one of the hardest workers of his time.'[9] Salisbury could speak on every subject which came his way in the House of Lords not only lucidly but in detail, all without reference to notes. Rarely a day passed between his receipt of a letter and the despatch of his reply. When in office, he lived to work. His hobbies were put aside. His only break took the form of recuperative holidays at his villa in France; and even there the red despatch boxes kept coming.

However close his attention to foreign affairs, Salisbury's surveillance outside his department extended well beyond those with business related to the Foreign Office, in other words beyond the armed services and the Colonial and Indian Offices. He had to involve himself in the conduct of departments which suffered from mismanagement and controversy, particularly the Home Office under Henry Matthews. He kept a critical eye on the niggling operations of the Treasury, kept fully abreast of Balfour's administration of Ireland, took the initiative in ecclesiastical legislation and eventually in education, and helped to shape contentious domestic legislation generally. The recollections of colleagues and comments of historians about Salisbury's lax supervision of his Cabinets are valid only for his last years and for 1885.

## i. W. H. Smith and the Leadership of the Commons

Still, his uninspiring colleagues in the Commons needed leadership, which he did not place himself on hand to give. This problem had bedevilled him ever since he succeeded Disraeli as leader in the Lords. Churchill's resignation forced the problem to the fore, both by dramatizing and compounding it; for the new leader would have to deal with Churchill's trouble-making on his flank as well as with Gladstone, Harcourt and Parnell across the aisle.

Salisbury had had enough of independent coadjutors in the Commons. He refused to put Hicks Beach back in Churchill's place, insisting that Hicks Beach was indispensable in Ireland. Instead, Salisbury reached into the herd, and selected W. H. Smith. Yet, except for the fact that Hicks Beach had been passed over, the selection of Smith was not a deliberate experiment. Salisbury chose him as a stop-gap until Goschen could take over. As soon as Goschen was elected to the Commons, an inner triumvirate of Salisbury, Smith and Goschen took shape. They exercised surveillance over the entire conduct of the Government; and when it came to foreign affairs, Smith tended to drop out of the conversation.

Smith, nevertheless, emerged as the undisputed second-in-command to Salisbury and the key to much of the Government's good fortune. His story, refreshing in a tale of intrigue, provides one of those rare instances where the meek inherit the earth. He had already acquired a vast amount of this world's treasure, by building up the firm of newsagents which, as a young man, he took over from his father. But in the still aristocratic world of politics, that achievement left his social standing as glamourless as his name. He was a tradesman: and he accepted the fact with just short of cloying humility, declining a G. C. B. in 1886 on the grounds that it was usually restricted to men of higher degree, and dining, when First Lord of the Treasury, with the Prince of Wales' tradesmen.[10]

He was without conspicuous talent, a reliable but unexciting administrator, a dull and diffident speaker. His one political distinction was his willingness to undertake disagreeable assignments whenever his party called. Never quite sure of his own mind, he was always anxious to prevent or patch up quarrels among colleagues of independent mind. Even in appearance he was hard to remember. There is one story, probably apocryphal, that Salisbury failed to recognize Smith across a dinner table after he succeeded Churchill; and another from the same period, unquestionably true, that a crowd which gathered on a railway platform to greet him failed to recognize him when he stepped off the train. He was always to some extent a figure of fun. Appointed by Disraeli to be First Lord of the Admiralty, he was the model for Gilbert and Sullivan's Sir Joseph Porter.[11] In his last years, his 'grave comicalities of mien'[12] endeared him to the House of Commons, where he was known as 'Old Morality.' Always in his seat, however late the hour and long the session, often with a rug over his knees, and toward the end of his life obviously in poor health, a martyr to duty, he became the most popular leader of the House of Commons in a generation.

No one foresaw this outcome when Smith met the Commons for the first time as its leader. The outlook was discouraging. Goschen had just suffered defeat at Liverpool. Churchill glowered below the gangway. The wolves of the Opposition eyed with hunger the lamb who stood up in front of them. 'Mr. Speaker', he began,

> I have, Sir, on rising to make an appeal to the House. Placed in the position in which I am, I desire to appeal to hon. Members for the indulgence and for that favourable interpretation of all my actions which are necessary to one who feels deeply his own deficiencies in following in the steps of the many great men who have held the important position that I now fill. I appeal to them in the hope that by the cordial support of my hon. Friends on this side of the House, and by the generous interpretation of my acts by right hon. and hon. gentlemen opposite, I may be enabled, to the best of my ability, to maintain the order and decorum of the proceedings of this House and the decencies of debate.[13]

The appeal proved gently powerful. The Opposition, bent on protracted debate, would have risen with eager fight against any displays of brilliance in the captain of the Government's forces. But there was no satisfaction in striking such a modest man. His appeals for decency and patriotic order in debate were disconcerting. His words were so few that the Opposition had little to latch onto. At the same time, he had a good sense of the strategic moment at which to move in the Commons, all the more effective because unexpected.[14]

Succeeding where Churchill failed, Smith demonstrated that, faced with a clear choice between brilliance and gravity, England still preferred gravity. But Sir Stafford Northcote had been a patently good and honourable man. Smith would not have fared better than Northcote as a leader in opposition. Reasonableness took the heart out of an Opposition; but earnestness, commitment to duty, and vulnerable lack of brilliance warmed the spirits of the new governing Conservative M.P.s and brought them out, night after night, to back him up. Though a tradesman, he appealed to and reinforced the Conservative country gentlemen's code of honour. They too thought of themselves as in Parliament only to serve. They too were incapable of anything brilliant. Smith embodied the respectability which old county and new urban Conservative M.P.s had in common.

Salisbury soon appreciated that the appointment of Smith was providential. Smith's first two years in his new position were the most straightforward that Salisbury ever enjoyed in his twenty-one years of collaboration with successive leaders of the party in the Commons. Smith's final three years became clouded, in 1890 seriously so. But Salisbury faced the prospect of replacing him, when his health gave way, with undisguised dismay. In a unique expression of emotion after Smith died, Salisbury spoke of him publicly as 'my beloved colleague'.[15]

His great virtue in Salisbury's eyes was that he was 'straight'. It was a political virtue to which Salisbury frequently referred. When he applied it to backbenchers, he meant tractibility.[16] Smith, when it came to the point, would always defer to Salisbury; but he was no rubber stamp. Smith was 'straight' in two other senses. He had no ulterior ambitions of his own; and he addressed himself solely to the job to be done. These qualities were reflected in his letters to Salisbury. Where Churchill's letters had been long, full of gossip, and warped by advice, Smith kept his letters even more terse than his speeches, often no more than a few sentences and strictly businesslike.

As a result, he kept Salisbury in touch with party opinion in the Commons more reliably than Churchill. He was particularly well qualified to keep Salisbury alive to those sections of the party with which the prime minister was least in tune. Though Salisbury prided himself upon descent from three Lord Mayors of London, and though he drew his economic ideas from the City, his reflexes were aristocratic. Moreover, his sceptical intellect tended to enervate him. Balfour was to compound this weakness. Smith corrected it. He shared the pragmatic, modestly reformist impulses of the industrial, mercantile and financial classes who consolidated themselves within the Conservative party during the years of Salisbury's leadership. Smith's transmission of their viewpoint was reinforced by some of the abler members of the Cabinet, C. T. Ritchie at the Local Government Board as well as Goschen, who came from the same class; and they were able to sway the less self-confident aristocratic majority. The result was domestic legislative proposals—the County Councils Bill, for instance, and the abortive temperance proposals—which bore the impress of this class of Conservatives. Despite obstruction in Parliament and occasional fai-

lure, they were able to put more on the statute books during Salisbury's
second Ministry than Chamberlain proved able to do after 1895.

For three and a half years, from 1887 until the summer of 1890,
Smith's lieutenancy allowed Salisbury unrivalled direction over his
Cabinet. The only threat to his position came from the renegade,
Churchill; and Salisbury took unrelenting care to keep him weak.
Initially, the prime minister benefited from a surge of loyalty among
Conservatives in reaction to Churchill's defection. Churchill had played
a powerful role in the selection of Salisbury's second Ministry, and had
advertised his influence while offices were being distributed by holding
'a daily sort of Cabinet at the luncheon table at the Carlton.'[17] At his
behest, two of the least effective survivors from Disraeli's last Cabinet,
Richard Cross and Frederick Stanley, were driven to the Lords, though
still with Cabinet office. He denied the squires' darling, Henry Chaplin,
a seat in the Cabinet; and Chaplin indignantly refused office under any
other terms. He kept Henry Cecil Raikes, a yeoman party organizer,
from the Home Office on which Raikes had set his heart, securing it for
his own client, Henry Matthews. Inevitably, men thus treated rallied to
Salisbury when Churchill resigned; and they remained grumblingly
loyal even when Salisbury continued to disappoint their ambitions.
Here, as over Iddesleigh's removal from the Foreign Office, Salisbury
managed to see that Churchill bore the blame for painful decisions
which were, in large part, his own.

Even the members of the Cabinet who had tended to side with
Churchill rallied to Salisbury. Lord George Hamilton, First Lord of the
Admiralty, put their reaction well:

> On local Government & foreign policy I incline to many of [Churchill's]
> views . . . [But] from the first I have felt that the duty of every member of your
> Cabinet was to try to keep the party together, & acting in that sense I
> will . . . subordinate my own views to the paramount object of keeping Gladstone
> out of office.[18]

Only one member of the Cabinet, Hicks Beach, had misgivings, but he
was worryingly significant. Salisbury had taken special pains to enlist his
support on the issue over which Churchill had resigned. But Salisbury's
letter to Hicks Beach was deceptive, and Churchill's resignation took
him aback. Uneasy at the outlook, he pressed harder than any other
member of the Cabinet for full coalition with the Liberal Unionists. The
limited result of Salisbury's negotiations with Hartington left Hicks
Beach suspicious of Salisbury's real intentions. Salisbury's explanation
for choosing Smith rather than Hicks Beach to lead the Commons—that
Hicks Beach was indispensable for Ireland—did not convince him.[19]
Still, the prime minister and the Irish Secretary drew together in the
opening months of 1887 over the coercion Bill; and when ill health

forced Hicks Beach to give up his Irish post, he remained in the Cabinet without office.

This arrangement was largely honorary. Cataracts had formed over both of Hicks Beach's eyes, forcing him to leave for treatment in Germany. He was not expected to recover, but the treatment proved effective. He returned to London in the autumn, uneasy once again, this time about Balfour's severe implementation of the Crimes Act. Hicks Beach still hoped for a reconstruction of the Ministry, in all probability to include Churchill as well as Hartington; and he felt increasingly dissatisfied with his position as a member of the Cabinet but without office. He therefore resigned, and drifted toward Churchill.

The as yet imperfect restoration of Hicks Beach's sight dimmed Salisbury's perception of the danger. Smith and Hartington opened his eyes. Early in 1888, before Hicks Beach had opened his mouth in Parliament, Salisbury made room for him in the Cabinet as President of the Board of Trade. The offer came almost too late. Hicks Beach wrote to Churchill, willing to join forces with him and turn Salisbury's offer down. Churchill, thinking that Hicks Beach might serve him in the Cabinet as a kind Trojan horse, advised acceptance of Salisbury's offer. Churchill did not have Hicks Beach's measure. Hicks Beach enjoyed administration. The work of his new office soon absorbed him, and reduced his interest in internal controversy. He remained in friendly contact with Churchill; but to that danger, Salisbury was fully alert.

Salisbury worked to keep Churchill powerless as assiduously as Walpole had done with Bolingbroke. Though few Conservatives sympathized with Churchill over his resignation, he retained some dangerous friends, including Lord Abergavenny, Borthwick, editor of the *Morning Post* and chairman of the conference of Metropolitan M.P.s, and for a while Saunderson, leader of the Ulster Unionists.[20] Even Smith canvassed the prospects for his return in 1888.[21] Though Churchill displayed failure of nerve at several critical junctures, his speeches could still stir the Commons[22] and rouse the country. It was in part to head off Churchill's continuing campaign against the army estimates that Salisbury authorized the appointment of a royal commission on the army. The Government's temperance proposals were intended to neutralize an agitation upon which Churchill as well as the Liberal Opposition were capitalizing.

Kept at more than arm's length, Churchill looked hungrily for signs of ill health whether in Salisbury or in Salisbury's colleagues,[23] whose departure might necessitate his recall. Unable, because of Salisbury's treatment, to follow Chamberlain's example of prodding the Government in private while upholding it in public, Churchill oscillated between defiance and support. It was the shows of support that worried Salisbury. Defiance he almost welcomed, for, as it grew less and less measured, it alienated more and more men from Churchill. In 1890, he failed to gain re-election to the Council of the National Union of Conservative Associations. By the time Smith died in 1891, Churchill was right out of the running to replace him.

## ii. Akers-Douglas and the Management of the Party in the Commons

The relationship between Smith and Salisbury, however effective, could not dispose of the difficulties which a prime minister in the Lords inevitably encountered in managing his party in the other House. The work of marshalling its forces and keeping the prime minister aware of its mood was a full-time job. Never was the job more demanding than in the 1880s. In order to make headway against obstructive opposition, ceaseless discipline was necessary. Despite the clear cut divisions between supporters and opponents of the Government on the major question of the day, morale on both sides was unstable, prone to excessive depression or elation over momentary setbacks or successes.[24] Smith, though attentive to this dimension of his responsibilities, had to give his first attention to the conduct of debate, which was conducted largely between the front benches, and to the shaping of legislation.

The impersonal character of Salisbury's Parliamentary leadership greatly increased his need for a good whip in the Commons. To most Conservatives in the lower House he was as inaccessible, to use a comparison one of them drew, as the Grand Llama of Tibet.[25] Not only did he absent himself from the lobbies and from most of the social life of London. He fulfilled his own social responsibilities grudgingly. To the select recipients of invitations to gatherings at Hatfield, Lady Salisbury was 'boundlessly hospitable',[26] but vast Parliamentary receptions at the Foreign Office stifled her native sociability: 'she would stand at the head of the broad marble staircase, and with an expressionless face, often half turned away, she would hold out a limp hand to each guest'.[27] Lord Salisbury's courtliness could not hide his boredom. 'Why', he complained, 'should I spend my evenings being trampled on by the Conservative Party?'[28] Apart from gatherings of this magnitude, M.P.s caught no more than glimpses of him crossing Parliament Square to the Foreign Office, when he looked like 'some learned literary recluse hurrying, after a visit to the British Museum, back to the study he had regretted leaving.'[29]

His hold upon his Parliamentary followers was indirect and emotionless. Among the Conservative electorate he inspired veneration, and this feeling worked indirectly on the party in the Commons. They were impressed by the lucid mastery of his speeches in the Lords, which they heard clustered on the steps of the throne or from the Lords' galleries—a compliment he did not return. They identified his prime ministership with their rights as a party. But he could not inspire affection among them, as even Northcote had done. When leaders of the Government gathered on ceremonial occasions which attracted people of their class, for example at the Guildhall or to receive honorary degrees at Cambridge, it was Balfour or even Goschen who drew the warmest applause. Educated men commonly remarked that Salisbury would have been happier in his great ancestors' time as a councillor responsible to the Crown rather than to Parliament; and the comment conveyed resentment as well as respect.

Nevertheless, the practice of voting occasionally against the party line all but disappeared among Conservative M.P.s[30] in the late 1880s and 1890s under Lord Salisbury's leadership. The sharp divide between parties on the central issue of Home Rule largely accounted for this situation to begin with. But it persisted after Home Rule ceased to be a pressing concern, indeed until Salisbury retired. The disintegration of the Conservative Parliamentary party after 1902 cannot be explained simply by Salisbury's retirement, any more than the cohesion acquired after 1885 can be credited simply to his presence. Even so, his achievement was remarkable.

But there was nothing miraculous about it. It was founded upon Salisbury's conception of his duty as party leader, upon extraordinarily good whipping, and upon social congeniality, not to be confused with sociability, between leader and party. A nobleman from a Tory family with illustrious forebears, Salisbury came from the class among which Conservatives wanted but rarely managed to find a leader. Regularly ill-supplied with men of talent, the Conservative party had an embarrassing reputation for following soldiers of fortune, most notoriously Disraeli. Even its more respectable leaders had flawed backgrounds. Peel came of manufacturing stock. Derby had served in the predominantly Whig Cabinet which enacted the Great Reform Bill. Now, for the first time since the death of Lord Liverpool, the Conservative party 'found itself in the comfortable embrace'[31] of a man who combined in equal measure competence and aristocratic dignity. Even Lord Liverpool had left something to be desired, for he was essentially a professional administrator. Castlereagh was more to the Tory party's taste, but he had not reached the highest office. It might be necessary to go back to Lord Clarendon to find as good a match between the self-image of the party and its leader as Lord Salisbury provided.

There was, furthermore, a fortunate correspondence between the conceptions about party leadership which Salisbury brought to the job and the particular character of partisan cohesion after 1885. He had insisted that a leader owed his party loyalty in the 1850s and '60s, when his message was inappropriate. Disraeli had ignored it, not from moral turpitude, but because, in that 'Golden Age of the private member', men of good will from one party did not hesitate to vote for some measures proposed by the party opposite. Cross-voting by the moderate men of both parties was much more common than rebellions among their immoderate hard cores. By 1885, the pattern was changing. The duel between Gladstone and Disraeli and the battle over Home Rule inspired new depths of partisan commitment. Harcourt on the Liberal side, never himself a devotee of Home Rule, recognized the consequence:

> No Government makes a *coup* which dissatisfies *its own* party; it is always repaid by sulky abstention. The idea that it is to gain by popularity with the other side shows a crass ignorance of practical politics . . . You can only have a strong Government by acting on the lines and in sympathy with the sentiments of *your own Party*.[32]

The danger to avoid now was not defections among men of the centre, but abstentions by partisans at the ends of the spectrum.

Salisbury welcomed the change. For reasons of his own, he wanted the Conservative party to be attentive to its diehards. Partly because of his action on Ireland, the party was ripe for his kind of leadership. When he insisted, as he frequently did, that the Government shape its policy to avoid alienating Tories whose first loyalty was to the ratepayers or to the landed interest or to the Established Church, he was playing realistic as well as principled politics.

The composition of the Parliamentary party was not, however, as tidy as such as analysis might indicate. Nationally the Conservative party embodied a broad coalition of social and economic forces which varied, moreover, from region to region. Until the 1880s, the composition of the Parliamentary party did not reflect that coalition, although for more than fifteen years it had been expanding beyond its original rural base to embrace urban men of property. The Parliamentary reforms of the mid-'80s accelerated this adaptation. The enfranchisement of agricultural labourers in 1884 weakened the hold of Tory landowners over rural constituencies. Meanwhile, a generation of businessmen was coming to the fore whose forefathers had built up their firms and who therefore felt free to devote themselves to politics. Their entry into the Commons was facilitated by the Corrupt Practices Act of 1883, which sharply reduced the cost of running for Parliament, and by the Redistribution Act of 1885, which created single-member constituencies more manageable in size and shaped along the lines of localities' social and economic composition. The Tory gentry were thereupon forced to share their Parliamentary ascendancy with 'the merchants and bankers who sat for the City, the stockbrokers, barristers and solicitors who sat for the inner ring of suburbs, and the bankers, brewers, merchants and manufacturers in the outer ring.'[33] The safest Conservative seats were no longer bucolic but suburban. The numerical strength of the Conservative Parliamentary came from the cities rather than from the countryside. Salisbury perceived the trend shortly before the general election of 1885 made it manifest. But he put it down to the superior formal education and political experience of city dwellers as much as to middle-class material interest. He never fully understood the phenomenon, and he never felt quite at ease with its spokesmen.

The make-up of the party in the Commons was still more complex. It included members for working-class constituencies, most notably in London, whose predilections in domestic policy were akin to Chamberlain's. It also included a contingent of Ulstermen, linked to another contingent of Irishmen sitting for English constituencies. Those Conservatives who owed their seats to Liberal Unionist support sometimes had further interests to consider, including Nonconformists and temperance advocates. Some of these groups sought strength through organization: there was a formally constituted 'Church party', and a regular association of Conservative M.P.s for metropolitan London.

Ceaselessly vigilant whipping was indispensable if this mêlée of representatives was to be marshalled in tight voting order over long months of debate. Salisbury's chief lieutenant for this purpose outside the lofty realm of policy formation, and even to an extent within that realm, was Aretas Akers-Douglas, M.P. for the St. Augustine division of Kent and chief whip in the Commons since 1885. Akers-Douglas did not owe his appointment to Salisbury. He was part of the 'Kentish gang' or organizers installed at the behest of that gnarled but affable veteran manager, Lord Abergavenny, just before Salisbury became prime minister. But their loyalty to Salisbury, or rather to the official leadership of the party, was unquestioning. Collectively they equipped him with an organization unsurpassed in its efficiency and discipline. Akers-Douglas, like Abergavenny, welcomed the vigour and popular appeal which Churchill brought to the party, and could have followed him as leader. But he could not excuse the stab in the party's back which Churchill's resignation inflicted, and he was slower than Abergavenny to allow for the possibility of Churchill's return. Akers-Douglas' sole concerns were the party's cohesion and success. He never showed the slightest inclination to use his capabilities to push the party in a direction opposed by the leadership, though occasionally he wrung his hands at the consequences of some of Salisbury's decisions and public remarks. Though gratified by his promotion to the Cabinet as First Commissioner of Works in 1895, he continued to serve—and to serve with entire contentment—as watchdog of the Parliamentary party.

His assignment was twofold, and was perfectly matched by his talents. An affable country gentleman, freed by an unhappy marriage from the temptation to spend his evenings at home, he was charged with ensuring that enough of the Government's voting strength in the Commons was in place, whenever necessary, to defeat Opposition motions or to impose closure. He and his harmonious team of young assistants kept the lax up to the mark, monitored the exits with looks, or words of disapproval, and in the process won backbenchers' affection. Akers-Douglas acquired more than affection. His ears were Salisbury's. The second part of his charge was to gather intelligence. In the course of bringing backbenchers back to their seats, he listened to their reactions to current party policy and transmitted this information to the leadership. Soon the leaders consulted him about probable reaction to policies they had under consideration. Salisbury as early as April of 1886 brought him into the ex-Cabinet's discussion of tactics against the Home Rule Bill. After Smith's appointment as leader in the Commons, Akers-Douglas and he became devoted to each other. When Salisbury appointed Smith Warden of the Cinque Ports, Smith asked Akers-Douglas to be his 'Prime Minister',[34] to advise him how to deal with the new calls made upon him. The pipeline from the backbenches through Akers-Douglas and Smith to Salisbury was unimpeded and straight.

## iii.  Lord Salisbury's Use of Power

The team of Smith and Akers-Douglas gave Salisbury his greatest opportunity to implement his principles. To what extent did he try to do so? To put it differently, what were the principles to which he tried to give effect in these years? Did he provide another instance of what he once described as 'the just Nemesis which generally decrees that partisans shall be forced to in office precisely that which they most loudly decried in opposition?'[35] Would he be able to avoid the path of Peel and Disraeli?

### a.  The blessing and the bane of Ireland

Opposition to Home Rule was the keystone of Salisbury's power. It was the sole policy which bound Radical Unionists to a Conservative Government. It was the supreme cause which gave heart to the Davids of the Conservative party against the Liberal Goliath. As Salisbury summed it up on the day Hicks Beach had to resign as Irish Secretary:

> It is not a question of this party or that; it is not a question of the career of statesmen . . . We are engaged upon a struggle on the issue of which depends whether our existence as a great Empire is to continue or not . . . .[36]

In a succession of speeches in 1887, Salisbury established defence of the Union as the cardinal, unifying strand in the banner of Conservative policy. Around it he wove the strands of imperial strength, economic security, and resistance to demagogic agitation. A banner composed exclusively of any one of these strands would not have been attractive enough to assemble a conquering army. Though maintenance of Britain's dignity as a power among nations had been a rising concern since 1870 when Bismarck undermined and Gladstone slighted it, imperialism was not yet a widespread popular sentiment. Talk of economic security held much less appeal for the urban working class than for the suburban middle class. The fear of mercurial popular government, Salisbury's deepest concern, was not a popular emotion. Woven together with defence of the Union, however, they made a moving appeal:

> If we have been able to maintain at one time an almost fabulous prosperity, if in this narrow island with a not too fertile soil, with an ungracious climate and limited space, we have been enabled to maintain a vast and gradually increasing population, it is because it has been the centre of a splendid Empire and a converging trade. If you once allow our Imperial strength to fall, if you once allow our Imperial fabric to be shattered, you proclaim it to the world that it is possible for importunity, for agitation, and unscrupulous conspiracy, to wring from you that unity which is your strength. Then, depend upon it, you Imperial power will vanish like a dream; in every part of the world your weakness will be known, your great dependencies on which your strength rests will learn the lesson that is taught them, and you will be left to meditate in fear, in affliction, in destitution, and under the loss of all the commercial and economic advantages by which this country has been distinguished, on the folly of neglecting the truth that commercial greatness depends on Imperial strength.[37]

It was the opportunity which defence of the Union gave Salisbury to interweave this variety of concerns which made him a dedicated Unionist. When Gladstone launched his crusade to gratify Ireland's just aspirations, Salisbury unfolded a counter-crusade to uphold the Union. But Salisbury's crusade did not reach down, as Gladstone's did, to the roots of his political concern. As indicated by his behaviour in 1885 and less clearly in 1886, Ireland was subordinate in Salisbury's mind to his concern about domestic English politics, to his primal fear that popular government would disintegrate the fabric of English society.

The common emotional bond between Salisbury and the support which he evoked against Home Rule was fear. Both responded to their fear with a proud assertion of strength, whether expressed with restraint as Salisbury usually did or aggressively as in the music halls. Whereas Gladstone placed the blame for Ireland's discontent on Britain's history of brutality, Salisbury placed it on Britain's history of vacillation.[38] Where Gladstone preached charity, Salisbury preached unflinching firmness: and the moral tide in Britain was with him. He insisted. 'Our national fault is that too much softness has crept into our councils';[39] and whenever he made the point, he met with loud cheers. The opposition to

Home Rule reflected and in turn contributed to a hardening during the last third of the nineteenth century in Britain's moral culture.

This moral deterioration affected Salisbury mainly in his fight against Home Rule, though it became evident later over the Boer War. The Conservative policy of a stiff maintenance of law and order in Ireland coupled eventually with generous economic amelioration bore Salisbury's stamp as much as Balfour's. Salisbury bolstered Balfour, not just with general support, but with close consultation and detailed advice. Just as Balfour responded to the killing of Nationalist demonstrators by police at Mitchelstown after the enactment of the coercion Bill with a quick expression of support for the police, so Salisbury responded to the coroner's decision that the police were to blame by urging Balfour to consider legislation reforming the appointment of coroners.[40] Balfour responded to the need to alleviate Ireland's economic distress more wholeheartedly than his uncle. But Salisbury grasped the point; and he preserved the Ashbourne Act, which Balfour jealously wished to replace with a dauntingly complicated one of his own devising.

The particular subject over which Salisbury's judgement deserted him was *The Times'* charge that Parnell had approved the use of violent intimidation in Ireland, and specifically had condoned the 1882 murder of T. H. Burke in Phoenix Park. The foundation for the charges was provided by none too cleverly forged letters which, with a readiness bred of hatred, *The Times* accepted as genuine. *The Times* publicised the letters through a series of articles on 'Parnellism and Crime'. Timed to coincide with the introduction of the coercion Bill, the articles served the Government's purposes in Parliament well. Assembled and distributed in pamphlet form, the articles also made effective electoral propaganda. The Government could have profited from the accusations without identifying itself with them; and a careful approach of this sort recommended itself to Balfour, Smith, Cranbrook and Hartington.[41]

Salisbury, however, embraced the charges as readily as *The Times*. Instantly and publicly, he referred to 'gentlemen who intimately knew Mr. Parnell [and] murdered Mr. Burke', and he asked

> What do you think will be the position of Mr. Gladstone going to the country when the electors have thoroughly realized that he accepts in political brotherhood men upon whom the presumption of conniving at assassination rests. . . .?[42]

With similar relish, he relayed the latest dark rumours about Parnell to the Queen.[43] The Cabinet decided to offer Parnell a commission of investigation whose mandate would extend to the illegal activities of the Nationalist leadership generally, but they were uncertain whether to insist upon such a commission if Parnell hesitated to accept it as a way to

exonerate himself. Salisbury induced them to stick to their guns.[44] He
sanctioned circumspect cooperation by the Irish administration with
*The Times*' efforts to substantiate its charges.[45] He overrode the scruples
of the Attorney General, Sir Richard Webster, about representing *The
Times* before the commission. Salisbury's temper on the subject was
reflected in a letter to Smith:

> I have a strong disinclination to be shouted down in this matter. According to
> existing practice the L[aw]O[fficers] have a clear right to take briefs in cases of this
> kind: & it seems very hard to debar The Times from obtaining the highest
> assistance—when the other side will undoubtedly have the highest assistance the
> Radical bar can offer.[46]

After the forgeries were exposed and *The Times* lay under a heavy cloud,
Salisbury whose instinct to defend friends and defy foes was always
quickened by adversity, wanted the Government to defray *The Times*'
legal costs;[47] but he was overruled by the Cabinet.

Responsibility for the discredit which implication in *The Times*' attack
upon Parnell brought upon the Government rested squarely on
Salisbury's shoulders, though his perpetual cloak of distance disguised
the fact. The load was heavy. The affair remained in the news for a year
after the forgeries' exposure, until the spring of 1890 when the
commissioners delivered their report. The Government then moved in
the Commons to receive the report and thank the commissioners for
their efforts. So uneasy were many Conservatives and Liberal Unionists
at the Government's behaviour that an amendment condemning *The
Times* might have carried. The debate circled dangerously close to
Salisbury, dwelling on the negotiations between Conservative leaders
and Parnell in the summer of 1885. Ironically, Lord Randolph
Churchill saved Salisbury. First, Churchill undermined support for the
one amendment which enjoyed considerable Conservative-Liberal
Unionist support—and, in doing so, alienated his last Conservative ally
in the Commons, Louis Jennings, the amendment's sponsor. Then
Churchill hissed his frustrated fury at the Government front bench in
words which shocked and repelled the Commons.[48] Though the
Government was thus spared from a humiliating rebuff, its grip over
Parliament weakened, and by summer came close to dissolving. If
Parnell had not been discredited by the scandal of the O'Shea divorce
later that year, Home Rule might well have come to pass.

### b. The rights of property

In the field of social legislation, except for housing, Salisbury was a
coordinator of partisan pressures and a critic, not an initiator. His
personal characteristics, convictions and talents conspired to deaden

interest in measures of social betterment. He was not socially insensitive so much as psychologically oversensitive. All too familiar with internal torment, he held a low estimate of the capacity of external rearrangements to increase happiness. Religion reinforced this inclination. The impact of Christianity upon him was socially enervating; the consolations of which man stood in urgent need were spiritual.

He found consolation in his family as well as from his faith. He could not be totally unaware of the material prerequisites of family life; and it is not entirely surprising that a man who retreated nightly to his own home should have been concerned about the housing of others. He was personally responsible for the Act of 1890, which empowered the newly created London County Council to enter into the house building business. However he conceived of the measure, it has entered the history books as the reverse of what he usually stood for—'a victory for the radical centralizing party which looked to the state and the municipality for help rather than for reactionary believers in self-help and the multiplicity of tiny independent local authorities.'⁴⁹

His interest in urban housing did not, however, affect the main body of his social policy. He was a firm though undogmatic devotee of *laissez-faire*. The classical economists' critique of the consequences of governmental tampering with the economy appealed to the cynic in him, and was reinforced by his veneration for the prerogatives of property. With his customary lucidity, he stated the common apologia for non-intervention in a speech delivered, appropriately, to the Associated Chambers of Commerce:

> Parliament is a potent engine, and its enactments almost always do something, but they very seldom do what the originators of these enactments meant. (Laughter.) The result, to use a technical phrase, is the resultant of composition of two forces, and the two forces are the enacting force of Parliament and the evading force of the individual. (Laughter.) If the enactment squares with the public interest and is agreeable to the public conscience, it will be carried out; if it has been adopted as the result of agitation, or at the bidding of a class, if it overrides the rights of minorities and tramples on the principles which the conscience of the nation approves, that Act of Parliament will have no effect in obtaining the objects for which it was made, but it will have an effect in surrounding the industry which it touches with precautions and investigations, inspection and regulations, in which it will be slowly enveloped and stifled.⁵⁰

He demonstrated his commitment to this philosophy on repeated occasions, but never more conspicuously than in 1887 on the subject of garden allotments for agricultural labourers. By everyone's calculation, the creation of garden allotments would be a national blessing. The fresh fruit and vegetables they produced would raise the income and improve the health of those who grew them. Allotments would also turn the rural proletariat into little yeomen farmers, and thus do on a small scale for England what tenant purchase was meant to do for Ireland. The canker was compulsion: provision for compulsory purchase of land for allotments where landowners were unwilling to reach voluntary arrangements. Radicals insisted upon compulsion as a hammer to beat the class enemy. But some Conservatives also insisted upon it, partly on the grounds that enough land to meet the need would not become otherwise available, partly as an earnest of their determination. Those like Henry Chaplin, a much loved squire and M.P. for the Sleaford division of Lincolnshire, who depended on the votes of agricultural labourers for electoral survival, pressed for the concession almost desperately. The subject gained prominence during the first months of Salisbury's second Ministry, and produced a tremor in Conservative Parliamentary ranks in the summer of 1887, at the very time that the survival of the Government was in doubt over the Irish Land Bill.

Almost alone, Salisbury resisted the pressure for compulsion. By examining the pertinent statistics, he attempted to demonstrate that the demand for allotments was not much greater than the already available supply of land. He argued, in the fashion of classical economists, that interference with landowners' freedom of action would be counter-productive. He pointed out the confiscatory features of compulsory purchase. But the heart of his argument lay deeper. Compulsory purchase for allotments would breach the wall of property rights against which the tide of popular government was pounding.

> Up to this time expropriation has been restricted to cases where it procures some direct benefit for the community, as where land is wanted for public health, or education, or communication, and so forth. Land has never been taken forcibly by Parliament from one individual merely to benefit another individual.[51]

There was an exception to this generalization, the Irish Land Act of 1881, though it dealt with property in the form of rent. With a conspicuous lack of enthusiasm but under pressure from his Unionist allies, Salisbury extended the principles of that Act in the Irish Land Bill of 1887. However much he disliked them, Salisbury could respect Liberal pressures from Liberal Unionists. To Conservatives who placed similar pressures upon him, he responded indignantly. He pinned on them

> the discredit of having adopted for electoral purposes a proposal, which is inconsistent with the rights of property as hitherto understood, and which some twelve months ago we were vehemently denouncing.

Contemptuously he drew the conclusion that,

> The extension to any class of men of the benefits of expropriation at their neighbour's expense will depend solely upon the possession of sufficient electoral power to disquiet a certain number of Conservative Members.

He found little support, however, even from Smith and Balfour. The pressure with which he had to contend grew intense in July 1887, when the Conservatives lost a by-election at Spaulding on Chaplin's doorstep in Lincolnshire. Salisbury's position was compromised at the same time by his decision to accept Chamberlain's amendments to the Irish Land Bill. Still he would not give in gracefully. He made the Cabinet and the backbenches uncomfortably aware of the strength of his convictions. 'Our men', pleaded Smith, 'are quite prepared to stand or fall with you. They are absolutely loyal as a body—but they would consider that a fall just now on this question would be disastrous in the present condition of affairs in England—and especially in Ireland.'[52]

At last, near the end of the session, Salisbury gave way. An allotments Bill was enacted with a compulsory clause. But the clause was safeguarded into innocuousness. Even so, Salisbury continued privately to dispute its necessity.[53] He had the satisfaction, over the next decade, of witnessing the lack of use made of this and subsequent measures, not for want of effectual compulsion, but because they were counteracted by deepening agricultural depression and outshone by the lights of the cities to which farm hands continued to migrate.[54]

Salisbury seldom resisted pressure within the Conservative party in so out-spoken and tenacious a fashion. He seldom needed to. It was not just because of him that during the 1880s the Conservative party became less elastic in social policy. Those who had imbibed the pure gospel of Disraeli had never been numerous. By the 1880s they were, like Lord Cranbrook and Lord John Manners, old, more inhibited by apprehension than invigorated by their dead leader's vision. Manners more than shared Salisbury's uneasiness about allotments. Cranbrook could still expound Disraeli's teaching. On the subject of local government, for example, he commented that, 'if representative institutions are needed we must face the full effect and I believe that guards & fences will fall.'[55] But he had always been an orator rather than a legislator; and the last years of his career were consumed in an anomalous fight with Salisbury over education. Disraeli's legacy to his party in the sphere of social reform deteriorated into complacent self-congratulation on the superiority of its record.

A loss of elasticity in social policy was the price the Conservative party had to pay for the consolidation of the propertied middle class within its ranks. In order to hold industrialists, merchants and bankers with themselves in a firm marriage, landed gentlemen had to foreswear their former flirtations with urban working men. Salisbury's role was merely to honour this marital understanding; and he did so readily, because the affair had disgusted him.

The initiative within the Conservative party for social reform came, not from scions of the aristocracy, landed gentlemen and country parsons as in the 1840s, but from capable administrators with a background in business, above all from C. T. Ritchie. Ritchie, after

sixteen years in his father's firm of East India merchants, entered
Parliament in 1874 as M.P. for the Tower Hamlets. He served in all of
Salisbury's Governments at a succession of posts, mainly domestic,
particularly the Local Government Board in the second Ministry, the
Board of Trade in the third, and the Home Office in the fourth. From the
early years of the second Ministry, he established himself as the staple
domestic legislator of the Conservative party. At each of his posts, he
sponsored a run of Bills, many of them conspicuous in the record of the
Ministry during which they were enacted, all of them solid.

Salisbury had come during the early 1880s to appreciate the importance
for the Conservative party of the kind of men Ritchie represented. Often
civic leaders, and concerned to extend popular agencies of civic improvement to the countryside, they wanted a thorough, nation-wide reform of
local government. Initially Salisbury had responded to the subject as a
rural landowner, with crippling precautions. But by 1884 his stance had
changed. His language about reform of local government was ringing
enough to excite mayors and town clerks.[56] Still, he presented the
demand in a way intended to reduce the hostility of the gentlemen
magistrates upon whose shoulders the responsibility for county government had hitherto rested. He talked of reformed local government not as
a democratizing measure, still less in the interests of collectivist social
action, but as a base for resisting the drift toward centralized government. 'The object of local government', he told the National Union,

> is to diminish central government. The object of local government is to place in
> the hands of the people of the locality the power hitherto exercised by
> departments in London . . . I hope there will be abundant elements of free
> election, but I do not consider that the important point.[57]

The restraint of the 1888 Local Government bill[58]—which Ritchie
piloted through the Commons—was as evident as its concession to the
demand for reform. The trouble it encountered within the Conservative
Parliamentary party came from what Salisbury called 'the left wing',
from friends of Churchill such as George Curzon and L. J. Jennings who
were ready to vote for Gladstonian amendmends removing restrictive
clauses. After two such defeats, rendered more ominous by by-election
losses at Ayr and Southampton, Salisbury summoned a meeting of the
party in the Commons to upbraid his 'left wing'. He warned them that if
they did not mend their ways 'it might be necessary for the Government
to . . . meet the difficulty by proposing only the mildest and most
unobjectionable form of legislation to Parliament.'[59] He was less afraid
of Tory Democrats than of 'the right wing',[60] in particular over local
government the country gentlemen. Soon after the Bill was introduced
in the Commons, he had commented to his secretary: 'I am afraid that
the squires are feeling nothing at all about it just at present, and that
very few of them will be conscious of any feeling on the subject at all for

the next two or three months; and then a sense of their unutterable wrongs will suddenly burst upon them, to our great embarrassment.'[61]

Salisbury rarely adopted one side in intra-party disputes as his own. He discussed them with his colleagues with seeming objectivity in terms of the Parliamentary and electoral weight of each side. However, his assessment commonly favoured the right wing, whether urban rate-payers or country gentry. He had little patience with the 'class of measures known from a celebrated instance as aiming at the result of "dishing the Whigs". . . the danger of such measures . . . is the risk of alienating old friends without conciliating any new adherents.'[62] 'Old friends' would not, of course, vote Liberal. But by staying at home during critical Parliamentary divisions or at election time, their disenchantment could be lethal. Salisbury had held this view in mid-century, when it had been impolitic. He adhered to it in the 1880s, when it began to coincide with Parliamentary realities.

Outside Wales the first set of elections for the new county councils went tolerably well from the standpoint of the owners of land. Those peers and country gentlemen who had served their counties conscientiously under the old dispensation and agreed to stand for election under the new, fared well. Justices of the peace made up just under half of the elected councillors, and more than half of the aldermen who were then coopted.[63] Still, the dismantling of the old order disturbed staid squires. Salisbury was not easy about his Government's handiwork. He argued that since previous governments had reduced to a mere shadow the powers that county magistrates had once exercised, the 1888 Act deprived them of extremely little, just the supervision of bridge repair.[64] But the argument convinced neither them nor himself.

The one irredeemable abomination, as Salisbury saw it, which the Act engendered was the London County Council. At Goschen's insistence, the Act applied to the metropolis. Salisbury soon regretted this extension as an accident which violated the main principle of the Act. He intended it as a decentralizing measure, and, outside London, it tended to that end. But as soon as the Liberals, under the guise of 'Progressives', won the first set of elections to the London County Council, it emerged as the focus of a new power concentration. Furthermore, Conservative or 'Moderate' councillors, undisciplined by the Gladstonian tradition of economy, acted with even greater financial profligacy than Liberals. Salisbury reacted by counselling his lieutenants to have nothing to do with the L.C.C. When Cadogan, one of the abler men on the Government's front bench in the Lords, asked his blessing for a campaign to win the chairmanship of the Council, Salisbury vigorously dissuaded him from running.[65] Lord Onslow, who ran in Cadogan's place, received meagre recompense after Salisbury returned to power in 1895.[66]

The London County Council became the *bête noire* of affluent metropolitan ratepayers. One of their representatives, George Bartley, M.P. for Islington North, wrote to Salisbury in 1891, inveighing against Ritchie over a Public Health Bill 'empowering the London County Council (that dreadful body) to ride roughshod over the Local Sanitary authority, creating armies of inspectors under the London County Council, setting free the common informer to aid the London County Council &c. &c.'[67] Salisbury forwarded the letter to Ritchie, who replied in kind: 'Bartley's letter is worthy of him. He is a good type of a pig headed, obstinate, unreasonable and most conceited politician.'[68] Pig-headed or not, Bartley reflected the opinion of a body of men whose energetic support Salisbury thought the Conservative party needed and whose predilections for small government he shared. The diet of legislation which Ritchie induced the Parliamentary party to swallow gave the Government a tolerably creditable record of accomplishment, but did not win party stalwarts' affection.[69]

As the time for a general election drew near, Salisbury intensified his efforts to minimize the measures or features of measures on the Government's agenda which disturbed the Tory faithful in rural or suburban constituencies. Their discontent was not a figment of his imagination. On the eve of the election, 'A Plain Tory' published a sharp attack on the policy of the Ministry, under the title of *Tory Democracy and Conservative Policy*. The author took up ground which Salisbury had held before his alliance with the Liberal Unionists. It was better, the 'Plain Tory' argued, for the Conservatives to be a minority party, resolutely upholding the principles and property rights in which they believed, than to submerge those principles in order to form a broad alliance:

> we are content to talk complacently about Lord Salisbury's 'strong Conservative Government', wholly ignoring the truth that it is strong, that it has a large majority, simply because it is *not* Conservative. Indeed, as things go at present, all strong Governments by whatever political label they may choose to be known, must be socialistic, must be against property, since large majorities are only to be obtained by bribery, and as bribes cannot yet be evolved from the ether of space, they must be extracted from the pockets of the wealthy. Wherefore all those who have no taste for being robbed must desire weak Governments which are less bepledged to confiscation and less powerful to affect it.[70]

The author then drove his point into Salisbury's breast:

> For this state of apathy and incapacity history will hold the spirit-of-the-time-serving marquis, the present Prime Minister, very largely responsible. Scientific opportunist as he is, he is quite unequal to the gigantic task of leading the Conservative forces of the country against the surging masses of Democracy . . . . He has led the Tory party in more than one memorable retreat, and a lengthened experience has taught him now to defy the enemy and avoid defeat by a dignified retrogression in slow time . . . . What Tolstoi tells us of armies is, of course equally true of political parties—the side which most strenuously believes in itself is the

side which conquers. Lord Salisbury is not at all the man to inspire this victorious self-confidence; his solid sentences and well-balanced flouts and jibes, his solemn strategy may discredit the enemy to some extent, but will never instill into his followers that desperate self-belief—the sure presage and token of victory.[71]

It was an incisive indictment. Written from a standpoint which he himself had shared and with his own pungency, it possessed the cruel insight of an alienated friend.

### c. The interests of the Established Church

The same personal characteristics that reduced Salisbury's concern for social reform heightened his concern for the Church of England. Through the Church he found most of what inner peace he knew. To measure the workings of religious faith on any man, let alone on one who was deeply reserved on the subject, is impossible: but the worship which formed part of the regular round at Hatfield bore its testimony about a man otherwise impatient of forms and ceremonies.

Far from being a separate compartment, his faith was of a piece with his general world view. He adhered to the teaching of the Oxford Movement because it swam against the popular tide and championed 'the Church of 18 centuries'[72] against the attempt to adapt theology to current intellectual predilections. He valued the Established Church for its effect on England's political culture: 'there is', he had written, 'no more formidable obstacle than the Established Church to the spirit of rash and theoretic change which we, almost alone among nations, have escaped. Her atmosphere is poison to the revolutionary growths that flourish so rankly in other lands.'[73] He linked the Liberal party with the anti-clerical parties on the Continent.[74]

Salisbury appreciated the reality of religious pluralism. In making Henry Matthews Home Secretary, he introduced the first Roman Catholic into a British Cabinet since the reign of James II. He did not couch his recommendations on the State's ecclesiastical policy in the language of a believer. Just as he handled questions of domestic reform in terms of the weight of interests on one side and the other, so he dealt with ecclesiastical issues as 'a balance of expediencies'.[75] But only the forms of his deliberation were neutral, not the substance. Just as he usually adjudged the weight on domestic reform to fall on the side of the propertied classes, so on ecclesiastical issues he usually reached the conclusion that the 'balance of expediencies' favoured action beneficial to the Church.

In neither case was his prejudice political folly. No commitment was more forceful in shaping the Conservative identity than commitment to the Established Church. The interests of property, which drew country gentry and city businessmen and suburbanities to the Conservative party, could also lead them to quarrel. But, with few exceptions such as the Ulster Presbyterians, all groups of Conservatives, urban as well as rural, Scottish as well as English, were loyal to their respective Established Churches. The ecclesiastical conflicts among English Conservatives were as adherents of rival traditions within the Established Church; and in the 1880s, after a searing experience in the previous decade,[76] these rivalries were not aggressively asserted. The active suburban Conservative was, if anything, more likely than his rural counterpart to be active in the affairs of his Church. His involve- ment in parochial or diocesan organizations often preceded his involve- ment in the affairs of the party. The clergy, for their part, rallied more than ever to the Conservative side. The Liberation Society's campaign for disestablishment reached its peak between the general elections of 1880 and 1885, all but capturing the Liberal party, with the result that Anglican clergy who supported the Liberals all but disappeared. In many parishes, the Conservative agent had no more resourceful ally than the local parson.

Virtually universal though commitment to the Established Church was among them, Conservatives were not unanimously enthusiastic about allowing it to fashion their political course of action. Religious neutrality was injected into the Conservative party, not by internal pluralism, but by the difficulties involved in legislative reform of the Church, and by the press of other business. Remembering the ill-fated Public Worship Regulation Act passed in 1874 under a Conservative Government, Churchill objected to a list of items of ecclesiastical legislation which Salisbury proposed at the end of 1885:

> Church reform which is the product of a Cabinet checked and controlled by party Whips and guided by House of Commons lobbies [Churchill wrote] is surely in its nature a monstrosity, possibly a profanity, certainly a farce.[77]

The 1887 conference of the National Union of Conservative Associations accepted a resolution calling for cooperation with the bishops to secure the legislation they wanted to reform the Church's administration; but the debate was perfunctory, and the resolution passed without enthusiasm.[78] Balfour wanted Salisbury in 1892 to give an India Councils Bill priority over a Clergy Discipline Bill[79] which the bishops and the Government had been trying to push through Parliament for five years.

Conservatives' lack of zeal for ecclesiastical legislation was reinforced by the Unionist alliance. Defence of the Established Church in Scotland was the backbone of Liberal Unionism there. South of the border, the situation was different. Though Hartington's contingent in the Commons was Anglican almost to a man, the churchmanship of most of them was of the tepid, Whig variety.[80] Chamberlain and the Radical Unionists had been active supporters of the Liberation Society, and some of their key supporters were Nonconformist ministers. Liberal Unionists of both sorts, accordingly, increased the weight of considerations tending toward an inactive ecclesiastical policy. These considerations also affected Conservative M.P.s whose seats depended upon the votes of Nonconformist Unionists.

Salisbury recognized with sadness that 'the Church is very weak with the present Conservative party'.[81] Throughout the nineteenth century the benefit which the Established Church derived from its association with Conservatives came, not from the party collectively, but from individual leaders, Sir Robert Peel in the 1830s and '40s, Sir Richard Cross in the '70s. Salisbury stepped into these men's shoes. In doing so he retarded the religious neutralization of the party: and delay was a gain he never scorned. The successive Conservative leaders in the Commons—Smith and Balfour as well as Churchill—were uneasy about his policy. Salisbury held his ground, and in doing so enhanced his party's otherwise hard visage as the party of property.

Each year during his second Ministry, he contributed ecclesiastical legislation to the Government's Parliamentary plans. His proposals fell into three categories: administrative reforms, attempts to settle the controversy over payment of tithes, and protection of denominational education. He cooperated with the Archbishop of Canterbury in pursuit of legislation to rid the Church of scandals connected with the exercise of private patronage and to set up more expeditious processes for removing criminous clergy. The difficulty with Bills of this sort was that, while not momentous enough to be placed at the head of the Government's agenda, they were quite controversial enough, whether to vested interests or to Nonconformist M.P.s, that they could not be dealt with in the spare moments of a congested timetable. The difficulty was compounded by the Archbishop of Canterbury, Benson, who had no gift for Parliamentary work. Measures which he drafted were internally inconsistent, offensive where they needed to be conciliatory, or created cumbersome machinery. When the Government proved unable to enact what had been agreed with him, he responded with petulance. The prime minister did not hesitate to knock the archbishop's proposals into shape. However much Salisbury appreciated the electoral influence of the clergy at large, he had a low opinion of their practical judgement.

The high order of priority which Salisbury assigned to protection of the Church, and the extreme difficulty of honouring that priority, were evident in his campaign to remove the most irritating features in the payment and collection of tithes. Tithes were a charge, attached by ancient legal custom to a large proportion of the landholdings of England and Wales, of roughly ten percent of the landholdings' annual worth, payable to the owners of benefices, who were commonly the local parsons. An unpopular charge, it was doubly so among Nonconformist tithepayers, and its unpopularity redoubled in the 1880s under the impact of agricultural depression. Still, the charge would not have become the focus of controversy but for two features in connection with payment. In the first place, legally the landowner was responsible for payment, but, by common custom, responsibility devolved upon tenant farmers as an addition to their rent. Secondly, the only process by which the titheowner could enforce his right was by physically distraining the property of the tithepayer. The spectacle of an Anglican parson carrying off the goods of a poor tenant farmer was too much, particularly for Nonconformist Wales. Rioting erupted; and in the winter of 1887-8 the Hussars had to be sent in.

Even before the violence reached this pitch Salisbury introduced remedial legislation. Its object, as he later explained, was 'to make the means of enforcing [the obligation to pay the tithe] as little injurious to the peace and harmony of the parish and the effectiveness of the clergyman's administration as we can'.[82] The Tithe Rent-Charge Bill of 1887 would have replaced direct distraint of possessions with action through county court. He ran quickly into resistance from landowners, not so much in the Lords as in the Commons, spearheaded by Sir Walter Barttelot, Member for the North-west division of Sussex. Their motive was economic interest, unalleviated by love for the Church. If, as the measure also provided, they were to relieve their tenants of effective responsibility for payment of tithes, they insisted that assessment of tithes be revised more frequently and hence lowered. Salisbury tried privately to warn them that downward revision of one kind of property right would set a dangerous precedent, but they were unmoved.

At the same time other clauses in the measure, those designed either to win landowners' acceptance or to reduce the size of the problem by encouraging tithepayers to buy themselves free of their obligation, drew a crossfire from the clergy. They received sharp support from doctrinaire defenders of the rights of property, led by a law lord, Lord Bramwell. This clash of interests among Lord Salisbury's customary supporters became further complicated, as the time for a general election drew near, by Conservative M.P.s for county constituencies who feared that tenant farmers would vote Liberal unless the burden of tithes was eased.

No better paradigm of legislative initiatives' consequences, as Salisbury usually saw them, could have been devised. He forged on, believing that the dividends from protecting the income and local reputation of the clergy were higher than the cost from landowners' annoyance. For four successive years he pressed tithes Bills on an apprehensive Cabinet and a reluctant, quarrelsome House of Commons, each time encountering failure to his deepening anger. The collapse of Parliamentary obstruction in the wake of the O'Shea divorce case at last gave Salisbury his reward, and in 1891 a Tithe Rent-charge Recovery Bill was enacted.

Conventionally, of all classes of Conservatives, the squires were supposed to be heartiest in their loyalty to the Established Church. But when that loyalty was tested economically over tithes, it proved to be less robust than the loyalty of the middle-class income tax payers when they were similarly tested over free education. Apologists for the squirearchy could plead the depression in agriculture, much more acute than in the urban economy. Even so, at least among the last generation of Victorians, the effective base of the identity between the Church of England and the Conservative party had moved from the countryside to the suburbs.

The subject of elementary education roused Salisbury to a height of enterprise.[83] What were known as the 'voluntary' or denominational schools, most of them run under the Church of England's auspices, still handled more than half of the elementary school children in England and Wales. Their religious significance was clear: only in these schools could denominational religious instruction be given. Politically their impact was not so obvious, but, as friend and foe sensed, it was great. Recent statistical analysis indicates that the Conservative vote in the elections of 1886 and 1895 bore a close relation to the proportion of enrollment in denominational schools.[84] At the same time the prospects for their financial survival were being undermined by the Education Department, and Liberals sought to undermine the denominational integrity of their religious instruction.

The predilections and proposals of the Education Department were shaped by social needs rather than by religious loyalties. The Department's staff wished to improve the quality of elementary schooling by steadily raising the requirements for receipt of financial support from the central government. Though not avowedly hostile to denominational schooling, they were not deflected from their policy by the knowledge that denominational schools, which were ineligible for support from the local rates, were going to the wall. The Department succeeded in imposing its conclusions upon its current overseer in the Cabinet, the Lord President of the Council, Cranbrook. Once an ardent high church Tory, but less interested in politics since Disraeli chose Northcote rather than him to lead in the Commons, and now addicted to hearth and home, Cranbrook was no longer alert and had lost his fighting nerve. 'The fact is', he observed after two years as Lord President, 'that things go in the Educ: Dept. without reference to the Chief until things are in such a condition that he is almost bound to follow the lead indicated.'[85]

Salisbury in 1888 sensed the Department's capture of Cranbrook, and immediately moved in effect to supersede him as the political moulder of educational policy. He obliged Cranbrook to revise a Technical Educational Bill, and was not satisfied when he did so: for the Bill still gave new power and income to the locally elected school boards which

ran the expanding network of civic schools. Salisbury looked upon
school boards as 'the natural enemy of the voluntary schools' and 'the
most recklessly extravagant bodies in England'.[86] This minor skirmish
was followed by a major battle, over a more demanding code which the
Education Department put forward to govern allocation of money from
Westminster to elementary schools regardless of type. Spokesmen for
denominational schools among the clergy and in both Houses of
Parliament cried ruin. Salisbury induced Cranbrook and the
Department to withdraw the code for reconsideration. An altered code
was introduced, with easier requirements and improved financial
provisions to allay denominationalists' fears. The revised code was
quickly accepted, but as a thumb in the dyke.

The denominational schools won a longer lease of financial life from
another, much bolder action which Salisbury took between the withdrawal of the first code and the acceptance of its revised replacement. In
a speech at Nottingham toward the end of 1888, he advocated a close
approximation to free, or what he preferred to call 'assisted', elementary education. His action took everyone by surprise. The Education
Department had been opposed to free education. Among Conservatives
there was virtually no pressure for and some outspoken opposition to it.
Though Chamberlain advocated it, it was one among several items high
in his current programme. Though pleased, he was almost as surprised
as Cranbrook. Chamberlain facilitated but did not stimulate Salisbury's
action.

What precipitated it was the Liberal party's movement in favour of
tax support for all elementary schools, including denominational ones,
but strictly on condition that denominational schools be subjected to
supervision by elected representatives from the locality. This requirement might lead to interference with the denominational character of
their teaching. The requirement was dear to the hearts of the Liberal
party's Nonconformist regiments, but was not otherwise in popular
demand. Free education would sugar the pill. Salisbury countered by
proposing to hand out the sugar without the pill, or, rather, to sweeten
his own pill. Denominational schools relied on fees in lieu of support
from the rates, for which only board schools were eligible. By using
national tax revenues to replace the income from fees, he could establish
something like free elementary education and at the same time place the
denominational schools on a firmer financial footing than they had had
for a decade. By doing so before he had to call a general election, he
would make it virtually impossible for the Liberals, who might then
form a Government, to impose popular control upon denominational
schools.

Free education had been a distinctively Radical policy. Salisbury's
talk of assisted education struck some Conservatives as an abandonment

of party principle. There was, however, a clearly Conservative logic to it. The rupture with the past, so Salisbury explained to Cranbrook, had taken place in 1876, when the Government made attendance at elementary school compulsory. Since that time, the poor had had a just grievance against the State, for the obligation to send children to school was not a natural duty of parents, like feeding children, but 'an artificial duty invented within the last sixty years'.[87] 1876 was to elementary education what 1867 was to the franchise: it inaugurated an irrevocably new order of things. Thereafter, Conservative statesmen were obliged to respond to the new order, not in the vain hope of restoring the old, but in such a way as to protect the interests committed to their charge. Usually Salisbury's concern with the logical implications of a reform, for instance of Gladstone's 1881 Irish Land Act, made him slow to accept further steps in the same direction. Very occasionally, as over the third Reform Bill and now over free education, this concern released rather than inhibited him.

His proposal at Nottingham was too startling for the Cabinet to settle on a Bill for the ensuing session of Parliament. Once the Education Department took hold of the proposal, they turned it into a draft Bill divest of the limitations which distinguished 'assisted' from totally free education. Much worse, the Department's draft provided for popular control of denominational schools. In the next year, 1891, the introduction of a Bill was held up until June, more than half way through the Parliamentary session, while Salisbury trimmed it of provisions he could not accept.

The principle of the Bill, even in trimmed form, did not pass unchallenged. Ten Conservatives divided the House of Commons against its second reading. They challenged Salisbury's contention that the Bill would strengthen the denominational schools' economic position. But their motivating concern was taxation. The budgetary surpluses which Goschen, assisted by a reviving national economy, had produced each year eliminated any need for an increase in the income tax to pay for free education. But if free education ate up the surplus, taxation might have to be increased prior to the general election likely to be called in 1892. George Bartley thought that any increase in the income tax could cost the Conservatives the election.[88]

The prospect of a general election brought the bulk of the Parliamentary party to the opposite conclusion. W. H. Smith, for one, had doubted the intrinsic merits of free education; but the sombre expectation that the Liberals would probably win the next election and would then grant free education coupled with popular control of denominational schools brought him round to Salisbury's view.[89] Members for rural constituencies, where denominational rather than board schools prevailed, thought that agricultural labourers, whose electoral loyalties were very much in flux, might be won over by free schooling.

The Commons as a whole—Conservatives as well as Liberals—came down in favour of free education even more heavily than Salisbury. The Bill was made more generous, particularly by extending the eligible age limit three years; and the safeguards for denominational schools were indirectly weakened. Cranbrook criticized Smith's willingness to give way before Liberal pressure at the expense of Tory interests, and the House of Lords prepared to restore something of the Bill's original character. But Cranbrook himself, influenced again by his department, was not stiff enough to suit Salisbury, who spoke out sharply at a meeting of the Cabinet.[90] The Cabinet managed to work out an agreement on amendments, which passed the upper House, and in attenuated form were accepted by the lower.

Salisbury's solicitude for the Established Church might well have exacerbated denominational divisions in the political arena. Nonconformists had formed one of the main divisions of the Gladstonian Liberal army. Salisbury regarded that alignment as natural and likely to persist. A rally which Nonconformist supporters of the Union held in London toward the end of 1888,[91] therefore, fascinated him. He kept referring to it in public for some months afterward as a remarkable phenomenon. His assumptions about the correspondence between denominational and political loyalties had blinded him till then to one of the consequences of Home Rule. Once Gladstone espoused Home Rule, the resolutions for example of the annual meetings of the Congregational Union lost their previously Liberal colour. Coercion might be condemned, but Home Rule was not endorsed.[92] To cite a more illustrious example, R. W. Dale, the Birmingham Congregationalist minister who had been a moving spirit in the councils of the National Liberal Federation, slipped into paralyzed indecision. The political allegiance of Nonconformists became enfeebled and perhaps even transferable.

In the wake of the O'Shea divorce scandal at the end of 1890, Salisbury bid directly for Nonconformist support. Parnell's adultery with Mrs. O'Shea shocked the Nonconformist conscience. Furthermore, the close cooperation between the anti-Parnellite majority of the Nationalist party and the Irish Catholic hierarchy aroused Nonconformists' Protestant susceptibilities. Salisbury exploited the latter reaction. In concert with Chamberlain, and with his eye on the impending general election, he warned repeatedly of the sway which the Catholic clergy would hold over Ireland if it received Home Rule. But this electoral tactic did not affect his ecclesiastical policy. As his behaviour after the Liberals won the general election of 1892 and again when he returned to office in 1895 demonstrated, his determination to act in the interests of the Church of England remained strong.

### iii. The Limits of Lord Salisbury's Power:
### The Crisis of 1890

Whether with regard to defence of the Union, to social reform, to the rights of property, or to the interests of the Established Church, the critical arena of battle was the House of Commons. The wishes and comparative strength of the varied interests within the Conservative and Liberal Unionist contingents there helped to determine the complexion of the legislative programme submitted each year by the Government, and more than helped to determine its outcome. The Liberal Opposition adopted a strategy of wearing the strength of the Ministerial bench and the spirits of the Conservative and Union backbenches down to the point at which they would resort to a general election. Salisbury, in a rare flourish of speech, described the struggle as 'between those who are able to talk and those who are able to endure; and those will win who can sit the longest listening to the dreary drip of dilatory declamation'.[93] Despite further tightening of the Commons' procedure, the talkers fared better than the endurers. The energies of Ministers in the Commons flagged under the double load of administration and debate. The spirits of their supporters drooped under the burden of responsibility, and could not be revived by unrestricted gratification of their prejudices. The Opposition flourished, increasingly confident that the Government had exhausted its popular mandate. The one ray of hope which Salisbury discerned was his Liberal counterpart's age and health. 'The life of the Ministry and the life of [Gladstone] are both ebbing', he observed to a confidante: '—the question is which will ebb the fastest.'[94]

The enervation of the Ministry by the end of 1889 was clear to many, including Churchill. 'The question now', he told Hicks Beach, 'is does Lord S intend to commence another session with WHS [mith] as leader of the H of C. If he does, why then, smash!'[95] It is impossible to know whether, if Smith had been in as good health in 1890 as in 1887, the success of his leadership could have been sustained. The fact was that he had been stricken with debilitating eczema. Weighed down by his duty to the Commons, never by temperament a fighter, and now physically enfeebled, Smith was more and more inclined to give way to the mood of the House and to reach accommodations with the Opposition front bench. The critical weakness of the Ministry was its lack of a leader in the Commons who had mastered the art of facilitating legislation, had command of each subject up for debate, and could keep his supporters in good heart. Someone was needed who could assess and impose his assessment of how much and what kind of legislation M.P.s, particularly those on his own side, could stomach. Events in 1890 were to prove that, because of different disabilities, neither Smith nor Salisbury could meet this need.

Sir William Harcourt, Gladstone's chief lieutenant in the Commons, demonstrated the ineptitude of the Treasury bench in 1889 by running circles around it over that year's Tithes Bill. It had been placed in the charge of the Home Secretary, Matthews, and the Attorney General, Webster, who, as Harcourt gloated, did not 'know the difference between a turnip and a cabbage, and hardly distinguish between a parson, a squire and a farmer'.[96] Smith contributed to the débâcle by oscillating on amendments, seeking to appease the Opposition but managing only to dishearten his own men. Salisbury burned with frustration over his inability to take charge, and he had to be calmed down by the Queen.[97]

Everyone in the Cabinet contributed to the near disaster of 1890. To begin with, the work which they set the Commons to accomplish depressed their supporters. Landowners resented the Tithes Bill which Salisbury had placed high on the agenda. No one loved Balfour's Irish Land Bill, with its eighty clauses that gave the Opposition endless opportunity to talk. The Government's refusal to make amends to Parnell on receipt of the special commission's report[98] brought sensitive Conservatives and Liberal Unionists to the verge of rebellion. Goschen then broke the camel's back by introducing, as part of his budget, a scheme of compensated reduction of licensed beverage outlets, for which the Queen's Speech gave no forewarning. The scheme pleased neither the licensed victuallers nor the temperance advocates, who drowned the Treasury bench with a torrent of petitions.

Smith had a sense of foreboding about the temperance proposals before they were introduced. He urged Goschen to abandon them,[99] but lacked the willpower to insist on his advice. The two men appealed to the prime minister; but because the question was one of tactics in the Commons, Salisbury responded with diffidence. He suggested embodying the licensing scheme in a separate Bill, apart from the budget.[100] Goschen accepted the advice, but it was not enough to avert embarrassment.

The morale of the party in the Commons had already shown signs of impending collapse, and Salisbury had convened a meeting of the Parliamentary party to win support for the Tithes and Irish Land Bills. The rot set in again deeper than ever when Goschen introduced his licensing scheme. The Government's majorities dwindled, not from defections but from abstentions, and threatened to disappear. Salisbury called another meeting of the Parliamentary party. He sympathized with its fatigue, and at the same time was exasperated by the repeated failure of the Tithes Bill and by the threat that the fiasco over Ritchie's temperance scheme of 1888[101] would be repeated. Accordingly, he proposed a radical departure in Parliamentary procedure, whereby Bills could be held over from one session for enactment in the next.[102] The change would have the effect of greatly strengthening the majority in the Commons against obstructive opposition. Incidentally it would have had the further advantage, from Salisbury's viewpoint, of strengthening the House of Lords by enabling it to defer action on Bills which the Commons set up: but on that point he said nothing. He offered the meeting an alternative, an autumn session to complete the year's work; but he argued against it because of the conspicuous toll which prolonged sessions were having upon M.P.s' health.

Decorously, the party mutinied. The proposed change in procedure grated against the traditions and prejudices of the House of Commons. The mutiny was led by an M.P. of peerless respectability, Sir John Mowbray,[103] hitherto a stalwart Conservative loyalist, a revered servant of the House in his capacity as chairman of two standing committees, and soon, by virtue of his years in Parliament, to be Father of the House. Smith's endorsement of the proposal at the meeting had no effect. For the moment he was regarded among Conservatives with much disappointment and some anger,[104] because of his failure to excise the unwelcome features of Goschen's budget, and also because of ill-considered remarks to which his exhaustion was making him prone. Far from reviving the spirits of the Parliamentary party, the meeting left them more depressed than ever. Four days later, taking advantage of the absence of many Tory M.P.s at Ascot, the Opposition forced a vote on one of the licensing clauses of the budget, and reduced the Government's majority to four. Ascot notwithstanding, the vote indicated that the Conservative rank and file in the Commons was losing the will to fight.

The Ascot vote shattered the nerve of the Cabinet in the Commons. The conspicuous dislike among the M.P.s for the licensing scheme, with which Ritchie as well as Goschen was identified, had already induced the two men to tender their resignations to the prime minister.[105] Smith's health was crumbling, and with it his courage. As Balfour sardonically observed: 'all the King's horses and all the King's men won't make Smith cheerful till he has been to a German bath'.[106] Remembering the remarks in times past about his indispensability as a leader, Smith refused rest and stuck doggedly to his bench. But he had lost hope of victory; he looked only for survival. The members of the Cabinet in the Commons, meeting alone, started to throw their legislative cargo overboard, beginning with the licensing scheme. A continuing run of adverse rulings by the Speaker and the Chairman of Committees deepened their demoralisation.

Their reaction was exaggerated, as the Chairman of Committees later commented. 'Considering they have a good majority and are not failing in their main policy of Irish Government, it seems absurd for the Unionist party to succumb like that to what is after all only comparatively a trifling blunder; but', he went on, 'the truth is there is no leader.'[107] This observation was even closer to the truth than he knew. The disintegrating morale of the party in the Commons made Salisbury only the more anxious to fight. He recoiled from lightening the Commons' agenda as a tactic which would further depress the spirits of supporters and embolden the Opposition. He pressed this view upon the Cabinet at a meeting on the 5th of July. The Cabinet disregarded his plea. Deferring to the unanimous advice of its members in the Commons, it threw virtually the entire legislative programme of the Government overboard, postponing the Irish Land and Tithes Bills to an autumn session. Salisbury took the reverse more seriously than his colleagues realized. Though he fought hard during the Cabinet meeting, he did not attempt to reinforce his view by threatening to resign. But he considered the option of resignation carefully, as he explained to the Queen that night:

> The situation is very abnormal, for under ordinary circumstances a Cabinet ought not to continue in office, when so grave a difference of opinion exists between the Prime Minister and his colleagues. But he thinks that great injury would be inflicted not only on the Party but on the Country, if a dissolution were to take place now. For the two years which remain they must get on as well as they can.[108]

This reverse showed Salisbury clearly for the first time the peculiar, inescapable limits on his power as prime minister. The limits were three. In the first place, the decision of 5 July indicated that, on questions involving the conduct of the Government in the House of Commons, the Cabinet would defer to the will of the Ministers in the Commons, if necessary overruling the prime minister in the Lords, even when the Government's credit was at stake, and even when the leader in the Commons possessed little autonomous, personal authority. The popularization of British politics had marked up another advance. As Lord Rosebery was to learn still more painfully, no peer-prime minister, however august or attractive, could any longer control his Government in the Commons.

The second limitation, implied in Salisbury's letter to the Queen, was equally impersonal. The mandate of this Government, as perceived not just by the electorate but more explicitly by the Government and its Parliamentary supporters, was to preserve the Union with Ireland. Salisbury may have espoused the policy of resistance to Home Rule, not so much on its merits as because it helped give effect to his aspirations for Conservative government. Nevertheless, fed by the rhetoric lavished upon it, support for the Union became the all subordinating cause. For Salisbury to precipitate the resignation of the Government and hence a general election on any other issue, at a time when the Opposition were sure to fare well, would be, like Churchill's resignation, apostasy. The Government's mandate denied him that freedom.[109]

The third limitation was entirely personal. It was reflected in Salisbury's comparatively passive acceptance of the other two. He could have imposed himself more forcefully upon the House of Commons, by keeping watch from the peers' gallery and cajoling in the lobbies. The fact that to do so would have been out of character only underscores the point. He could have imposed himself more forcefully upon the Cabinet. It was not until four days after the critical meeting that Goschen, for one, realized how deeply it had disturbed the prime minister.[110] To threaten resignation without meaning it was perhaps unwise, as Churchill had discovered. Still, Salisbury's failure to make his colleagues aware of the intensity of his feeling reflected an inability or—what amounted to the same thing—an unwillingness, to act fully up to the role of leader.

The action of 5 July did not stop the rot in the Commons. On 23 July, again in response to what he took as its mood, Smith foreswore any intention of including questions on religious affiliation in the forthcoming census, questions which the Church of England desired in the belief that they would prove it to be more popular than Nonconformists cared to concede. Salisbury responded by despatching his one thoroughly angry letter to Smith.[111] Next day, whether or not because of this latest evidence of Smith's pusillanimity, the House was 'so demoralised. . .that anything might have happened.'[112]

There was one indignity which Salisbury was able to spare himself: readmission of Churchill to the Cabinet. More than a year earlier, Salisbury had contemplated a reconstruction, elevating Smith to the Lords, Goschen to the leadership of the Commons, and Hamilton to the Exchequer.[113] But he had persistently rejected the notion of bringing Churchill back, even in a minor post. To invite him now would be a confession of failure, without any confidence that the new arrangement would work. Talk of the need for a reconstruction, probably including Hartington as well as Churchill, received the *imprimatur* of *The Times* late in June,[114] and reached epidemic proportions in the lobbies at Westminster during July. Cabinet reconstruction was, however, the prerogative of the prime minister; and Salisbury refused to budge.

The deadly fog of obstruction lifted suddenly and unexpectedly, just before Parliament reconvened on 21 November for its autumn session. Parnell had been cited in the O'Shea divorce case in 1889; but, partly because one of the counsel retained against him was the Conservative Solicitor-General, little heed was paid to the case until November 1890, when it came up for hearing. Parnell's failure then to contest the charge of adultery, and the revelation of details of his liaison with Mrs. O'Shea, including facial disguises and a hurried escape from her bedroom window, eroded his hold upon the leadership of the Irish Nationalist party. By the time Parliament reconvened, Nationalist M.P.s were at each other's throats, debating the leadership in committee room nineteen and hence away from the floor of the Commons. The Liberals were non-plussed by this setback, soon underscored by a turn toward the Conservatives in by-election results. Parnell repudiated his alliance with Gladstone, and took care to demonstrate his independence by voting for the Government's reintroduced Irish Land Bill. Debate on the address from the throne lasted three hours; and the Irish Land and Tithes Bills were read a second time within two weeks.

The lifting of obstruction was not the only dividend of Parnell's discomfiture. It also broke the spirit of resistance in Ireland behind the Plan of Campaign, already enfeebled by Balfour's administration of the Coercion Act.[115] Moreover, the disintegration of the Home Rule alliance between Parnellites and Liberals enabled Salisbury to maintain that it had always been a mismatch, doomed to break up at the first serious test.[116] The contrast between their sharp dispute and the firm cooperation among the Unionist allies under the strains of the previous summmer, even over the temperance scheme,[117] was indeed impressive. As Goschen had put it:

> We have all worked together with such harmony & cordiality for more than two years of great anxiety yet of great success in many ways, that I feel the utmost confidence that we should find common ground on almost every conceivable subject.[118]

The good fortune which the O'Shea divorce brought to the Government disguised the implication of the crisis of mid-1890, turning it seemingly into darkness before a new dawn. At least with regard to Salisbury, the appearance was deceptive. What had begun for him was a long afternoon. His advice had been rejected in June by the Conservative Parliamentary party, and in July by the Cabinet. By indicating the limits of his power, the crisis of 1890 brought the noontime of his primacy to an end. The limits were never spelled out by the rest of the Cabinet. They were not to be demonstrated again until a further six years had passed: Salisbury's inclination was always to avoid confrontations. Still, after July 1890, those limits formed part of the Conservative inner council's experience. They entered the category of unspoken assumptions.

## NOTES

1. Quoted in Arthur Hardinge, *The Life of Henry Howard Molyneux Herbert, Fourth Earl of Carnarvon* (London, 1925), III, p. 235.
2. Lady Gwendolen Cecil, *Life of Salisbury*, III, pp. 340–1.
3. Salisbury to Churchill, 14 January 1887, copy, Salisbury papers.
4. Speech at the inauguration of the National Conservative Club, *The Times*, 7 March 1887, 7b.
5. Northcote's diary for 6 February 1886, in R. R. James, *Lord Randolph Churchill* (New York, 1960), p. 208.

6. Cranbrook to Salisbury, 23 November 1886, copy, Salisbury papers.
7. Holland to Salisbury, 28 December 1886, Salisbury papers.
8. *Hansard*, 3rd ser., CCCLV, 1521–1522 (17 July 1891).
9. Rosebery, *Miscellanies Literary and Historical* (London, 1921), I, p. 267.
10. Kenneth Rose, *Superior Person* (London, 1969), p. 133; Herbert Maxwell, *Life and Times of the Right Honourable William Henry Smith* (Edinburgh, 1893), II, p. 342.
11. When he went to Cambridge to receive an honorary degree, undergraduates lined the route waving pinafores. Harrowby papers LXXIII: f. 250b.
12. Henry Lucy, *A Diary of the Salisbury Parliament, 1886–1892* (London, 1892), pp. 430–1.
13. *Hansard*, 3rd ser., CCCX, 70 (27 January 1887).
14. See e.g., Viscount Chilston, *Chief Whip* (London, 1961), pp. 272–3.
15. Speech at Guildhall, *The Times*, 10 November 1891, 10e.
16. Salisbury once remarked, 'Independent members are members that nobody can depend on.' Arthur S. T. Griffith-Boscawen, *Memoirs* (London, 1925), p. 36.
17. Viscount Cross, *A Political History* (privately printed, 1903), p. 107.
18. Hamilton to Salisbury, 23 December 1886, Salisbury papers.
19. A. B. Cooke and John Vincent, 'Select documents: XXVII, Ireland and party politics, 1885–7: An unpublished Conservative memoir', *Irish Historical Studies*, XVI, 63 (March 1969), p. 335.
20. Abergavenny to Churchill, 23 September 1889, Churchill papers; Reginald Lucas, *Lord Glenesk and the 'Morning Post'* (London, 1910), pp. 293–301, 314–16, and 329; Reginald Lucas, *Colonel Saunderson, M. P.* (London, 1908), p. 127 and *passim*.
21. A. E. Gathorne-Hardy, *Gathorne Hardy, first Earl of Cranbrook* (London, 1910), II, p. 290.
22. H. W. Lucy, *A Diary of the Salisbury Parliament, 1886–1892* (London, 1892), p. 427.
23. J. L. Garvin, *op. cit.*, II, p. 315; Chamberlain to Churchill, 19 October 1887, and Hicks Beach to Churchill, 27 October 1887, Churchill papers.
24. 'the House of Commons is in so unstable a condition, on account of the present acrimony of party politics and the absence of any fixed majority, that any small rush of adverse opinion, even upon a matter not connected with politics, might be very inconvenient.' Salisbury to the Queen, 6 February 1888, in *Letters of Queen Victoria*, 3rd ser., I, pp. 380–1.
25. Helen Evelyn, *The History of the Evelyn Family: with a special Memoir of William John Evelyn, M. P.* (London, 1915), p. 435.
26. Viscountess Milner, *My Picture Gallery, 1886–1901* (London, 1951), p. 79.
27. Maud Wynne, *An Irishman and His Family* (London, 1937), p. 175.
28. Quoted in Lucille Iremonger, *The Fiery Chariot* (London, 1970), p. 136.
29. Lord Rosebery, *Miscellanies Literary and Historical* (London, 1921), I, p. 268.
30. Hugh Berrington, 'Partisanship and dissidence in the nineteenth-century House of Commons', *Parliamentary Affairs*, XXI, 4 (Autumn 1968). The Lords proved harder to manage: see chapter VII, section v, and chapter VIII, section i.
31. Lord Rosebery, *Lord Randolph Churchill* (London, 1906), p. 123.
32. A. G. Gardiner, *The Life of Sir William Harcourt* (London, 1923), II, p. 151.
33. J. P. Cornford, 'The Parliamentary foundations of the Hotel Cecil', in Robert Robson, ed., *Ideas and Institutions of Victorian Britain* (London, 1967), p. 286. This article contains a masterly analysis of the Conservative Parliamentary party's components at the turn of the century.
34. Smith to Akers-Douglas, 7 May 1891, Chilston papers.
35. *Essays: Biographical* (New York, 1905), p. 5.
36. Speech at the inauguration of the National Conservative Club, *The Times*, 7 March 1887, 7b.

37. Salisbury at Norwich, *The Times*, 28 July 1887, 7c.

38. Speech at Liverpool, *The Times*, 12 January 1888, 7d.

39. Speech at the inauguration of the National Conservative Club, *The Times*, 7 March 1887, 7c.

40. Salisbury to Balfour, 14 October 1887, copy, Balfour papers (Whittinghame), 33.

41. L. P. Curtis, Jr., *Coercion and Conciliation* (Princeton, 1963), p. 183; S. H. Zebel, *Balfour* (Cambridge, 1973), p. 74; Viscount Chilston, 'The Tories and Parnell, 1885–1891', *Parliamentary Affairs*, XIV (1960–1), p. 68; T. W. Moody, '*The Times* versus Parnell and Co., 1887–90', *Historical Studies, VI* (London, 1968), p. 166.

42. Speech to the Primrose League, *The Times*, 21 April 1887, 8b.

43. Salisbury to the Queen, 21 April 1887, Royal Archives A 65/74.

44. Salisbury to the Queen, 23 July 1888, in *Letters of Queen Victoria*, 3rd ser., I, pp. 431–2.

45. L. P. Curtis, Jr., *Coercion and Conciliation:* A study in Conservative Unionism (Princeton, 1963), p. 284. My discussion of the Irish policy of Salisbury's second Ministry generally draws upon Professor Curtis' able work.

46. Salisbury to Smith, 22 December 1889, Hambleden MSS.

47. T. W. Moody, *op. cit.*, p. 165.

48. The heart of the offence was his analogy of the forger, Pigott, to a 'bloody rotten, ghastly foetus.'

49. J. N. Tarn, *Working-class Housing in 19th century Britain* (London, 1971), p. 46.

50. *The Times*, 5 March 1891, 6c.

51. Note of Objections by Salisbury for the Cabinet on the Allotments Bill, 6 December 1886, P. R. O. CAB 37/18, pp. 4–5. Cf. Salisbury to W. A. T. Amherst, 28 July 1886, Salisbury papers, Secretary's notebook.

52. Smith to Salisbury, 6 July 1887, Salisbury papers.

53. Salisbury to Smith, 7 May 1890, copy, Salisbury papers.

54. J. L. Garvin, *Life of Chamberlain*, II, pp. 422–3.

55. Cranbrook's diary, 16 January 1887, Cranbrook papers.

56. Granville to Gladstone, 12 October 1885, in Agatha Ramm, ed., *The Political Correspondence of Mr. Gladstone and Lord Granville, 1876–1886* (Oxford, 1972), II, p. 410.

57. Salisbury at the National Union's annual conference, *The Times*, 24 November 1887, 6e.

58. *Supra*, p. 127.

59. Report of a meeting of the Conservative Parliamentary party, *The Times*, 22 June 1888, 9f.

60. He used this term again at the meeting of the Parliamentary party in June 1888 and again in a letter to Balfour of 6 February 1889, Balfour papers, B. L. Add. MSS. 49689.

61. Salisbury to Lord Granby, 1 April 1888, in Lady Gwendolen Cecil, *Life of Salisbury*, IV, p. 148.

62. Salisbury to Blundell Maple, M.P., 14 March 1892, copy, Balfour papers, B. L. Add. MSS. 49690.

63. J. P. Dunbabin, 'Expectations of the new County Councils, and their realization', *Historical Journal*, VIII, 3 (1965), pp. 360–1.

64. Salisbury at Carnarvon, *The Times*, 11 April 1888, 12c.

65. Salisbury to Cadogan, 13 January 1892, Cadogan papers.

66. Onslow to Salisbury, n.d., copy, and Salisbury to Onslow, 1 July 1900, Onslow papers.

67. Bartley to Salisbury, 1 June 1891, Salisbury papers, with Ritchie's letters to Salisbury.

68. Ritchie to Salisbury, 2 June 1891, Salisbury papers.
69. Ritchie could not find a seat in the Commons from 1892, when he was defeated at the general election, until the spring of 1895 when he was adopted for Croydon.
70. *Tory Democracy and Conservative Policy* (London, 1892), p. 4.
71. *Ibid.*, pp. 14–15.
72. Salisbury to a group of churchmen conferring about a memorial to Dr. Pusey, *The Times*, 17 November 1882, 6a.
73. Quoted in Paul Smith, ed., *Lord Salisbury on Politics*, p. 67.
74. Salisbury to H. Lowthian, 14 November 1884, Salisbury papers, Secretary's notebook.
75. 'I do not know whether you look on the Deceased Wife's sister question as a matter of conscience. If so, pray do not read this letter any further.
    But if, like me, you regard it merely as a balance of expediencies . . . .' Salisbury to Viscount Barrington, 28 May 1883, Duke University Library MSS.
76. See P. T. Marsh, *The Victorian Church in Decline* (London, 1969), chaps. 7 and 9.
77. Churchill to Salisbury, 9 December 1885, in W. S. Churchill, *Lord Randolph Churchill*, II, p. 20.
78. National Union Annual Conference Minutes, 22 November 1887, pp. 116–25.
79. Balfour to Salisbury, February 1892, Salisbury papers.
80. There were outstanding exceptions, particularly Lord Selborne and his son, Lord Wolmer.
81. Salisbury to the Duchess of Rutland, 16 July 1891, copy, Salisbury papers.
82. *Hansard*, 3rd ser., CCCXXV, 307 (24 April 1888).
83. A great deal of the following discussion is derived from Gillian Sutherland's *Policy-Making in Elementary Education, 1870–1895* (Oxford, 1973).
84. P. F. Clarke, 'Electoral sociology of modern Britain', *History*, LVII, 189 (February 1972), p. 46.
85. Cranbrook's diary, 27 July 1887, Cranbrook papers.
86. Salisbury to Cranbrook, 11 February and 4 March 1888, copies, Salisbury papers.
87. Salisbury to Cranbrook, 10 December 1889, in Lady Gwendolen Cecil, *Life of Salisbury*, IV, p. 157.
88. Bartley to Salisbury, 1 June 1891, Salisbury papers, with Ritchie's letters to Salisbury.
89. Smith to Harrowby, 6 February 1891, Harrowby papers.
90. Cranbrook's diary, 16 July 1891, Cranbrook papers.
91. Reported in *The Times*, 15 November 1888, 7a–f.
92. J. L. Lindsay, 'The Liberal Unionist party until December 1887', University of Edinburgh Ph.D. dissertation, 1955, p. 206.
93. Speech at the Royal Academy banquet, *The Times*, 2 May 1887, 7c.
94. Salisbury to Alfred Austin, 21 March 1889, copy, Salisbury papers.
95. Churchill to Hicks Beach, 9 November 1889, copy, St. Aldwyn papers.
96. Harcourt to Morley, 19 August 1889, in A. G. Gardiner, *The Life of Sir William Harcourt* (London, 1923), II, p. 110.
97. Lady Gwendolen Cecil, *Life of Salisbury*, IV, p. 155.
98. *Supra*, p. 158.
99. Smith to Goschen, 9 April 1890, copy, Salisbury papers, with Goschen's letters to Salisbury.
100. Telegram from Salisbury in response to Goschen's letter of 10 April 1890 to Salisbury, copy, Salisbury papers.
101. *Supra*, p. 128.
102. The meeting was fairly fully reported in *The Times*, 13 June 1890, 9f.
103. Chaplin to Salisbury, June 1890, Salisbury papers.

104. See Herbert Maxwell, *Life and Times of the Right Honourable William Henry Smith* (Edinburgh, 1893), II, p. 278.
105. Lady Gwendolen Cecil, *Life of Salisbury*, IV, pp. 154–155. Salisbury said that three colleagues were talking of resignation, but did not name the third.
106. Balfour to Salisbury, 23 June 1890, Salisbury papers.
107. Leonard Courtney in his journal, 2 July 1890, in G. P. Gooch, *Life of Lord Courtney* (London, 1920), p. 289.
108. Salisbury to the Queen, 5 July 1890, copy, Salisbury papers.
109. Cf. Salisbury to J. W. Maclure, M.P., *The Times*, 30 March 1889, 7e: 'What [the Separatists] long for is a dissolution, where the fate of the Union shall be decided on issues with which the Union has nothing to do. Conservatives have no more urgent duty at the present time than that of keeping before the minds of the electors the necessity of subordinating all minor motives for political actions to the one momentous question.'
110. Goschen to Salisbury, 9 July 1890, Salisbury papers.
111. Salisbury to Smith, 23 July 1890, copy, and Smith to Salisbury, same date, Salisbury papers.
112. Quotation from Leonard Courtney, in G. P. Gooch, *loc. cit.*
113. Extract from the Queen's Journal for 5 April 1889, in *Letters of Queen Victoria*, 3rd ser., I, p. 490.
114. *The Times*, 26 June 1890, 9b.
115. L. P. Curtis, Jr., *op. cit.*, pp. 264–265, and 330, F. S. L. Lyons, 'John Dillon and the Plan of Campaign, 1886–90', *Irish Historical Studies*, XIV, 56 (September 1965), p. 344.
116. Salisbury at Rossendale, *The Times*, 4 December 1890, 6d.
117. *Supra*, p. 128.
118. Goschen to Salisbury, 9 July 1890, Salisbury papers.

CHAPTER 6

# THE MIDDLETON MACHINE

> What we want is a professional and competent person who. . . knows how to turn to the best account the political forces which it is not his business to call into existence, which it is not his business to direct in matters of policy, but which it is his business to bring to the polls when the day of trial comes.
>
> *Balfour to the National Society of Conservative Agents, 14 December 1892*

On the eve of the general election of 1880 Salisbury laboured under all the patrician prejudices against 'wirepullers', the men who organized and were supposed to manipulate the popular electorate to partisan ends. Though a Member of Parliament for fifteen years before he inherited his peerage, he had no first-hand experience of popular elections, since the constituency for which he had sat, Stamford, was a Cecil family borough and his election was never contested. He shared the fear of many of the second Reform Bill's critics that a predominantly propertyless and uneducated electorate would make wirepullers sovereign.[1] Gladstone's willingness to make use of Chamberlain's National Liberal Federation raised before Salisbury's eyes the still more sinister spectre of a 'growth of the power of the wirepuller, centred in the caucus, [acting] under the directions of a Prime Minister, master of the House of Commons, master of the House of Lords, nay, yielding but apparent and simulated obedience to the orders of the Sovereign, gathering into his own hands every power in the State, and using them so that, when the time of renewal of power comes his influence may be overwhelming and his powers may be renewed.'[2]

The abysmal performance of the Conservatives in the 1880 election began to change this reaction. The party's managers had encouraged the calling of the election with rosy predictions, which afterward placed their judgement in question; and the election revealed disarray and unpreparedness in the party's constituency organization.[3] As soon as the election was over, the certainty that the leadership of the party would soon pass to new hands, and the possibility that it might pass to Salisbury's, led him to turn his attention to party organization as one of his prospective responsibilities.

Liberals gave credit for the victory to their organization, Chamberlain to his National Liberal Federation, the *Edinburgh Review* to the Liberal whip, W. P. Adam. Salisbury saw good reason to agree with such claims, and not just because to do so was easier than to admit that the electorate had repudiated the Conservative Government's policies. He did not dispute the electorate's verdict.[4] That still did not account, in his estimation, for the magnitude of the disaster, or rather its seeming magnitude. Ever since his days as a critic of proposals to extend the 1832 franchise, Salisbury had paid close attention to voting statistics. 'Is Robert still doing his sums?', Lord Derby asked scornfully of Lady Salisbury in 1867 just after her husband had resigned from the Cabinet. In 1880 Salisbury was quick to observe that, though the Liberals had won a huge majority in the House of Commons, the election had been closely fought. In 72 of the Liberal victories, Conservatives had polled within 10 per cent of the Liberal total:[5] or, as he added it up, 2,000 votes, if cast for Conservatives rather than Liberals, would have reinstated a Conservative Government.[6] A swing of 2,000 votes was within the capacity of efficient organization. Lady Salisbury summed up the drift of his thought in a remark to Disraeli: 'We must have "caucuses".'[7]

After Disraeli's death, during Salisbury's probation as leader in the Lords, he acquired a heightened sense of the utility of popular constituency associations of Conservatives. To judge by Gladstone's second Ministry, Liberal Governments were sensitive, spinelessly so, to expressions of popular opinion. Or, if one wished to be charitable, one could concede that a majority of the members of Liberal Cabinets wished to be moderate, and therefore welcomed evidence of Conservatively inclined public opinion as grounds for resisting the demands of their Radical colleagues and supporters. In either case, if Conservatives would organize themselves to hire and fill public halls and pass resolutions, much could be achieved. 'It is here, in associations of this kind', Salisbury told the South Essex Registration Association, 'that the policy of the Empire is made; this is the workshop in which it is constructed. It may receive its finish, its edge, its polish, in the Houses of Parliament, but it is here that its main outlines are rough-hewn.'[8]

The same words could have come from the lips of Chamberlain, then at the summit of his career as a Radical. Chamberlain heralded his federation of Liberal associations as an instrument to popularize national politics, to bring the will of the people more effectively to bear upon Parliament. It was precisely this mobilizing of Radical pressures, and the feebleness of the Liberal Government in resisting them, that alarmed Salisbury. He turned Chamberlain's methods against him. Salisbury seized upon Conservative constituency associations as a vital addition to the meagre devices for resistance against the onrush of radical democracy. They could help make democracy safe for England.

Salisbury was by no means the only Conservative who recognized the need to pay greater attention to the party's popular organization. Disraeli appointed a blue ribbon committee (on which Salisbury served) in the wake of the general election to rejuvenate the organization. Then Churchill made his bid to capture the National Union of Conservative Associations. He was happy to collaborate with dissident leaders in the National Union, not simply to advance his personal power, but also to enliven and advance the thinking of the party. Salisbury wished only to bring out whatever conservatism was latent in the electorate. 'At all times', he wrote, 'I believe that those who wish to preserve greatly outweigh those who wish to destroy, but the difficulty is to awaken the Conservative classes to a sense of the danger in time to repel active assailants of our institutions.'[9] Churchill soon lost interest in the National Union; Salisbury's interest in electoral organization proved lasting.

Moreover, his understanding deepened. Nothing in his personal experience or philosophy had led him to question the wisdom of continuing to employ the arts of electoral influence by which local grandees had made their desires effective. He did not recognize—what John Gorst knew from his term as Principal Agent in the '70s—that legislation against these practices would emancipate and hence invigorate local associations. Salisbury was uneasy about the Corrupt Practices Bill of 1883,[10] and let it pass the House of Lords only in deference to the judgement of members of the Commons such as Gorst with an intimate understanding of constituency politics. In the following year, Salisbury forced up the limits on expenses proposed in the Corrupt Practices Bill for municipal elections.[11] By 1887, however, he had the full measure of local associations' responsibilities: propaganda; selection of the right agent, candidate and local chairman; and an organization, ready to be set in motion on short notice, 'to bring every sluggish elector into the field.'[12] Careful organization was even more important for Conservatives than for Liberals, he argued, placing his personal impress on the subject. For, whereas Anglican clergy tended to keep their support for the Conservative party discretely informal, Nonconformist denominations and trade unions did not hesitate to place their organization at the disposal of Liberals. Salisbury urged upon Conservatives the duty of 'perfecting your organization, to furnish a complete and legitimate substitute for these advantages.'[13] By the end of the decade, he was a complete convert to the new style of organization, even against the old patrician one. 'Under the old franchise', he instructed the Queen, organization 'was managed locally, generally by the family solicitor of the principal person in the place. Since the franchise was changed in 1867, and afterwards in 1885, there has been the greatest difficulty in inducing these persons, who are entirely incompetent, to give place to more active men. We are doing it gradually: but it requires time: and there is the greatest possible reluctance on the part of the local magnates to admit any central interference at all.'[14]

## i. The Skipper

Salisbury acquired this understanding under the tutelage of R. W. E. Middleton, an organizer of unsurpassed skill in the history of British politics. Middleton became Principal Agent for the Conservatives just before Salisbury first became prime minister. The coincidence was accidental. Middleton was part of the 'Kentish gang', a group of Conservative organizers led by Lord Abergavenny and including Akers-Douglas and the preceding Chief Whip, Sir William Hart-Dyke. The Kentish gang sponsored Middleton's appointment. It completed a reconstruction of party headquarters which had been going on, with a succession of experimental appointments, since the disaster of 1880. Apart from the test of strength with Churchill over the National Union, Salisbury had not been deeply involved in this reconstruction, though awakening to its significance. Until he became leader of the entire party and not just of the Lords, the business of party organization tended to fall within the orbit of the leaders in the Commons; and they were his rivals. Stanhope, who looked after county organization in the early '80s, was a devotee of Northcote. Gorst and Bartley, Middleton's predecessors as Principal Agent, were under Churchill's influence. The Kentish gang kept fairly well clear of these rivalries, concentrating their talents on the craft of party organization. The appointment of Akers-Douglas as Chief Whip and of Middleton as Principal Agent equipped Salisbury, on his accession to the party leadership, with a harmonious pair of organizational lieutenants at party headquarters, eager to employ their skills in the service of the party, and ready to give their loyalty to the leader of the party, whoever he might be. Rarely has a new party leader been so fortunate.

Given Lord Salisbury's peculiar style of leadership, this piece of luck was vital to his success. Under the guise of 'the Hertfordshire Man', Salisbury is the hero in a Conservative play of 1887 entitled *Which Shall We Have?* But the Hertfordshire Man never appears on stage. The play concludes with an announcement that he 'has just sent a message . . that he is very much engaged looking after our business.'[15] Clearly the playwright found Salisbury's remoteness, as well as his dedication, attractive. Another observer explained: 'Lord Salisbury was far less oracular and mysterious than Lord Beaconsfield, but he had that certain aloofness which, in those days, both parties liked in their leaders.'[16] The playwright exaggerated Salisbury's absence from the public platform. By campaigning in the general elections of 1885 and '86 until the eve of voting, Salisbury shattered the convention which prohibited a peer from intervening personally in an election after the issue of the writs. He made regular speaking tours through the provinces, and used them as opportunities to engage local leaders in conversation about their concerns. Still, he did not possess the temperament of a demogogue. 'At Edinburgh', he told his secretary on one occasion, 'they have recently proposed that I should attend a ceremony of twenty minutes which is to consist of uncovering *my own bust* . . . I have rebelled.'[17] The setting in which he delighted was not the public platform, nor even the House of Lords, but his own overheated study. The temperature which he liked, and the exhausting regimen of work to which he subjected himself, made him unusually susceptible to drafts, with the result that he had to be handled on his speaking tours like a hothouse plant. Even at banquets, care had to be taken that he was not seated with his back to a door which would be frequently opened.

His physical remoteness from the public could have deprived him of knowledge of its reflexes and moods; and such detachment would have been fatal, if not to his party, certainly to his own career. However, he came to possess shrewd judgement about what the electorate would allow, more particularly about what would keep up Conservative voting strength, and eventually about the requirements of the Unionist electorate as a whole. Part of this gift came to him by instinct. He possessed a rarefied version of that native sense of the public will which had enabled squires and landed aristocrats to govern England for so long. But Middleton supplied the data upon which this talent worked. The attention which Salisbury had always given to voting statistics made him receptive to Middleton's instruction. Salisbury's seat in the Lords released him for frequent conferences with Middleton. While protracted debate tied Ministers in the Commons to their seats, Salisbury was free to walk over to party headquarters in St. Stephen's Chambers. There, the rest of the staff withdrawing to a respectful distance, the two men would sit, pouring over returns from a by-election or reports which constituency agents had been ordered to compile.[18] Middleton was one of the few men who had free access to Salisbury, and he saw Salisbury more frequently than all but the major Cabinet Ministers.

Middleton was not the formal chief at party headquarters. That was the traditional responsibility of the Chief Whip, and Akers-Douglas' presidency at party headquarters was no mere formality. One division of his duties, supervising the selection of Parliamentary candidates, was his direct responsibility because of its bearing on the personnel of the House of Commons. He also supervised day-to-day disbursement of the national party budget,[19] dividing it largely between payment for propaganda and partial reimbursement for candidates' electoral expenses. Salisbury turned to Akers-Douglas when Middleton's salary was under consideration. The Chief Whip presided over general planning and strategy sessions at party headquarters, and maintained a supervisory eye on Middleton. But just as Smith, though generally responsible for the party's performance in the Commons, left the business of whipping largely to Akers-Douglas, so Akers-Douglas left electoral organization largely to Middleton.

There was another intermediary between Salisbury and the party organization outside as well as inside Parliament: his principal private secretary. His first private secretary was his colleague, Lord John Manners' eldest son, Henry. From the outset Salisbury made it clear that Henry Manner's primary function was to serve as intermediary with the rank and file rather than to handle correspondence; and Manners was quickly nominated to the Carlton Club. He had already been active in a minor way in the National Union, and he spent much of his time as secretary away from his desk, seeing the whips and others on party business. His health, however, was not good, his personal affairs preoccupyingly difficult for a while, and his judgement was not always sound.[20] When his father succeeded to the Duchy of Rutland in 1888, Henry found himself with the courtesy title of Marquis of Granby and private means enough to take over his father's seat in the House of Commons.

From then until Salisbury's retirement in 1902, with two brief interruptions, Salisbury was served by Schomberg McDonnell, a younger son of the Earl of Antrim. McDonnell was less sociable than Manners, and could be prickly outside his circle of friends.[21] He spent more time than Manners had at his desk in Salisbury's anteroom. Still, he frequented the Carlton Club, and there was a steady shuttling back and forth between his office and party headquarters. Before the end of Salisbury's second Ministry McDonnell had become an indispensable cogged wheel relating the larger rotations of the prime minister and the 'wirepullers'. He mastered the business of party management so well that he could discuss critically with Salisbury the advice which came from Middleton. He became the third in an amicable, inner council of the national organization, who knew each other as Bob (Akers-Douglas), Pom (McDonnell), and Skipper (Middleton).

On the social scale, Middleton was the lowest of the three. Like the solicitors who, earlier in the century, had managed elections in most constituencies, Middleton's sphere was in the half-light between the governing classes and the governed. There is something not quite reputable, or at least patronising, in his being referred to as 'Captain' Middleton though he had never risen in his naval career higher than lieutenant. He remains a shadowy figure. The known biographical facts about him are few.[22] Born in 1846 the son of an official at the Admiralty and grandson of an admiral, he joined the navy at the age of fifteen. The official magazine of Conservative agents in the 1890s placed him among those responsible for the invitation which led to Disraeli's famous speech of 1872 in the Manchester Free Trade Hall.[23] Actually in that year he was repressing the slave trade off the east coast of Africa in a vessel called the *Flying Fish*. Shortly afterward he resigned his commission to get married. Wollaston Pym, an outstandingly successful Conservative agent in Middlesex and one of the first non-solicitors to do this kind of work, took Middleton on as an apprentice.[24] In 1882 Middleton took charge of a large suburban Conservative club, and in 1883 became agent for West Kent. When he died in 1905 he left a widow and five children, one of whom Salisbury had helped to a commission in the navy. Middleton's salary as Principal Agent was not high, but after the general elections of 1895 and 1900 he was presented with two bulging purses of £10,000 a piece. Through the additional munificence of one backbencher,[25] he was well off in his last years. Yet he never received a mark of honour from the Crown. McDonnell, on the other hand, was knighted, while Akers-Douglas was raised to the Privy Council, then to the Cabinet, and eventually to the House of Lords.

Nevertheless, of the three Middleton's accomplishment was the most remarkable. Akers-Douglas and McDonnell rendered traditional kinds of service, though with enviable facility. Middleton stimulated and supervised the development of partisan electoral organization to a pitch of refinement unmatched before and perhaps since. Both Akers-Douglas and Middleton were valued, not just for their organizational skills, but even more for their ability to interpret the information they gleaned about opinion in their spheres, respectively the backbenches and the electorate. Of the two, Middleton's sphere was the more opaque, and never more so than at the end of the nineteenth century. From the end of open balloting in 1872 until the birth of systematic public opinion polling, interpreters of electoral opinion had to work in unusually intense darkness. 'The Ballot'. Salisbury once remarked, 'is the régime of surprises.'[26] Middleton was a priest who knew what auguries to select and how they should be interpreted to discern the mood of Britain's new political god, the populace, whom Salisbury feared and wished to make peaceable. Middleton spread a network of professional agents across the kingdom to gather detailed information about the factors which would determine the outcome of an election in single constituencies and hence in the country at large: the state of the rival organizations and of the electoral register, the proportion of electors likely to vote, the local connections and reputation of the candidates, economic conditions, the affect of the time of year, and particular grievances about which the locality felt strongly, often matters of administration such as a defence contract rather than of high policy. Equipped with this information, he could divine its electoral meaning. With uncanny accuracy he could predict what the vote totals in a by-election would be and—though not quite so precisely—the size of the margin of victory or defeat throughout the kingdom in a general election. Unlike his Liberal counterpart, Francis Schnadhorst,[27] indeed unlike most organizers, he never mistook smoothly running party machinery as tantamount to electoral victory. When his predictions erred it was on the side of pessimism, a leaning which Salisbury appreciated and shared.

Middleton, like Akers-Douglas, possessed another quality golden to Salisbury: undeviating loyalty. The organizers of party support in Britain never acquired the independent base of power enjoyed by their American counterparts. Patronage in Britain since the eighteenth century had become too insubstantial,[28] and government was too centralized, to give rise to American-style bosses. Still, the skills of Akers-Douglas and Middleton were their own, and could have been put to use by factions within the party. Gorst and, to a lesser extent, Bartley had done so, and they had also tried to use the office of Principal Agent as a stepping stone in their political careers. The National Liberal Federation under Schnadhorst's direction was the first prize for which Gladstonians and Liberal Unionists contended as soon as they split with each other.

Middleton had no political ambitions for himself, and he placed himself and his organization devotedly at Salisbury's disposal. Though in the 1890s he ran successfully for a seat on the London County Council, he did so only for the added leverage it gave him for his purposes as Principal Agent, and he gave it up after a few years. He could not excuse the stab which Churchill inflicted in the party's back by resigning office, and he had no dealings with the renegade until 1893 when Churchill was back in harness. Middleton was an old fashioned Tory brought up to date in his thinking only where electoral considerations dictated. Salisbury was a leader after Middleton's heart, 'the Old Man' he called him with affection; and he placed a high estimate upon Salisbury's hold over the Conservative electorate.

Salisbury never left any doubt that he appreciated his team of organizers. 'Douglas and Middleton', he testified, 'have never put me wrong.'[29] What passed unobserved was the close attention Salisbury paid to initiatives in their sphere. The prospect of a general election naturally quickened his concern. He urged Middleton to cooperate with a campaign which Lord Wolmer planned in 1892 for systematic heckling of Gladstonian candidates.[30] The Liberals' victory kept Salisbury's concern about extra-Parliamentary partisan activity lively, and he prodded forward an enterprise of Middleton's to solicit funds from Indian maharajahs for the Conservative war chest.[31] But victory and the burdens of office did not drive the party's popular organization from his mind. His red 'S' and occasional comments can be found on Middleton's and Akers-Douglas' reports and proposals just as on ambassadorial reports.

Indeed one of the more remarkable facts about the Middleton machine was the position of the Parliamentary Conservative party while it was being built. Advances in party organization commonly follow severe electoral defeats such as those of 1832 or 1945, and almost always coincide with periods in opposition. Construction of the Middleton machine, by contrast, began during Salisbury's first Ministry and was completed during his second. This fact can be explained by referring to the third Reform Act's enlargement and radical redistribution of the electorate, to the unsettlement of party loyalties among the electorate over Home Rule, and to the treatment of by-elections during the second Ministry as referenda on Irish policy. By-election contests became showcases for rival efforts in electoral mobilization. The Middleton machine was built, tested and refined during a decade of almost ceaseless electioneering. In addition to general elections in 1885, '86, '92, and '95 and to intervening by-elections, there were triennial County Council elections after 1888 modestly invested with national significance, as were the parochial and district council elections after 1894. In November of that year, *The Tory* commented:

> The heart of a London Agent must rejoice to judge from the amount of work to be got through in the next six or seven weeks. In November, 11 Elections, to select 55 members of the School Board; in December, 235 Elections, to select 3,247 parochial substitutes for the ancient Vestrymen. In addition, the election of an untold number of Guardians whilst the City will continue to hold its ancient Wardmotes on St. Thomas Day. To sum up this tale of woe, next spring the County Council Elections take place.[32]

The realm of electoral politics was rapidly expanded in these years, and parties had to develop their organization to cope with this expansion. It was not until 1895, when a majority of Conservatives even apart from their Liberal Unionist allies was returned to Parliament, that the atmosphere of perpetual electioneering came to an end.

Still, John Gorst had learned after the Conservative victory of 1874 that, in spite of the best efforts of an able manager at headquarters, a good organization could deteriorate rapidly without the collaboration of the leader of the party. Disraeli had cooperated cordially with Gorst until 1874. Then the aging prime minister failed to tend the organization, particularly in dispensing offices and patronage, and devoted his attention instead to high politics. Salisbury, prime minister with the added responsibility of the Foreign Office, carried a heavier administrative load than Disraeli had ever borne, and attended to it more assiduously. Admittedly he came to the premiership at a younger age than Disraeli. It is nonetheless true that Salisbury kept a closer eye on the party machine than any other nineteenth-century prime minister had done; and to that extent he deserved credit for its accomplishments. Even after the decisive victory of 1895 he continued to lay the heaviest responsibility for 'establishing, on a firm foundation, the institutions which we love...not upon Ministers, not upon members of Parliament,but upon Conservative organizations.'[33] The fact that he never appeared to be an oiler of the machinery's wheels was just another manifestation of the aura of honour and detachment which served him so well.

He lubricated the electoral as well as the Parliamentary organization generously in dispensing honours. From his first accession to the premiership, he exploited every category of title or honour. As luck would have it, two special sets of Royal Jubilee honours, those of 1887 and 1897, came his way during his terms as prime minister, in addition to the annual New Years and Royal Birthday honours. His purpose in distributing them was not always partisan. He provided ample honours for the expanding civil service, and set precedents for rewarding distinction in the arts and sciences. Even so he maximized the opportunities for political patronage at the disposal of a prime minister. He encouraged his colleagues to include political service among their considerations in disposing of the appointments at their control.[34] McDonnell kept a register of proposals for honours, the last volume of which is still preserved among his papers, from which it is clear that Middleton was the source of many nominations and was asked to assess others. During the lifetime of the second Ministry, Salisbury restrained the flow of honours for M.P.s to avoid causing discontent among those passed over, until the dissolution. But after 1895, in response to that decade's uninhibited 'rage for distinctions',[35] he avoided discontent by dispensing honours lavishly, creating 'so many knights and baronets as to justify the saying that you cannot throw a stone at a dog without hitting a knight in London.'[36] If McDonnell and he took care to avoid discredit by weeding out mere party hacks,[37] they took at least equal care that service in the constituencies as well as in Parliament was amply rewarded.

## ii. Constituency Agents

'All the excitement, and all the enthusiasm, were absolutely wasted', said Middleton at a meeting of the Midland Union Association of Conservative Agents,[38] 'unless there was one man at the head of affairs cool-headed, calm, and clear, who had in his mind the whole scheme he wished to work out, and who could direct all the energy and enthusiasm into the channel where it would have the greatest effect.' That statement summed up the style of Conservative party management in Salisbury's day. It could have been applied to Middleton or in some senses to Salisbury. Middleton intended it to describe the function of his full-time, professional agents in the constituencies. The network of them which he elaborated was the outstanding development of British party organization in the last fifteen years of the nineteenth century.

Middleton's network was a wry yet natural consequence of the electoral reforms of the first half of the 1880s. The Corrupt Practices Act of 1883 was intended to emancipate the electorate from manipulation by wealth through the hiring of assistants and payment for services. The hope was that these forces could be replaced by voluntary enterprise. Detailed regulations were laid down severely limiting expenditure and the number of agents who could be paid during an election in any constituency. But the statutory regulation was so close—'It bristles with shoals and pitfalls in every section, sub-section, and line'—and the penalties upon infringements were so stern, that 'to pilot a candidate successfully through its meshes requires all the tact, energy, and ability of an agent who has devoted some years of his life to election work.'[39] Furthermore, the voluntary activity which the Act hoped to elicit was not likely to spring forth at election time unless it was nourished in the dog-days between elections. What was needed was someone steadily employed to kindle interest, build voluntary associations where they did not exist, and see that this machinery did not fall into disrepair.

By extending the borough franchise of 1867 to the counties, the Franchise Act of 1884, in spirit akin to the Corrupt Practices Act, destroyed the ability of territorial magnates, already weakened by the agricultural depression, to control county elections. Party machinery in rural constituencies had to be built up, often from scratch. In most borough constituencies, too, the machinery had to be revamped because the Redistribution Act of 1885 covered most of the country for the first time with single-member constituencies, leaving few old boundaries unchanged. As a result of the Franchise and Redistribution Acts, furthermore, no one could rely on past electoral behaviour as a guide to future voting. There was a sharp drop in the general election of 1885 from the usual number of constituencies left uncontested, and a corresponding drop in the number which could safely be left unorganized. In all of these ways, the electoral reforms of the early '80s created an acute need for an able organizer in every constituency.

Middleton sought to satisfy this need in such a way as to enhance the power of party headquarters. Not only did he encourage the appointment of full-time, professional constituency agents wherever possible; he also brought them into closer connection with headquarters. He did so partly through his own correspondence, and by initiating the practice of assigning agents to constituencies with which they had no previous personal connection. But his chief device was to appoint regional deputies to supervise the work of the agents and popular associations in every constituency within their assigned provinces. These regional lieutenants provided the link which turned the proliferating company of constituency agents into an effective network. That network, in turn, provided the nervous system of an increasingly elaborate national organization. At every level—constituency, regional, and national—the professional agent served and hence supervised the corresponding popular association of party stalwarts and volunteers. Well trained and competent constituency agents gave the party another advantage. They provided a combination of services—voter registration, mobilization of volunteers, and propaganda—which were available singly but at greater cost and without coordination.

Middleton's agents were not new either in being full-time or in their professionalism. The need for professional expertise had been created by the rules laid down in the first Reform Act for registration of the electorate, too onerous for civic officials to cope with and further complicated by successive statutes. By the turn of the century, registration was governed by 118 Acts and over 650 judicial decisions, and 60 different official forms were involved.[40] Partly because of such technicality, constituency agents between the first and third Reform Acts were usually solicitors, who handled the work on a part-time basis. The emergence of full-time agents was a result of the expansion of the electorate. There were full-time agents by 1868 in some large towns and a few counties. In the 1880s they became common in the wealthier constituencies.[41] With gentle but persistent pressure, particularly through the National Society of Conservative Agents, their use was extended until, by the century's end, full-time agents were employed in at least half the constituencies.[42] And their influence extended still more comprehensively through regional associations.

The swelling band of agents tended to link themselves into cooperative networks. As early as 1872, a North of England Conservative Agents' Association had been formed,[43] and it operated effectively under the vigorous superintendence of its secretary, Isaac Lyons. Middleton took the next step with the appointment of his regional agents, including Lyons. The initiative for a national federation came in 1890 from Lyons' North of England Agents' Association. In the meantime other regional associations of agents had been created, in Yorkshire, the Midlands, East Anglia, the West, and Scotland. Late in 1891, with Middleton's encouragement, the National Society of Conservative Agents was founded.[44] Immediately it became the prime institution through which Middleton, with yeoman assistance from Lyons,[45] undertook to complete the conversion of constituency agents into a network of full-time professionals.

The most conspicuous feature of the National Society was its concern to establish and strengthen its members professional stature. For these purposes the National Society fell midway between a craft union and a professional society. It laid down rules for membership; required newcomers to undergo a brief apprenticeship and pass a rigorous examination, mainly on registration law; discouraged the employment of gentlemen amateurs or of solicitors handling election work on a part-time basis; limited the number to take the qualifying examination, in order to protect the jobs of certified agents already in possession; provided for expulsion on grounds of persistent professional or moral misconduct; and tried to set the minimum annual salary at £150. Middleton initiated a benefit fund to help retired members or their widows who found themselves in financial distress. Apprenticeship and examination were part of a larger effort by the National Society, including conferences and the publication of a monthly journal called *The Tory*, to increase the knowledge and skill of its members.[46] The members of the National Society of Conservative Agents wished to add themselves to the list, which had grown rapidly in the nineteenth century, of recognized professions. So keen was the desire to gain recognition as a profession that the secretary of the Society of Certified Liberal Agents suggested to Lyons that the agents of both parties might eventually combine for the purpose.[47] The suggestion fell on stony ground, in part because of the Conservative agents' greater self-assurance.

Middleton cordially sympathized with his agents' aspiring professionalism. Nonetheless, at party headquarters the professionalizing of agents was of interest primarily because it sharpened them for electoral management. Mastery of registration, the strongest proof of agents' professionalism, was more than an arcane craft. Registration was the primary device retained under the Franchise Act of 1884 to keep the electorate to less than democratic proportions. The other restrictive requirements of the Act, involving type of residence, especially tricky for lodgers, and length of residency, hard on migrant workers or men without secure employment, were enforced through registration. Together these requirements and the hurdles of registration excluded enough of the poorer population from the vote to keep the electorate below sixty per cent of Britain's adult males—to say nothing of females. Though Salisbury and Middleton did not defend this percentage directly, they contrived to keep it from rising. Whenever Liberals brought up the subject, Salisbury warded it off by arguing, not entirely mischievously,[48] that womens' enfranchisement should be dealt with first. Middleton upheld the complications of registration as checks against casual voters with too little concern to make sure that they were on the register.[49] Tutored by the National Society of Conservative Agents, the Parliamentary party defeated Liberal efforts at reform.

Registration was not just a restrictive mechanism. It also provided enterprising agents with a powerful tool for electoral management. At a time when few constituencies were won or lost by margins of more than three figures, careful attention to the electoral register could make a critical difference. The door-to-door work of registration provided an opportunity for personal evangelism, and enabled the agent to compile a marked list of electors so that he could identify and bring out the full Tory vote come polling day. In addition to its restrictive provisions, the Franchise Act enhanced the electoral power of property owners by allowing electors who lived in one county constituency and owned property in another to vote in both. Plural electors tended, after the Liberal split over Home Rule, to be Conservative or Unionist;[50] and Middleton's network of agents mobilized this source of strength by serving as an exchange of information about them.

Registration, therefore, bulked large in the annual routine of an agent. Yet it was not primarily the need to register, but rather the need to organize the expanded electorate which led to the proliferation of full-time agents and to the network which Middleton fostered. Registration was but one of the prerequisites to delivery of the maximum number of Conservative votes in ballot boxes, which was the object of the whole enterprise. In addition, intelligence about voter desires and party strength had to be fed into party headquarters to enable the leadership to formulate tacts and, when in power, to time elections wisely. In 1894, for example, when the leaders were pondering what tactics to adopt toward the Liberal Government's Employers' Liability Bill, they directed Middleton to make enquiries in manufacturing districts to gauge the electoral importance of an agitation which was being conducted against 'contracting out.'[51] Middleton and his agents brought constituency organization to a height of refinement, from which it was forced to recede a generation later. The third Reform Act made the electorate too large to be dealt with by part-time agents; the extension of the franchise to all adult males and to women after World War I would make the electorate too large for close-combing management even by full-time agents. In the interim the work of registration, the complexities of which were hard to reduce until every adult had the vote, provided agents with a fine mesh through which to sieve their constituencies.

Full-time agents were costly, more so than part-time solicitor agents, though sometimes paid at a lower rate. But the Corrupt Practices Act had released money to foot the bill by suppressing the old ways in which wealth had made itself electorally effective. Now that the holders of industrial and mercantile wealth were moving over to join the owners of land in the Conservative party, it was for the first time very much richer than its rival.[52] The Liberal Act of 1883 merely prodded Conservatives into deploying their superior wealth in more effective ways.

Although a network of professional agents was beautifully suited to the purpose and resources of the Conservative party, recognition of its significance came slowly. It was impeded by one of the network's most valuable features: inconspicuousness. The National Liberal Federation had been founded with fanfare, and quickly became a focus of national debate. Chamberlain trumpeted its virtues, Conservatives blackened it as an American-style caucus. The prominence of the controversy put men on their guard about the Federation, and also created an impression that it was Liberals who were masters in political organization. The impression was accurate in the early 1880s. But it lasted into the 1890s, after the mental powers of Schnadhorst, the executive secretary of the National Liberal Federation, had waned,[53] and Conservatives were setting the pace both in the extent of their organization and in its refinement.

The Liberals still could accomplish great things at by-elections, for which they concentrated their organizing talent on single constituencies. But by bringing in star organizers who left when the by-election was over, they ran the risk of undermining the local machine, upon which they would have to rely in a general election. Middleton, able to equip himself with more professional constituency agents than the Liberals could afford, was willing to pull his punches at by-elections in order to keep local organizations in good shape for the supreme arbitrament of a general election.[54] It was the Conservatives also who first instituted a qualifying examination, started a monthly magazine, set up a pension fund. Nevertheless, as late as 1894 Sir Henry James, the architect of the 1883 Corrupt Practices Act, now a leading Liberal Unionist, assumed that the emergence of professional agents was a largely Gladstonian phenomenon.[55] Conservative M.P.s who were asked to speak at dinner of the National Society commonly confessed previous ignorance of its existence. They tended to treat the assembled agents as they might an association of butlers, good fellows who deserved to be commended though an association for them seemed a bit odd. The inconspicuousness of Middleton's network was disarming. Like the aura of disinterestedness which surrounded Lord Salisbury, it camouflaged a formidable arsenal of weapons.

These weapons were at Salisbury's disposal. The kind of loyalty which Middleton gave to Salisbury radiated through the agents' ranks. The particular complexion of their politics tended to be the same as his, a hearty Toryism, lubricated in the evenings after their meetings with plentiful toasts, unembarrassed by association with the temperance lobby. Many of them had working-class origins, and the assignment for most of them was to mobilize working class electors: some agents, therefore, had Disraelian or Tory Democratic leanings. But, more often, they had received their first taste of organizational work on behalf of the Church of England, for instance through the Church Defence

Institution.[56] Middleton summed up their thinking after one of their banquets:

> He believed that the various gentlemen present in the room that night were all actuated by but one motive in the work they had undertaken . . . It was true they had to look to their appointments . . . but for the Agent there was only one real stimulant, and that was the conviction that he was fighting the cause of his God, his country, and his Queen. (Loud applause.)[57]

Apart from questions of organization and registration, the agents evinced no wish to guide the party. That was the business of M.P.s and of the leadership. When it came to running elections, agents looked down on M.P.s as horses to be directed by their agent-riders,[58] but they were content to see the roles reversed in the business of government. They would happily funnel up information about local feeling, act on requests for the calling of meetings to pass resolutions in line with Conservative policy, make speeches upholding the cause, and in some cases run for local office; but further they did not go.

### iii. Popular Organization

Though the network of agents was the Conservative electoral organization's nervous system, it would have been useless without a body. Associations or clubs of supporters in each constituency, federated within the National Union of Conservative Associations, were the organization's flesh and blood. They were the focus of attention between 1884, when Churchill attempted to capture the National Union, and 1886, when Middleton took the National Union in hand.

Salisbury did not forget the institution which had given him so much trouble. The experience of 1884, and the possibility that the alliance with Liberal Unionists might give rise to even worse insubordination within the popular electoral organization, particularly over free trade, made him anxious for the National Union to shape its organizing efforts 'so that the various sections of which this great Unionist party is composed may always pull in parallel lines, and may never waste their respective energies by divergent efforts or by friction.'[59] Yet he wished to do more than render the National Union tractable. Without massive, enterprising assistance from the National Union, he could not hope to succeed in the Herculean task of winning commanding support for the Conservative party from an electorate which, however cribbed by registration, seemed predisposed by nature to a Liberal allegiance. In the proposal which he made to Churchill in April 1884 to canalize the energies of the National Union, Salisbury outlined what he had in mind. 'The chief object for which the associations exist', he wrote.

> is to keep alive & extend Conservative convictions; & so to increase the number of Conservative voters. This is done by acting on opinion through various channels:

by establishment of Clubs—by holding meetings—by securing the assistance of speakers & lecturers & by the circulation of printed matter in defence of Conservative opinions—by collecting the facts required for the use of Conservative speakers & writers, & by the invigoration of the local Press.[60]

The work of propaganda which the National Union handled after 1884 adhered remarkably closely to this prescription.

The reorganization of the National Union in 1886 was not Salisbury's handiwork. It bore close resemblance to proposals made by provincial leaders within the Union before Churchill made his debut.[61] The final design of the revised constitution, and its implementation, were the work of Middleton. Still, the National Union's approval of its new design could not have been given when it was, in May of 1886 at the height of Parliamentary debate over the Home Rule Bill when everyone was bracing himself for another general election, unless Salisbury had blessed the enterprise.

The new design was an organizational masterpiece. The terms of affiliation with the National Union were lightened and made automatic so that all manner of constituency associations and clubs would be embraced within it. It was to be the one complete national federation of Conservative electoral societies. Secondly, the National Union was divided into nine Provincial Unions, perhaps in order to make a repetition of Churchill's attempted coup more difficult, but ostensibly to increase opportunities for intercourse between constituency associations. The third and cardinal feature of the new design was the placing of Middleton and his nine provincial sub-agents in position to serve and hence to scrutinize, stimulate and unify the Union's activities. Middleton became honorary secretary on the National Union's governing council, his lieutenants served as honorary secretaries for the Provincial Unions' governing councils. The councils welcomed them because they were capable men and served without charge. They received their salaries as Middleton's supervisors over the constituency agents within their provinces, and in that capacity they reported to Middleton weekly. They also tended to be selected to take charge of the provincial branches of the National Society of Conservative Agents. On the bottom rung of this hierarchy stood the constituency agent. His responsibilities for his local Conservative association were comparable to Middleton's for the National Union and to his subagent's for the Provincial Unions.

Inevitably, the redesigned National Union did not function exactly as the blueprint implied. The Provincial Unions enjoyed different degrees of health, depending upon the indigenous popular strength of Conservatism and the degree of sophistication in party organization, whether Liberal or Conservative, within their regions. They never became foci of popular activity to the extent envisioned in 1886. Nor did

Middleton's sub-agents turn out to be uniformly excellent, though only one of them, W. H. Meredith in Wales, proved unsatisfactory. Despite unevenness, the Middleton machine became a model, one upon which subsequent generations of Conservatives elaborated, but from the essentials of which they would never depart for long.

Propaganda became the chief work of the National Union, as Salisbury had prescribed in 1884. The 1885 election led him to re-emphasize the critical importance for the Conservative party of efforts to educate the popular electorate. Conservatives had done well in urban seats, thus disposing for ever, so he assured an audience in March 1886, 'of the idea that we have any cause to fear the judgement of the working men.' But the party had done poorly among the newly enfranchised, and hence inexperienced, agricultural workers.

> What we have cause to fear [he went on] is the uninformed judgement of the working men. What we want is more discussion, more information, more light. The more light there is thrown on any political question, the more the working men discuss it, the more opportunity they have of comparing the experience of their fathers with their own, the more certainty there is that they will steadily and surely verge to the Conservative cause.[62]

Middleton taught his agents that the simple electioneering cries of yore were no longer adequate.[63] A Tory trade unionist echoed the theme in speaking at the 1890 conference of the National Union: 'it will always be necessary, for the Conservative party to do more educational work than for the Radical party.'[64]

The National Union spent from half to two-thirds of its budget each year for literature and lecturers; and the proportion was higher if the Provincial Unions' expenditure of their national grants was included. Middleton almost doubled the annual rate of publications under the National Union's auspices in his first year as Principal Agent. The number of publications doubled again in 1886, and in 1895 redoubled. Middleton and his men attempted to leave some literature at every home in England, and also to make it available at low prices through commercial booksellers. If Morley's *Life of Cobden* sold for a shilling, then the popular *Life of Salisbury* must be reduced from half-a-crown. The resourcefulness of this effort was also evident in its packaging. In Scotland, colporteurs held discussions with those to whom they distributed literature, both to reinforce the message and to accumulate information on electors' party loyalty.[65] Remote areas, for instance in East Anglia, were evangelized from lecture vans equipped with magic lanterns to illustrate the glories of the empire or the barbarities of Irish Nationalists.

The literature designed for popular consumption was weeded to eliminate items 'too prosy for the General Public.'[66] But there was another category of National Union publications which Salisbury's prescription of 1884 had foreshadowed: collections of 'facts required for the use of Conservative speakers and writers.' This group of largely unadorned, dense compilations was begun in 1885 with the *Constitutional Year Book*, followed from 1892 by a *Campaign Guide*[67] for each general election, and in 1893 by 'National Union Gleanings'. The nature of these publications was accurately described when 'Gleanings' was launched: 'to supply politicians with a list of speeches made by leading statesmen and prominent members of Parliament, to furnish a classified list of magazine articles of importance, and to provide in a convenient form a handy means of reference to the sayings and doings of those who occupy the position of political leaders.'[68]

There was a final item in Salisbury's prescription for propaganda by the National Union: 'invigoration of the local press.' Until 1886, a heavy majority of the newspapers throughout the country either espoused Liberal opinions or adopted an independent stance more friendly to Liberals than to Conservatives.[69] As soon as Salisbury and Churchill reached their concordat on the National Union, it addressed itself to this situation. The Provincial Unions followed suit once they were set up, as did the National Society of Conservative Agents. Yet, except by drawing attention to the problem, general efforts of this sort proved futile. Newspapers were by nature impressed with their individuality. They had to be founded, captured or cultivated one by one. An attempt by party headquarters in 1883 to deepen the loyalty of the editors of Conservative newspapers by inviting them to a conference at the Carlton and a banquet with Salisbury and Northcote backfired, at least among the great metropolitan editors, who were repelled by anything which might look like 'nobbling.'[70] Further experience taught Salisbury how difficult it was to cultivate steadily friendly relations with newspapers, and taught Akers-Douglas and Middleton how costly and unreliable the purchase of newspapers could be. Middleton repeatedly refused requests from promoters of takeovers for financial contributions from the party treasury.[71]

Still, stalwarts of the National Union and the leaders of the party threw themselves into the endeavour at various levels. Ashmead Bartlett set a popular example by founding the weekly, *England*, in 1880. Stanhope, in line with his concern about county organization, bought control of two periodicals influential among landowners and tenant farmers. Some constituency associations bought control of local organs. Middleton became chairman of the *Birmingham Gazette*. By the end of the 1880s, the change in the weight of press opinion, especially in London, was distressingly apparent to Liberals. But this had more to do with defections among the Liberal press over Home Rule than with successful takeovers by Conservatives.

The influencing of the great metropolitan papers was left to the party leaders, above all to Salisbury. By 1887, he had impressed *The Times* as 'the Prime Minister most accessible to the Press. He is not prone to give information: but when he does, he gives it freely, & his information can always be relied on.'[72] His most important relationship was not, however, with *The Times*, but with the *Standard*, through Alfred Austin. The relationship between Salisbury and the *Standard* was complex and ambiguous. For Austin was not the paper's editor; he was the author of a regular number of leaders each week, and wrote primarily, though not always, about foreign policy. Mudford, the owner, was a prickly individual and fretful lest his paper be regarded simply as Salisbury's mouthpiece. Not infrequently, he edited Austin's leaders. The editorial line of the paper, as a result, oscillated. Though occasionally embarrassing, this situation suited Salisbury, for it enabled him to disclaim responsibility whenever he wished. Despite the inconsistency and Salisbury's many disclaimers, the relationship was close. On occasion, he too edited Austin's leaders. Often he directly inspired what Austin wrote. Austin, an ardent Tory without originality and gratified to be in the confidence of the prime minister, possessed a version of that quality which Salisbury prized in Smith: he was straight. The relationship persisted until 1896 when Salisbury, in a display of aesthetic insensitivity, made Austin Poet Laureate. Luxuriating in his elevation, Austin promptly dropped 'Lord' from his mode of addressing Salisbury, and gradually withdrew himself from the terrestrial work of leaderwriting in order to compose bad verse.

The surveillance which Middleton's network of agents exercised over the National Union, and the primacy of propaganda among its activities, have left an impression that, after the reorganization of 1886, the National Union 'went quietly to sleep,'[73] until 1903 when it found new life as a hive of tariff reformers. It is true that during the Boer War the National Union failed to transmit to the party leaders the distress felt among its membership, particularly about the army's performance.[74] The leaders of the National Union throughout these years were justly disparaged as 'third-rate politicians who took ample revenge for their failure in the House of Commons by practically monopolising the platform on the occasions of the annual gathering.'[75] The National Union did not attain, or even aspire to, the heights of influence enjoyed by the National Liberal Federation, especially at its Newcastle conference in 1891 when Gladstone was obliged to endorse a wide range of special interests' demands in order to maintain support for Home Rule. Middleton could tune the local platforms of the National Union for Lord Salisbury as well as the pulpits of the Established Church were tuned in the days of Lord Salisbury's great ancestors: indeed much better. Before Balfour introduced the Irish Coercion Bill of 1887, Middleton alerted his provincial deputies to the need for meetings to offset the expected Radical agitation.[76] A decade later, Salisbury approved Middleton's proposal to organize demonstrations of Conservative support for the Government's handling of the Cretan question, to counteract Liberal demonstrations of sympathy for Greece.[77]

Even so, the National Union was no mere echo chamber or amplifier for the policy pronouncements of the party's Parliamentary leaders. Repeatedly during the years between its reorganization and the Boer War, the National Union's annual conferences passed protectionist resolutions, undeterred by the leader's warnings and by the obvious offence to Liberal Unionists.[78] A delegate from Blackpool to the annual conference of 1890 refused to withdraw a motion critical of any free or assisted education which might imperil the existence or impair the efficiency of voluntary schools. Salisbury wanted to fight the motion and instructed Middleton accordingly, but it was passed unanimously.[79] The annual conference of 1891 carried a resolution recommending creation of a separate Labour Department under a Labour Minister, over the qualified objections of Stuart Wortley, Under-Secretary for the Home Office.[80] The chairman of the 1898 conference, Sir Benjamin Stone, had some justification for his claim that the annual conferences 'served the admirable purpose of bringing to the front questions that, if not ripe for discussion in Parliament, were generally in a preparatory form.'[81]

Though theoretically all-inclusive in its coverage, the National Union continued to flourish most vigorously in the social soil of its birth, in cities and suburbs. In the countryside, Conservatism was cultivated by the Primrose League, acclaimed by the end of the century as 'the most permanently successful of all the political organizations that have ever been known in England.'[82] Royalists in France attempted to duplicate it.[83] Its genius was quite distinct from that of the National Union, though some of their activities overlapped. In spite of a ban from the Ruling Council on direct involvement in elections, 'Habitations' of the Primrose League commonly undertook the work of canvassing and registration. They arranged transportation for Conservative electors to the polls,[84] an activity over which the official constituency machine could run into difficulty as a result of the Corrupt Practices Act. In a few instances, a Primrose Habitation functioned as the constituency association, and as such was directly affiliated within the National Union. Such assimilation into the National Union was a development which Middleton wanted to arrest.[85]

For the Primrose League contributed to the Conservative cause what no regular party organization could give. Salisbury epitomized the difference when he explained that, 'The Conservative associations act mainly by public speaking. The Primrose League acts by private

intercourse.'[86] Both were propagandist organizations, but whereas the
National Union did its teaching straight, through pamphlets and
lectures, the propaganda of the Primrose League was 'disguised with a
coating of popular entertainment, or was so surreptitiously introduced
into the evening's gaiety as to be almost unnoticed.'[87] Into rural society,
made seemingly more bleak and lonely by the bright lights of the city,
the Primrose League brought colourful Mason-like ceremonial and gay
festivities, whether smoking concerts or soirées or garden fêtes. Lord
Salisbury had initially raised his eyebrows at the garish ribbons and
titles lavished from top to bottom of the Primrose League's hierarchy.
He surely winced on a train journey from Wrexham to Welshpool in the
spring of 1885 when 'a clergyman and several ladies came to his
lordship's carriage, and showered upon him clusters of primroses'.[88]
But he learned to appreciate the popular appeal of the Primrose
League's ritual. 'Of course, it's vulgar', Lady Salisbury remarked:
'that's why we are so successful.'[89]

The Primrose League managed to give new vitality to the landed
classes' electoral influence which the Corrupt Practices Act and the third
Reform Act had been expected to undermine. 'The coming of democracy in the counties destroyed the old system of landed control, and
it greatly weakened "influence" in the quasi-technical sense of mid-
nineteenth century electioneering', an able historian has noted, 'but it
left landed society with all the advantages of wealth and status.'[90] These
were the advantages which the Primrose League brought into play. Its
fêtes and Habitation meetings brought the ranks in rural society
together, thus nourishing deference. It also unleashed the electoral
influence of women. Though, from time out of mind, individual ladies
had brought their influence to bear upon local electorates, no party
hitherto had made use of women collectively. Almost from its inception
the Primrose League admitted women as members. Organized both
separately and together with men, the wives and daughters of Tory
peers, squires and parsons gave new political effect to the social power
they had always possessed. The Liberals tried to follow suit, but could
not attain the same success. Friend and foe alike testified to the effect of
the Primrose League, particularly of its 'Amazons recruited from the
drawing-rooms of the wealthy.'[91] The statistics of membership bore the
testimony out. The League grew almost faster than its central organization could handle, from less than a thousand in 1884 (its first year) to
nearly a quarter million in 1886, more than half a million in 1887, and
over a million in 1891. By 1890 there were Habitations in every county of
England. The second half of the '80s were its great years. Thereafter,
though the statistics of membership continued to raise, its income slowly
declined.

The same blend of sociability with propaganda which the Primrose League brought to the countryside, Conservative clubs brought to working men in the cities. In the countryside, the house and garden of squire or parson were at the Primrose League's disposal. In cities, Conservative clubs enjoyed the social advantage over Liberals of greater freedom in the use of alcohol. These clubs should not be confused with the handful of grand West End institutions like the Carlton and the Constitutional which served the Parliamentary party and its hangers-on, nor with the replicas of the Carlton in the largest provincial cities. Situated in working and lower middleclass residential districts, and accommodated in small brick buildings, these clubs were built, by and large, during the generation following the enactment of the second Reform Bill in order to reach the newly enfranchised borough householders. Initially they had a fairly serious sense of political purpose, as a refuge for Conservative electors in a hostile Liberal environment, or as a base upon which to erect electoral machinery. Toward the end of the century, no longer beleaguered, their social activities tended to predominate. On the eve of the general election of 1900 the *Conservative Clubs Gazette* felt it necessary to appeal to its members to get out and vote.[92]

When Middleton became Principal Agent in 1885, the clubs' heroic period was drawing to a close. He had begun his political career as secretary to a well established club in South London. Now he supervised the last few years of intensive club formation, attempting to keep the initial plans for each new one very simple and inexpensive.[93] In 1894, seeking further vitality and political value he launched the Association of Conservative Clubs.[94] It was his last creation as an organizer. Already the clubs in Oldham and in Birmingham had formed municipal associations for themselves. Middleton's national Association concentrated on London to begin with. Within eight years, it had established centres in Birmingham, Manchester, Leeds, Glasgow and Edinburgh as well as London, and embraced at least two-thirds of the Conservative clubs in the country among its affiliates. The Association served a number of functions. With the assistance of the great West End clubs, it fostered political education by forming a lending library for affiliates. It improved their efficiency by providing advice on how to conduct their business. It enhanced the pleasure which affiliates could offer their members, by organizing sports and games competitions and out-of-town excursions beyond the capacity of a single club. The crowning touch was to stimulate the formation of cycling clubs, not merely to harness the latest sporting craze, but to train despatch riders for use on election day. Conservative club cyclists were fitted out with tunic, knickerbockers, hat, and silver badge.

## iv. Lord Salisbury and the Machine

It is rarely if ever possible to measure with much exactitude the contribution of party organization to the outcome of elections. The debt which Lord Salisbury and the Conservative party owed to their organizers is particularly hard to fathom because, during its heyday, the Middleton machine never became an object of contemporary debate and hence analysis. It managed to put an end to the controversy raised by Lord Randolph Churchill over the National Union. Not till the beginning of the new century did the conduct of the National Union provoke criticism from the press.[95] Not till the tariff reform debate, after Salisbury's and Middleton's retirement, did the major parts of the machine, no longer closely coordinated, become a forum and an object of attack. Not till the repeated Conservative defeats of 1910, when the Middleton machine was a thing of the past, was it held up as model to be envied and emulated. The fact that Middleton's term as Principal Agent coincided with a period of unprecedented, almost unbroken electoral success for Conservatives might have led men to draw the apparent conclusion. However, inclined as always to credit their own policies and actions for their fortune, politicians in both parties gave the chief credit for Conservatives' success to their opposition to Home Rule and to the consequent Unionist alliance.

Middleton himself echoed this verdict. It was part of the genius of the machine that he insisted that Conservative electoral successes were victories for the Government and policies of Lord Salisbury. And certainly there was no direct equation between the amount of organizational vigour and the level of Conservative electoral success in the various regional divisions of his machine. Only in Wales did Conservatives' organization and their electoral performance match each other: both were feeble. The organization in Ireland and, to a lesser extent, Scotland enjoyed a degree of autonomy unknown in England and Wales, and assumed distinctive characters. The National Union formed a more powerful part of the Scottish than of the English organization.[96] The Scottish National Union was a more aristocratic, less popular body than its English counterpart, and on the whole less effective. In Ireland, Conservative party organization either assumed a confessional character, being inextricably entwined with the Orange Order,[97] or, where it avoided religious controversy, as the Irish Loyal and Patriotic Union attempted to do, it existed for British more than for Irish purposes, providing Irish propaganda against Home Rule for English and Scottish consumption. Within England, Conservative organization was at its most intense in Chamberlain's Duchy, through the contagion of Chamberlain's machine and the requirements of the

Unionist alliance, as much as through native Conservative electoral strength; and Chamberlain carried away most of the electoral fruits. Conservative organization was lively and sophisticated in the North and in East Anglia, but in both areas the Conservative electoral record was patchy. In the south-east, the heartland of Conservative electoral strength, party organization did not attract a great deal of attention after 1885, in part because it was already well developed.

There was reason underlying this uneven pattern. Organization could make little difference in safe seats, whether Liberal, Conservative, Irish Nationalist, or Orange. But it could make the difference between victory and defeat in the marginal constituencies of East Anglia and the North. The regional unevenness within the Middleton machine, accordingly, provides a measure of the size of its contribution to the Conservatives' electoral success. But to arrive at a measurement on this basis alone would be to underestimate the contribution. All of the general electoral contests of the last twenty years of the nineteenth century were close, including the seeming landslides. Even taking uncontested constituencies into account, the Conservative majorities elected to the House of Commons in 1895 and 1900, like the Liberal majority in 1880, were out of all proportion to the victorious party's lead in total of votes cast in the kingdom. Seemingly small considerations could make a large difference. To cite an example: Middleton contributed to the timing of the elections of 1892 and '95 by urging that they be called for harvest time, when agricultural labourers, a disturbingly uncertain quantity in his calculations, would be distracted from voting:[98] and Henry Pelling has remarked upon the high level of non-voting in rural constituencies in the general elections of 1892, 1895 and 1900.[99] In general, whether through registration or the timing of elections or a combination of both,[100] Middleton employed the restrictive devices available within the electoral system to disfranchise Liberal or unreliable voters and thus to minimize the hostile potentialities of a popular electorate.

Very occasionally, and even then before a select audience, the Conservative party testified to its debt to Middleton. The £10,000 given him after the triumph of 1895 was solicited through a discrete though extensive canvass. Enclosed in an inscribed, silver casket, the cheque was presented by Salisbury at a banquet in the Constitutional Club attended by two dukes and a bevy of other Conservative peers and M.P.s. Middleton usually shunned such prominence. Gruff, down to earth and businesslike, he made few speeches, and then only at conferences of the National Union or of the National Society of Conservative Agents. He was most as ease, hearty and convivial, in the company of his agents.

This inconspicuousness of conduct was, as noted earlier, a quality which Middleton and his machine possessed in common with Lord

Salisbury. And it was not the only characteristic which they shared. In his speech upon presenting the silver casket, Salisbury pointed, among Middleton's admirable qualities, to 'that knowledge of the world which will guard a man from the pitfalls into which too eager partisanship is ever likely to lead men.'[101] This was an unusual quality to single out for praise in the captain of the party's popular organization; but it was very much like his own observant detachment. Salisbury was also as exacting a professional and as sensitive to the significance of detail in his conduct of foreign affairs as Middleton was about electoral behaviour. The correspondence of the Middleton machine with Salisbury's needs and style as party leader was still closer. Just as Salisbury needed Akers-Douglas' ears to keep him abreast of opinion in the Parliamentary party, so he needed Middleton's intelligence network to keep him abreast of the electoral mood: even more so, for ultimately Salisbury's ability to command the allegiance of the party in the Commons depended upon his ability to gauge the tolerance of the electorate. Furthermore, Salisbury's wisdom in assessing the limits of this tolerance helped him to retain the respect of the Cabinet even after his capacities for work began to fail him. Middleton nourished that wisdom.

There was no anomaly in the building of an exemplary electoral organization while Lord Salisbury was prime minister. Lacking the magnetism of a Disraeli or even a Peel, Salisbury never suffered from the illusion that he could personally absorb the attention of the body politic. He recognized his need for organizational reinforcement in the House of Commons and among the electorate at large. In spite of his occasionally derogatory comments about mere partisanship, he was dependent upon the Conservative party, both in Parliament for his leadership of the Unionist alliance, and in the country for the performance of the electorate. In addition to greasing the wheels of organization with honours and occasional counsel, what this dependence demanded of him was loyalty to the support thus organized. And that was what he had demanded from party leaders ever since he entered public life. Finally, the Middleton machine reflected something of Salisbury's purpose as a statesman, in that it was a means for controlling and steadying the electorate. In comparison with Liberal organization, the emphasis in the Conservative organization was less on arousing and more on educating and curbing the electorate. The spirit in which constituency agents worked was professional rather than popular; and Conservatives set the pace in professionalizing their occupation. The Conservative network of agents quickly became the dynamic part of the Conservative machinery, while the National Union of Conservative Associations, though continuing to press certain policy predilections of its own, was fundamentally docile. Within the Liberal party, the situation was reversed. The National Liberal Federation was the dominant part of the

Liberal organization, and was capable of forcing the party leaders' pace. Developed in response to the emergence of a popular electorate, the Middleton machine helped an anti-popular statesman steady and restrain the power he feared.

## NOTES

1. Lady Gwendolen Cecil, *Life of Salisbury*, I, pp. 270–1.
2. Salisbury at Glasgow, *The Times*, 2 October, 1884, 7d.
3. The organization was not quite as unenterprising as the 1880 election results seemed to imply. In a perhaps foolish attempt to disperse Liberal energies Conservative candidates had been fielded in hopeless Scottish boroughs. Still, the Principal Agent, W. B. Skene, proved ineffectual. The Chief Whip, Sir William Hart-Dyke, fell ill shortly before the election. No record was kept of financial commitments made during its course. Trevor Lloyd, *The General Election of 1880* (London, 1968), p. 145; Robert Blake, *The Conservative Party from Peel to Churchill* (London, 1970), p. 149; Northcote's diary, 28 May and 5 June 1880, Iddesleigh papers, B. L. Add. MSS. 50063a; H. J. Hanham, *Elections and Party Management* (London, 1959), p. 363
4. *Supra*, p. 6.
5. Trevor Lloyd, *The General Election of 1880* (London, 1968), p. 135.
6. 'Ministerial embarrassments', *Quarterly Review*, CLI (April 1881), p. 541. Cf. Trevor Lloyd, *op. cit.*, p. 136.
7. Lady Salisbury to Disraeli, 17 April 1880, Beaconsfield papers.
8. *The Times*, 25 May 1882, 12c.
9. A letter from Salisbury on the formation of a new Conservative Association, *The Times*, 19 July 1882, 8d.
10. *Hansard*, 3rd ser., CCLXXXIII, 700–4 (16 August 1883).
11. *Hansard*, 3rd ser., CCXCI, 1146 (31 July 1884), and 1716–17 (5 August 1884).
12. Salisbury at Norwich, *The Times*, 29 July 1887, 8a.
13. Salisbury to the Constitutional Club, *The Times*, 23 May 1887, 12a.
14. Salisbury to the Queen, 18 October 1889, Royal Archives, A67/93.
15. F. M. C., *Which shall We Have? Mrs. G. O. M.—The Grand Old Madam—or the Hertfordshire Man!*, (Hoddesdon, 2nd ed., 1887), p. 11.
16. Ian Malcolm, *Vacant Thrones* (London, 1931), p. 5.
17. Salisbury to McDonnell, 12 October 1894, McDonnell papers.
18. A Privy Councillor (J. S. Sandars), *Studies of Yesterday*, (London, 1928), p. 167; Lady Gwendolen Cecil, *Life of Salisbury*, III, p. 197.
19. The party's central fund was managed by three trustees: Akers-Douglas, Abergavenny, and the Whip in the Lords. The last two also took responsibility for raising the funds, especially before general elections. Salisbury kept personal control over a considerable portion of the budget. Middleton to Salisbury, 5 August 1890, and a note by McDonnell, 8 December 1890, Salisbury papers, with Middleton's letters to Salisbury.
20. See Agatha Ramm, ed., *The Political Correspondence of Mr. Gladstone and Lord Granville, 1876–1886* (Oxford, 1972), I, p. 351.
21. There was an ardent streak in McDonnell that led him first in the early 1890s to join the volunteer force armed to fight for Ulster if Gladstone's second Home Rule Bill should carry, then to volunteer for and see active duty in the Boer War, and finally to rush off in 1915 at the age of fifty-four to Flanders, where he was killed.

22. See *Who Was Who* (1897–1916); *The Times'* obituary on 28 February 1905, 10d; and *Conservative Clubs Gazette*, C (July 1903).
23. *The Tory*, XXXIX and XL (April & May 1896), p. 4.
24. Lord George Hamilton, *Parliamentary Reminiscences and Reflections* (London, 1916), I, pp. 9–10.
25. Sir John Blundell Maple, M.P. for the Dulwich Division of Camberwell. Middleton had sat for Dulwich on the London County Council.
26. 'Disintegration', p. 316.
27. Barry McGill, 'Francis Schnadhorst and Liberal party organization,' *Journal of Modern History*, XXXIV, 1 (March 1962), p. 28. But see also A. B. Cooke and J. R. Vincent, *The Governing Passion* (Brighton, 1974), p. 424.
28. 'It is a most singular fact, that the only influences having an affinity for the old corruption, which still survive in Great Britain, are such as can be brought to bear on those exalted regions of society, in which stars, garters, ribands, titles, and lord-lieutenancies, still circulate.' Sir Henry Maine, *Popular Government* (N. Y., 1886), p.105. For a more accurate assessment of the amount and character of patronage at this time, see H. J. Hanham, 'Political patronage at the Treasury, 1870–1912', *Historical Journal*, III (1960), pp. 75–84.
29. A Privy Councillor (J. S. Sandars), *Studies of Yesterday* (London, 1928), p. 161.
30. Lord Wolmer to McDonnell, 26 February 1892, and McDonnell's note on it, Salisbury papers.
31. *Infra*, pp. 224–5.
32. *The Tory*, XXII (November 1894), p. 5.
33. Salisbury to the National Union, *The Times*, 20 November 1895, 7d.
34. Lady Gwendolen Cecil, *Life of Salisbury*, III, pp. 192–3.
35. Salisbury to Sir Henry Ponsonby, 23 March 1890, Royal Archives L7/64.
36. J. M. Maclean, *Recollections of Westminster and India* (Manchester, 1902), p. 126.
37. See G. W. E. Russell, *Collections and Recollections* (London, 7th ed., 1904). pp. 188–9.
38. On 1 June 1897 (sic), in *The Tory*, LI and LII (April and May 1897), pp. 11–13.
39. *The Tory*, XVII (1 June 1894), pp. 2–3.
40. *The Conservative Agents Journal*, 1 (January 1902), pp. 21–2.
41. H. J. Hanham, *Elections and Party Management*, pp. 233 and 248.
42. Dr. Hanham makes this estimate *(Elections and Party Management*, p. 242), which almost certainly errs on the low side since he excludes solicitor agents from the ranks of the full-time. Quite a few solicitor agents served full-time. One was elected in 1894 to be chairman of the National Society's Council.
43. *Ibid.*, p. 240.
44. *The Tory*, I (June 1892), p.4.
45. The Letterbook of the Secretary of the National Society of Conservative Agents, 1891–1895, preserved in the Westminster City Library on Buckingham Palace Road, provides an intimate record of Lyons' work. This library also possesses a Minute Book of the Society from 1895 to 1903.
46. *The Tory* opened a correspondence column for subscribers. One wrote in: 'Having utilized popular actresses, of untarnished fame, as canvassers, I can confidently recommend them to brother Agents. Their beauty appeals where logic fails.' *The Tory*, III (20 September 1892), p. 109.
47. *The Tory*, XVII (1 June 1894), p. 30.
48. *Infra*, p. 286 n. 34.
49. National Union Annual Conference Minutes, 14 December 1892, pp. 147–8.
50. Neal Blewett, 'The franchise in the United Kingdom, 1885–1918', *Past & Present*, XXXII (December 1965), pp. 44–50.
Balfour to Salisbury, 12 January 1894, Salisbury papers.

52. As late as 1880, Gorst could comment to Northcote: 'When the contest becomes one of money we are in most places no match for our opponents.' Gorst to Northcote, 15 September 1880, Iddesleigh papers, B. L. Add. MSS. 50041.
53. Barry McGill, *op. cit.*, 38–9.
54. *The Conservative Agents' Journal*, VII (July 1903), p. 73.
55. *The Tory*, XVII (1 June 1894), p. 2–3.
56. There are biographical sketches of many of the agents in the pages of *The Tory* and of Ashmead Bartlett's weekly newspaper, *England*.
57. *The Tory*, XXIII (December 1894), pp. 15–16.
58. As Middleton put it: 'A good candidate was one who devoted his time to making himself popular, and a bad candidate, one who was always interfering in details.' *The Tory*, XXIII (December 1894), p. 22.
59. Salisbury to an assembly of Scottish Conservatives and Liberal Unionists at Edinburgh, *The Times*, 1 December 1888, 8a.
60. Salisbury to Churchill, 1 April 1884, copy, Churchill papers.
61. James Cornford, 'The transformation of Conservatism in the late nineteenth century', *Victorian Studies*, VII, 1 (September 1963), p. 46.
62. Salisbury at the Crystal Palace, *The Times*, 4 March 1886, 10a. Cf. Byron Reed in his opening address as chairman of the National Union: 'whilst Gladstonianism can find a convenient foothold in rustic credulity the Conservative cause finds warmth and welcome and strength in the great urban constituencies in the country, and points to the great centres of intelligent population as the great strongholds of the Conservative party.' National Union Annual Conference Minutes, 24 November 1891.
63. Middleton to the Midland Union Association of Conservative Agents, 1 June 1897 (sic), in *The Tory*, LI and LII (April and May 1897), pp. 11–13.
64. Remarks by a Mr. Waddington from Barnsley, National Union Annual Conference Minutes, 18 November 1890, p. 113.
65. Memorandum on the ' "Campaign" Fund,' Salisbury papers, with Reginald MacLeod's letters to Salisbury.
66. Middleton to Mr. Saumarez, 8 October 1885, Chilston papers, Middleton's copybook.
67. Brought out initially by the Scottish organization.
68. *The Tory*, XV (15 April 1894), pp. 15–16.
69. National Union Conference Minutes, 23 July 1884, p. 117; H. J. Hanham, *op. cit.*, p. 112.
70. Reginald Lucas, *Lord Glenesk and the 'Morning Post'* (London, 1910), pp. 304–6.
71. Middleton to Lord Dartmouth, 16 February 1887, Chilston papers, Middleton's copybook.
72. Edward Hamilton's diary, 5 February 1887, XVI, p. 102, B. L. Add. MSS. 48645, f. 102.
73. Robert Blake, *The Conservative Party from Peel to Churchill* (London, 1970), p. 156.
74. Robert McKenzie, *British Political Parties* (N. Y., 2nd ed., 1964), p. 177.
75. John A. Bridges, *Reminiscences of a Country Politician* (London, 1906), p. 174.
76. Middleton to the Secretaries of the Provincial Unions of the National Union, 23 March 1887, Chilston papers, Middleton's copybook.
77. Middleton to McDonnell, 9 March 1897, with notes by McDonnell and Salisbury, 9 March 1897, Salisbury papers.
78. B. H. Brown, *The Tariff Reform Movement in Great Britain, 1881–1895* (N. Y., 1943), pp. 67–81; National Union Annual Conference Minutes, 1895, 1896 and 1900.
79. Papers in the National Union program of 1890, with notes by McDonnell and Salisbury, 6 November 1890, Salisbury papers, with Middleton's letters to Salisbury; *The Times*, 20 November 1890, 4a.

80. National Union Annual Conference Minutes, 24 November 1891, pp. 91–114.
81. National Union Conference Minutes, 29 November 1898.
82. Herbert Paul, *History of Modern England* (London, 1904–6), IV, p. 192.
83. *Birmingham Daily Gazette*, 5 October 1888.
84. J. H. Robb, *The Primrose League, 1883–1906* (N. Y., 1942), pp. 56 and 118. Much of the following information is derived from this source.
85. Middleton to Mr. Read, 24 May 1886, Chilston papers, Middleton's copybook.
86. Speech at Ormskirk, *The Times*, 19 October 1893, 8a.
87. J. H. Robb, *op. cit.*, pp. 88–9.
88. *The Times*, 23 April 1885, 7e.
89. A. L. Rowse, *The Later Churchills* (London, 1958), p. 294.
90. Janet Howarth, 'The Liberal revival in Northamptonshire, 1880–1895', *Historical Journal*, XII, 1 (1969), p. 97.
91. James Annand, 'The reorganization of liberalism', *New Review*, XIII, 78 (November 1895), p. 496.
92. *The Conservative Clubs Gazette*, LXVII (October 1900).
93. 'Clean, bright rooms, with the means of playing drafts & bagatelle is the chief want—For Reading Rooms—hire one or two good rooms & furnish as simply as possible—get all your friends to send their papers as soon as finished with—spare books, etc.—you must buy a few daily papers. . . all our successes begin in this way.' Middleton to Lord St. Oswald, 8 March 1887, Chilston papers, Middleton's copybook. £40 was suggested in 1895 as enough to get started. Entrance and annual membership fees were kept very low, most commonly to one shilling. Association of Conservative Clubs, *Monthly Circular*, VIII (November 1895).
94. *The Tory*, XIX (August 1894), pp. 2–3.
95. Robert McKenzie, *loc. cit.*
96. Unionist Organization Committee Report, June 1911, pp. 30–1; D. K. Irwin, 'The development of the Conservative party organization in Scotland until 1912', *Scottish Historical Review*, XLIV, 138 (October 1965), p. 109.
97. D. C. Savage, 'The general election of 1886 in Great Britain and Ireland', University of London Ph.D. dissertation, no. 21842, 1958, p. 440; D. C. Savage, 'The origins of the Ulster Unionist party, 1885–6', *Irish Historical Studies*, XII, 47 (March 1961), pp. 185–208.
98. Middleton to Salisbury, 3 April 1890, Middleton's copy book, Chilston papers: 'If your wish to give . . . [a peerage] is such that you do not mind the risk of a reduced majority, the best time for creating such a vacancy would in my opinion be about the first week in May so that the election would take place about the 20th May or a little later—the labourers will thus have had two or three months of good wages and the hay harvest will not be engrossing the attention of the Farmers which might be the case in June.'
99. Henry Pelling, *Social Geography of British Elections, 1885–1910* (N. Y., 1967), p. 428.
100. P. F. Clarke, *Lancashire and the New Liberalism* (Cambridge, 1971), p. 122.
101. *The Tory*, XXXVIII (March 1896), p. 10.

# CHAPTER 7

# EMPOWERED BY DEFEAT, WEAKENED BY VICTORY

> Morley (after he had replaced Balfour as Chief
> Secretary for Ireland): What is more and more
> clear to me is that you cannot know the House of
> Commons to good effect unless you are actually in
> it and at work. The detached man is no use.
> Balfour: Yes, and the curious thing is that men
> who have been in the House of Commons, when
> they go into the House of Lords, seem quite to
> forget the temper and the ways of the House of
> Commons.
>
> *Viscount Morley, Recollections, I, 228*

There was a martial quality to the experience of the forces defending the Union in the first half of the '90s. The collapse of Irish Nationalist unity over the O'Shea divorce revived Unionists' spirits. They held the victory of the Home Rule alliance in the general election of 1892 to such narrow dimensions that it deprived the new Government of authority to insist upon its legislative programme. For the next three years, the Unionist forces intensified their opponents' weakness by conducting themselves as if always on the eve of a general election. This energy and enterprise won its reward in 1895 with the formation of a coalition Unionist Ministry immediately hailed as the strongest Government of modern times and confirmed in office by the most sweeping electoral victory since 1832. But the grip of the Unionist captain upon his forces fluctuated in inverse relation to the ebb and flow of battle. His ability to control his forces was increased by their loss of a governing majority in 1892 and was reduced by their electoral victory in 1895.

## i. The Changes of Unionist Leadership in the Commons

Nothing proved more ironic in this tale than Salisbury's appointment of his own nephew, Arthur Balfour, to lead the Government in the House of Commons after W. H. Smith died in October, 1891. The intimate relative would never enable Salisbury to direct the party in the Commons with as little intermediary distortion as Smith had done. Though Balfour was the popular choice, Salisbury felt some uneasiness about the charges of nepotism to which he would be open in making the appointment. If Smith had died during the summer while Parliament was still sitting, Salisbury would have handed over to a meeting of the Parliamentary party the task of selecting a successor.[1] But fear of appearing nepotistic was never a dominant emotion in him. The obligation of making the selection himself during the Parliamentary recess threw Salisbury into turmoil both because of the man he had to select and because of the man he had to pass over.

George Goschen had entered the Ministry on the tacit understanding that, once the Conservatives in the Commons grew accustomed to him on the front bench, he would take Smith's place. Smith's success as leader delayed Goschen's elevation much longer than anyone initially expected. Still, whenever Smith was absent from the House, Goschen served as his deputy, and Goschen looked forward to the reversion. At stake was the leadership not only in the Commons but perhaps eventually also of the whole Unionist alliance. Within days of Smith's death it became apparent that, in spite of Goschen's years of critically valuable service, he possessed no personal following whatsoever. Far from identifying Liberal Unionist interests with Goschen, Hartington and Wolmer expressed an emphatic preference for Balfour.[2] Even the financial community, from whose ranks Goschen had entered politics, was less impressed by his orthodoxy at the Exchequer than it was irritated by his small innovations. His colleagues on the Treasury bench had found his whispered commentary on debate in the Commons distracting, and were exasperated by his indecisiveness. The conclusive drawback was his failure to attract cordial support from the Conservative backbenches. His elevation to the leadership would take the heart out of the party in the Commons just as it entered what might well be its final session before a general election.

The case for passing over Goschen in favour of Balfour was overwhelming. It filled Salisbury, nevertheless, with uneasiness. Salisbury was, in fact, the one person who sympathized with Goschen's desire for the leadership. Neither Goschen nor Balfour would be as malleable as Smith had been. Still, the reflexes of Goschen and Salisbury, particularly on domestic policy, were closely akin, and they treated Chamberlain with the same sceptical caution. Balfour, on the other hand, had left his uncle in no doubt about his sympathy for many of Chamberlain's proposals. At last, conquered by mounting evidence of the antagonism of Conservative M.P.s, Goschen put Salisbury out of his misery by conceding that he would be unacceptable as leader and agreeing to serve under Balfour.

The urbanity of Balfour's relationship with his uncle disguised critical differences in perspective. They enjoyed each other's company, and were sharpened by their intellectual interplay. Both men had an eye for the general issue at stake in particular points of controversy. Both were dissecting and cynical in their method of analysis. Both observed the man around them with detachment. Their differences were related to these very affinities. In the first place, Salisbury was the greater cynic. Balfour's cynicism was not as profound—nor as fine—as his uncle's. His conclusions, as a result, were less firmly rooted and more tentative than Salisbury's. And Balfour was susceptible to Chamberlain's enthusiasm for programme construction. Secondly, Balfour was more of a philosopher, fascinated by ideas, and less of a scientist, fascinated by facts, than his uncle. Quite apart from whatever instinctive understanding Salisbury may have possessed of the English public, Balfour lacked Salisbury's perpetual concern for detailed information about electoral opinion and behaviour. Finally, detached behaviour was less appropriate for the nephew in the Commons than for the uncle in the Lords.

The drawbacks of Balfour in his new position became apparent soon after Parliament reopened. His detachment had served him well as Irish Secretary, for it made him impervious to the waves of emotion produced by ugly incidents inevitable in any coercive administration, and also to the torrent of abusive questions which Nationalist M.P.s hurled at him in the Commons. Conservative M.P.s delighted in his performance, and even Home Rulers accorded him grudging respect. He emerged enhanced from an office which had shattered the health or political prospects of a string of predecessors. But Ireland was comparatively calm now. The virtue of cool self-possession under fire was no longer at a premium. His new assignment was to rally the tired ranks of the Conservative party in the Commons for one last session before Parliament was dissolved.

The Government's slate of legislation made the task more difficult. Two main measures, a Small Holdings Bill and an Irish Local Government Bill, were framed, not so much to hearten the troops for the election, but to reconcile the conflicting interests of Chamberlain and the English and Irish landowners. Chamberlain treated the subject of small holdings, that is to say the creation of very small farms, on the same basis as garden allotments, and wished to see compulsory clauses in Bills on both. The Conservative M.P.s of Henry Chaplin's stamp, who sat for rural constituencies and were nervous about the agricultural labourer's vote, agreed whole-heartedly with Chamberlain about garden allotment, but were very uneasy about forcing landowners to sell larger portions of their property for small holdings. The Small Holdings Bill of 1892, by excluding compulsion, fell between two stools. English landowners considered it at best a disagreeable political necessity, while Chamberlain endorsed it merely as better than nothing.

At least the Small Holdings Bill reached the statute books. An ignominious fate awaited the Irish Local Government Bill, which bore a similar political complexion. Any concession to the demand for indigenous institutions of government in Ireland aroused the fears of Irish Unionists and the suspicions of the English Conservative right wing. On the other hand, the elective local governing authorities which the Bill proposed for Ireland were so hedged with safeguards that they failed to satisfy Radical Unionists and those Tories who thought that some concession to Irish nationalism short of Home Rule might solve the problem. Gladstonians and Nationalists greeted the Bill with hoots of derision. Balfour's airy candour in presenting it made matters worse. Even Conservatives tittered with embarrassment when he extolled the 'very great advantages in doing a stupid thing which has been done before, instead of doing a wise thing that has never been done before.'[3] Having failed to kindle enthusiasm in any part of the House, the Local Government Bill was allowed to die after a second reading.

Weakness in the leader in the Commons was not entirely undesirable from Salisbury's point of view. What made the change of Conservative command in the Commons more disturbing was its connection with a parallel change in the Liberal Unionist command. Both allied parties in the lower House entered the session of 1892 under new leadership, the larger under Balfour, the smaller under Chamberlain. The partnership between the two men created a concentration of Unionist power in the House of Commons which reduced Salisbury's powers of control. The crisis of 1890 had already demonstrated his inability to impose his will in a matter of vital moment upon the leaders in the Commons. Balfour and Chamberlain were now in positions which would eventually enable them to make that limitation upon Salisbury's power permanent.

Lord Hartington succeeded his father as Duke of Devonshire in December 1891. His removal from the Commons institutionalized a shift of power which was already taking place within the Liberal Unionist leadership. Hartington, now Devonshire, was going the way of Goschen. Salisbury valued his counsel and found him much more agreeable to work with than Chamberlain. But the electoral contribution of Liberal Unionists to the allied cause depended on their appeal to voters who retained Liberal leanings on issues other than Home Rule. Concerned to maintain cordial relations with the Conservative leaders, Devonshire had always taken care to ascertain the limits of their tolerance before speaking in public. Chamberlain reversed this order of precedence, aware that his power rested less upon the good graces of the Conservative leaders than upon the electoral and hence Parliamentary support which he brought to the alliance. The by-election reverses suffered by Liberal Unionists were interpreted, whether correctly or not, as underscoring the need for Chamberlain's approach and the inadequacy of Devonshire's.

Although Devonshire retained his position as national leader of the

Liberal Unionist party and also took over from Lord Derby as the leader of the Liberal Unionists in the House of Lords, that did not compensate for his loss of immediate control over the conduct of his contingent in the Commons. Devonshire's loss was also Salisbury's. Now the two national leaders, weakened by their seats in the Lords, had to deal with two leaders in the Commons who strengthened and complemented each other.

The relationship between Salisbury and Chamberlain never settled down. It twisted and turned from the early '80s when each abused the other as the embodiment of the enemy he fought, through various phases of mistrust and cordial cooperation, to Salisbury's deathbed when he decried the havoc Chamberlain was wreaking among the Unionist forces which he had sedulously kept together. When Chamberlain became Liberal Unionist leader in the Commons, the two men still knew little of each other from face to face encounter. They had been kept in touch through two members of Salisbury's family circle, Balfour and Wolmer. Still, Salisbury and Chamberlain had more in common than opposition to Home Rule. When things were going against the Unionist alliance, both had the instinct not to appease the enemy, but to fight. In the crisis of 1890, for example, Chamberlain heartily endorsed Salisbury's attempt to allow Bills to be carried over from one session to the next, while Hartington collaborated with the Ministers in the Commons urging abandonment of the Government's legislative programme. Salisbury and Chamberlain, as Disraeli might have put it, were men of courage.

They shared, furthermore, a pragmatic approach to the alliance. In the case of Chamberlain, the Radical demagogue turned Unionist, this opportunism, as it was more often called, was obvious and brought ceaseless cries of apostasy down upon him from Gladstonians. Salisbury was more circumspect and never generated strong emotion. But on occasion he deliberately exposed his pragmatism to the public. In 1888, in an attempt to induce Conservatives to adjust their thinking to changes taking place in party loyalties, he asked a Primrose League audience 'whether we do not attach somewhat too much importance to the names of parties in the present time'. He went on to suggest an answer:

> Remember that the problems of the age are changing as we live, that the things for which we fought when we were young no longer remain to be fought about when we are old... there are other questions that are arising... To my mind we are coming to a state of things where two questions above all will occupy the minds of statesmen and the efforts of political men. One is the condition, constitution, defence, and upholding of the Empire which we hold among the nations of the world. The other one is one that is related to the former—very closely related. How shall we maintain our extended commerce, or, in other words, how shall we furnish employment for our teeming millions?[4]

As he had done with Ireland, so he was now doing with Empire. He was testing a bridge to link the expanding popular sentiment of nationalism with defence of the economic order, a bridge which Liberal Unionists and Conservatives could occupy with equal ease.

Chamberlain took to this bridge with ever deepening enthusiasm. He and Salisbury approached the subject of Empire, however, with differing degrees of confidence. In odd contrast to the personal impression which each man conveyed, Salisbury had the greater confidence, not only in Britain's imperial strength but also in the resilience of the existing economic order. The industrial disturbances of the late 1880s did not alarm him. He predicted that the socialist virus would lack staying power[5] or that its remedies would be exposed as fallacious, and that in either case capitalism would win. Chamberlain was much more apprehensive. He sensed a need to consolidate Britain's imperial claims and to shore up the economic order with beneficent labour legislation and social insurance. Chamberlain's whole approach to domestic policy was summed up in the term 'programme.' Even the use of the word to denote a number of proposals calculated to appeal to a variety of economic and social interests within the electorate was his coinage.[6] In Chamberlain's mouth the word was filled with a spirit of urgent construction. As the lifespan of the Parliament elected in 1886 drew toward a close, he unfolded a programme including an eight-hour day for miners, small holdings for the agricultural labourers, workmen's compensation for industrial accidents, legislation to enable working men to own their homes, and extension of elective local government to the parish and district level.

Salisbury responded to this, as to all of Chamberlain's programmes, in piecemeal fashion. He rejected those items which, in his estimation, would destroy economic confidence or alienate Conservatives of Bartley's stripe, whatever their appeal to Chamberlain's Radicals. He excised unacceptable features of others; and he endorsed the remaining few. When an eight-hours Bill was first proposed, he flatly turned it down:

> To make such a law would be an unpardonable interference with the freedom which Englishmen of all classes have established for many generations, would interfere with the natural relations of trade, would drive capital out of trade, and would be ultimately ineffective because it would ultimately lead to a general redistribution of wages all around.[7]

Small holdings legislation he would tolerate as a harmless gesture, but only if compulsion were excluded. On that point he dug in his heels, playing for time until the general election, which he thought the Conservatives would probably lose. 'I have', he told Balfour, 'a strong conviction that I can get better terms for property out of office, than I can in office, upon this point. Compulsion must end in taking land at an artificially low valuation : otherwise it will be useless.'[8] Old age pensions, which Chamberlain approached with a modest pilot scheme, Salisbury met with similar modesty, proposing to reinforce the existing benefit societies,[9] an alternative which Chamberlain was willing to try.

The extent of the difference between Salisbury and Chamberlain was not too great to overcome. But it could have led equally well to war; great parties have fought over less. In 1892 Salisbury did not know which it would be. In building his own platform for the general election Salisbury accommodated the demand for social reform, to the extent that he did, out of deference, not so much to Chamberlain, as to reformers within his own party. In the Lords' debate on the Factories and Workshops Bill of 1891, Salisbury had had to ward off attack from two directions; one from Lord Wemyss who opposed any governmental regulation of industry, and the other from the Tory Democrat, Lord Dunraven, who wanted to extend the Bill to embrace laundries.[10] The Conservative Campaign Guide for 1892 took pride in the Government's record of social legislation, which included a Cotton-Cloth Factories Act to protect the homes of textile workers against excessive damp and dust, and an Act tightening safety regulations on the railways. Conservatives, Salisbury among them, used these measures to demonstrate the wisdom of Parliament devoting its attention to improvements in material wellbeing rather than to perpetual tinkering with the constitution. Chamberlain publicly claimed credit for the progressive features in the Government's domestic record, in particular for the Local Government Act of 1888 and for free education. But when a backbench Conservative, H. H. Howorth, wrote Salisbury to complain about these supposedly humiliating concessions to Chamberlain, Salisbury could justly reply that they were the fruit of widespread Conservative concern. He could also observe that the need which Chamberlain felt to publicize his claim provided 'some proof that it is not self-evident, & requires a good deal of special pleading to make it out.'[11]

In the two years between his elevation to the Liberal Unionist leadership in the Commons and the general election, Chamberlain pressed Salisbury hard; but Salisbury responded with equal, and ultimately more efficacious, vigour. Until the eve of the formal campaign, they conducted their dialogue on English domestic issues in public. At last, in June 1892, Salisbury contacted Chamberlain, first through Wolmer and then directly, pressing him to cease stamping the Government's legislative record in public with a Liberal Unionist rather than a Conservative impress. His letter was courteous but firm in its assertion of his own claim. He denied the need for Conservatives to reproach themselves for having 'deserted their colours and changed their coats... though', he went on, 'I believe it is true that they have

proved—and that you have found them—more liberal on many points
than in 1885 you could have imagined.'[12] Chamberlain acceded to the
request, and for the rest of the campaign concentrated attention upon
the issue of Home Rule.

It was not so much by main force as by influencing the thinking of
Conservatives, particularly of Balfour, that Chamberlain could mould
the domestic policy of the alliance. Though the framing and implementation of the measures to aid the Irish economy, for example, were
Balfour's work, they received their inspiration from plans which
Chamberlain had laid out. Balfour was similarly impressed by other
parts of Chamberlain's programme, enough at any rate to contemplate
'ambitious legislation'.[13] Throughout the second Ministry, Salisbury
preserved Conservative predominance by presiding over two councils:
an informal one of the leaders of the allied parties, who seldom met as a
group but conducted their negotiations in pairs or by letter; and the
formal, essentially Conservative Cabinet. The separation of these
councils, which suited Salisbury's purposes, struck Balfour as dangerously divisive. In 1888 Balfour contemplated using the subject of
Smith's deteriorating health to raise the possibility of a coalition.[14] In
the brief interlude between receipt of the returns from the 1892 election
and the fall of the Government he relayed to Salisbury in a sympathetic
manner Chamberlain's talk about closer collaboration between the
allied parties, including the possibility of fusion.[15] But as Balfour
expected, Salisbury did not yet welcome such a course, which he was
easily able to avoid.

## ii. The Leverage provided by the Lords

The outcome of the general election placed Salisbury in the strongest
position of his entire career because the swing against his Government
was held to creditably narrow proportions while the Parliamentary base
of Conservative power shifted from the House of Commons, over which
he had indirect control through independently minded colleagues, to
the House of Lords, where he was in undisputed command. The election
also gave Salisbury less concrete dividends. The campaign drew the
Unionist alliance together. Once Salisbury had induced Chamberlain to
mute the annoying features of his talk about domestic issues, the two men
in their speeches struck similar chords. In addition to declaiming against
Home Rule, both men wooed the Nonconformists. What drew
Nonconformists to the side of Home Rule was the moral appeal with
which Gladstone invested it, but the revelation of Parnell's liaison with
Kitty O'Shea had undermined that appeal. The conspicuous influence
of the Catholic clergy within the subsequent, anti-Parnellite majority of
Irish Nationalist M.P.s increased the possibility that a Home-Rule

Ireland would be priest-ridden. Nonconformity in 1892 seemed to be a detachable body of opinion. Chamberlain's title to woo them, dating back more than twenty years to his leadership of their campaign against the voluntary school system, was hard to impeach. Salisbury was an improbable suitor but he played without restraint upon Nonconformists' 'fiercest prejudices' against 'ecclesiastical domination'.[16]

The election-time concord between Salisbury and Chamberlain could be lost, however, as quickly as it had been found. It was from the specific results of the voting in the general election of 1892 that Salisbury derived the greatest advantage. Conservatives and their Unionist allies fared no worse than the supporters of any Government which had borne the responsibilities of office for six years were likely to do. The narrowness of Gladstone's victory and his dependence on the Irish Nationalist contingent for a governing majority dispelled many doubts about the electoral viability of opposition to Home Rule. At the same time the loss of a Conservative and Unionist majority in the Commons made the undiminished Conservative majority in the Lords of decisive importance in shaping Conservative and Unionist strategy. The power to control the alliance came to rest as never before or afterward in Salisbury's hands.

The election of 1892 was fiercely contested. It stayed in Middleton's mind as the hardest fought of his career[17] though both sides entered it tired from a Parliament which had run almost its full statutory term. The only impact of that fatigue upon the election was on its timing. Toward the end of May Salisbury convened one of the rare meetings of the Conservative and Liberal Unionist party leaders and organizers—Balfour, Akers-Douglas and Middleton as well as himself for the one side, Devonshire, Chamberlain and Wolmer for the other—to settle the date for dissolution. All but the two ardent fighters, Salisbury and Chamberlain, insisted on a speedy dissolution and a July election because of M.P.s, weariness and increasing preoccupation with their constituencies. Salisbury and Chamberlain, sensing that the electoral tide was moving in their favour, wished to push the Government's legislative proposals through, and go to the polls in October. But the electoral auguries were so hard to read—Chamberlain had never known them to be so obscure—and support in the Commons was so listless, that the two men did not insist upon their view.

The three British parties rose to the election in fighting trim. The Liberals had been ready and eager for a contest since 1888, and had largely recovered from the O'Shea divorce and Parnell's desertion, though the Irish Nationalists were still at each other's throats. Liberal Unionists had to prove their viability as permanent occupants of the electoral landscape. What the Whig Unionists lacked in numbers, they

tried to make good through financial contributions from their disproportionate share of wealthy supporters, and through Wolmer's organizational acumen. Chamberlain concentrated on his Duchy.
Middleton's organization had been purring powerfully, and now sprang
into action.

What the outcome would be was tantalizingly uncertain. The best
informed Unionist estimates were for a combined Gladstonian and Irish
Nationalist majority of between 28 and 40. Salisbury, though aware of
the advantages in losing office, always fought to win. He was, therefore,
initially disappointed when the county returns began to turn against
him. Nor can he have been completely happy about Chamberlain's
ability to reverse the national trend within his Duchy, increasing
his personal majority and wresting three additional seats from the
Gladstonians. It was Liberal Unionist resilience which prevented the
Liberal party from recovering its former vigour. The fall in the number
of Liberal Unionist seats nationally from the 79 of 1886 to 47 only
augmented Chamberlain's powers within his party. But these were faint
shadows on what was, from Salisbury's point of view, an otherwise
almost perfect result. Gladstone's margin in his own constituency of
Midlothian, where he expected a majority of 3000, fell to an embarrassing 690. The total number of his victorious supporters in the new House
of Commons, 270, was all but matched by the 268 successful
Conservatives. England declared itself emphatically against Home Rule
by 262 seats to 194. Only the Irish Nationalist contingent of 81 gave
Gladstone 'a motley majority'[18] of 40 with which to govern, and the
Nationalists were divided, nine of them still carrying Parnell's banner.

These results lent some delicacy to Salisbury's task of extricating his
Government from office. To resign before Parliament met would lend an
impression of decisiveness to the electoral verdict, which he had no wish
to convey. No one, in fact, knew whether Gladstone would be able to
carry a Home Rule Bill through the House of Commons. There was just
enough plasticity about the new Parliament to raise the possibility that a
Unionist Government could retain office. Such a Government, however,
would have to extend its ruling core to include Chamberlain and
Churchill, thus placing Salisbury's leadership in jeopardy, and would
have to woo possible Liberal defectors with advanced legislative
proposals. Salisbury wished, therefore, to transfer power to the Liberals
but without dispiriting the outgoing Government's supporters.

He acquitted himself with fair success. In order to avoid legislative
proposals which might divide his men and help to unify their opponents,
Salisbury insisted upon a strictly formal Queen's speech, devoid of any
substantive content. The Liberals had to drive him from office with the
straightforward confidence motion which he wanted. The only advantage
they could pluck from his proceedings was the month's delay between

the last election results and the fall of his Government, a month which they needed to induce a coy Lord Rosebery to accept the Foreign Office. That did not disturb Salisbury, for by placing foreign affairs in the hands of a man whose leading desire was to carry Britain's policy on without rupture, it removed foreign policy from the prospective agenda of party controversy. Salisbury's only slip was his disappointing if understandable lack of vigour in the Lord's debate on the Queen's speech[19] and that was quickly forgotten. Privately he could not disguise the lightness of heart he felt at his escape from office. The change of Government would test the pledges of the Liberals and the cohesion of the Home Rule alliance while enabling the Unionist alliance to avoid a similarly searching test. In view of the new Government's slim and motley majority, the House of Lords need feel no hesitation about rejecting legislative proposals which it felt to be intolerable, and in doing so it would magnify his Parliamentary power. After nearly seven years as prime minister the change allowed him to replenish his physical and mental resources: he confessed soon to his secretary, 'I mainly employ myself in sleeping'.[20] Even the unregulated workings of the economy moved in his favour. The slight downturn since 1890, which had contributed to the results of the election, deepened to distress his opponents.

Every department of the party and alliance responded to the holiday with renewed vigour. Some read the outcome of the election as proof of the Liberal's organizational superiority. Though confident that the charge was unjust, the Middleton machine undertook an inquest into the weak points revealed by the election. Alive to the possibility of a snap election any time after the Lords' rejection of the Home Rule Bill, *Campaign Guides* were published in 1894 and again in the early spring of 1895. His national machinery well in hand, Middleton extended his activity to fields which he had not yet ploughed. Until the mid-'90s, Conservatives and Liberal Unionists played down the bearing of the metropolitan politics of London upon the national scene by disguising their own participation in the London County Council under the label of the Moderate party. The disguise was never convincing, and the inclination to treat County Council elections as a barometer of the national weather increased, particularly when the Liberals gained much of their ground in the 1892 general election in the metropolitan constituencies. Ignoring the disguise, Middleton decided to run for a safe Council seat himself. And, in preparation for the Council elections scheduled for December 1894, he pressed Salisbury either to launch the Moderates' campaign or to permit Balfour to do so. The label of Moderate papered over a division between Liberal Unionists and Conservatives, of which Middleton was sharply conscious. There was talk of Chamberlain launching the campaign. Akers-Douglas and

Middleton wanted Salisbury or Balfour to preempt the initiative and place a restrained Conservative complexion upon the Moderates' programme before Chamberlain could develop it to his liking.[21] Middleton's stress on the national import of the campaign, and his own suspicions of the use to which Chamberlain might put the opportunity,[22] finally overcame Salisbury's dislike of anything to do with the London County Council. He did as Middleton bid, but in a disconcerting way. Unable to imagine what good the London County Council could do, he could not suggest to his metropolitan audience at the beginning of the local election campaign how the Moderates who might be elected to the Council ought to act. Instead he inveighed against its constitution and its evil tendencies: 'It is the place where Collectivist and Socialistic experiments are tried. It is the place where a new revolutionary spirit finds its instruments and collects its arms.'[23] So black a picture did he paint that the mover and seconder of the vote of thanks to him for his speech entered demurrers.

Middleton extended his organizational enterprise not only to the London County Council but much farther afield, to the exotic shores of India; and Salisbury, the former Indian Secretary, threw himself into this enterprise without any of the reservation he displayed over the London County Council. Soon after the 1892 election, Middleton received a contribution to the party coffers from an Indian prince, the Rajah of Bobilli. Pleased at this windfall but aware that the practice might carry implications which Salisbury might not welcome, Middleton reported it to him. First tacitly, then whole-heartedly, Salisbury bestowed his approval. His experience of paternal Indian government in the 1860s and '70s had confirmed his distrust of popular government at home. Recent developments both in India and at home reasserted this connection in his mind. From the early '80s, he had deplored the tendency of British Liberals to introduce elective councils into the fabric of Indian government and to widen their scope. Reaching for the general point at issue, Salisbury argued that the Liberals were displaying toward India the same willingness 'to place individual rights, & liberties...at the mercy of a mere numerical majority'[24] that they wished to apply to Ireland through Home Rule. The birth of the Congress party in India deepened his alarm. He embraced the Indian princes in the same spirit in which he embraced the propertied, Protestant minority of Ireland.

Middleton responded to this encouragement and cultivated other rajahs by sending them parcels of Conservative literature. During the London County Council campaign toward the end of 1894, he put Salisbury in touch with an ardently Conservative Englishman named Turner who was about to return to India where he had many friends among the princes. Turner left for India with a letter from Salisbury for

his princely friends in which Salisbury appealed to the princes' concern
about 'the maintenance of private rights and of national traditions . . .
The struggle before us', he concluded, 'is so severe that we need to enlist
on our side all our natural allies'.[25] Turner came back in April to report
that the princes had responded with great interest, and that they had
also cast covetous looks at the responsibility of Parliamentary representation in the Lords or the Commons.[26] Representative government,
however, was what Salisbury feared; and the Indian princes had to
content themselves with personal letters from the man soon again to be
prime minister.[27] The money from India began to flow in time for the
1895 election. Middleton followed on after the election by proposing to
appoint a Conservative party agent in India; and an Indian Carlton
Club was established in London for the convenience of visitors from
India, both Indian and English. Lord George Hamilton, the Secretary
of State for India in the new Unionist Government, opposed these
activities for fear that the princes would turn their contributions into a
form of bribery. 'No Englishman', he warned, 'is a match for an
intriguing Hindoo.'[28] Salisbury refused to be deterred, and Middleton
continued to accept contributions, at least until 1897.

The Indian scheme was more symptomatic of Conservative enterprise
during the Liberal interlude than an intrinsic source of strength. The
critical battles had to be waged on the conventional terrain of
Parliament and the constituency platforms, and with the conventional
weapons. Liberals had familiarized Britain with the use of persistent
platform oratory to reinforce their Parliamentary campaign during
Salisbury's second Ministry. The Conservatives now followed suit, and
with even greater intensity. While Gladstone's Home Rule Bill was
before the Commons, Middleton orchestrated a series of great rallies in
London, and Devonshire stimulated meetings in the provincial towns.

The great set piece of the Liberal interlude was the rejection of Gladstone's second Home Rule Bill. It was the House of Lords' part in this
rejection that interested Salisbury, not the rejection itself, for about that
there was no doubt. Even before the general election, after observing the
cornucopia of other promises which Liberals offered to the electorate, he
had stipulated that he would not take his party's defeat as a mandate for
Home Rule. The results of the election made it easy for him to stand by
this challenge. Now he wanted the defeat of the Bill to take place in the
House of Lords in order to demonstrate that, at least on the great issue of
Home Rule, the House of Lords represented British opinion in the new
Parliament better than the House of Commons. Even before the
Government changed hands he announced to the upper House that 'in
the year that is coming the centre of interest and the centre of action will
be found within these walls.'[29] During Parliament's autumn recess,
while the new Ministry prepared its legislation, he reiterated his bid to

make the Lords rather than the Commons the decisive theatre of action. In an article in the *National Review* on 'Constitutional Revision', he argued for general acceptance, on constitutional as well as passing political grounds, of the Lords' right to reject a Home Rule Bill. Some passages of his constitutional argument were quaintly reminiscent of his godfather, the Duke of Wellington, on the unreformed House of Commons. Excusing some of the anomalous characteristics of the upper House by pointing out the arbitrariness and folly of treating the lower as a steadily reliable index of public opinion, Salisbury drew the conclusion that 'it is the English constitution *as a whole*, that has succeeded. The illogical provisions of one part of it have balanced the illogical provisions of another'.[30] His political appeal was nonetheless robust:

> We are at the present juncture asked to adopt one of the most vital changes to which a nation can submit. We are to cut our country in two; and, in the smaller portion, we are to abandon a minority of our own blood and religion to the power of their ancient enemies, in spite of their bitter protest against the debasing and ruinous servitude to which we propose to leave them.[31]

When Parliament came back into session, Salisbury threw cold water on Chamberlain's suggestion that, in the event of protracted collision between the two Houses, Unionists should insist upon a referendum.[32] He was equally uninterested in tactics of debate in the Commons designed to split up the majority behind Gladstone's Bill by concentrating on the provisions about which Nationalists and Gladstonians were most likely to quarrel. Sir Edward Clarke, Solicitor General in the previous Ministry, believed that enough uneasy Liberal M.P.s could have been won over to defeat the Bill in the committee stage in the Commons if the Opposition had not fostered the assumption that the House of Lords could be relied upon to prevent the Bill's enactment.[33] The very assumption which Clarke regretted, Salisbury did his best to encourage.

He worked instead to maximize the number of peers who would vote against the Bill when it reached their House. Everyone knew that the Lords could defeat the Bill soundly because of the regular Conservative and Liberal Unionist preponderance there. Salisbury wanted a display of extraordinarily wide concurrence. The Unionist Whips took such pains to make sure that every one of their supporters, regardless of age or health, turned up to vote, that the saying went round that only two stayed away without compelling excuse: one shooting lions in Somaliland, the other killing rats at Reigate.[34] Salisbury extended his efforts beyond the serried ranks of his and Devonshire's supporters to embrace all but the diehard Gladstonian peers and office holders. Accordingly, he sought to please the episcopal bench by refraining from giving a partisan Conservative colour to the Church of England's Anti-

Home Rule rallies[35] and by leaving to the Archbishops rather than to the Conservative Whip the task of urging the bishops to cast their votes against the bill instead of abstaining. Devonshire and he canvassed the thirty-six Liberal Peers who had not yet made it clear whether they were Gladstonian or Liberal Unionist. The success of these efforts was complete. When, after six months in the Commons, the Bill reached the Lords, they took four days to debate it, and then threw it out by 419 votes to 41. It was the largest vote in the history of the House of Lords. The proportions of the defeat, better than ten to one, exceeded the Conservative Whip's best estimate. Every bishop, virtually all of the previously uncommitted Liberal peers, and even five of those reckoned to be loyal Gladstonians, trooped into the Opposition lobby. More than half of the minority held official positions from the Government. For one of the few times in his life,[36] Salisbury was the darling of the London crowds, and they cheered him through the streets as he made his way home after the vote.

The Lords' action gave their House the last spell of popular acclaim it was ever to enjoy. It owed its current state of health, the precarious features as well as the strong ones, largely to its leader. Simply by being there Salisbury heightened the importance of the House of Lords. He and, much more briefly, Rosebery were the last two men to pass their term as party leader entirely in the upper House. Salisbury's debating skill and power of speech lent weight to the otherwise brief, often desultory, proceedings of the Lords. What he gave his House was, of course, much more than a casual by-product of his talent. His creed and personal advantage led him to assert the rights of his House to the full and to cultivate appreciation of the Lords' contribution among the public. He also fostered the political talent available in the Lords, encouraging young peers when they entered into debate, quickly rewarding nascent enterprise with junior office, if not in the Ministry, then at court. He found it hard to promote many peers beyond this level. It was not a matter of talent: there seemed sometimes to be more Conservatives of intermediate Ministerial calibre in the Lords than in the Commons. But Salisbury felt obliged to maintain equal numbers of peers and commoners within his Ministries. This consideration blighted the careers of several peers, most notably Lord Cadogan.

Reform of the composition of the second chamber could increase its health still further, and might even aggrandize its weight at the expense of the Commons. The democratization of election to the House of Commons had rendered a second House composed of hereditary landowners precariously anomalous. Yet Salisbury approached reform of the Lords' composition cautiously. He had given conspicuous support in 1869 to Lord Russell's Bill for adding a leaven of life peers to the upper House. But when Rosebery raised the subject in 1884, just days before the Lords were to receive Gladstone's Bill extending the franchise for election to the House of Commons, Salisbury backed away.[37] To pay attention at that moment to the need for reform of the House of Lords would cast doubt on its right to resist the franchise Bill as he intended to do. The Liberal split over Home Rule greatly strengthened the case for reform. For it was in the House of Lords that the defections from Gladstone proved most numerous. Even before the split Conservative peers enjoyed a majority over Liberals in the neighbourhood of 60: the number of Conservative peers was put at 276, of Liberals at 216.[38] Afterwards the number loyal to Gladstone shrank to 40, with another 35 or so whose allegiance remained uncertain.[39] The Lords became an almost one-party House. Salisbury's insistence that this was a fleeting phenomenon produced largely by opposition to the policies of the one man, Gladstone, carried little conviction.

Rosebery moved for a committee of enquiry in 1888. As in 1884 he was not thinking simply of the good of the House. He wished to divert attention from Home Rule and also from the Local Government Bill which promised credit to the Ministry he opposed. He timed his motion to coincide with Ritchie's introduction of the Local Government Bill in the Commons. Rosebery's motion placed Salisbury in some difficulty. The nub of the matter was the addition of an elective element to the upper House. Such an addition would greatly strengthen the Lords *vis-a-vis* the Commons, and would therefore provoke fierce resistance among the Radical wing of the Liberal party, who would press instead for abolition of the upper House. On the other hand, any scheme of reform which did not provide such an elective addition would deeply disappoint not only Liberals of Rosebery's colour but also Radical Unionists and, still more seriously, ardent constructive spirits on the Conservative side such as the Earl of Dunraven and George Curzon. In short, Rosebery's motion placed the existing title of the House of Lords in question without much hope of replacing it with a stronger one.

Salisbury, therefore, attempted to render the movement for reform of the upper House innocuous. He turned down Rosebery's motion, and also a concrete scheme which Dunraven introduced, but promised to introduce a measure of his own. After protracted debate in the Cabinet, indicative of the issue's divisive potentialities, he presented the Lords with two Bills. One provided for the appointment of a number of life peers, never more than a total of fifty, and no more than five in any one year. The other Bill would give the Lords the power to expel 'black sheep'—those who went into insolvency or were thought to have brought discredit upon the House through scandalous behaviour—for the duration of each Parliament. The very limited scope of the measurers disappointed many Conservatives in the Lords and provoked some derisory comment among Conservatives in the Commons.

Salisbury's well-remembered response to Russell's Bill of 1869 had led them to hope for more. The Lords took up the Bills, though without enthusiasm, and were about to give the Life Peerages Bill its second reading, when the whole effort ended abruptly. At the very time that the Lords were debating the second reading of the Life Peerages Bill, Gladstone on the floor of the House of Commons offered to facilitate passage of the Local Government Bill and the accompanying Finance Bill on condition that Smith postpone legislation on reform of the Lords until a new session, when Parliament could devote its full energies to the subject; and Smith promptly agreed. His action, hurriedly conveyed to the upper House, embarrassed Salisbury, who criticized Smith's action, gently in public, sternly in private.[40] But Salisbury did not attempt to break the agreement between the two leaders in the Commons, which enabled him to blame Gladstone for the failure of the reform.

Salisbury discouraged all subsequent talk of reform. But quietly he used his power of recommending new peerages to effect a somewhat similar end. In one regard his use of his power aggravated the problem. He could have prevented the one-party character of the House of Lords from growing more pronounced if he had kept the number of his nominations small. Instead his annual rate of creation of new peerages rose even higher than the Liberals' rate during their intervening periods in office.[41] Conservative appetites after a half century of mainly Liberal Governments, and the demands of the Unionist alliance, could explain but did not excuse his extravagance. The failure of the Lords to reflect the extent of Liberal opinion in the country did not disturb him. But he was disturbed by the Lords' failure to reflect the variety of propertied interests. During the Caretaker Ministry, he inaugurated a policy, which Gladstone promptly adopted for himself, of assigning more than fifteen per cent of his creations to men who derived their wealth, not from land, but from commerce and industry.[42] Salisbury also pressed, sometimes against royal resistance, for the ennoblement of a sprinkling of distinguished men in the arts, medicine, and science. He took care too that the upper House contained experienced and articulate naval as well as army officers. His appointments did nothing to prepare the House of Lords for the day when the Liberals might win a potent majority in the House of Commons, but he brought the composition of the Lords into line with the composition of the Unionist alliance in the Commons.

The very widespread approval of or acquiescence in the rejection of the second Home Rule Bill by Salisbury's House of Lords seemed to bear out the claims which he had made on its behalf. But a much more searching test of these claims and hence of Salisbury's Parliamentary power was already in store. The Liberal Government had attempted to sugar Home Rule by promising a substantial assortment of domestic legislative reforms in the same Queen's speech that heralded the Home

Rule Bill. After the Lords rejected the Home Rule Bill, the Government honoured these promises by pressing forward with Bills on Employers Liability and on Parish Councils. The Bills posed a critical challenge to Salisbury. They confronted him with those sorts of domestic questions which, on the morrow of the general election, he had feared were 'destined to break up our Party.'[43] On the other hand they came at a time when the Lords could claim to represent the country better than the Commons and when his control of the upper House gave him that power within Unionist councils which electoral victory would have given to Balfour and Chamberlain.

Salisbury met the challenge deftly. As far as the principles involved in the substance of the two Bills were concerned, he made his own preferences clear. But he did not set his course in strict accordance with these policy preferences, which other Unionist leaders were entitled to dispute, but rather upon calculation of the political pressures with which all the Unionist leaders had to reckon. The pressures of which Salisbury made use came from the electorate and the House of Lords. In order accurately to gauge the balance of opinion and the strength of concerns in these two spheres on the forthcoming legislation, he put Middleton's intelligence network in motion in the constituencies, entered into close communication with the bench of bishops through the Primate, and kept abreast of opinion among the Conservative peerage through his whip, Lord Limerick. He left the House of Commons to Balfour, but kept Balfour thoroughly informed and won the approval of the Conservative party in the Commons. As Salisbury expected, the two Bills brought out the line of cleavage between Conservatives and Liberal Unionists, and in both Houses the two parties held separate meetings as they had not done for several years. Though this division produced some embarrassing moments in each House, a reassertion of Conservative distinctiveness held no terrors for Salisbury. Still, he kept the Unionist cleavage within bounds by frequent, detailed correspondence with Devonshire and more remote but still direct dealings with Chamberlain.

On employers' liability, the critical matter was 'contracting out'. In other words, the Conservatives insisted that already existing private schemes of compensation for industrial accidents should be allowed to continue wherever employer and employees so agreed, in lieu of the otherwise mandatory scheme prescribed by the Bill in obedience to the demands of the trade unions. Salisbury wanted to take up high, uncompromising ground on this issue. Middleton's intelligence provided evidence that he could do so. Middleton reported that more electoral support would be acquired by insisting upon 'contracting out' than would be lost if the Government dropped the Bill rather than accede to the Lords' demand.[44] Some queasy Liberal Unionists led by Lord Northbrook did not want to take the gamble.[45] But Chamberlain, with few reservations, backed Salisbury, because Chamberlain's intelligence came up with the same findings as Middleton's.[46] Chamberlain added his imprint to Unionist policy by upstaging the Liberals without abandoning 'contracting out'. He called for a workmen's compensation measure more comprehensive than the current Liberal Bill, and Salisbury in turn backed Chamberlain.[47]

Impaled from both sides, the Government dropped its Bill without credit to itself or loss to the Lords. The Employers Liability Bill had elicited a perfect demonstration of Salisbury's power. He had combined his control over the House of Lords, some ambivalance in electoral opinion, and the compatibility between his own negative criticisms of the Bill and Chamberlain's much more ambitious criticisms of its deficiencies into a force great enough to induce the Government to acquiesce in the loss of part of its English programme on top of the centrepiece of its programme for Ireland.

Salisbury's experience with the Parish Councils Bill indicated, however, that he could enjoy sustained success only if he kept together all three of the ingredients which he had combined against the Employers Liability Bill. Equipped simply with control over the Conservative majority in the Lords, he could secure no more than marginal modifications in the second piece of English legislation. Of the two, the Parish Councils Bill was much the more complex, and hence raised a sufficient number of controversial issues to eliminate the possibility of a wide consensus within the Parliamentary Opposition. The Bill would give to the new councils compulsory power to acquire land for allotments, control over parochial charities including those founded with specifically Anglican intent, and supervisory authority over the administration of Poor Law relief. If the Opposition used its majority in the House of Lords to refuse all of these provisions, it would acquire an electorally damaging reputation for general anti-popular obstruction.

All of the Opposition's leaders recognized the sovereignty of the popular electorate as a determinant in their choice of course of conduct, a determinant which was especially pressing under a weak Government which might seize upon the first good prospect which came its way of increasing its Parliamentary majority through a general election. But they could not agree upon which of the Bill's provisions was most offensive nor about the bearing of electoral opinion upon their choice. Goschen and some Conservative and Liberal Unionist peers, for example, felt more hostile toward the Poor Law than toward the allotment clauses.[48] But Salisbury refused to concentrate his fire upon the Poor Law provisions after Middleton informed him that agricultural labourers, upon whose votes the outcome of an election in the critical rural constituencies might well depend, cared more about the Poor Law than about the allotment clauses.[49] The Liberal Unionist high command, including Devonshire as well as Chamberlain, carried this sensitivity about electoral response much farther. They doubted the wisdom of insisting on any amendments which the Government would rather drop the Bill than accept.[50] These doubts had the effect of undercutting Salisbury's power. Though, to his surprise and dismay,[51] Devonshire defied him outspokenly in the House of Lords, Salisbury still had enough Conservative votes there to outweigh the combined strength of Gladstonians and Liberal Unionists. But the Liberal Unionist defection deprived him of the moral authority to defy the Government's majority in the House of Commons. Defiance of the Government by the Conservative peers alone could be discounted as blind intransigence or mere partisanship. It was Liberal Unionist cooperation which had given the Lords' opposition to the Home Rule and Employers Liability Bills the appearance of thoughtfulness and of concern for more than sectional interest. Deserted by the Liberal Unionists, some even of the Conservative peers were afflicted by doubts. Though Salisbury succeeded in pressing the Government to accept more amending to the Parish Councils Bill than Liberal Unionist peers were willing to insist upon, what he secured amounted from his point of view to no more than peripheral improvements.

Devonshire and Salisbury switched roles over the third domestic controversy of 1894,[52] the death duties introduced in Sir William Harcourt's budget. These duties posed a double threat to inheritors of large landed estates. Harcourt laid down a steeply graduated scale for the duties. Even more seriously, he proposed to assess the duty on land, not as heretofore upon an estimate of the life-interest of the legatee, but upon the full capital value no matter how frequently the land changed hands through death. Devonshire, who had inherited one of the greatest estates in the kingdom, conducted an agitation outside Parliament against the scheme, and the Conservatives in the Commons voted against it. The Finance Bill, in which the scheme was embedded, had to be passed by the Lords; and though they could not amend a money Bill, they had never abandoned their theoretical right to reject one *in toto*. Salisbury eleven years earlier had refused to admit that the House of Lords was incapable of throwing out a money Bill 'directed toward the attainment of any object of popular policy.'[53]

Yet on this occasion he did nothing to impede the Bill's enactment. Two considerations held him back.[54] A substantial new source of revenue was needed to pay for naval construction sufficient to enable England to retain its supremacy against the newly formed Dual Alliance between Russia and France. Salisbury was prepared to acquiesce in the death duties as 'an injustice which may be excused by the serious need.'[55] In the second place rejection of the death duties by the Lords would add a dangerously persuasive economic ingredient to the campaign which the Liberals were only to anxious to launch against the rich as well as obstructive peerage. Salisbury therefore dampened Devonshire's campaign out of doors by holding open the possibility of repealing the death duties after the next change of Government.[56] With similar intent, he said nothing to the Lords until the Bill was about to leave their House. Only then did he make a statement[57] objecting to the principle of graduated death duties, belittling the moral authority of the present House of Commons, and repudiating any implication that the Lords lacked the right to reject a Finance Bill.

The Parliamentary warfare of 1893 and '94 ended in a draw. The setback to the Government over the Employers Liability Bill was offset by the success of Harcourt's budget. When Gladstone at last retired in March 1894, neither the fears nor the hopes of Unionists were borne out. The fear that some Liberal Unionists—Sir Henry James' name was mentioned[58]—might return to the Liberal party soon proved groundless. At the same time the Liberals' hold on office proved much firmer than Unionists had ever anticipated. Admittedly no one could contain Liberal Cabinet Ministers' propensity to internecine quarrelling as Gladstone had done. Deeply offended by Lord Rosebery's elevation to the premiership, Sir William Harcourt as leader in the Commons made no pretence at cordial cooperation with him, and sullenly pursued his own way. The party in the Commons, however, behaved with greater self-discipline than its leaders. Chamberlain's rhetoric in the lower House served the Government's purposes even more than his own, for while he whipped Unionist ardour to fever pitch, he also drove the governing majority together in anger. Furthermore, though Liberals lost ground in municipal elections, in Parliamentary by-elections they more than held their own.

The ground had not shaken when Gladstone retired as it had been expected to do. There was, in fact, a curious stillness to the political air after Parliament rose in 1894. The obvious gage of battle was the pretentions of the House of Lords. But the Liberals hesitated to pick it up. Gladstone had pressed the Cabinet to do so after the Lords had in effect rejected the Government's Employers Liability Bill and had trimmed back the one on Parish Councils. That opportunity, though far from ideal, was the best the Liberals could count on. The Cabinet rejected his advice, sensing that popular reaction to the Lords' action was equivocal, knowing also that Gladstone wanted to distract attention from the need for increased naval estimates upon which the rest of the Cabinet insisted. Virtually forced to resign because of this twofold rejection of his advice by the Cabinet, Gladstone used his last speech in the Commons to urge the case against the Lords. Unsupported, his voice only accentuated the silence of the men beside him. The circumstances justifying the appeal soon deteriorated as a result of the Lord's restraint over Harcourt's budget. Lord Rosebery, nevertheless, appropriated the issue during the autumn recess. He was goaded to do so by his humiliating powerlessness in the House where he himself sat, and also by his desire to divert attention from the rival causes of Home Rule, which John Morley championed, and temperance, which Harcourt tried to push forward. The Cabinet, however, refused to honour Rosebery's public demand for a resolution by the House of Commons censuring the behaviour of the House of Lords.

But in the brief interlude between the first intimation that Rosebery intended to concentrate his fire on the Lords and the failure of his attempt, it came close to tripping Salisbury up. As soon as Rosebery notified the Queen of his intention she wrote in alarm to Salisbury. Improperly, she had already been in touch with the Leader of the Opposition in the summer of 1893 about the constitutional rectitude and the partisan expediency of insisting upon a dissolution of the House of Commons. Salisbury, while upholding her constitutional right to do so, had advised her that it would be premature.[59] When she notified him of Rosebery's plan in October 1894, however, Salisbury encouraged her to dissolve Parliament.[60] Rosebery's plan worried him. Salisbury knew that the public supported the House of Lords not in itself but for what it prevented, particularly Home Rule. And the Liberals were managing to stay in office long enough for the threat of Home Rule to recede from the public mind. Rosebery was, in all probability, quite right in calculating that given time to divert attention from Home Rule to the virtually one-party composition of the House of Lords he could enhance his Government's electoral appeal. Accordingly Salisbury assured the Queen that the Unionist party was ready for an election and would probably fare better 'now than later, when a lengthened agitation against the House of Lords has banished the Irish question from men's minds.'[61] He reinforced his advice by sending her a letter he received, unsolicited, from the Duke of Rutland to similar effect.[62]

Salisbury's advice was short-sighted, for if the Queen followed it her action, regardless of the immediate electoral outcome, would add the Monarchy to the House of Lords as an object of partisan controversy. Fortunately for her own interests and for those of constitutional stability she also consulted her favourite Liberal Unionist, Sir Henry James. He argued[63] that Rosebery would reject the Queen's demand for a dissolution, and would then have to resign, in effect dismissed by the Queen. 'Dismissal would render the Government popular, and a Dissolution by the new Ministers would be far less favourable to the constitutional cause than if it occurred after the Government of Lord Rosebery had been overwhelmed by their own difficulties and had been defeated.' This advice, ultimately reinforced by Devonshire, Argyll, Chamberlain[64] and Balfour brought the Queen to a better mind. Only the high degree of confidentiality which enveloped the Queen's inquiry kept Salisbury's aberration in judgement from damaging him at a time of otherwise gratifying success. The Cabinet's eventual refusal of Rosebery's plan for a campaign against the House of Lords, and the calmness with which the public received his spirited denunciations of the upper House, implicitly testified that Salisbury's vigorous use of the House of Lords since the last election had not exceeded public tolerance.

### iii. Tensions within the Alliance

Unable to reach internal agreement on a single, overriding objective, the Government was reduced to what Balfour called 'ploughing the sands', introducing all sorts of legislation which no one expected the Lords to pass. And yet the Government did not collapse. This stalemate produced divided counsel within the Unionist Opposition, each faction hopeful that its particular trumpet would shatter the walls of Jericho and annoyed that other trumpets were distorting the clarity of its sound. At the same time Liberal Unionists and Conservatives, confident that sooner or later the walls would fall, tried to establish rival claims for the spoils of victory. As a result, in the last eight months of Rosebery's Ministry, the Unionist alliance came close to the kind of rupture that had enervated the Home Rule alliance in the last year and a half of Salisbury's second Ministry. The passage of the Parish Councils Bill largely as the Government fashioned it had shown Salisbury once again the critical importance of Liberal Unionist support for Parliamentary, let alone for electoral success. But he continued to show much greater reserve than Balfour in meeting the desires of Liberal Unionists, particularly of Chamberlain.

Chamberlain was the first to sound his distinctive horn. The Liberals' firm showing in by-elections deepened his conviction that it was not enough to parry the initiatives of the Government through the House of Lords. In order to woo the swing voters who he assumed would make the difference between triumph and perpetuation of the current stalemate, he urged Unionists to rival the Government's programme of domestic legislative proposals by adopting a programme of their own. Of the two the Unionists programme, he argued, ought to be more substantial; but its most telling attraction would be the knowledge that a Unionist Government could enact its programme without risk of dilution by the Lords and would not give purely political and constitutional measures priority over social ones, as Liberal Governments invariably did. The list of subjects on which Chamberlain proposed action was formidable: alien immigration, shopkeepers' hours, industrial relations, labour exchanges, working-class housing, railway transportation for working men, workmen's compensation, technical instruction in agricultural areas, and temperance. In an attempt to combine his brand of politics with Salisbury's, Chamberlain not only concentrated on social rather than political reforms but placed Salisbury's one legislative initiative in the current Parliament, a Bill to curb alien immigration, at the head of his list, and also placed great emphasis on working-class housing. He suggested to Salisbury that substantial amounts of the programme be introduced, not as mere promises, but in the more substantial form of Bills in the House of Lords in the forthcoming session.[65]

Salisbury responded to Chamberlain, and at the same time kept his distance, by agreeing in principle with the course of action which Chamberlain proposed while subjecting the practicalities of it to withering analysis. First privately through Lord Wolmer and then publicly at Edinburgh, Salisbury voiced a sympathetic if cautious response to Chamberlain's program.[66] But when it came to an exchange of detailed memoranda between the two men, Salisbury struck the note to which he commonly resorted when he wished to dispose of Tory Democratic or Liberal Unionist initiatives. Except on temperance and shopkeepers' hours, he avoided criticizing the substance of Chamberlain's proposals, but he challenged Chamberlain's faith in the swing vote:

> My fear is that some at least of these measures will provoke the hostility of those of whose support we should otherwise be secure. The question then follows—would these measures gain for us an adequate compensation among those who otherwise would vote for us. As a general rule, I should not believe in that compensation. Our loss would be due to unreasonable fear, & in some degree to resentment. Our gain, if any, would come to us from those who had imagination enough to realize the advantage of our measures: & believed we were the only persons from whom they would be obtained. In most cases the unreasonable fear is the most susceptible mental affection of the two.[67]

Moreover, fearful of creating new grounds for demanding reform of the House of Lords, he questioned the wisdom of the use to which Chamberlain wanted to put it:

> ...we are defending the House of Lords as a checking—not an originating—chamber. ...I doubt whether we should impress its claim to be considered a good drag chain—by showing that, on occasion, it can pull on its own account.

The positive note with which Salisbury concluded the letter was faint:

> two or three of the measures proposed in your minute might be very reasonably brought on for discussion there, with advantage to the party, & to the subjects themselves.

His sandcastles washed flat, Chamberlain abandoned the arts of attraction for the arts of force. He turned to Sir Henry James, his intermediary with Devonshire, and opened discussion about the demands which Liberal Unionist ought to make if and when the time came for Conservatives to invite them into a coalition Ministry.[68]

Minor currents of discord in the Unionist alliance set back its hopes of defeating the Government quickly at the opening of the 1895 session of Parliament. Salisbury and Balfour, intending to capitalize upon resentment in Lancashire about India's imposition of a 5% tariff on imported textiles, arranged for an appropriate motion of censure during the debate on the speech from the throne. Though Henry James was chosen to introduce the motion, the whole tactic was arranged without thorough consultation on the Liberal Unionist and Conservative front benches. The debate in the Commons was a disaster and the vote worse. James, ambivalent about the manoeuvre, muffed his lines. Goschen spoke against the motion. The Liberal Unionists defected almost to a man, and about 50 Conservatives joined them. The Government carried the day with a majority of almost 200, more than ten times its normal size. Lord George Hamilton commented angrily to Salisbury, 'I think before we again embark in a joint enterprise with the Lib. Un. We should have some guarantee that they mean business.'[69]

By springtime Radical Unionists and Conservatives were still allied to each other, but each was determined to insist on their distinctive rights. Aggressive defence of denominational education by the Moderate party in the recent London School Board elections had offended Nonconformist Unionists.[70] But Chamberlain was the main focus of the allies' internal strain. Some Conservative M.P.s held him responsible for the continued survival of the Government. They sensed the angry cohesion he gave to the Home Rule benches, or blamed him for the failure to precipitate a general election over the Parish Councils Bill. Squires among them resented the support he had expressed for Harcourt's death duties, while his equally articulate support for Welsh disestablishment outraged the Church party. His renewed talk of a National party,[71] whose domestic policy would bear his imprint, worried others. His insistence on maximum Liberal Unionist claims within his electoral Duchy bred sullenness among Conservative associations, particularly in the Midlands but elsewhere too. Akers-Douglas and Chamberlain issued public statements of their rival claims.

The storm broke at the end of March over these constituency disputes. Akers-Douglas claimed the seat at Hythe vacated by the death of Sir Edward Watkin. His claim was immediately challenged, because Watkin's brand of Unionism, though locally said to be Conservative, was so indistinct that even the Conservative *Constitutional Yearbook* had listed the seat as Liberal Unionist. On the other hand, the quick claim which Chamberlain made to the constituency of Warwick and Leamington, vacated by the retirement of the Speaker of the House of Commons was still shakier. The Speaker, A. W. Peel, had risen to his office as a Liberal before the Home Rule split, and though thereafter he was deemed a Liberal Unionist, he continued his financial contributions to the Gladstonian association. Fearful of compromising the Speaker's non-partisan office, the Liberal Unionists in the constituency had refused to create a separate organization. The work of Unionist organization was delegated, by mutual consent, to the Conservatives. One of their men, Montagu Nelson, nursed the constituency faithfully in the general expectation that he would take the seat whenever Peel retired. Wolmer understood the situation;[72] but an attack of 'flu prevented him from making it known to Chamberlain when the moment of Peel's retirement arrived. Falling, as the constituency did, within Chamberlain's Duchy, Chamberlain immediately offered it to his client, George Peel, the retiring Speaker's son. The one precaution Chamberlain took was to secure Balfour's support. Balfour failed to consult Akers-Douglas and Middleton before issuing a public letter on behalf of Chamberlain's nominee. The Conservative constituency reacted with angry defiance.

Its reaction took on national significance when two metropolitan Conservative organs, the *Standard* and the *New Review*, adopted it as the occasion for attacks upon Chamberlain. Of the two, the *Standard's* attack[73] had the greater impact, for Salisbury's influence with the *Standard* was widely known and as widely exaggerated. But the *New Review's* article[74], published anonymously, written in fact by George Curzon, was much more sweeping and bitter. It launched its attack with tasteless condescension:

> Mr. Chamberlain has never to this day quite freed his garments and phylacteries from the fustiness and the flue which men observe in the back-parlour of the Provincial Mayor.

Burying his youthful admiration for Churchill, Curzon went on to lump Chamberlain together with Churchill as unprincipled demagogues and to question the genuineness even of their opposition to Home Rule. Curzon linked this general criticism to the business at Warwick and Leamington by commenting on Chamberlain's assiduous attention to his organizational machine:

> it is to wire-pulling that he has devoted his narrow and powerful intelligence, and he has done so to such a purpose that he has in his hands more constituencies than a rich patron in the old, bad days could ever carry in his pocket.

Curzon did not call for an end to the alliance with Chamberlain. Instead he demanded that, when the Unionists regained power, Chamberlain must be subjected to the harness of Cabinet office. Curzon concluded with a claim that he had 'talked with many politicians about this matter, and the views of most are the views I have set forth.' Though exaggerated, the boast did not lack substance, as the reception of the article promptly proved. Though disapproving of excesses, such solid Conservatives as Hicks Beach responded to the attack as articulating thoughts which they had till now suppressed.[75] Approving letters found their way into the correspondence columns of *The Times* as well as the *Standard*. The Constitutional Club decided to postpone a banquet in Chamberlain's honour until the quarrel at Warwick and Leamington was settled.[76] When Howard Vincent, as chairman of the National Union but on his own initiative, asked Chamberlain and Devonshire to another banquet in their honour, he met with angry growls of disapproval.[77]

These demonstrations of Conservative hostility came as a revelation to Chamberlain. They hurt him deeply. Already depressed, he was unable to gauge exactly how deep the antagonism lay. Had Salisbury inspired the *Standard's* editorial? When Wolmer hastened to see him, Chamberlain poured out his feelings, displaying an almost bewildered need for reassurance. But even in this cry there was steel. Whatever the intrinsic merits of his case at Warwick and Leamington, the attacks of the *Standard* and the *New Review* rendered compromise more odious to him than ever.

No one doubted Balfour's eagerness to mollify Chamberlain. But Balfour could not speak for the party since already over Warwick and Leamington he had shown himself to be out of touch with the party's supporters and organizers. Wolmer and Sir Henry James wrote posthaste to Salisbury, who was on holiday in Beaulieu. He did not respond by contacting Chamberlain directly, while his letters to the intermediaries were remarkably sardonic and did not yield much ground. 'My dear Willie', he wrote to Wolmer,[78]

> Many thanks for your most interesting account of Chamberlain's emotions. I sincerely pity him—if that is not too big a word to use—for he has got himself into a peck of troubles. That unlucky letter over the Welsh Church[79]—& his speaking in favour of the death duties last year—were proceedings better suited to the innocence of the dove than the wisdom of the serpent. If he wishes for a following—which is purely a question of taste—he has no choice now except to put as far into the shadow as he honestly can his anti-Church & anti-land opinions. I think he has got himself into trouble largely from a very common defect of earnest men—he cannot believe in earnestness on the other side. He does not really believe in a convinced Churchman, or a squire who retains his opinions honestly: & he does not—or rather did not—realise that they would be impervious to his powers of persuasion.
>
> I do not, however, look upon this part of his troubles as serious. Undoubtedly, if he means to shape his political life on the Birmingham view of Church & squire—those two authorities will in the long run refuse to take him for one of their leaders. But, if he will put that philosophy in the lumber-room for the present, as Pitt did his views on reform, or Canning & Castlereagh their views on Catholic emancipation, this little breeze will very speedily be forgotten.
>
> The compact is a much more urgent question—& may be a much more

dangerous one. . . .We looked at the matter purely from a Parliamentary point of view. We saw that the continued existence of the Liberal Unionist party was probably desirable, & certainly inevitable: & therefore we pledged Conservative support, to assure a certain number of seats to it. . . .We were imitating the state craft of the potentates of the Congress of Vienna, who strove to establish the balance of power, by exchanging slices of territory certified to contain so many million souls. As Jefferson observed at the time, these marketable souls would in the end have the deciding voice, whether the bargain of which they were the subject should endure or not.

. .It is a case in which the interests of the whole Unionist party are on one side, & the interest of parts of it are on the other. In such a conflict of interests the whole ought to prevail: but it very rarely does.

Salisbury wrote at such length in an attempt to induce Wolmer as the Liberal Unionist Whip to join Akers-Douglas in drawing up a definitive compact, constituency by constituency, to avoid quarrels in future. In writing to Akers-Douglas,[80] Salisbury did not encourage over-generosity:

I think some of our people are ungrateful to [Chamberlain]: but after all his policy has been very peculiar. To sit upon the fence for nine years is an unprecedented achievement: but he can hardly complain because we will not hold his legs to prevent him tumbling upon either side.

Wolmer could not accept his father-in-law's assessment. Regarding the Unionist alliance as natural and essentially healthy, looking forward indeed to the day of fusion, Wolmer replied to Salisbury that eruptions of discontent in the constituencies could be avoided simply by more attentive observance of existing procedures.[81] That was easier for a Liberal Unionist to say, as Salisbury observed, than for a Conservative. 'Your view', he replied,[82]

. . . in effect places the solution in the difficult cases upon the backs of the C. leaders. For their position in preaching a concession to their people is much the most formidable: for they have to enforce the submission of the majority to the minority.

His final comment on Chamberlain's feelings was scarcely sympathetic.

I have known one distinguished statesman who went half-mad whenever he was caricatured in Punch: and another who wished to resign his office, because he was *never* caricatured in Punch . . . But I never met any one before who was disturbed by articles in the Standard; except the foreign ambassadors.

The storm died down when George Peel, against Chamberlain's advice, withdrew his candidacy, a partial victory for the Conservatives at Warwick and Leamington which made them willing to accept an alternative Liberal Unionist nominee, Alfred Lyttelton. Balfour stroked Chamberlain's feathers with a speech at the end of April in which he bore generous witness, reinforced by quoting from a letter which Salisbury wrote for the purpose, to Chamberlain's service to the alliance.[83] In Parliament the allied forces pulled more closely together, quickened by evidence that the factions which made up the Government's majority were falling apart. The Primrose League concluded its annual May meeting by passing a resolution expressing confidence in 'the Unionist leaders.'[84]

## iv. Coalition

Others might dismiss April's storm as an ephemeral flash. To Salisbury, it was only the latest in a series of episodes which reflected the tensions inevitable in an alliance between the Conservative party, with its hard core of squires and parsons, and the Radical from Birmingham. Never, from the first days of the Liberal split, had Salisbury welcomed Chamberlain's adherence. Until the change of Government in 1892, he recoiled at the prospect of a full coalition Ministry. He welcomed the results of the 1892 election because they enabled him to avoid that possibility a little while longer.

But the Liberals' showing in that election, however inadequate from their own point of view, began to teach Salisbury and to convince his party that Chamberlain's participation in the supreme councils of the Unionist alliance was an unavoidable necessity, as inevitable as the tensions it would cause. The events of the next two years pushed Salisbury slowly, more slowly than many other Conservatives, to the conclusion that the Parliamentary as well as electoral support which Liberal Unionists brought to the alliance was indispensable to its success. If only in the spirit of Curzon's *New Review* article, he accepted the necessity, preached from a thousand Liberal Unionist and Conservative platforms, of incorporating Liberal Unionists, including Chamberlain, in a coalition Ministry as soon as the Liberal collapse should occur. When the Queen approached him about a dissolution in the autumn of 1894, Salisbury reinforced the impression that he would head the Unionist Ministry which she contemplated. The death of Churchill a few months later, killed by his dread disease, eased Salisbury's way. In June, when the moment to form a Government finally came, he did not hesitate.

Nevertheless, the decision to create a coalition Ministry produced not only a blurring of the distinction between Conservatives and Liberal Unionists, which Salisbury did not welcome, but more importantly a loss of control for himself. Hitherto he had utilized separation as an operating principle, whether between the allied Parliamentary parties in 1887, between the Cabinet and the Unionist leaders' council subsequently, or, since 1892, between Lords and Commons. The principle had served its two related purposes well: it had buttressed his own power, and it had maintained Conservative predominance within the alliance. The prospect of a coalition sharply reduced the principle's utility. Salisbury was forced to rely instead upon sources of strength which were either less substantial or less reliable than his party. He fell back upon his native dexterity and upon increased departmentalization of authority within the Cabinet. Both were to prove inadequate for the task of keeping Chamberlain within acceptable bounds.

Acceptance of coalition did not eliminate Salisbury's room for manoeuvre. Speed, in fact, was of the essence. He did not spend a moment questioning the need for a coalition, nor did he pause to hammer out a concordat. To do so would not ward off the inevitable, and would give the Liberal Unionists opportunity to present their demands. When the Queen's summons to form a Government arrived—itself a testament to Conservative predominance in the alliance—Salisbury acted upon it so fast, and a day later launched into negotiations with Devonshire and Chamberlain with such breezy self-possession, that he caught both men off-balance. If he could not restore the happy old arrangement of a Conservative Government backed by Liberal Unionist support in Parliament, at least he could employ every opportunity which the Queen's summons gave him to fashion the coalition Ministry. But whatever the immediate advantage, within a month his speed turned out to have been a mistake.

The Liberal Government was defeated on a Friday night, 21 June, both to its own and to the Conservatives' surprise, on a motion to censure the War Secretary, Henry Campbell-Bannerman, over an alleged shortage of cordite. Though the designers of the motion informed Salisbury and Balfour that it might well trip up the Government,[85] Conservative whipping was lax; but the Liberal Unionists were on the alert; and the Government, deserted by its military supporters, fell seven votes short of a majority. This vote could easily have been reversed. But it saved the Ministry from a much more embarrassing defeat within a few days over its scheme for Welsh disestablishment, which Gladstone and the Welsh Nonconformists, for opposite reasons, were expected to oppose; and Rosebery tendered his Government's resignation on Saturday evening, 22 June. The Queen's handling of the resignation flawed Salisbury's prospects more seriously than either he or she could have realized at the time. She could have pressed Rosebery to dissolve Parliament, because the present Parliament had voted lack of confidence in both alternative Ministries, Salisbury's in August of 1892 and Rosebery's now. In her eagerness to rid herself of a Ministry she distrusted, however, the Queen accepted Rosebery's resignation then and there. Salisbury would have preferred a dissolution of Parliament by the Liberal Government. But he was quite willing to form a Government, so long as the Queen clearly understood that its first order of business would be a dissolution. The necessity under which a new Government would labour, of securing interim financial supply from a House of Commons which it could not control, disconcerted him much less than it did his colleagues. He seems never to have contemplated the possibility of being in a position to secure better terms for the Conservatives within a Unionist coalition Government after the general election than before. He forfeited that option by agreeing to form a Government immediately.

By Sunday 23 June, when the Queen's emissary brought Salisbury her invitation to form a Government, he had already decided the basic lines on which he wanted to construct it. In addition to the premiership, he wanted charge of a substantial imperial department himself, either the Foreign Office or supervision of the armed forces through the Presidency of the Council. He wanted a Conservative leader of the Commons in the person of Balfour, a decision everyone expected. Royal suggestions to the contrary, he was also determined to give important places to the men, now all Conservatives, who had given him the most welcome and able support in his last Ministry: Goschen, Lord George Hamilton, and Lord Halsbury.[86] Halsbury's reappointment as Lord Chancellor had the additional advantage of keeping the third-ranking Liberal Unionist, Sir Henry James, out of the senior position for which his legal talent otherwise made him the natural choice.

Salisbury dispatched letters asking Devonshire and Chamberlain to meet Balfour and himself in his Arlington Street house at noon on Monday, a bare three hours before he was due at Windsor. Meanwhile he had time to aquaint Balfour with his views,[87] so that Balfour could second his suggestions during the conference. When the four men met at Arlington Street, Salisbury directed the discussion with the same aplomb that had impressed Gladstone eleven years earlier during the conferences in the same house on the third Reform Bill. Salisbury began by asking whether the Liberal Unionists would join the Government.[88] When Devonshire replied by saying yes but asking for assurances on policy, Salisbury airily averted discussion by replying that there was no difficulty as to principles—a lovely touch—and no difficulty he could foresee on general lines of policy, that the Established Church would remain an open question, and that details had necessarily to be left open. Turning immediately to the composition of the Cabinet, he proposed four seats for Liberal Unionists which they could fill as they liked, specifying only that Balfour would be First Lord of the Treasury. He went on to suppose that either of two offices would suit Devonshire—either the Foreign Office, or the Presidency of the Council including the chairmanship of a Committee of Defence to coordinate the armed forces—asserting that he would take whichever of the two Devonshire declined; and in view of Salisbury's preeminence in foreign affairs, Devonshire accepted the Lord Presidency. Salisbury then offered

Chamberlain his pick of what was left, assuming that he would want a domestic department.

Chamberlain's response stored up much more difficulty for Salisbury than he appreciated at the time. Turning his back on domestic posts, Chamberlain expressed a desire for the Colonial Office, adding that 'if it was thought that under present circs. I could be more useful in War, I wd. take that'. Surprised, Salisbury suggested the Home Office, and Balfour, more generously, assured Chamberlain that he could have the Exchequer if he wished. When Chamberlain repeated his preference, Salisbury, not sure that Chamberlain was speaking his true mind, suspended the discussion, saying that 'perhaps we would give a decided answer tomorrow'. He then indicated his wish to retain the Lord Chancellorship for Halsbury, and left for Windsor. Salisbury was slow to credit the intensity of Chamberlain's concern about the Empire. A week later, in offering Wolmer, now Earl of Selborne, the Under-Secretaryship for the Colonies as a man with whom both Chamberlain and he himself could work, Salisbury commented:

> My impression is that Chamberlain's interest in the Colonies is entirely theoretic & that when he gets into office he will leave the practical work entirely to you.[89]

Salisbury had had some success in trimming Chamberlain's pro-grammes of social legislation down to tolerable size, and had therefore contemplated the prospect of Chamberlain being in charge of some domestic department with equanimity. He had not reckoned with the possibility of Chamberlain devoting his energies to a department intimately connected with his own.

The conference of the Unionist leaders was resumed on Tuesday 25 June, this time extended to include four more Conservatives:[90] Hicks Beach, Goschen, Halsbury, and Akers-Douglas. The vagueness about policy was preserved, Chamberlain insisting only upon appoint-ment of a small expert committee on old age pensions, and depriving even this subject of urgency by reflecting that legislation would have to await a budgetary surplus.[91] Since Salisbury had by now accepted Chamberlain's desire for the Colonial Office as genuine, other offices were distributed, in committee as it were, Hicks Beach taking the Exchequer after Goschen declined it in preference for the Admiralty.

Salisbury maintained his rapid pace in completing the Cabinet and Ministerial appointments. Devonshire could not keep up. '*He is extraordinarily precipitate in his arrangements*', the Duke complained to Sir Henry James, 'and assumes off-hand that everybody will take office which they do not want'.[92] Devonshire had trouble securing for James even the Chancellorship of the Duchy of Lancaster, because Salisbury had already promised it for the Queen's favorite Conservative, Cross. Because of the trouble at the War Office over which the Liberal

Government had fallen, Salisbury attempted to secure the seals of the office from Campbell-Bannerman before the full change of Government took place, only to provoke a protest in Parliament and a formal note of disapproval by the Queen.[93] She too felt hurried. After the Tuesday conference, Salisbury wired her in cypher that he was coming to Windsor to kiss hands, and he arrived while the telegram was still being decyphered.[94] Before the Queen had time to comment on either decision, the appointment of Goschen to the Admiralty and of St. John Brodrick, a Conservative whose capacity for executive decision Salisbury always admired, to be Under-Secretary for War, were made public.[95]

The Liberals did not obstruct passage of the financial Bills, which they themselves had prepared; and Parliament was quickly dissolved. Both sides launched their election campaigns just before the formal dissolution, Rosebery with a speech to the Eighty Club, Salisbury just afterwards at the last session of the House of Lords. A note of confidence, quite new to his treatment of popular government, entered Salisbury's manifesto. He presented the election as an opportunity for the electorate to put the long generation of 'muffled civil war', which had begun over the first Reform Bill, behind them. The Liberals' failure over the last three years to capitalize (as he interpreted their strategy) upon regional and class divisions within the kingdom, and the public's quiet reception of the House of Lords' efforts to defeat that strategy, allowed him to wonder, as he had never dared before, whether that generation might indeed be at an end. He felt able to claim for the House of Lords

> the thanks of the country for its recent action. . . that it has helped to clear the field of the sterile and angry conflicts which had become a bad habit with some of our legislators, and has invited us to the more remunerative industry of considering and promoting the social amelioration of the people.[96]

He also used his manifesto to restrain and reorder Chamberlain's programme. At the head of the list of subjects needing attention from the new Parliament, Salisbury placed a distinctively Conservative item entirely missing from Chamberlain's programme: help for agriculture, in particular relief from the heavy burden of rates on land. To this he added two items from Chamberlain's programme, one on a subject, working-class housing, which had long been his own, the other, on small holdings, a genuine concession to Chamberlain. Salisbury mentioned but did not elaborate upon the need to revise the Poor Law, and about Chamberlain's many other proposals he said nothing. Though, in the heat of electioneering, many Conservatives might adopt further items from Chamberlain's programme, the pledges to which the Ministry was committed were remarkably few and imprecise.

The electorate was not whipped up by promises, nor by unprecedented organizational effort. Middleton's Association of Conservative Clubs went into electoral action for the first time, and the Primrose League lifted its prohibition on direct electioneering. Still, the Conservative and Unionist coffers for this election were not as full as three years before, while the Liberals' treasury had been replenished, partly through contributions from the men they had recently elevated to the peerage; and in some parts of the country Liberal organization was at a peak of efficiency.[97] The Liberal party, nonetheless, was demoralized. It leaders dashed off in contrary directions, Rosebery for reform of the House of Lords, Morley for Home Rule, and Harcourt for temperance. None of their appeals rang with conviction; for their failure in 1893 and '94 to take up the many gauntlets thrown down by the Lords by dissolving Parliament, and the alacrity with which they abandoned office without attempting either to reverse the censure on Campbell-Bannerman or to appeal to the electorate, belied their claims to confidence in the voters. The most revealing evidence of Liberal demoralization was the number of seats they left to Conservatives and Liberal Unionists without contest: 130, as against 41 in 1892. In many other constituencies, Liberal candidates were put up too late to set the local electoral machinery running efficiently.[98] Even so, the Liberals expected, if not to defeat the Unionists, at least to hold the Unionist victory within small compass. After all, until shortly before the dissolution, they had done remarkably well in by-elections. In forming his Ministry Salisbury had acted on the universal assumption that he would need Liberal Unionists to command a majority in the House of Commons.

The results, therefore, took everyone by surprise. The Conservatives won 341 seats, enough to give them a working majority on their own. With the further 70 seats won by Liberal Unionists, almost as many as they had won in 1886, the Government commanded a majority of 259, the largest since 1832. Morley and Harcourt were defeated in their own constituencies. The magnitude of the victory could not but occasion some regret at Hatfield and at Chamberlain's Highbury. However many of the Conservative victories may have been produced by Liberal Unionist votes, however inevitable a coalition may have been regardless of the Conservatives' independent majority, the existence of that majority justified greater Conservative preponderance within the Ministry, at least among the offices below Cabinet rank, than Salisbury had been able to require before the election. But there could be no revision now in the terms of the coalition. Even so, the size of the victory made Chamberlain fearful of a loss of Liberal Unionist influence within the existing Ministry.[99] Whatever the feeling between the two Unionist contingents, the Government's huge majority would allow factions more room to go their own way.

In spite of such reflections, the results of the election gratified
Salisbury. As so often when looking for a parallel, his mind went back to
Pitt,[100] in this case to the election of 1784 when Pitt and the House of
Lords, whose action had helped bring Pitt to power, received a
resounding vote of confidence from the electorate. The results of the
election of 1895, interpreted in the light of the events of the immediately
preceding years, demonstrated to Salisbury's satisfaction, as he later
told the Primrose League,

> That for the future, when assaults are made upon the integrity of the Empire or
> upon any of our vital institutions, assaults to which the full and undoubted assent
> of the people has not been obtained, the resistance of the House of Lords can be
> calculated upon as a secure political force, and that no political force exists in the
> country which can overwhelm it.[101]

He saw even farther-reaching significance in the election. Before the
year had ended he was announcing[102] that the election had brought an
end to a period of nearly eighty years during which the dominant
concern in British politics had been expansion of the electorate. The
Liberal party had identified itself with that policy in the
expectation—which he had gloomily shared—that, 'if they once got the
mass of the English people within the boundary of the suffrage the first
desire of the latter would be to upset the institutions they found here'. To
his amazed relief, 'The result has turned out exactly the other way.' The
English public had indeed 'desired to be admitted to a share in the
government of the country, but, when admitted, they had no sort of
notion of destroying what they had been admitted to share in.' The only
source of electoral discontent with British institutions which he could
now discern came from 'portions of the country where, owing to
historical causes, the assimilation of races has not reached the point
which is, happily, reached in England, and where deep-seated religious
differences cut the population horizontally in two.'[103] In England, the
'base of operation', popular government had come of age much sooner
than he had ever dreamt possible. An unexpected sense of some security
about the electorate calmed Salisbury after the election of 1895. It
lowered his combative instincts just when, through the coalition, his
ability to control the Unionist forces was reduced.

## v. The Débâcle of 1896

Salisbury's talk during the election campaign about 'promoting the
social amelioration of the people', though it assigned priority to
Conservative interests and was less comprehensive than Chamberlain
would have liked, was not empty rhetoric. If Salisbury had intended to
do little, the foreign and colonial eruptions during the remainder of

1895—Turkish butchering of Armenians, President Cleveland's ultimatum about British Guiana, the Jameson raid and Kaiser Wilhelm's
telegram to President Kruger—could have been used to excuse a very
modest domestic program for Parliament in 1896.

In spite of these distractions overseas, the Government submitted an
'unusually ambitious'[104] programme of legislation. The political complexion of the programme was also significant, for it bore the mark of
Balfour and Salisbury rather than of Chamberlain. The subject of
employers' liability, with which Chamberlain had long been identified,
was deferred, after preliminary debate, to another year. The measures
which the Government pressed were an Agricultural Land Rating Bill
to ease the burden of local taxation on the farming interest, a Diseases of
Animals Bill which gratified protectionist sentiment as well as the
farmers by stiffening the regulations governing importation of cattle, an
Irish Land Bill which bore Balfour's stamp, and an Education Bill in the
interests of the voluntary schools and religious instruction. The prime
minister was determined to use the vast Parliamentary majority which
he possessed in both Houses to honour his commitments.

The size and self-assurance of that majority, particularly in the House
of Commons, defeated him. Poor management of Parliament contributed to the defeat. Parliament was not convened till mid-February,
late enough to raise from the outset a disheartening prospect of
protracted sitting deep into August. The Government could not launch
its legislative proposals immediately because of pressing financial
business left over from the interrupted session of 1895. The agricultural
Bills encountered no more than predictable amounts of opposition, and
they reached the statute books; but precious time was consumed by the
Rating Bill's sponsor in the Commons, Henry Chaplin, who, as the wags
said, 'seemed to consider it not a Rating but a *pero*-rating Bill'.[105]

The trouble over the Irish Land Bill was more serious. Designed to
make the terms for purchase of their holdings more attractive to tenants,
the Bill was of a piece with Balfour's legislation in the second Ministry.
Salisbury had again treated him as overseer for Irish affairs,[106] and the
Chief Secretary for Ireland was his brother, Gerald. But the need for
economically ameliorative legislation for Ireland, which had kept
Conservative M.P.s and peers grudgingly in line during the second
Ministry, was no longer obvious. If the election of 1895 had made
anything obvious, it was the British electorate's persistent rejection of
Home Rule. Furthermore, Ireland was quieter than at any time at least
since mid-century; and the Irish Nationalist ranks, still bitterly divided,
were not the force to reckon with that they once were. Irish landowners
and their many English Conservative sympathizers could see no need
now for further sacrifices. Still, apart from pockets of protest, the
Commons acquiesced, even when Gerald Balfour, under Irish

Nationalist pressure, abandoned amendments which he had meant to introduce in the landlords' favour.

It was in the Lords that the protestors took over. There the Government whip, as Salisbury explained, was 'without a lash. . . . He has no chairmen or local secretaries whom He can set in motion. . . . For rousing distant or lazy Peers he is very useful: for converting Peers who have taken a turn the wrong way he is of very little avail.'[107] Even during the second Ministry, Salisbury could not always get his way with the Lords on matters of less than vital moment; and the Irish peers were an especially restive lot. On the present occasion, they found, in Lord Londonderry, a prominent Conservative more than willing to lead their mutiny. The immensely rich proprietor of large estates in Ulster and of mining property around Durham, Londonderry had entered the Government's service as Lord Lieutenant for Ireland during the early years of Salisbury's second Ministry. Upon his return to England he had thrown himself into the work of party organization in the north east, and earned considerable respect within the National Union. His estimate of his own importance soared. Salisbury had offered him the Privy Seal in 1895 with a seat in the Cabinet; but, wanting control of a major department of state, Londonderry refused.[108] Unhappy at Salisbury's failure to give him an office which matched his estimate of himself, Londonderry responded quickly to the opportunity for making trouble which the Land Bill offered.

Salisbury had foreseen the possibility of trouble on the subject of Irish land. As soon as word that Gerald Balfour was drafting a Bill on the subject reached him, he had dispatched cautionary notes to Cadogan, Gerald Balfour's immediate superior. 'I earnestly hope', he wrote, 'that [the Bill] may not recall 1887 to our minds. That was a Bill containing some very bad provisions—but they were the price of obtaining the votes of the Lib[eral]. Un[ionist]s, & of the left wing of our party, for the Crime Act. We have no such costly favour to purchase now: & I trust we shall pay no such price.'[109] Once the Cabinet had agreed to the Bill, Salisbury laid careful plans for its presentation in the House of Lords. He assigned its introduction to the Secretary for War, Lord Lansdowne, as an Irish landowner highly respected by his fellows. Lord Ashbourne was to lie 'in wait for any discontented Ulster peer, [and overwhelm] him with legal thunder.'[110] But Salisbury himself took no part in the debate, either because he never entirely liked the Bill, or because he under-estimated Londonderry's capacity to make mischief. If the latter was the case, Londonderry came close to proving Salisbury right. During debate on the Bill, the rebel convulsed the Lords by declaring, 'This is the reason why you have failed to settle the Irish land question in the future as you have done in the past', and later on, 'This is the keystone of the Bill, are you going to kill it?'[111] However amused at their leader, the mutineers forced many amendments into the Bill over the Government's protests. Because the Conservative majority in the Commons sympathized with the mutiny,[112] Gerald Balfour had to accept the amendments either entirely or with modifications in order to salvage the Bill. Even so, the mutineers in the Lords came close to rejecting his modifications, which survived only as a result of lobbying by Arthur Balfour and some others who came up from the Commons for that purpose. Balfour had good reason for suspecting that Salisbury's heart was not altogether with him.[113]

Salisbury was moved much more by the fate of the Education Bill. The grant of free education in 1891 had given the voluntary schools only a brief respite from the devouring competition of the board schools. When the Liberals regained power in 1892, the Education Department reverted to its natural policy of raising standards, regardless of the burden on voluntary schools, whose rate of collapse quickly accelerated. Salisbury had blamed this unwelcome development upon the soaring ambitions of the teaching profession as well as upon the Department, and also upon the deliberate policy of its current Liberal chief, Arthur Acland. The steady supersession of voluntary by board schools snapped Salisbury's patience with the compromise of 1870, which had laid down the basic rules governing the relationship between the two kinds of school. He made his mind known to the public in the spring of 1895, when he announced that 'the idea of the voluntary school as it is now conceived and managed, and the idea of the Board school as it is conceived and managed, are not consistent with each other, and the Board School seems to me to be losing its hold on the affection and the opinion of the people.'[114] A week before the fall of the Rosebery Government, Salisbury promised Anglican supporters of denominational education 'a better law which shall place you under no religious disability.'[115]

In his initial discussion with Devonshire and Chamberlain about forming the coalition Ministry, the one subject which he reserved as an open question was the Established Church. In keeping with this requirement, and in view of the untested cohesion of the coalition at the beginning of the election, he made no mention of education in his electoral manifesto of 6 July. Balfour, however, inserted it among his pledges. The plight of the voluntary schools bulked large among the concerns of those who worked hard for the Conservative party in the constituencies. Harcourt lumped parsons[116] with publicans as the two groups who worked most actively against the Liberal party in the campaign. As the Conservatives won victory upon victory, Chamberlain acknowledged the parsons' contribution by opening a discussion with Hicks Beach as Chancellor of the Exchequer about ways to improve the voluntary schools' financial lot, short of giving them aid from the rates.[117]

In constructing the Ministry, Salisbury had allowed responsibility for Cabinet level supervision of educational policy to be ill-defined. The day-to-day work of the Education Department would fall under the Vice-President of the Council, Sir John Gorst, who did not sit in the Cabinet. Theoretically Devonshire, as President of the Council, would serve as Gorst's overseer in the Cabinet. But Salisbury expected Devonshire to be preoccupied with military policy: he assured Gorst of 'an independence more than usually complete, as [Devonshire's] hands will be full of other matters.'[118] Though Salisbury could scarcely take formal responsibility for education on top of the Foreign Office and the premiership, he proceeded to treat Devonshire as he had formerly treated Cranbrook,[119] though with much more tact. Salisbury met and responded to deputations about education on behalf of the Government, careful only to arrange for Devonshire to accompany him. The handiwork in education would be Gorst's, but Salisbury intended to infuse it with a spirit of his own.

He gave voice to that spirit in three speeches during November. First, in an address to the National Union of Conservative Associations, he assured himself of secular support by appealing to those who bore 'the tremendous burden, and the increasing burden, which the education rate is laying upon many communities in this country.'[120] Immediately afterward, he received a memorial which the archbishops of the Church of England presented on the voluntary schools' behalf;[121] and he 'carried [the deputation] away with the fervour of his Churchmanship and readiness to help.'[122] Then, taking the bull by the horns, he met a deputation from what he hoped might be the least hostile Non-conformist denomination, the Wesleyans.[123] He made no attempt to disguise his ecclesiastical loyalties from this company, and he rejected a cardinal Nonconformist assumption that a generally acceptable, non-denominational form of religious instruction could be devised. He observed that Anglicans' insistence upon teaching the distinctive features of their creed, far from diminishing, was 'very much more intense now than it was thirty years ago, and that the difficulty, therefore, of providing what is called unsectarian religion that shall be sufficient for all kinds of religious belief had increased in recent years, and my impression is that it is going on increasing.' But that observation only quickened his appreciation of the equally fervent beliefs of Nonconformists who found themselves in districts served only by Anglican schools and had, consequently, to endure the grievance of choosing between 'a religious teaching which they do not believe or no religious teaching at all.' That dilemma stimulated the prime minister to suggest his own solution, namely

the multiplication of denominational schools. I should like to see, wherever there was a population which could in any sense be called sufficient to sustain a

> Nonconformist school, that school assisted for the purpose of giving education to the parents of those children[sic].

He was, however, 'fully conscious of the enormous practical difficulties'[124] which limited his ability to secure all he wanted in the interests of the ratepayers and of denominational education. When Chamberlain refused to tolerate financial aid for the voluntary schools from the rates,[125] Salisbury did not press the point. The Education Bill of 1896 reflected Balfour's anxiety to raise the calibre of English elementary education, and Chamberlain's strong sense of the limits beyond which his Nonconformist supporters could not be pushed, as well as Salisbury's concern. The Bill offered the voluntary schools, particularly the poorer ones, modest increases in financial aid from the central exchequer, and exempted their property from liability to rating. It wooed the ratepayers by subjecting educational expenditures to tighter supervision. It moved toward a uniform, decentralized administrative system by creating a network of new authorities, education committees for each county and county borough, which would assume immediate responsibility to assist voluntary schools and were expected eventually to absorb the school boards. Finally, it granted permission to parents to secure denominational religious instruction for their children, whichever type of school they attended.

Supported by Catholic Nationalist M.P.s from Ireland, the Bill secured a resounding endorsement on its second reading.[126] But thereafter it was slowly strangled by opposition in Salisbury's own camp, the kind of internal division which, on secular issues, he was careful to avoid but which, on ecclesiastical issues, he was ready to fight, as his behaviour over tithes and free education had already indicated. In return for the benefits to denominational education, the Bill conceded some authority over the voluntary schools to the new education committees. But the Church party in the House of Commons, led by Salisbury's son, Lord Cranborne, rejected any form of secular supervision as admitting the enemy into the sanctuary. The rebellion in the Commons over the Education Bill was much more dangerous than that in the Lords over the Irish Land Bill, because the Church party's fire upon the Treasury bench was reinforced from various sides. Howls for rejection from Nonconformists, from the National Union of Teachers fearful of tightened limits on expenditure, and from school boards, rejuvenated the Liberal Opposition. Even among Conservatives, the Church party did not exhaust the ranks of critics. Metropolitan Conservatives, for example, deplored the threat to the London School Board, which they controlled, while others criticized the amount of the increase in state aid for voluntary schools as inadequate. The debate bogged down in a welter of amendments, eventually rising to four figures.

Matters were brought to the breaking point by Balfour's cavalier demeanour in the House. Sauntering in late one evening, unaware that shortly before his arrival Gorst had rejected a backbench Conservative amendment to oblige all boroughs and not just county boroughs to appoint education committees, Balfour accepted the amendment for the larger boroughs. His action not only necessitated amendments to other clauses of the Bill, but also compounded the Conservative and Unionist disarray. The Government attempted to regroup its forces by calling a meeting of the party in the Commons. Balfour proposed at the meeting that the Bill be put aside, and that Parliament, instead of being prorogued in August, be adjourned then until January, when it could concentrate on the Bill. His hope was that Parliament would enact it before March, when a new session would have to begin to deal with that year's financial supply. The only person to voice doubts about the plan was the maverick Liberal Unionist, Leonard Courtney.[127] The rest silently acquiesced but without conviction. For the plan did not deal with the substantial points at issue. It also did not remove the possibility of the Liberals renewing the obstruction in January. Balfour could not remove that threat, for he had already promised not to gag opposition by using the device of closure by compartments.

The situation in the Commons continued to deteriorate. Unable or unwilling to push the Bill aside immediately, the Government sank deeper into the mire of amendment and counter-amendment. Lord George Hamilton wrote to Salisbury in desperation:

> We have now sat for five consecutive days. . . & we carried 13 words in the 1st clause. . . .
>
> Our men are getting impatient at our impotence, & I say frankly that there seems to be no course open to us but to withdraw our bill, remodel it & under new & more favourable conditions reintroduce it. . . .Our men are disheartened, & divided, & unless we in a very short time cut the rope of the noose round our necks we shall be strangled.[128]

The rest of the Cabinet in the Commons soon reached the same conclusion, that there was no hope for enactment of the Bill this session even if the session were to be reconvened in January, that the Bill must be withdrawn outright, reconstructed, and introduced in a later session. This counsel filled Salisbury with dismay. It would throw into question the vigour of the Government and the cohesion of its massive Parliamentary support in the first full session of the new Parliament. Reinforced vigorously by the Queen and, to a lesser extent, by the metropolitan press, he urged the Cabinet to stick to its guns. But he met with solid refusal among the members of the Cabinet in the Commons.

The situation now recalled the crisis of 1890,[129] when the members of the Cabinet in the Commons had forced Salisbury, even though he thought the credit of the Government was at stake, to accept the withdrawal of the legislative programme for that year. The stake in 1896 was even higher because Parliament was in its opening, not its closing years. Still, as in 1890, Salisbury could not enforce his will against his colleagues in the Commons, because the substance of the matter at issue was the conduct of legislation in the lower House. Now that the Conservative and Unionist forces possessed a majority in the Commons as well as the Lords, he no longer possessed the same control over his party which he had enjoyed between 1892 and '95.

Salisbury eventually bowed to the decision of the Cabinet, as he had done in 1890; but there were significant changes in his manner of doing so. In the first place, he did not contemplate even the possibility of resignation. The discussion which he had had with the Queen in 1890 about resignation reflected the unsettlement then about alignments within and between parties. Churchill was still very much alive; and the electoral viability of Liberal Unionism, and Chamberlain's commitment to it, were open to doubt. By 1896, the alliance had been consummated by coalition. Whatever its internal strains, few of its adherents were prepared to precipitate a serious revision in their alignment. In any case, the criticism of the Education Bill had been much more outspoken among Conservatives than among Liberal Unionists. But though Salisbury did not think of resignation, he fought much harder and more openly against the Cabinet's decision in 1896 than in 1890. This time he left his colleagues in no doubt about the strength of his feeling. And when the Cabinet insisted on its decision, he refused to chair the meeting of the Parliamentary party at which it was announced.[130] Since Balfour had, however, sometimes presided over meetings of the party in the Commons as distinct from the entire Parliamentary party, the meaning of Salisbury's gesture was not recognized much beyond Cabinet circles.

By acquiescing in the Cabinet's decision yet refusing to preside over the party meeting when it was announced, Salisbury set a style of behaviour to which this Ministry subsequently adhered. Each member of the Cabinet would, in the final analysis, prove willing to subordinate his will to the common enterprise. But gestures of disapproval or, as Chamberlain later demonstrated, words expressing opinions with which the Cabinet did not agree, were permissible. The style was initiated, not by Chamberlain over foreign policy, but by Salisbury over domestic.

## NOTES

1. *Letters of Queen Victoria*, 3rd ser., II, pp. 49–50.
2. Salisbury to the Queen, 20 and 22 October 1891, copies, Salisbury papers; Wolmer to Akers-Douglas, 12 October 1891, Chilston papers.
3. *Hansard*, 4th ser., I, 713.

4. *The Times*, 1 December 1888, 8e.
5. Salisbury to Alfred Austin, 2 December 1888, in Lady Gwendolen Cecil, *Life of Salisbury*, IV, pp. 206–7.
6. Peter Fraser, 'The Liberal Unionist Alliance', *English Historical Review*, LXXVII, 302 (January 1962), p. 53.
7. Speech at Nottingham, *The Times*, 27 November 1889, 6d.
8. Salisbury to Balfour, 28 January 1892, Balfour papers, B. L. Add. MSS. 49690.
9. Salisbury's speech at Exeter, *The Times*, 3 February 1892, 6b.
10. *Hansard*, 3rd ser., CCCLV, 1038–1040 (13 July 1891), and CCCLVI. 83 (23 July 1891).
11. Salisbury to Howorth, 3 and 12 December 1891, copy, Salisbury papers, Secretary's Notebook.
12. Salisbury to Chamberlain, 22 June 1892, copy, Salisbury papers.
13. Balfour to Salisbury, 23 November 1888, draft, Balfour papers, B. L. Add. MSS. 49689.
14. *Ibid.*
15. Balfour to Salisbury, 24 July 1892, copy, Balfour papers, B. L. Add. MSS. 49690.
16. Ashbourne to Salisbury, 3 February 1892, Salisbury papers; Salisbury at the Guildhall, *The Times*, 10 November 1891, 10e.
17. *Conservative Agents' Journal*, VII (July 1903), p. 73.
18. Salisbury, 'Constitutional Revision', *National Review*, XX, 117 (November 1892), p. 289.
19. *Letters of Queen Victoria*, 3rd ser., II, p. 140.
20. Salisbury to McDonnell, 26 August 1892, McDonnell papers.
21. Akers-Douglas to Salisbury, 6 October 1894; Middleton to Salisbury, 9 October 1894; and Middleton to Balfour, 9 October 1894, copy, with Middleton's letter to Salisbury, all in the Salisbury papers.
22. 'He would have played the devil with our party in London as I am told that he would have gone hot against the City.' Salisbury to McDonnell, 19 November 1894, McDonnell papers.
23. Quoted in *The Times*, 8 November 1894, 4b.
24. Salisbury to Mr. Turner, 17 November 1894, draft, Salisbury papers with Middleton's letter to Salisbury. (The letter was sent: Middleton to Salisbury, 20 November 1894, Salisbury papers.)
25. *Ibid.*
26. Middleton to Salisbury, 22 April 1895, Salisbury papers.
27. Salisbury to the Maharajah of Darbhanga, K.C.I.E., 16 May 1895, draft, Salisbury papers with Middleton's letters to Salisbury.
28. Hamilton to Salisbury, 10 November 1895, Salisbury papers.
29. *Hansard*, 4th ser., VII, 58 (8 August 1892).
30. 'Constitutional Revision', *loc. cit.*, pp. 298–9.
31. *Ibid.*, p. 295.
32. J. L. Garvin, *Life of Chamberlain*, II, p. 577. Cf. Salisbury to A. V. Dicey, 26 November 1892, Salisbury papers, Secretary's Notebook.
33. Sir Edward Clarke, *The Story of My Life* (London, 1918), pp. 310–11.
34. Patrick Buckland, *Irish Unionism* (Dublin, 1973), II, p. 19.
35. Salisbury to Archbishop Benson, 18 May 1893, Benson papers, vol. 121, f. 328.
36. See *infra*, p. 279.
37. *Hansard*, 3rd ser., CLXXXIX, 963–7 (20 June 1884).
38. Geo. Panton, *House of Lords, 1882* (Manchester, 1882), p. 7.
39. J. L. Lindsay, 'The Liberal Unionist Party Until December 1897', University of Edinburgh Ph.D. dissertation, 1955, p. 170.

40. *Hansard*, 3rd ser., CCCXXVIII, 871–2 (10 July 1888); Salisbury to Smith, 10 July 1888, copy, Salisbury papers.
41. R. E. Pumphrey, 'The Introduction of Industrialists into the British Peerage', *American Historical Review*, LXV, 1 (October 1959), p. 6.
42. *Ibid.*, p. 8.
43. Salisbury to Balfour, 26 July 1892, in B. E. C. Dugdale, *Arthur James Balfour* (London, 1936), I, p. 213.
44. Lord Limerick to Salisbury, 21 January 1894, Salisbury papers.
45. Devonshire to Salisbury, 30 December 1893 and 25 January 1894, Salisbury papers.
46. J. L. Garvin, *Life of Chamberlain*, II, pp. 586–7.
47. Salisbury in Cardiff, *The Times*, 30 November 1893, 8b.
48. T. J. Spinner, Jr., *George Joachim Goschen* (Cambridge, 1973), p. 181; Lord Limerick to Salisbury, 21 January 1894, Salisbury papers; Salisbury to Balfour, 30 January 1894, Balfour papers, B. L. Add. MSS. 49690.
49. Balfour to Goschen, 20 and 30 January 1894, Goschen papers, Bodleian Library Dep. C. 183.
50. Devonshire to Salisbury, 21 February 1894, Salisbury papers.
51. Alfred Austin to Salisbury, 26 February 1894, Salisbury papers.
52. The Government protracted the session begun in 1893 until the beginning of March, 1894, and then initiated the new year's session on March 12.
53. *Hansard*, 3rd ser., CCLXXXII, 1613–4 (6 August 1883).
54. Considerations which were equally applicable but forgotten by the Lords in 1909.
55. Memorandum by Salisbury, 17 May 1894, quoted in Lady Gwendolen Cecil, *Life of Salisbury*, V (typescript in Salisbury papers), p. 13.
56. Salisbury in St. James's Hall, *The Times*, 9 June 1894, 11b.
57. *Hansard*, 4th ser., XXVII, 1222–9 (30 July 1894).
58. Lord Limerick to Salisbury, 6 March 1894, Salisbury papers.
59. *Letters of Queen Victoria*, 3rd ser., II, pp. 282 and 297–9.
60. *Ibid.*, pp. 433–4.
61. *Ibid.*
62. Rutland to Salisbury, 12 November 1894, Royal Archives A70/89; Salisbury to the Queen, 13 November 1894, Royal Archives A71/1.
63. *Letters of Queen Victoria*, 3rd ser., II, pp. 442–4.
64. Who had, however, taken issue with the similar line of advice tendered by Salisbury in the summer of 1893. *The Letters of Queen Victoria*, 3rd ser., II, p. 282.
65. Chamberlain to Wolmer, 12 October 1894, copy; and Chamberlain to Salisbury, 29 October 1894, and attached memorandum, copies all in Chamberlain papers.
66. Wolmer to Chamberlain, 15 October 1894, Chamberlain papers; Salisbury at Edinburgh, *The Times*, 31 October 1894, 7c–d.
67. Salisbury to Chamberlain, 9 November 1894, Chamberlain papers.
68. Chamberlain to James, 11 December 1894, in J. L. Garvin, *Life of Chamberlain*, II, pp. 618–19.
69. Hamilton to Salisbury, 22 February 1895, Salisbury papers.
70. D. Spratt to Middleton, 1 December 1894, and enclosure, Salisbury papers with Middleton's letters to Salisbury.
71. Bernard Semmel, *Imperialism and Social Reform* (Anchor Books, 1968), p. 83.
72. Wolmer to Chamberlain, 4 April 1895, Chamberlain papers.
73. *Standard*, 3 April 1895.
74. 'Z', 'Two demagogues: A parallel and a moral', *The New Review*, XII, 71 (April 1895), pp. 363–72.
75. Wolmer to Salisbury, 7 April 1895, Salisbury papers.

76. P. G. Cambray, *Club Days and Ways* (London, 1963), pp. 34–5.
77. Akers-Douglas to Balfour, 22 April 1895, Balfour papers, B. L. Add. MSS, 49772; Austin Chamberlain to Joseph Chamberlain, 24 April 1895, Chamberlain papers.
78. Salisbury to Wolmer, 13 April 1895, Selborne papers, Bodleian Library, I MSS. Selb. 5.
79. Chamberlain had written a letter, eventually published, to the editor of the *Aberystwyth Observer* in January, advising Unionists to accept disestablishment of the Welsh Church on terms economically advantageous to it.
80. Salisbury to Akers-Douglas, 16 April 1895, in Viscount Chilston, *Chief Whip* (London, 1961), p. 266.
81. Wolmer to Salisbury, 18 April 1895, Salisbury papers.
82. Salisbury to Wolmer, 20 April 1895, Selborne papers, Bodleian Library, I MSS. Selb. 5.
83. *The Times*, 27 April 1895, 9a.
84. *The Times*, 23 May 1895, 6d.
85. Earl of Midleton, *Records & Reactions, 1856–1939* (New York, 1939), pp. 87–8.
86. Notes by Sir Arthur Bigge on change of Government, June 1895, Royal Archives C40/20.
87. Devonshire and Chamberlain also had a hurried exchange of views at Devonshire House before heading to Arlington Street.
88. Chamberlain's notes on the meeting, 24 June 1895, Chamberlain papers JC6/6/D/2.
89. Salisbury to Selborne, 30 June 1895, Selborne papers, Bodleian Library I MSS. Selb. 5.
90. Henry James was ill.
91. Chamberlain's notes on the meeting of 25 June 1895, Chamberlain papers JC6/6/10/3.
92. Devonshire to James, 25 June 1895, copy, James papers.
93. Note by the Queen, 4 July 1895, Royal Archives C40/86.
94. Sir Arthur Bigge to the Queen, 25 June 1895, Royal Archives C40/24.
95. Notes by Sir Arthur Bigge on change of Government, *loc. cit.*; Salisbury to Bigge, 2 July 1895, Royal Archives C40/99.
96. *Hansard*, 4th ser., XXXV, 265–71 (6 July 1895).
97. Janet Howarth, 'The Liberal revival in Northamptonshire, 1880–1895', *Historical Journal*, XII (1969), p. 95.
98. J. S. Sandars to Balfour, 23 July 1895, Balfour papers, B. L. Add. MSS. 49760.
99. J. L. Garvin, *Life of Chamberlain*, II, pp. 639 and 642.
100. *Hansard*, 4th ser., XXXVI, 52 (15 August 1895).
101. Salisbury to the Primrose League, *The Times*, 5 May 1898, 7a.
102. Salisbury at Watford, *The Times*, 31 October 1895, 10b.
103. Salisbury in Brighton to the annual meeting of the National Union, *The Times*, 20 November 1895, 7b.
104. G. P. Gooch, *Life of Lord Courtney* (London, 1920), p. 333.
105. Sir A. T. Griffith-Boscawen, *Fourteen Years in Parliament* (London, 1907), p. 98.
106. Salisbury to Balfour, 22 June 1895, Balfour papers (Whittinghame) 71.
107. Salisbury to McDonnell, 17 August 1896, McDonnell papers.
108. Londonderry to Salisbury, 27 June 1895, Salisbury papers.
109. Salisbury to Cadogan, 22 November 1895, Cadogan papers. Also Salisbury to Cadogan, 2 October 1895, Cadogan papers.
110. Salisbury to Cadogan, 20 February 1896, Cadogan papers.
111. Quoted in the *Evening News*, 28 January 1902. These remarks were deleted from the version of the speech as edited by him and published in *Hansard*.

112. Sir A. T. Griffith-Boscawen, *op. cit.*, p. 108.
113. Balfour to Lady Elcho, 16 August 1896, in Kenneth Young, *Arthur James Balfour* (London, 1963), p. 174. Cadogan later hailed Salisbury as 'the Champion of the Ulster Landlord Interest': Cadogan to Salisbury, 22 April 1900, Salisbury papers.
114. Salisbury in London at a meeting on behalf of Church day schools, *The Times*, 22 March 1895, 5e.
115. Salisbury to the National Society, *The Times*, 13 June 1895, 12b.
116. A. G. Gardiner, *The Life of Sir William Harcourt* (London, 1923), II, p. 371.
117. Chamberlain to Hicks Beach, 20 July 1895, St. Aldwyn papers.
118. Salisbury to Gorst, 1 July 1895, copy, Salisbury papers.
119. *Supra*, p. 169.
120. Reported in the *School Guardian*, 23 November 1895.
121. Reported in *The Times*, 21 November 1895, 4b-d.
122. A. C. Benson, *The Life of Edward White Benson* (London, 1900), II, p. 663.
123. Reported in the *School Guardian*, 30 November 1895.
124. Salisbury had used these words back in March: *The Times*, 22 March 1895, 5f.
125. J. L. Garvin, *Life of Chamberlain*, III, p. 153.
126. The number of favourable votes exceeded the negative ones by 267, 'the largest ever known': *Letters of Queen Victoria*, 3rd ser., III, p. 43.
127. G. P. Gooch, *op. cit.*, p. 332.
128. Hamilton to Salisbury, 19 June 1896, Salisbury papers.
129. *Supra*, pp. 175–6.
130. McDonnell to Sir Arthur Bigge, 24 June 1896, Royal Archives A73/16.

# CHAPTER 8

# AMBIGUOUS ACHIEVEMENT

> . . . the world, however slowly—I might say at the moment very slowly—is travelling to the point where the government of all races will be done, not by organized force, but by regulated and advancing public opinion. . . .
>
> *Salisbury on the bicentenary of the Society for the Propagation of the Gospel, 19 June 1900*

The formation of a coalition Ministry and the majority which it won in the Commons left Salisbury without a distinctive partisan or Parliamentary base. He never found another, at least not one comparable with the Conservative party or the House of Lords. His role would never again be as well defined. He continued to possess many sources of strength: the office of prime minister which included presidency over the Cabinet's deliberations, the Foreign Office, the leadership of the Lords, the loyalty of Middleton, and his own august popular image. But these, though in sum substantial, were fragments of power rather than a naturally coherent whole.

He accepted the position with something approaching equanimity. The fighting spirit which had characterized his leadership until the mid-'90s was replaced by a blanket of imperturbability. The change could not be accounted for simply by age. He began his third Ministry at 65, not particularly old for a prime minister, and his health showed no signs of giving way until 1897 or '98. The accommodations which he had made as the price of power—with Churchill in the mid-'80s, and since that time with the Liberal Unionist and with his Conservative colleagues in the Commons—had undoubtedly blurred the edges of his original creed and extended the limits of his tolerance. Still, as the flow of sardonic observations in his letters continued to show, his perceptions were too acute, and his native pessimism was too deep, to enable him to put up with a thoroughly repugnant situation calmly. His new confidence in the sobriety of the electorate did much to calm him. The election of 1895 gave him a few years of relief from his terror of popular government. However ineffectively the majority in the new House of Commons might behave, whatever failure of nerve his colleagues might display, however frustrating the distribution of power within the Ministry, the fruit of the electorate's decision remained intact, the Cabinet did not fall apart. The

Queen's diamond jubilee in 1897 invigorated popular patriotism. Salisbury voiced rare contentment in his speech to the Lords on the occasion:

> The impulse of democracy, which began in another century in other lands, has made itself felt fully in our time, and vast changes in the centre of power and the incidence of responsibility have been made almost imperceptibly without any disturbance or hindrance in the progress of the prosperous development of the nation.[1]

A revitalization of the Liberal party might have reawakened Salisbury's primal fear. But the feud between Rosebery and Harcourt did not abate when they moved into Opposition or even after they resigned their positions of leadership. The division between Liberal Imperialists and Little Englanders spread far beyond personal rivalry, leaving the party weaker than ever. Even so, Salisbury assumed that the Liberals would gain a small majority at the next general election. But the prospect of a small, internally divided Liberal majority in the Commons checked by the strong Unionist majority in the Lords could not disconcert him after his experience between 1892 and '95. The contentment he derived from the electorate's behaviour in 1895 persisted until the closing weeks of 1899.

This confidence or, more accurately, reduction in fear undergirded Salisbury's willingness to adapt himself to the limitations upon his power in his third Ministry. During its lifetime and the lifetime of its successor, the base of governing power was neither one of the allied parties nor one of the Houses of Parliament, but, to an unusual extent, the Cabinet. The lines of demarcation between Conservative and Liberal Unionist grew increasingly confused after 1895 at every level. Among constituency stalwarts, grating differences in life-style, for example between imbibing Tories and teetotal Liberal Unionists, persisted;[2] but in the critical business of fighting elections, their cooperation was intimate. On the back benches in Parliament, suspicions of Chamberlain remained very much alive; but they existed as much—or as little—among Whig Unionists as among Conservatives, and Chamberlain drew his Parliamentary power not so much from the Liberal Unionist minority as from aggressive imperialists in both of the allied parties. As for the distribution of power between the two Houses of Parliament, the Unionists' acquisition of a majority in the Commons certainly reduced the importance of the House of Lords. But the Lords' loss was not entirely the Commons' gain. The majority in the Commons never fully rescued itself after its demoralizing performance in 1896. Thereafter, national preoccupation with colonial and foreign affairs diverted attention from Parliament, for, short of overthrowing the Ministry, the House of Commons could not direct but only comment upon the actions of the Ministers in charge.

The power which the allied parties and the Houses of Parliament did not exercise devolved upon the Cabinet, a fact which its members sensed. The Cabinet conducted itself with a consciousness of supreme yet diffused authority. Even its seating arrangement around the council table acquired more than formal significance. Breaking tradition, Salisbury placed the Duke of Devonshire rather than the leader of the Commons directly opposite him: the two imperturbable party leader peers held the centre, face to face. To Salisbury's left sat Balfour and, next to Balfour, Chamberlain: the two party leaders in the Commons were side by side at the council table as on the Treasury bench. Lesser men observed closely where members were placed and whose opinion was sought on general matters.[3] Those whom Goschen jealously labelled the 'quartet'[4]—Devonshire, Balfour, Chamberlain, and the prime minister himself—spoke most freely on general policy and commanded the greatest deference. Still, the opinion of the lesser men could prove decisive, since Salisbury allowed important questions including those in his own department to be decided even against his wishes by majority vote. Chamberlain too, with studied courtesy,[5] referred questions to the Cabinet and accepted its arbitration. To satisfy the requirements of both allied parties and yet retain a reliable Conservative ballast, Salisbury had appointed the unprecedentedly large number of nineteen men to the Cabinet. This size contributed to the diffusion of authority within the Cabinet by increasing the tendency toward departmentalization to which Salisbury was prone in any case. No Cabinet secretariat existed to counteract the tendency. Cabinet committees on specific problems which gave rise to controversy or involved several departments were few, and they rarely lasted from one Parliamentary session to the next. The Treasury's authority to review all departmental expenditure could have provided a form of coordination, but the only coordination which the truculent Hicks Beach produced among his colleagues was against himself. No one resigned from this Cabinet largely because no one controlled it; it possessed a kind of impartiality which commanded all its members' deference.

Nothing reflected the lack of prime ministerial coordination as much as the authority which Balfour and Chamberlain acquired over the House of Commons. When questions of how to proceed there arose in Cabinet, Salisbury refered them to Balfour and Chamberlain almost as though the Commons was their department.[6] Never a frequenter of the galleries or lobbies of the lower House, the prime minister reached the point where he did not know one in ten of the Conservative and Unionist M.P.s by sight.[7] His remoteness, and his bad eyesight, became proverbial. M.P.s consoled themselves by recounting tales of his failure to recognize W. H. Smith across a dinner table, of his mistaking a footman in a fez for the Shah of Persia, and of his mistaking a photograph of the Prince of Wales, who happened to be his host on the occasion, for one of the Boer War general, Sir Redvers Buller. Even in the House of Lords, Salisbury asserted his preeminence sparingly, though it remained a pervasive reality. He intervened in debate less frequently than before. On one occasion he cavalierly referred the Lords to speeches in the French Chamber of Deputies for a statement of the policy which the powers of Europe, including Britain, were pursuing toward Crete.[8]

The erosion of the House of Lords as a base of power was not arrested by the peers' rebellion over the Irish Land Bill. A second rebellion by Lord Londonderry, over the Workmen's Compensation Bill of 1897, attracted a little concern toward the upper House. Thereafter, apart from prime ministerial statements and an occasional sally by Rosebery, the focus remained upon the House of Commons. The leaders of the Cabinet in the Commons began to behave with the same lack of concern for the needs of debate in the Lords that Gladstone had displayed, and that Salisbury had defied, in the early 1880's. Lord James finally exploded to Salisbury after helping, in the premier's absence, to ram a Factories Bill through the upper House at the tag end of the 1901 session:

> We had to ask the House of Lords to forego all its legislative functions and become a mere machine to register the decision of the House of Commons.
>
> The Factories Bill contained 169 Clauses. There were in it upwards of 100 new provisions materially affecting labour interests. The Bill was not distributed in time for any member of the House to read it.
>
> Within a few hours of it being printed all its stages had of necessity to be passed through. . . .
>
> Is it not to be feared that if the House of Lords accepts this position the public will soon say that they agree in regarding the institution as useless—and be careless of its existence?[9]

Though sympathetic, Salisbury met James' outburst philosophically:

> I abound in the sense of your denunciations: but what is to be done? It does not seem possible that you and I should censure our colleagues: and yet how could we stop the Bill without doing so? This is the business of the Opposition. . . .we are 'muzzled'.
>
> There is this trifle of consolation. I am old enough to remember that in Peel's Ministry not one but many important Bills were pushed through, sometin es in September, with a similar abuse of consideration and decorum: and critics used to prophecy [sic] evil results very much in the language you are using now. But the House of Lords has not grown weaker. It has a quite peculiar political organism—peculiar I fear to the lowest class of creation. It is very difficult to stimulate it: but it is almost impossible to kill it.[10]

The lack of coordinating, enforcing purpose in Salisbury's third Ministry inevitable made its character indistinct. Its *mélange* of styles was aptly epitomized by an experience of St. John Brodrick, at a slightly later date, when as Secretary for War he received, late on a Saturday night, Lord Kitchener's telegram announcing the end of the Boer War.

He despatched special messages to the 'quartet' asking for instructions as to publication.

> Lord Salisbury deprecated haste, urging that such communications were often erroneous. 'Wait till Monday.' A. J. B. [alfour]. said: 'Decide as you think best.' Chamberlain asked: 'Why have you not published it at once?' No reply from the Duke of Devonshire.[11]

While the Agricultural Rating and Education Bills gave the Parliamentary session of 1896 a Tory complexion, the Workmen's Compensation Bill and the attention attracted by the South African Committee's report placed Chamberlain's impress on the session of 1897. From then on, the legislative proposals of the Government struck even loyal supporters as 'of the makeshift and temporary expedient order.'[12] The Ministry's failure to give its Parliamentary supporters a clear lead, and the rivalries among the leaders of the Opposition, gave rise to an 'air of listlessness' in the House of Commons. The festivities connected with the Diamond Jubilee drew M.P.s away from their place in the Commons chamber, setting a pattern of slackness in attendance rarely known during the previous decade and in sharp contrast to the discipline displayed during the Golden Jubilee when the Irish Coercion and Land Bills were under debate. The problem was not that the Government presented a weak image, but that it presented several different images of varying individual strengths. Unlike Salisbury's second Ministry, his third contained a high proportion of widely known and able men. Devonshire, Hicks Beach, who had regained his old vigour, and Balfour, as well as Salisbury and Chamberlain, had strongly marked characters familiar to the public. Unquestionably the most arresting personality was Chamberlain, with his monocle, orchid and impeccable grooming, his trenchancy of phrase, and his shattering will power.

But Salisbury's image, though much less rousing, made almost as evocative a contribution as Chamberlain's to the impression which the Ministry conveyed. Massive in height and weight, bent by his years over a desk, 'one of the worst-dressed men of his order in London',[13] with a great grey mane and beard, he was 'irresistibly reminiscent of one of Michelangelo's versions of God.'[14] His countrymen took pride in his stature as a statesman when he spoke for Britain in the council of nations. At the same time his cynical turn of phrase was appealing as Victorian values gave way to Edwardian. There was a sardonic undercurrent to the pride dominating Britain's political climate during the late 1890s, an undercurrent reflected by Rosebery, Harcourt and Balfour as well as Salisbury.[15] Sir Henry Lucy, more impressed with the sage of the 1890s than with the party leader of the 1880s, described Salisbury's favourite attitude in the Lords for the readers of *Punch*:

> his head sunk on his chest, his clenched fists dug into the cushion of the bench supporting his ponderous figure. This post has special advantages, inasmuch as it implies close attention, whilst affording opportunity for decently dropping asleep.[16]

The stance conveyed an amused but shrewd sense of proportion. Salisbury's demeanor and, still more, his manner of speech were well adapted to the limiting circumstances in which he found himself. The caustic high Tory of mid-century broke through less and less frequently. That figure was replaced by one that spoke more and more deliberately, 'the mellowed and majestic statesman', 'the philosopher meditating aloud'. 'It seemed a mere accident that the reflection was conducted audibly and in public rather than in the recesses of the library at Hatfield.'[17]

Other sources of influence lent substance to this impression. Salisbury retained a remarkable capacity for work. St. John Brodrick, who became Undersecretary for Foreign Affairs in 1898 after recurrent bouts of 'flu had reduced Salisbury's reserves of strength, learned with awe of the regimen which his aging chief continued to follow:

> though not by nature inclined to early rising, he would, when at Hatfield, despatch considerable correspondence before breakfast. From ten to one he slaved at innumerable Foreign Office boxes, and his subordinates knew to the moment when the business they had sent down overnight would be returned to them. From four o'clock to eight-fifteen, the work of the Prime Minister and the Foreign Office papers just received from London were dealt with. From 10 p.m. to the early hours of the morning, this slavery was resumed.[18]

Salisbury simply knew more than any of his colleagues, at least so far as written communication could convey knowledge. Furthermore, even when age began to weaken his will, his judgement lost none of its acuteness. Finally, Middleton's intelligence network continued to keep Salisbury abreast of developments on the electoral front. However others might respond to the coalition of parties and diffusion of power within the Cabinet, Middleton remained staunchly Salisbury's man. In June of 1899, when the skies over South Africa were darkening, the South African Association, at Chamberlain's behest, issued a circular to Conservative associations throughout the country, 'urging the immediate summoning of meetings to denounce the Transvaal Government and to demand action on the part of H. M. Govt.' The local agents, ready to take such instructions only from Middleton, wired him for clarification. Middleton ordered them to hold back. Though Chamberlain reacted to this interference as 'preposterous', Middleton, unruffled, would not lift the ban until he received instructions from Salisbury.[19] If the internal dynamics of the third Ministry restrained the prime minister, they also fettered his colleagues.

## i. The Record at Home

Nowhere was the mixture of purposes and mutual restraints within the Ministry more apparent than in domestic policy. In response to the welter of concerns among the majority in the Commons over education in 1896, the Cabinet had prevented Salisbury from securing a Bill he dearly wanted. Chamberlain underwent a somewhat similar experience with his Workmen's Compensation Bill of 1897, for though the Bill reached the statute books, the victory was a pyrrhic one. From the moment the Bill reached the Cabinet's drafting board it accentuated the ambiguity of the Government's mandate. The division reached back to the debate on the Employers' Liability Bill of 1893. Chamberlain and Salisbury had collaborated in shooting it down, but whereas Chamberlain had emphasized the inadequate comprehensiveness of the Bill, Salisbury had dwelt on its prohibition of 'contracting out'.[20] This difference in emphasis persisted among their respective supporters during the election campaign of 1895. Comprehensiveness was the leading characteristic of the Bill which, in due course, Chamberlain brought before the Cabinet. The draft which he presented did not contain any clause providing for 'contracting out.'

The attack on the Bill came in two stages, each mounted by a man outside the Cabinet but deeply entrenched in the Conservative organization. Middleton, who was apprised of each phase of the drafting, launched the first attack while the Bill was before the Cabinet. Chamberlain accounted for the character of his Bill by claiming that the majority of Unionists had pledged themselves at the election to the principles contained in it. Middleton countered with an array of citations from electioneering pronouncements which dwelt on the importance of 'contracting out'.[21] He explained the social and economic significance of the point by praising private industrial schemes as a bond between masters and men and by arguing that the increased costs which industries would incur under Chamberlain's Bill would cause a rise in prices. He also argued—with greater foresight than Chamberlain—that the process laid out by the Bill for settling disputed claims would prove slow and expensive, with the result that the Bill would not secure its principal object, the gratitude of the working man. All that Middleton achieved for his pains was a contracting-out clause which was in fact illusory: the Bill provided for state-regulated compensation on more generous terms than existing private schemes, and would soon, therefore, drive these schemes out of existence.[22]

The torch of attack passed to Lord Londonderry. Though a less able man than Middleton, he was capable of at least equally worrisome opposition because of his combination of positions: in the coal industry, in the party organization, and in the Lords. At the beginning of the year he had refused, after three years of losses, to renew the lease which he held from the Ecclesiastical Commissioners for the Rainton Collieries in Yorkshire, because their best seams had been worked out. As a result, these collieries were closed down. The experience lent substance to the cry of distress from mine owners, whose industry would be most affected by the supersession of private insurance schemes. Londonderry had a strong political base in the Northern Union of Conservative Associations whose efforts he had nursed for years and of which he was currently President. Finally, as over the Irish Land Bill of 1896, Conservative discontent could enjoy freer play in the Lords than in the Commons. With greater lucidity and oratorical effect than he had ever displayed before, Londonderry first voiced his opposition to Chamberlain's Bill from the platform of a Conservative demonstration in Westmoreland. Breaking the restraints of the coalition, he spoke as a Conservative to Conservatives. While praising the loyalty of Liberal Unionists over the past decade and welcoming their participation in the Ministry, he drew attention to their numerical weakness in the Commons and to the Conservative majority there. Assuming, on that basis, that the electoral strength behind the Ministry was predominantly Conservative, he revived the warning, which Salisbury had emphasized in years past, about the folly of attempting

> to conciliate our opponents at the expense of our friends and supporters [or] to embrace Radical principles in hopes of securing Radical votes. Both are impolitic, for embracing Radical principles by the Conservative party will not secure any votes from Radicals, and will most certainly alienate our own people.[23]

He applied this general warning to the particular subject of workmen's compensation. Then he mobilized his provincial base by putting his presidency of the Northern Union on the line. The prospect of his resignation evoked dismayed expressions of grassroots support. When the Bill reached the Lords, Londonderry appealed to Salisbury personally, urging him not to 'allow Conservative principles to be subordinated to Radical principles of the deepest dye'.[24]

Londonderry's mutiny gave Chamberlain an experience of the circumstances which made him dependent on Salisbury. The critical arena was the House of Lords where Chamberlain could not speak, and the source of disaffection was among Conservatives for whom, on such a subject, he had no appeal. Salisbury not only took charge of the debate on the Bill in the Lords, but also assumed authority to decide what amendments to accept or reject.[25] The usual relationship between the leaders of the two Houses was reversed. Chamberlain had to acquiesce in the subordination, or lose his Bill. In the debate in the House of Lords, Salisbury, attempting to split Londonderry and disaffected

Conservative peers from the rigid classical economists of the Liberty of Property League led by Lord Wemyss, directed attention toward the question of Conservative principle which Londonderry had raised. The premier did so by appealing to the party's hallowed tradition, all the more revered because rarely and cautiously invoked, of willingness to uphold the rights of health and life when they conflicted with the rights of property. Londonderry as well as Salisbury had applied this tradition to the subject of working men's housing. Salisbury sought to extend it to industrial accidents.

> Where property is in question I am guilty, like [Lord Wemyss], of erecting individual liberty as an idol, and of resenting all attempts to destroy or fetter it; but when you pass from liberty to life, in no well-governed State, in no State governed according to the principles of common humanity, are the claims of mere liberty allowed to endanger the lives of the citizens.[26]

He reinforced the point by mocking Wemyss lightly as the leader of a one-man band and then by summoning up the shades of Shaftesbury and Disraeli. Salisbury and Londonderry played by the rules of their club. The rebel declined to vote against the Government on the second and third readings, confining his mutiny to the pursuit of amendments in committee; and the Leader went part way to meet him there. He was happy to do so, for the Lords' amendments gave him opportunity, all too rare now, of imposing his will upon the Commons.

Londonderry was not entirely appeased by the arrangement, and continued to press his attacks upon the Government's behaviour. His campaign bore delayed fruit. For in the autumn it was joined by an influential spokesman for Conservative backbenchers in the Commons, James Lowther, and was rejoined by Middleton. Even before the Bill left the Lords, Middleton reported to Salisbury[27] that many coalmasters were withdrawing their names and subscriptions from the party. Two months later, the Government did badly in a by-election in East Denbighshire. Londonderry promptly issued the predictable explanation.[28] It hit home because Middleton privately substantiated it: his detailed *post mortem* 'attributed the result practically to the lack of interest taken by landowners & employers in the Unionist cause'.[29] Lowther then used the annual conference of the National Union of Conservative Associations to deliver a speech drawing the general conclusion. "What had aroused some feeling of misgiving among the party at large," he insisted,[30]

> had been the fear that a departure had taken place from the understanding which had resulted from the last general election, that there had been rather more than enough of far-reaching and subversive legislation, that they had had too much of ambitious departmental administration, and that what the country required was a much-needed repose. (Cheers.) . . . Feeling as he did that a frank explanation of views was a more straightforward policy than grumbling in corners, he desired to

put before the conference what he believed to be the opinion not only of the great
majority of the delegates, but of many thousands of the party throughout the
country. (Cheers.) That opinion was that there should be anti-Radical administration, and non-Radical legislation (Cheers.) . . . .

The sluggish reflexes of the Conservative party had given Chamberlain
a longer run in 1897 than Salisbury had enjoyed in 1896, but the veto,
when it came, was more explicit.

Chamberlain took it seriously. The vetos of 1896 and '97 deprived
each of the two leading personalities within the Ministry of confidence in
his power to infuse its domestic program with his distinctive sense of
purpose. The Cabinet fell back upon a mechanical policy of honouring
the specific commitments which they had given during the general
election. Official propaganda boiled the electioneering rhetoric of 1895
down to a list of fourteen subjects, on eleven of which it could be claimed
that action had been taken by the time this Parliament was dissolved.[31]

The most substantial and the most embarrassing of the fourteen was
old age pensions. Chamberlain had given public attention and private
study to the subject since the early '90s. The caution of Salisbury's
response had not been prohibitive, and the subject drew sympathetic
comment from most Unionist platforms in 1895. But Conservative
reaction to the Workmen's Compensation Act made Chamberlain
apprehensive. A governmental commission of experts reported in 1898
that they could not discover any non-compulsory scheme for old age
pensions which would benefit the industrial population without discouraging thrift. Chamberlain publicly confessed himself daunted.
Unwilling simply to abandon their pledge, the Government resorted to
another commission, this one Parliamentary, under the inept chairmanship of Henry Chaplin, President of the Local Government Board.
Though no one was satisfied by the committee's report, its more
optimistic conclusion renewed Chamberlain's determination to secure
some enactment, and Balfour backed him up, making the commitment
official. But the Ministry was far from agreed on how substantial or how
little a measure they should sponsor. The outbreak of the Boer War did
not immediately release the Cabinet from a sense of obligation on this
subject. In December 1899, on the eve of the most disastrous week of the
war, the Cabinet wrestled with their dilemma,[32] torn between electoral
anxieties voiced by Chaplin and the financial protests of Hicks Beach.
The war finally saved them. Though Chaplin remained nervous, the
war's unexpected gravity, length and cost made Hicks Beach's case
compelling and diverted public attention from all other subjects.

The legislative record which this Parliament built up was one of
colourless, deflating compromise. The list of Acts passed contained two
deliberately uncontentious measures on working-class housing, one
bearing Salisbury's stamp, the other Chamberlain's. The Workmen's

Compensation Act was extended in 1900 to embrace agricultural labourers, which was more than the Minister in charge, Ridley, wished but less than Chamberlain had urged. Salisbury had heaped scorn in the House of Lords upon a Bill to provide seating for female shop assistants in Scotland:

> In such matters as facility for standing up and sitting down, we have hitherto trusted to the instincts of humanity, believing that people could manage them themselves. . . .I do not see the logical process by which we should confine [application of the Bill's principle] to warehouses and shops where female assistants are engaged in retailing goods to the public. The image of the housemaid crosses my mind. How often she must desire to sit down. Are you prepared to have an army of inspectors to examine the house of every householder to see that there are a sufficient number of chairs placed at stated intervals, so that at each moment of exhaustion the housemaid may sit down in comfort?[33]

Yet, overcoming their dismay at the thought of chairs strewn up and down stately staircases, the Lords passed and the Commons accepted a Seats for Shop Assistants Bill embracing the entire country. The Government succeeded in keeping two subjects, a statutory eight-hour day for certain industries and women's suffrage, at bay by treating them as questions upon which the Ministry need not take a collective stand.[34] A high proportion of the Ministry's legislative accomplishments emanated from Ritchie at the Board of Trade. But his measures, such as the Railways (Prevention of Accidents) Act of 1900, were unspectacular, and the aura of legislative competence which he bestowed upon the Ministry was counteracted by Henry Chaplin's performance at the Local Government Board. 'H.C. does not adorn his office', Salisbury groaned to Balfour, '—and he will get into worse trouble . . . if we have any Social Legislation. Happily that seems to be at a discount'.[35]

Salisbury and the Conservatives rebels of 1897 were content with this generally unprepossessing performance which, indeed, they had helped to produce. It conformed to the requirements which Salisbury had laid down at the outset for the Ministry's social legislation: it was 'careful and tentative', not inspired by belief 'in ethereal doctrines and high-flying theories'.[36] Furthermore, by minimizing their tinkering with economic relationships, the Government could foster what it believed to be an economically productive sense of stability. Confidence was the code word of the Conservative prime minister as well as the rebels:

> That [Salisbury declared] is the vital thing. That is the lifeblood of the body politic and the body commercial. Where confidence is there is prosperity and civilization. Where confidence is not you are on the rapid road to anarchy and ruin.[37]

As if to vindicate this belief, the pall of depression, which had contributed to the Liberal defeat in 1895, seemed to lift after the new Government was ensconced in office. In fact it had begun to lift before the change of Government, but the early improvement had not commanded attention. In the spring of 1897, Salisbury claimed some credit for the return of prosperity.[38] The Conservative mutineers disputed the claim that year, but upheld it thereafter when the Government avoided ambitious legislation.

The Irish policy of Salisbury's third Ministry, like its domestic record, had a composite character to which Salisbury contributed in a manner agreeable to his diehards. The main Irish legislation, the Land Act of 1896 and the Local Government Act of 1898, bore the impress of the Balfour brothers. But Salisbury's sympathy with the disaffection of the Irish landlords, particularly over the first of these measures, deepened, and he hardened the Government's response to Irish discontent. Before 1896 was over he wrote to Lord Cadogan, the Lord Lieutenant of Ireland, bemoaning that year's 'disastrous Land Act. . . which adds so much to our difficulties now, & which almost disables me for the future from defending the rights of property in Ireland'.[39] The prime minister contrived the following summer to convey his feeling publicly by assuring the Lords that the Government wanted to 'do what un-doubtedly we have so much at heart—namely, improve the position of those who have been so much injured by recent legislation—as the Irish landlords.'[40] But when a commission appointed by the previous Liberal Government reported that Ireland paid a disproportionate share of the kingdom's taxation, and the Irish landlords joined in the general Irish agitation to remedy this state of affairs, Salisbury rejected the demand out of hand. Cadogan and Gerald Balfour wanted to appease the agitators, at least by appointing another commission of enquiry. Salisbury could scarcely contain his contempt.

> The Irish peasant, by drinking more than other people, had paid what he considers an excessive contribution to the Exchequer. ... Do you imagine . . . that the British tax payer would be so patient that he would increase his own burdens in order that the Irish peasant might get drunk more easily?[41]

He forced the Irish Ministers to respond to the agitation directly 'by resisting it'. Indirectly, however, the agitation was undermined by increased financial generosity toward Ireland, in the form of grants for Irish agriculture and local government. These same grants served also to ease Irish landlords' distress at their loss of political power under the Local Government Act of 1898. They were by no means completely appeased. They forced the House of Lords in 1899 and 1900 to pass resolutions endorsing landowners' claims to compensation, and in 1900 they reduced the tithe rent charge. But Salisbury retained their grudging confidence. He took care to soften the Ulster leader, Colonel Saunerson, with a Privy Councillorship in 1898, and in 1900 to silence Londonderry and his ally in the House of Commons, Edward Carson, by making them respectively Postmaster General and Solicitor-General.

Salisbury and Arthur Balfour never locked horns over Ireland. They usually kept their disagreements on this subject tacit, restricting their contrary advice to private communications with Gerald Balfour and Cadogan. There were, nonetheless, not two but three quite distinguishable chief consuls within the Cabinet: Balfour as well as Salisbury and Chamberlain. Devonshire, the fourth member of what Goschen called the 'quartet', had passed his prime. His precedence was more formal than substantial, since he did not reinforce it with vigour even within his assigned province of imperial defence. The top level in the Cabinet consisted of a triumvirate, not a quartet. The lines of alliance within the triumvirate changed from issue to issue. Balfour might have expected to find himself always allied with one or the other, either through blood and some temperamental affinity with Salisbury, or through sympathy for programmatic politics and his close relationship in the Commons with Chamberlain. But on occasion he found himself the odd man out. Salisbury and Chamberlain, the master politicians, could find common ground in opposition to Balfour when he adopted the role of enterprising administrator.

This happened during the autumn of 1896 over elementary education. The Government had withdrawn its Bill earlier in the year with a pledge to push a fresh Bill through Parliament in its next session. Chamberlain responded to the first session's experience by checking his political sums. John Boraston, his organizational lieutenant, reported[42] that, while their Nonconformist supporters would tolerate a grant of additional state aid to foundering denominational schools, they would not tolerate either the introduction of denominational religious instruction into board schools or financial assistance for denominational schools from the rates. Even a measure to release the property of denominational schools from the liability to pay rates would repel Nonconformist Unionists, Boraston reported; and any change in the local administration of education, to say nothing of a direct attack on the school boards, would arouse their apprehension. Chamberlain concluded that the new Bill should be confined to financial relief for poor denominational schools, coupled, he hoped, with similar relief for poor board schools. Salisbury too concluded from the fate of the first Bill that the second should attempt no more than, as Devonshire put it, 'to maintain the existence and improve the efficiency of Voluntary Schools until the constituencies are in a position to decide whether they are to be permanently maintained, and on what conditions'.[43] Salisbury was determined to secure financial relief for poor denominational schools, particularly in rural areas, for which he felt the greatest sympathy. At the same time, with the taxpayers as well as the Church in mind, he wanted the financial relief to go strictly for denominational education, uninflated by the insatiable appetite of one of his *bêtes noires*, the educationists.

> The educationist [ he told Balfour] is one of the daughters of the horse leach [sic]: & if you let him suck according to his will, he will soon have swallowed the slender increase of sustenance you are now tendering to the voluntary schools. So long as you leave to him to determine what improvements shall be exacted, you are giving no relief at all to the voluntary schools. . . . You had much better give no grant at all, & let the money go to build an ironclad.[44]

Like Chamberlain, Salisbury justified his prejudices by referring to the electorate: 'stimulating the efficiency of the schools—in itself a very good object [is] not the one which was in view at the election'.[45]

But that was the very object which Balfour had at heart. He wanted to frame the regulations governing the additional grant so as to raise the quality of the education provided by denominational schools. To that end he pressed for distribution of the grant through regional associations of denominational schools working in cooperation with the Education Office at Westminster. His proposed arrangement alarmed his fellow triumvirs, Chamberlain because of the associations' ecclesiastical character, Salisbury because of the regulatory power they gave to educationists. Balfour also wanted more of the aid to go to urban than to rural schools, pointing out in passing that the recent Rating Act had helped agricultural but not urban property owners.[46] He thus revealed his uneasiness about the one distinctively Tory achievement of 1896. He demonstrated similar insensitivity to Chamberlain's political constituency by canvassing ways to give denominational schools direct rate aid.[47] The Bill, as Balfour drafted it, was much more complex than the simple measure which Chamberlain and Salisbury wanted, and raised questions which they wished to avoid. The controversy plunged the Cabinet into many sessions of protracted discussion fed between times by memoranda from the protagonists. By a majority of 10 to 8, the political calculations of Salisbury and Chamberlain won the assent of the Cabinet,[48] but Balfour remained in charge of the drafting. Predictably, the eventual Bill was a compromise. It increased the grants for denominational schools, and relieved their property from liability to rates; it established a diluted version of the administrative arrangements Balfour desired; and it was quickly followed by a measure to help needy board schools. The question of a permanent settlement was put off for another five years.[49]

## ii. The Shifting Balance of Executive Power over Foreign Policy

Until 1898, the Government conveyed a firm sense of purpose in foreign and imperial affairs that compensated for its lacklustre performance at home. Concern for the Empire and for Britain's international position had played only a secondary part in Unionists' electioneering in 1895, reinforcing their main call for a halt to Liberal efforts at constitutional revision. Still, Salisbury's return to the Foreign Office, and Chamberlain's surprising selection of the Colonial Office, gave an implicitly higher priority to overseas than to domestic affairs. Before the year was out, the public moved toward a similar order of priorities under the press of spectacular events abroad: recurrent massacres of Armenians in the Ottoman Empire, President Cleveland's special message over the border dispute between British Guiana and Venezuela, the Jameson raid, and the Kaiser's telegram of sympathy to President Kruger in disregard of Britain's claim to suzerainty over the Transvaal. Salisbury and Chamberlain met these challenges in a way that gratified the promptings of national pride without shocking Liberal sensibilities. Though Chamberlain sought to convince the public as never before of the cardinal importance of the Empire and of the need to cultivate and consolidate it, for two or three years Liberal observers could not quite make up their minds whether he or Salisbury was the more reasonable proponent of British interests overseas. At the same time, the ring of Chamberlain's language began to give Conservative imperialists the impression that, of the two, he was the more congenial to themselves. These distinctions, however, were matters of shading. The Ministry as a whole seemed to know where it was going, and the direction commanded national respect.

That direction was not the result of discussion about overseas affairs between Salisbury and Chamberlain before the change of Government in 1895. In the course of their negotiations with each other during the Liberal interregnum, they had said virtually nothing about the foreign and colonial sphere. Their silence indicated that they did not feel any pressing need to deal with the possibility of serious conflict here. But they were not in each other's confidence on overseas affairs, and Salisbury had no way of knowing about Chamberlain's as yet largely unspoken dream of Empire. For two years after they took office they worked together without serious friction, largely because in those critical matters where the development of the colonial Empire and Britain's foreign relations overlapped, Chamberlain was prepared to defer to the renowned judgement of Salisbury.[50] Salisbury did not exploit his prestige. He soon recognized the folly of his early assumption that Chamberlain's interest in the colonial Empire was superficial. The energizing hand which Chamberlain displayed in his management of the colonies confirmed Salisbury's inclination to respect the departmental autonomy of his colleague, and he readily deferred to Chamberlain's judgement on matters about which the Colonial Secretary could be expected to be much better informed than himself.

But the flow of deference was mainly the other way. While the Colonial Secretary was new to his work, Salisbury was regarded, now that Bismarck had gone, as the premier international statesman of Europe. Chamberlain could not refrain from making suggestions on foreign policy, for example to enlist American intervention over the Armenian massacres, which struck Salisbury as wild.[51] But the naivete of the suggestions rendered them harmless, and Chamberlain, recognizing his inexperience, did not press them. He was even willing to be overruled by Salisbury on questions of the tactics to be used in warding off the German threat to British dominance over southern Africa.

Salisbury did not have things all his own way in foreign affairs. Before the Cabinet was many months old, it hobbled his policy in the Middle East by refusing, on the advice of Goschen as First Lord of the Admiralty, to prepare to meet with naval force a Russian threat to the freedom of the Straits.[52] During the Parliamentary session of 1897, when Greece and Turkey locked horns over Crete, Salisbury could not concentrate simply upon the sources of that unrest and the threat that war would spread through the Balkans. He also had to bridge the gulf of sentiment at home between philhellenists and Turcophiles. The division of sentiment affected the Cabinet, where it tended to bring out the old division between Liberal and Conservative.[53] Lord James and Chamberlain championed the Greek side[54] and fretted under Salisbury's pacific caution. Yet, in the midst of the controversy, Lord James 'praised Lord Salisbury in the highest degree, and said the one wish of the Cabinet was to support him in all his difficulties, for he was so very wise and calm, and so dispassionate, really at the present moment the only great stateman in Europe.'[55] The dexterity with which Salisbury worked out step-by-step solutions to the combination of domestic and foreign controversy over Crete, and the steadiness with which he implemented his proposals, bred within the Cabinet a deepened sense that his leadership was indispensable. The Cabinet might place unwelcome fetters upon some of his policies overseas; but dealing with fetters was the stuff of foreign policy as Salisbury conceived of it. The initiative remained in his hands. Possession of the Foreign Office strengthened his premiership, as it was intended to do.

In 1897, however, his health began to fail and his will to falter. In March, when the Cretan business was at a delicate stage, he had to go abroad briefly to recoup his strength. This evidence of fatigue was followed closely by the first stirrings in Chamberlain of dissatisfaction with Salisbury,[56] in this case with his reluctance to insist on maximal British claims in a dispute with France over the extent of the two countries' Nigerian possessions. Salisbury's desire for a mutually acceptable compromise with France over West Africa raised doubts in Chamberlain's mind about the validity of the premier's reputation and about the whole cast of his foreign policy. Fortified, nevertheless, by his management of the controversy over Crete, Salisbury enjoyed enough support within the Cabinet to have his way over West Africa. Devonshire, as his own influence declined, was increasingly impressed with Salisbury's indispensability. Goschen and Hicks Beach went out of their way to endorse Salisbury's strategy of conserving Britain's strength for the much more important conflict with France over the Nile. When Chamberlain pressed Salisbury to keep his West African demands high, Salisbury could have followed established practice and referred the disagreement to the Cabinet, confident that he would be upheld. But he simply gave way.

His unwillingness to press for acceptance of an integral though subordinate part of his imperial strategy undermined the Cabinet's confidence in that strategy on the eve of a new and graver challenge. The Kaiser seized Kiaochow in November 1897, and precipitated a scramble for China among the major powers, thereby challenging British preeminence in the Chinese trade. Because this challenge involved more powers and larger commercial interests, Salisbury treated it as more serious than the one in West Africa. Yet he was willing to narrow Britain's sphere in China down to the Yangtze valley where British commercial interests were most fully developed. This willingness was based upon an assessment of British power and a ranking of British priorities which Chamberlain found repugnant. Salisbury doubted Britain's ability to maintain the fringe areas of its commercial empire in China, so far from British shores, particularly against Russia which was poised to penetrate south over its long border with China. Britain was similarly poised to press south, not in China but in Egypt, aiming to turn the Nile, from its headwaters to Alexandria, into an axis of British imperial power. Control of the Nile was the chief unsecured interest which Salisbury considered vital to the British Empire. He wanted to keep other imperial interests subordinate, at least until this one was secured. Britain needed, in his estimation, to husband its material power and diplomatic capital to that end.

The scramble for China brought on a collision between Salisbury's and Chamberlain's brands of imperialism. Salisbury, no less than Chamberlain, was a genuine imperialist. There was, admittedly, an element of domestic political utility in his imperialism. He recognized its value as a cause, like defence of the Union with Ireland, capable of transcending domestic divisions of class and religion. In 1896, after the spectre of Home Rule had receded, and just before his Government introduced an Education Bill sure to disturb Nonconformists, he presented the cause of Empire to the Nonconformist Unionist Association in the same fashion which he had used to woo Nonconformists over Ireland:

I do not ask you, I do not myself propose to alter my opinions or my wishes on any grave subject to which I have been led to defend convictions; but I ask you to consider which are the most urgent subjects for our immediate care. . .If we allow the Empire under whose shelter we are all gathered to be shattered, and to whose interests we devote so much care and give so much enthusiasm, it will be dissipated and lost.[57]

There was, nevertheless, a fine but revealing difference between Salisbury's maintenance of the Union and his maintenance of the Empire. His crusade against Home Rule had led him to excesses, particularly in his treatment of Parnell, which did not bespeak an entirely easy conscience: there was, if anything, more utility than conviction to his defence of the Union. There was more conviction than utility to his maintenance of the Empire. True to character, the very restraints with which he asserted the interests of Empire testified to this deeper commitment, particularly when his restraint cost him the confidence of his Cabinet and of previously ardent supporters.

Imperialism was the affirmative, overseas side of his fear of the disintegration which he expected popular government to produce. In this case what he feared was a conjunction between Liberal sympathies at home and nationalist stirrings within the farflung territories of the Empire. Gladstone had sought just such a conjunction, partly in order to prevent any extension of the Empire which might strain rather than strengthen Britain, partly from his conviction that the strength of the Empire depended upon cultivation of goodwill among its components, if need be by concession to local aspirations. Salisbury shared the first of these concerns, but disagreed profoundly with the second. It clashed with his premise, whether in domestic or imperial politics, that concession never appeased enemies. It clashed with his premise, whether in international or imperial affairs, that a policy was no stronger than the physical force behind it. It clashed with the respect which he had acquired at the India Office for resolute, authoritarian, government of imperial dependencies. It clashed, finally, with his racist assumption that only Teutonic peoples were capable of self-government. He had maintained these beliefs more rigorously than most of his Conservative colleagues and Liberal Unionist allies during the second Ministry. He decried, for example, the decision of Lord Cross and Lord Lansdowne to create modestly representative councils within the Government of India.[58] The erection of tariff walls around the developed nations of the West injected a lively economic ingredient into his imperialism. As he told an audience at Manchester, 'if you are being shut out by tariffs from the civilized markets of the world, the uncivilized markets are becoming more and more precious to you.'[59]

Still, Salisbury's imperialism was a reasoned, conservative, and limited faith, not a visionary one. It did not inspire him to strive, like

Chamberlain, to rise above the impediments with which the white dominions blocked the way to imperial federation. However that goal might excite the imagination of others, it left Salisbury pragmatically sceptical. Similar practicality curbed his racism. He deplored the 'damn nigger' attitude common among Englishmen resident in the tropical Empire; he warned repeatedly that the gratuitous 'sensations of subjection' which such an attitude aroused would build up a terrible threat to the Empire in the future.[60] The circumspect character of Salisbury's imperialism did not reflect a dimly burning belief. It reflected his assessment of the sensibility and prudence required to deep Britain and its Empire among the living rather than the dying nations.

Chamberlain took Salisbury's cautious treatment of imperial affairs of supine folly. Just as he was more apprehensive than Salisbury about the viability of capitalism in a democratic polity, so he entertained a lower estimate than Salisbury about Britain's prospects for survival as a great power unless it maximized its imperial potential. The Colonial Secretaryship gave Chamberlain some departmental claim to insist upon an uncompromising policy of this sort in West Africa. China, however, fell almost entirely within Salisbury's domain at the Foreign Office because, apart from Hong Kong, the British presence there was not colonial but commercial and informal. The scramble for China induced Chamberlain for the first time to invade Salisbury's sphere. This time the Cabinet inclined to the Colonial Secretary's side. Because the challenge in China was unexpected and affected greater commercial interests, it caused much more consternation within the Cabinet than West Africa had done. Salisbury did not want to turn Russia, the ally of France, into an active enemy barely months before he challenged France on the upper Nile. But because China was not a direct French concern, its bearing upon British preparations to recapture the Sudan was not obvious, even to members of the intimate family circle at Hatfield. Moreover, Salisbury's loss of nerve over West Africa undermined Cabinet confidence in his resolve, in his command of affairs, and hence in his wisdom over China.

Then, in March, while the Cabinet was wrestling with this problem, Salisbury was stricken with influenza. He returned to work before he had fully recovered, suffered a relapse, this time more serious, and was forced into convalescence in France. These events, occurring at a time of widespread discontent in the Parliamentary party with his China policy,[61] created an opportunity politely to suggest that he ought to retire, at least from the Foreign Office. The suggestion reached the editorial columns of *The Times*.[62] But Salisbury's will to power had not slipped to the extent of willingness to surrender either of his offices. 'Of course I have no intention of changing my position in the Govt.,' he wrote to his private secretary. Still, he had an uneasy sense that the work of the Foreign Office—'very heavy and . . . getting heavier'[63]—was perhaps becoming too much for him. 'I am trying to persuade myself', he told Balfour,[64] 'that my influenza was the result of drains—& therefore that it will not attack me again.' His appointment of Balfour to deputize for him at the Foreign Office during his now periodic absences on the Continent institutionalized his weakening grip. This arrangement was especially weakening when the centre of attention shifted from particular geographic spheres of interest to the general desirability of a great power alliance, which Chamberlain urged but Salisbury rejected as disadvantageous and unnecessary; for Balfour inclined to Chamberlain's rather than to Salisbury's estimate of British strength.

Balfour managed to preserve the semblance of agreement within the Cabinet during Salisbury's absence in the spring of 1898. When Salisbury came back, the situation deteriorated rapidly. Salisbury used the opportunity afforded by the annual meeting of the Primrose League to deliver a speech—one of his most famous, on 'the living and the dying nations'—in which he attempted to put across the wisdom of his imperial viewpoint. It provoked Chamberlain into an equally famous rejoinder, his 'long spoon' speech in which, without challenging the prime minister explicitly, he took issue with Salisbury's reassuring estimate of British strength. Salisbury allowed the challenge to pass without rebuke either public or private. When pressed in the Lords to comment on Chamberlain's remarks, he replied that he had not read them. To Chamberlain personally he said nothing. Unchastised for his rebellion Chamberlain pressed it into the inner sanctum of great power diplomacy. He convened a rebel council including three of the Cabinet's Conservative stalwarts—Lord George Hamilton, Henry Chaplin, and Goschen—and his own Under-Secretary, Selborne, who was Salisbury's son-in-law, plus the British ambassador to Germany. Through the ambassador the council approached the Kaiser with nothing less than a proposal for alliance. Only the folly of the proposal prevented it from convulsing the Ministry. The proposal was focused upon China against Russia, and, as Salisbury could have predicted, the Kaiser saw no advantage for Germany in China, where German interests were as yet small, to compensate for the permanent estrangement of Russia which the proffered alliance would bring about. In fact a quarrel between Britain and Russia over China might well work to Germany's advantage.

Germany's rebuff to the rebels in the Cabinet did not arrest the deterioration of Salisbury's control over foreign policy. On the contrary the dissidents 'not merely frustrated policies which Salisbury wished to follow but actually forced the reluctant Prime Minister to acquiesce in an agreement of their own choosing'.[65] The subject at issue was

Portugal's colonial possessions in southern Africa. Britain wanted to cut off the flow of overseas arms to the Transvaal through the Portuguese port of Delagoa Bay. Germany intervened in the negotiations, demanding compensation if Britain secured control over Delagoa Bay. Salisbury wished to reject the demand as illegitimate. But Chamberlain and, still more, Balfour responded to Germany's intervention as an opportunity to cultivate the closer relationship with Germany that had eluded Chamberlain over China. Taking advantage of a second period of convalescence by Salisbury in France, and bolstered by decisive support within the Cabinet, Balfour signed an agreement with Germany in August of 1898, just before Salisbury's return. Grudgingly the prime minister acquiesced.

He was on the verge of his most popular international success. Nine years earlier he had concluded that supremacy over the Nile must be a paramount British objective. With ceaseless vigilance since that time he had exploited every opportunity to reach his goal. He had ridden roughshod over usual Treasury practice in order to drive a railway north through Uganda.[66] Overcoming the apprehensions of Balfour and Chamberlain, he had leapt to the aid of Italy after its defeat at Kassala by the Ethiopians in order to launch an Anglo-Egyptian military advance south to Dongola. He selected its commander, Sir Henry Kitchener, and supervised its advance. To his own political cost, he sought to minimize all other quarrels so that Britain would be free to insist upon its will over the Nile. He was fully prepared for the showdown with France, which came in September 1898, when Kitchener confronted the tiny French force of Captain Marchand at Fashoda just south of Khartoum.

Even at this long-awaited juncture, Salisbury could not impose his design for a solution upon the Cabinet. He sought to enable France to climb down with grace. Knowing that humiliation poisoned relations between victor and vanquished, he may have contemplated granting France a colonial border near if not on the Nile. But the confrontation's drama, which worried the prime minister,[67] hardened the pleasure of the Cabinet. They refused to allow France any substantial recompense for its eventual retreat from Fashoda. Only the courtesy with which Salisbury treated France, and his refusal to turn Egypt and the Sudan into a formal British colony, eased the French surrender. Unaware of his distaste for the glamour of the victory which so gratified them, the public lifted Salisbury to the pinnacle of popularity. All the stars in the political galaxy attended a special banquet in November at the Mansion House in Kitchener's honour, but the one for whom the crowd in the streets saved its cheers was Salisbury.[68] Nevertheless, the events of the past year left the Cabinet's confidence in him permanently eroded.

## iii.  The Costs of National Consensus

There was more to Salisbury's popularity than fleeting illusion. The same events which had undermined Cabinet confidence in him and sent the attitude of jingoistic Unionists toward him through extreme fluctuations had bred calm trust in him among Gladstonian Liberals. The prominence of imperial affairs between 1895 and '98, and his response to them, had built up an amount of respect for him among Liberals which he could never have acquired over domestic issues. It turned him into a national more than a partisan statesman. But this stature could not at all fully compensate for his other losses of power since 1896, and it produced a further set of enfeebling ambivalences in the Government's performance.

Murmurs of Gladstonian approval had been audible from the first year of the Ministry. Gladstone sensed Salisbury's desire to do as much for the Armenians as he himself would have wished, and more than Rosebery would have done.[69] On the question of Crete, which evoked distinctively Liberal sympathies more than any other issue of these years, Harcourt approved of Salisbury's general policy and censured only his supposed weakness in pursuing it.[70] Dilke and Courtney, two of the most incisive Liberal[71] critics of the Government's foreign policy, were quick to recognize Salisbury's aversion to jingoism.[72] Liberal Imperialists such as Rosebery and Grey sought to take advantage of his failures to gratify imperialist sentiment, while uncompromising Little Englanders such as Morley and Labouchère refused to blunt their criticism of him. They spoke, however, for the extreme wings of their party. Harcourt, though prickly personally, spoke on foreign affairs for the larger central Liberal contingents later led by Campbell-Bannerman, and he gave Salisbury discrete by increasingly trustful support. In a New Year's letter of 1898, Harcourt explained himself to the doubtful Morley:

> The condition of things in Europe, Asia, Africa and America is such as to make me bless my stars that it is the other fellows and not we who have the responsibility of dealing with them. What a mess we should have made of it! I believe Salisbury to be by nature and conviction a man of peace, and I at least will be no party to vex him on that account.[73]

Liberal applause could embarrass Salisbury, and he took every opportunity to denounce Liberal departures from the national consensus. He blasted the hundred M.P.s who signed a message of support for Greece in connection with the Greco-Turkish war of 1897,[74] and he stepped harshly on the mild-mannered, usually supportive Liberal leader in the Lords, Lord Kimberley, when Kimberley repudiated maintenance of the integrity of the Ottoman Empire as a principal to which British policy in the Middle East must adhere.[75] But Salisbury did not issue these denunciations to gratify his own partisans so much as to keep Liberals within the boundaries essential for a bipartisan foreign policy, and hence to guarantee British policy some stability in spite of fluctuations in popular sentiment.

Salisbury feared popular sentiment as a guide in foreign affairs, not so much because of its radical propensities, but because it blinded men to sober international realities and because it was singularly unreliable. It oscillated between assertive and pacific phases, as many Ministries had learned to their cost. Through most of Salisbury's Parliamentary career, the pacific impulse had been the stronger; and in his first years as leader of the Conservative party, he had drawn repeated attention to the deplorable consequences of the policy of self-denying philanthropy in overseas affairs which John Bright and Gladstone erected upon that pacific base. Since the mid-1880s, the assertive impulse had grown stronger, and Salisbury had welcomed the consequent balance. But in 1898 over China and Fashoda, the assertive impulse manifested itself as dominant, certainly among many Unionists, perhaps also in the country. The new imbalance could lead in any of three directions as Salisbury analysed it, all of them alarming. If some of the varied hosts of Unionists refused to succumb to the new spirit, it could split the party.[76] If the party succumbed but not the country, the party would be subjected to a terrible beating, as in the election of 1880, once the costs of an assertive policy, say in China, became apparent to the public. If the whole country succumbed to the new spirit, the scope of the disaster could be national and not just partisan.

In a pair of speeches at the beginning and end of 1898, Salisbury drew attention to the fact that the public was in the throes of 'a reaction from the Cobdenic doctrines of 30 or 40 years ago, and [was toying with the belief] that it is our duty to take everything we can, to fight everybody, and to make a quarrel of every dispute.'[77] He pleaded for the sober middle ground, for a foreign policy which trod along

> the narrow line that separates an undue concession from the rashness which has, in more than one case in history, been the ruin of nations as great and powerful as ourselves.

He tried to offset the fears about Britain's comparative international power which made imperialists of Chamberlain's sort truculent. Salisbury warned that truculence, far from demonstrating strength, bred enemies. He warned, as Gladstone had done, of the 'danger. . .lest we should overtax our strength'. He appealed, as Cobden had done, to the experience of private enterprise.

> The more our Empire extends, the more our Imperial spirit grows, the more we must urge on all who have to judge that these things are matters of business and

must be considered upon business principles. The dangerous temptation of the
hour is that we should consider rhapsody can be made an adequate substitute for
calculation.[78]

Fashoda proved that Britain was able to assert its imperial claims
against a determined challenge. Fashoda therefore gladdened and
emboldened the jingoes, and they paid no attention to the restraints by
which Salisbury had husbanded British strength for the confrontation.
One of the most convincing proofs of British determination over
Fashoda came from the many Liberals who proclaimed their solidarity
with the Government as it stared France down. Unionists joined in
applauding Campbell-Bannerman's subsequent boast that 'we ranged
ourselves as one man in determining to resist aggression.'[79] Salisbury
closed the year by achoing Unionists' praise of their opponents. But he
told the Unionists to

> turn that doctrine round. If it is true that the unanimity of the people gave us an
> enormous strength when it was thought by certain persons that we might have to
> go to war, it is equally true that if that unanimity is absent it is very difficult for the
> Government to treat any question as one on which they will go to war.[80]

His remarks posed the dilemma with which his Government was about
to wrestle over the prospect of war in South Africa.

Thunder clouds had hung over South Africa from the beginning of
Salisbury's career as leader. The unavenged defeat of Britain by Boers at
Majuba Hill took place just before Disraeli died. Two conventions
regulating the relations between Britain and the Transvaal were
concluded, under a rain of Conservative criticism, during the remainder
of Gladstone's second Ministry. Salisbury in his Caretaker Ministry
contemplated a showdown between the Boers and the South African
blacks backed by Britain.[81] His third Ministry was shaken in its early
months by the abortive Jameson Raid and the Kaiser's telegram to
Kruger. Since that time, relations between Boer and Briton had
continued to deteriorate. Boer reaction to the Jameson Raid enabled
Kruger to tighten his grip on the Transvaal and accelerated his quest for
arms. The Raid compromised the claims of the uitlanders, many of them
British, who had entered the Transvaal in order to harvest its fabulous
resources of gold and diamonds and then demanded equal rights of
citizenship with the earlier, farming Boer settlers; it intensified the
alliance between the two Boer republics; and it destroyed the title of the
indigenous British leaders in the Cape Colony, preeminently Cecil
Rhodes, to enough Afrikaner support to give them a majority in the
colonial assembly. Then in 1897, a new British High Commissioner,
Alfred Milner, arrived in South Africa. A Liberal Unionist, Milner was
despatched with the blessing of the leaders of both British parties. They
hoped that he would gather together whatever remnants of goodwill

could be found amid the ashes of the Jameson Raid. However, he soon concluded from what he saw that a decisive confrontation between the aspirations of Boer nationalists throughout South Africa and Britain's imperial need for supremacy there was inevitable, and that, from Britain's point of view, the sooner the confrontation came the better. Accordingly, he deployed his considerable, abrasive talent to stir one up.

Milner was Chamberlain's subordinate, and the two men had much in common, both in temper and in philosophy. But while Milner knew his own mind on South Africa and pressed his conclusion in and out of season, South Africa put Chamberlain in two minds. As an imperialist, he agreed with Milner. But as a politician, Chamberlain was apprehensive about the reception which colonial war, particularly against a kindred Anglo-Saxon or Teutonic people, would find among the electorate at home. He dealt with his uncertainty by granting Milner considerable discretionary responsibility. There were elements in Chamberlain's relationship with Salisbury on South Africa similar to this relationship with Milner. Age and the events of 1898 tended to confirm the prime minister's practice of departmental devolution. Then in July Lady Salisbury suffered a mild stroke, from which she failed to recover, and the deterioration in her health took first place in her husband's mind. Explaining two months before the outbreak of war that 'the moment has passed when Chamberlain could with any advantage be urged to alter his plans of delivering his despatches', Salisbury confessed to Hicks Beach, 'I do not know enough of the details.'[82]

But the laxity of Salisbury's supervision, and the measured tone of his public references to the South African negotiations, created a misleading impression. The margin of disagreement between Salisbury and Chamberlain on South Africa was narrower than that between Chamberlain and Milner. In the first place both the prime minister and the Colonial Secretary were concerned about public reaction in Britain to war with the Boers, though Salisbury extended this concern to embrace the impact of war upon Boer opinion throughout South Africa including the Cape Colony. Secondly, the two men's strategies of empire, divergent on China, overlapped on South Africa. Salisbury adhered to the traditional British calculation that supremacy in South Africa was an indispensable link in Britain's chain of empire.

The dispute between the Transvaal and Britain brought out a debilitating inconsistency in Salisbury's calculations about the bearing of public opinion upon foreign policy. On the one hand, his fear of producing unnecessary 'sensations of subjection' throughout the Empire, and his desire for bipartisan agreement at home, made him wish for a negotiated settlement tolerable to both countries. On the other hand, he had often worked, especially but not solely in domestic partisan politics, on the premise that concession did not appease enemies. This premise seemed particularly applicable to the Transvaal. Gladstone's refusal to avenge the defeat at Majuba Hill had taught the Boers to discount British determination. When, on the contrary, Britain stiffly resisted Kruger's wish to impose draconian sentences upon rebellious uitlanders after the Jameson Raid, Kruger had backed down. Salisbury, therefore, doubted the Boers' will resist British demands to the point of war.

He was, of course, wrong. And by stiffening Britain's negotiating posture, he reduced whatever chance there may have been for a peaceful settlement. On 18 July 1899, the Volksraad of the Transvaal passed a measure granting uitlanders a seven-year retrospective franchise, only two years longer than the British had demanded. Chamberlain responded to the concession as a victory. Milner dismissed it as a sham but his now well-known prejudice against the Boer leaders reduced the weight which his assessment carried. Salisbury, however, arrived at a similar assessment. He saw the Volksraad's action as an indication that President Kruger would give way when convinced that Britain meant business, and he urged Chamberlain to increase the military pressure on the Transvaal. It was Salisbury who led Chamberlain to change his mind about the concession. Under their joint leadership, the Cabinet approved a comprehensive demand, not just for continued discussions on the franchise, but for settlement of the remaining differences through a conference between Kruger and Milner, and for the creation of a Tribunal of Arbitration to resolve all future disputes about the requirements of the London Convention of 1884 which governed the relations between the two countries. These demands convinced Kruger, and subsequently the Boer moderates, that Britain was using the uitlanders' agitation as a lever to exact from the Boer republics a submission to British supremacy far more extensive than they had endured since 1881. The Boer reaction, in turn, convinced Salisbury that Milner's analysis of the situation in South Africa was basically correct. Salisbury elaborated his course of thought for Leonard Courtney:

> At first I accepted the favourable theory of the Dutch proceedings. But watching the course of negotiations I became convinced that Kruger was using the oppression of the Outlanders as a lever to exact from England a renunciation of suzerainty; and the conduct of President Steyn[83] and Mr. Schreiner[84], of the Afrikaners generally and of their sympathisers in Europe, has brought home to me the belief that there is an understanding among the leaders of Dutch opinion, and that their aspiration is the restoration of South Africa to the Dutch race.[85]

If the British Government had gone to war with no better case than its record in the negotiations with the Transvaal, the British public would not have responded with anything approaching bipartisan support. It took the Boer ultimatum of 9 October, demanding terms which no British

Government could accept, to galvanize British opinion behind the war. Even then, the published record of the discussions with the Transvaal was sufficiently unsatisfactory to drive 135 M.P.s, including a Conservative and a Liberal Unionist,[86] to vote for Philip Stanhope's motion expressing 'strong disapproval of the conduct of the negotiations.' Liberal Imperialists upheld the case for war and voted with the Government. But the Liberal leader in the Commons, Sir Henry Campbell-Bannerman, abstained, and privately encouraged his followers to vote with Stanhope.[87]

Ironically, the Government's concern for opinion at home, while not enough to impose an appropriate consistency upon its negotiations, was sufficiently strong to impede its military preparations, again with nearly disastrous consequences. The tactics of keeping pressure upon the Transvaal while negotiating with it would logically have justified substantial mobilization long before a breakdown in the talks appeared probable. But mobilization would give rise to charges that the British Government was not negotiating in good faith or was bullying the Transvaal, charges which would create partisan division at home even before it came to a question of peace or war. In June and again in July 1899 the Commander-in-Chief of the army, Lord Wolseley, asked the War Secretary, Lord Lansdowne, for permission, first simply to assemble food and stores in South Africa, then to despatch 10,000 men to Natal and the Cape Colony. Both times Lansdowne turned him down. Not till August was a small contingent of 2,000 men sent to Natal. Not till 8 September, when the hardening responses of the two Governments made war very probable, did the Cabinet seriously turn its attention to military preparation.

This delay, the weeks of sailing time between England and the Cape, and the further two or three months 'which the extraordinary futility of the War Office interposes between us and any effective action',[88] made Salisbury apprehensive. His diplomatic house was in good order: Britain, so he told Lord Granby,[89] had no quarrel on its hands at the moment with any other country. But that was not security enough. Until the eve of the Transvaal ultimatum, Chamberlain could not believe that the Boers would take the offensive, '—nor do I fear a British reverse if they do'.[90] Salisbury and Balfour were more apprehensive about the military situation, and they urged Chamberlain to slow down the pace of the final diplomatic exchanges with the Transvaal so that Britain could put its armed forces in position. Kruger, alive to his military advantage, precipitated the outbreak of war. The Boer ultimatum was diplomatic folly but militarily astute. And the great military difficulty which Britain experienced before it could defeat the Boers revived the doubts which the ultimatum had suppressed about the war's justice.

## NOTES

1. *Hansard*, 4th ser., L, 418–9 (21 June 1897).
2. John A. Bridges, *Reminiscences of a Country Politician* (London, 1906) pp. 169–70
3. Lord Askwith, *Lord James of Hereford* (London. 1930), p. 255.
4. T. J. Spinner, Jr., *George Joachim Goschen* (Cambridge, 1973), p. 183 and *passim*.
5. A. B. Cooke and A. P. W. Malcolmson, comp., *The Ashbourne Papers, 1869–1913* (Belfast, 1974), p. 31.
6. Lord Askwith, *loc. cit.*
7. Sir Arthur S. T. Griffith-Boscawen, *Fourteen Years in Parliament* (London, 1907), p. 129.
8. *Hansard*, 4th ser., XLVII, 745 (16 March 1897).
9. James to Salisbury, 17 August 1901, copy, Lord James of Hereford papers.
10. Salisbury to James, 19 August 1901, copy, Lord James of Hereford papers.
11. Earl of Midleton, *Records & Reactions, 1856–1939* (New York, 1939), p. 112.
12. Sir Arthur S. T. Griffith-Boscawen, *loc. cit.*
13. Justin McCarthy, *British Political Leaders* (London, 1903), p. 47.
14. Lucille Iremonger, *The Fiery Chariot* (London, 1970), p. 133.
15. Goschen remarked in 1896 to Gladstone's daughter: 'It is England's great misfortune that the four men most nearly concerned with the Government, the present and the late Prime Minister, Lord Salisbury and Lord Rosebery, the present and the late Leaders of the House of Commons, Mr Balfour and Sir William Harcourt, were all four, in the main, cynics.' Mary Drew's reminiscences of Balfour, typescript, p. 56, Balfour papers (Whittinghame).
16. H. W. Lucy, *A Diary of the Unionist Parliament, 1895–1900* (London, 1901), pp. 334–5.
17. Lord Curzon, *Modern Parliamentary Eloquence* (London, 1913), p. 35.
18. Earl of Midleton, *op. cit.*, pp. 106–7.
19. McDonnell to Salisbury, 14 June 1899, Salisbury papers.
20. *Supra*, p. 230.
21. J. S. Sandars to Balfour, 3 March 1897, Balfour papers, B. L. Add. MSS. 49760; Middleton to McDonnell, 7 April 1897, Middleton's note on it, and enclosures, Salisbury papers.
22. Sandars to Balfour, 26 April 1897, Balfour papers, B. L. Add. MSS. 49760.
23. Speech at Levens, 10 June 1897, Londonderry papers, vol. of newsclippings, D/L0/F/148.
24. *Hansard*, 4th ser., LI, 537 (20 July 1897).
25. Sir Matthew Ridley to Salisbury, 12 July 1897, Salisbury papers.
26. *Hansard*, 4th ser., LI, 1436–7 (29 July 1897).
27. McDonnell to Salisbury, 20 July 1897, Salisbury papers, with Middleton's letters to Salisbury.
28. Londonderry's speech to annual conference of the Northern Union of Conservative Associations at Berwick-upon-Tweed, *The Times*, 16 October 1897.
29. J. S. Sandars to Balfour, 6 October 1897, Balfour papers, B. L. Add. MSS. 49760.
30. National Union Annual Conference Minutes, 16 November 1897, 1–2.
31. J. H. Robb, *The Primrose League, 1883–1906* (New York, 1942), p. 68.
32. Salisbury to the Queen, 8 December 1899, P. R. O. CAB 41/25.
33. *Hansard*, 4th ser., LXX, 1285 (4 May 1899).
34. This understanding did not prevent Salisbury from delivering a remarkably fervent, though unsuccessful, protest against the elimination of women's eligibility to serve as aldermen and local councillors. *Hansard*, 4th ser., LXXIII, 546–51 (26 June 1899).
35. Salisbury to Balfour, 22 August 1898, Balfour papers, B. L. Add. MSS. 49691.

36. Salisbury to the annual conference of the National Union, *The Times*, 20 November 1895, 7c.
37. Salisbury at Bradford, *The Times*, 23 May 1895, 6c.
38. Salisbury to the Junior Constitutional Club, *The Times*, 19 May 1897, 12b.
39. Salisbury to Cadogan, 22 December 1896, Cadogan papers.
40. *Hansard*, 4th ser., LI, 871 (23 July 1897).
41. Salisbury to Cadogan, 22 December 1896, *loc. cit.*
42. Memorandum by John Boraston, 22 October 1896, on the Education Bill of 1896, Balfour papers, B. L. Add. MSS. 49769.
43. Memorandum to the Cabinet by Devonshire, 7 November 1896, P. R. O. CAB 37/43.
44. Salisbury to Balfour, 20 November 1896, Balfour papers, B. L. Add. MSS. 49690.
45. Memorandum to the Cabinet by Salisbury, 30 November 1896, P. R. O. CAB 37/43.
46. Balfour to Salisbury, 23 November 1896, copy, Balfour papers, B. L. Add. MSS. 49690.
47. Memorandum for the Cabinet from Balfour, 8 November 1896, P. R. O. CAB 37/43.
48. Note by Chamberlain, 2 December 1896, Chamberlain papers JC 5/5/25.
49. Elementary schooling did not exhaust the divisive potentialities of the subject of education for the Ministry. Salisbury tangled with Devonshire over schemes, prepared by the Charity Commissioners and presented by Devonshire in his capacity as Lord President of the Council, to make more efficient use of educational endowments by lessening the ecclesiastical requirements laid down by the original donors. Backed by the bishops as well as his customary Conservative support, Salisbury, to Devonshire's taciturn embarrassment, easily induced the House of Lords to reject two of these schemes. *Hansard*, 4th ser., LI, 267–86 (16 July 1897), and LIII, 844–58 (17 February 1898).
50. See Andrew Porter, 'Lord Salisbury, Mr. Chamberlain and South Africa, 1895–9', *Journal of Imperial and Commonwealth History*, I, (October 1972), pp. 3–26.
51. Chamberlain to Salisbury, 24 December 1895, Salisbury papers; Salisbury to Balfour, 27 December 1895, Balfour papers, B. L. Add. MSS. 49690.
52. Peter Marsh, 'Lord Salisbury and the Ottoman massacres', *Journal of British Studies*, XI, 2 (May 1972), pp. 74–80.
53. Though Hicks Beach was an ardent Hellenist, and Goschen and Balfour had Hellenic leanings. *Letters of Queen Victoria*, 3rd ser., III, p. 146; and Lady Gwendolen Cecil, *Life of Salisbury*, V, p. 191, typescript in the Salisbury papers.
54. Lady Gwendolen Cecil, *Life of Salisbury*, V, typescript in Salisbury papers, pp. 183–4.
55. *Letters of Queen Victoria*, 3rd ser., III, p. 135.
56. The following discussion draws heavily upon J. A. Grenville's compelling analysis in *Lord Salisbury and Foreign Policy* (London, revised ed., 1970), and, to a lesser extent, upon the masterpiece by Ronald Robinson and John Gallagher, *Africa and the Victorians* (London, 1961).
57. *The Times*, 1 February 1896, 10b.
58. Salisbury to Cross, 14 February 1889; note by Salisbury, n.d.; Memorandum by Salisbury on 'The Indian Reform Bill', n.d.; Salisbury to Cross, 21 July 1892, Cross papers, B. L. Add. MSS. 51264, ff. 28, 38–44 and 89.
59. *The Times*, 17 April 1884, 6a.
60. Lady Gwendolen Cecil, *Life of Salisbury*, I, pp. 206–7, and II, 67; *Letters of Queen Victoria*, 3rd ser., III, pp. 485–6 and 488; Salisbury to Lord Northcote, 8 June 1900, copy, Salisbury papers, Drafts.
61. Sir Arthur S. T. Griffith-Boscawen, *op. cit.*, p. 135.

62. *The Times*, 30 April 1898, 11e.
63. Salisbury to McDonnell, 5 April 1898, McDonnell papers.
64. Salisbury to Balfour, 9 April 1898, Balfour papers, B. L. Add. MSS. 49690.
65. J. A. S. Grenville, *Lord Salisbury and Foreign Policy* (London, 1970), p. 178.
66. Ronald Robinson and John Gallagher, *Africa and the Victorians* (London, 1961), p. 351; Lady Gwendolen Cecil, *Life of Salisbury*, IV, p. 309.
67. He loathed the trophies that excited jingoistic imperialists. After the victory of Omdurman, when only 48 Anglo-Egyptian officers and men lay dead on the field as compared to at least 12,000 dervishes, he commented: 'The 'butcher's bill' is ghastly. The only consolation is that they were sustaining the worst and cruellest Government in the world. I hope it will calm some of the feverish aspirations on the back benches. A slaughter of 16,000 ought to satisfy our Jingos for at least six months.' A. E. Gathorne-Hardy, *Gathorne Hardy, First Earl of Cranbrook* (London, 1910), II, pp. 368–9.
68. *The Times*, 5 November 1898, 12c.
69. Malcolm MacColl, *Memoirs and Correspondence*, ed. G. W. E. Russell (London, 1914), p. 159.
70. A. G. Gardiner, *The Life of Sir William Harcourt* (London, 1923), II, pp. 440–1.
71. Courtney was a most independently-minded Liberal Unionist.
72. G. P. Gooch, *Life of Lord Courtney* (London, 1920), pp. 354, 375 and *passim*; Stephen Gwynn and G. M. Tuckwell, *The Life of the Rt. Hon. Sir Charles W. Dilke* (London, 1917), II, p. 310.
73. A. G. Gardiner, *op. cit.*, p. 449.
74. Salisbury to the Junior Constitutional Club, *The Times*, 19 May 1897, 12c.
75. *Hansard*, 4th ser., XLVII, 1013–4 (19 March 1897).
76. Salisbury to Alfred Austin, 17 August 1898, Austin papers.
77. *Hansard*, 4th ser., LIII, 43–4 (8 February 1898).
78. Salisbury to the Constitutional Club, *The Times*, 17 December 1898, 12b.
79. Quoted in Ronald Robinson and John Gallagher, *op. cit.*, p. 377.
80. Salisbury to the Constitutional Club, *loc. cit.*
81. 'I should intimate to the authorities of the New Republic that their allotments were all encroachment on the territory of our allies the Zulus. At the same time I would let a ship show itself on the Zulu coast.
    If the Boers continued encroaching—& we survived, I should proclaim a protectorate over a strip along the whole coast: & put a resident there if there is any wholesome place in which we could live. I should instruct the Resident to tell the Zulus that the New Republic had no sort of right to the farms they occupied: & if the Zulus chose to defend their native soil, I should facilitate their being provided with arms & ammunition. But I would not declare British protection or sovereignty over any place, we could not conveniently reach from the coast.' Salisbury to Frederick Stanley, 18 December 1885, Hobbs papers.
82. Quoted in J. A. S. Grenville, *op. cit.*, p. 235.
83. Of the Orange Free State.
84. Premier of the Cape Colony.
85. Salisbury to Courtney, 5 October 1899, in G. P. Gooch, *op. cit.*, pp. 377–8.
86. J. M. Maclean and Courtney. Sir Edward Clarke, Conservative M.P. for Plymouth, took a prominent part in the preliminary onslaught upon the Government's negotiating record, but abstained from the final vote.
87. G. P. Gooch, *op. cit.*, p. 386.
88. Salisbury to Chamberlain, 29 August 1899, quoted in J. A. S. Grenville, *op. cit.*, p. 255.
89. Salisbury to Granby, 5 October 1899, Rutland papers.
90. Chamberlain to Hicks Beach, 7 October 1899, in Lady Victoria Hicks-Beach, *Life of Sir Michael Hicks-Beach (Earl St. Aldwyn)* (London, 1932), II, pp. 108–9.

# CHAPTER 9

# DISINTEGRATION

Freedom, the underlying principle of a democratic society, requires a commitment to restraint, a willingness not to do anything to
undermine the basic set of conventions which
enable men of different values and interests to live
together.

Seymour Martin Lipset, 'The paradox of American
politics', The Public Interest, XLI (Autumn 1975),
p. 165.

The Boer War was the first and greatest of a series of developments at
the turn of the century which heightened impatience with the craft of
Conservative government that Salisbury and his older colleagues had
mastered in the 1880s. All the practitioners of the old craft, including
Goschen and Hicks Beach, at a lower level Middleton, and in a sense, the
Queen, were nearing the end of their lives. The primary purpose behind
the craft was to curb the excesses and vagaries of popular government
which had come into being in their lifetime. Maintenance of the rights of
property was inextricably mixed up with this objective, to which most of
the practitioners also added defence of special interests, particularly the
Established Church. The craft was conventional rather than innovative
in its assumptions. It was more concerned with the accommodation of
interests than with the promotion of governmental efficiency. It
assumed a thoroughly civilian state, permeated with concern for
economic prosperity rather than for military might. In spite of the
envious glances Salisbury cast at the essentially military autocracy of
imperial government in India and Egypt, he had never contemplated
Bismarckian cures for the fevers of popular government in Britain. The
only foreign model he had held up for admiration was the American one
with its Senate and Supreme Court, so much stronger bulwarks against
popular fancies than the House of Lords, and he cited the American
constitution simply to underscore the need to keep the House of Lords in
full vigour.

All of the old craftsmen, Goschen and the Queen as much as the
others, had come to rely upon the Conservative party as the main,
though not the sole, instrument for their purposes. They had also
learned—some much earlier than others, Salisbury more slowly than the

rest—that in order to secure their supreme objective, they had to adapt themselves to less than congenial allies, even at a cost to subordinate interests. Hicks Beach had curbed his independent spirit and his admiration for Lord Randolph Churchill in order to work under the loose but safer harness of Salisbury. Salisbury had learned the most: first to work in cooperation with cautious Conservative peers such as the Duke of Richmond; at periodic but always painful moments to defer to the requirements of his Cabinet colleagues in the House of Commons; in 1887 to acquiesce in the failure of the Unionist alliance to congeal into a party of resistance; last, and most slowly of all, to appreciate the implications of Nonconformist Unionism.

The Boer War exposed glaring limitations in this approach to government. Ardent spirits, already impatient with its restraints and now emboldened by the inglorious course of the war, extended their challenge to non-military spheres. Too old or tired to fight back, those master craftsmen who were not carried off by death, retired: Goschen in 1900, Salisbury and Hicks Beach in 1902, Middleton in 1903. And with them went their craft, rejected wholly or in part by their successors. Both because of the shrewdness and because of the limitations inherent in the abandoned craft, these successors were soon innundated by disasters.

## i. The Boer War

The defeat of a British force by the Boers at Nicholson's Nek at the end of October 1899, three weeks after the formal commencement of hostilities, disturbed the British public only mildly. The main expeditionary force, under General Buller, was still on the high seas, and Englishmen awaited its deployment with confidence. This mood of confidence was shattered and transformed into grim determination by 'Black Week', the second week in December, when the Boers repulsed three major British forces, including one under Buller's personal command, within five days. Three long months were to pass before British forces could send home word of their first major victory.

'Black Week' revealed the incompetence of the commanders on the spot, preeminently Buller. Upon arrival at Capetown, he had split his expeditionary force into three divisions rather than concentrate it, and had then deprived the divided force of unified command by heading off personally with the eastern division. But Buller was quickly replaced by the joint leadership of Lord Roberts and Lord Kitchener. The long vigil from December into mid-February drew persistent attention in Britain to the inefficiency of the military policy-makers at home and the military administrators in Capetown. In preparation for the outbreak of hostilities, army headquarters had sent two commanders, Buller and Sir George White, from England to South Africa without ensuring that the two men held consultations with each other prior to departure, without precise clarification of their mutual relationship, and virtually without instructions. This lack of preliminary coordination by army headquarters was the result in part of a long-standing feud among senior officers between partisans of Lord Roberts and partisans of the Commander-in-Chief, Lord Wolseley. The quarrel was perpetuated in South Africa. Furthermore, there was a pitifully small intelligence staff of eighteen at army headquarters, and in the field a lack of good maps and trained guides. Time after time, contingents of British troops mistook their position and fell into traps laid by unseen Boer riflemen.

Shortcoming such as these brought discredit upon Lord Salisbury's Ministry, both for failure earlier in its term to put the army's house in good order, and for the inadequacy of its wartime leadership and supervision. True to his belief that Britain's power overseas depended ultimately on force rather than on good will, Salisbury had paid attention to the capacity of the army and navy from his first months as prime minister. But the scale of warfare which he had contemplated was small, limited to narrowly defined actions, for example on the western approaches to India or up the Nile. To ensure effective military capacity at this level, he had in the past exerted fairly steady, sometimes innovative pressure on the agencies of government. He had defended expenditure on coaling stations against Churchill in 1886. He had welcomed the scale and extraordinary guarantees of sustained expenditure laid down in the Naval Defence Act of 1889. He had impressed the Queen with the debilitating consequences of the addiction of her cousin, the Duke of Cambridge, as Commander-in-Chief, to seniority in awarding promotions.[1] He had suggested the desirability of approving the estimates for the service departments in lump sums in order to release them from minute, throttling supervision by the Treasury.[2] The pace which his Government set in military reform and expansion during the '80s was far enough in advance of the Parliamentary consensus to be controversial and to reduce the spokesmen for still greater speed to the political adventurers, to Sir Charles Dilke discredited by a seamy divorce case, to Lord Randolph Churchill, and to the impulsive Lord Charles Beresford.

When forming his third Ministry, Salisbury, again in line with the maturing thought of the pundits on military affairs, gave the Duke of Devonshire special responsibility to coordinate the activities of the services and related departments through a new Defence Committee of the Cabinet.[3] The appointment was not a mere gesture, for Devonshire in 1887 (when still Lord Hartington) had been appointed to chair a royal commission of enquiry into the army's organization. Though intended partly to head off attacks by the adventurers, Hartington's Commission tackled its subject boldly. Its most imaginative recommendation was for the creation of a Committee of Defence such as that Devonshire was now called upon to lead. The innovation of 1895, enhanced by the prestige and political weight of its president, was enough to reassure the advocates of reform.

The Committee proved worse than useless, for it quieted apprehensions without dealing with their substance. Its failure to accomplish more reflected the functional weakness of Salisbury's Cabinet as an executive. The Committee's mandate ran counter to the Cabinet's pervasive mode of operation as a honeycomb of largely autonomous departments. In the case of each of the service departments, this mode was reinforced by entrenched interests, peculiar organization, long traditions, and mutual jealousy. The struggle of the Secretary of State for War, Lord Lansdowne, to cope with internal conflicts within the army deprived him of energy for the further work of subordinating the army to the needs of imperial defence. Goschen, at the Admiralty, was downright hostile to subordination of the navy.[4] The navy was at a peak of efficiency, in which he took pride, and his jealousy of the 'quartet' within the Cabinet deepened his resistance to any encroachments upon the navy's autonomy. If he had been overridden, he would almost certainly have resigned.

Lansdowne's lack of energy and Goschen's hostility enervated Devonshire. The critical failure of the Defence Committee lay with its chairman. The Hartington Commission had envisioned a committee chaired by the prime minister. Salisbury had been prepared to assume that responsibility instead of the Foreign Office: Devonshire became chairman of the Defence Committee by his own choice. The nature of the coalition then obliged Salisbury to leave the conduct of the Committee in his leading ally's hands. Salisbury participated fully in the discussion in the autumn of 1895 about the extent of the Committee's authority, and, like Devonshire, he favoured an ambitious definition. He did not request a seat on the Committee for himself as Foreign Secretary. Such an arrangement would have strengthened the Committee, but would also have impinged upon Devonshire's province as well as upon the autonomy of the Foreign Office. Significantly, Devonshire did not ask him to participate. Goschen asked Salisbury to do so, but only in order to drive home to him the ignominy of subordinating the navy to the Committee, and Goschen's suggestion was therefore passed over. In spite of Goschen's dogged non-cooperation, Devonshire might have made progress if he had led the Committee with something of the energy Chamberlain invested at the Colonial Office. But Devonshire's talent, in contrast to Chamberlain's, was for commonsense political judgement rather than for bold administration, and he had also passed his prime. Even his weight in the deliberations of the Cabinet was diminishing, for he was growing deaf and had difficulty catching all that was said. The Committee lapsed into inactivity, broken only by occasional meetings to resolve minor disputes, usually brought about by the Treasury over expenditure.

Had Devonshire and the Committee acted with more energy, they could still not have saved Britain from embarrassment in the Boer War, since the Committee was limited not just in energy but also in vision. The scale of operations which the Committee persistently envisaged did not rise above the small engagements on the fringes of empire which Britain had experienced over the previous generation; and Britain had a good record in military campaigns of these dimensions. The Government presumed that the Boer War would be a little larger campaign but of the same sort. No responsible British politician had reckoned with the requirements of war on the scale which all Continental powers took for granted, a scale which the Boer War eventually approached. The Boer War did not inject the Defence Committee with new vitality. The Committee went on, as before, dealing 'with technical military matters, not broad strategy and the reconciliation of departmental aspects of imperial policy.'[5] After the reconstruction of the Ministry in 1900, the Defence Committee was virtually superseded by a larger War Committee composed of Salisbury, Balfour, Hicks Beach, Chamberlain, Lansdowne, now at the Foreign Office, and the new service Ministers, still under the chairmanship of Devonshire.[6]

The executive capacity of the Ministry in the opening months of the war was further though briefly impaired by Lord Salisbury's grief over the death of his wife. After several years of worsening health, Lady Salisbury had suffered a stroke in July 1899. Her buoyancy, irrepressible enjoyment of company, and complete dedication to her husband's welfare, and the religious faith which they shared had saved him from psychological anguish and ineffectuality. Her illness came first in his mind, displacing even the war. He could not accept the facts which the doctors gave him about the impossibility of her recovery; for once he clung to a baseless optimism. She died late in November 1899, just when Buller's force was landing in South Africa. Balfour quietly took over the prime minister's responsibilities for a short space of time, including 'Black Week'. Mercifully, Salisbury was laid low with 'flu on the day his wife died. As McDonnell reported at the beginning of December to Lord Curzon:[7]

> this obliged him to go to bed where he remained until after the funeral: and his body and mind have now been so far rested that he is nearly well again, though he will not begin his work once more for a few days... He *looks* tired and old, white and unhappy; but he is still full of vigour, and when a little time has passed I think he will devote himself to his work with even greater care than before.

McDonnell's assessment was borne out right after Black Week when the Ministry decided to replace Buller with Lord Roberts. It was Salisbury who insisted that the Ministry make a joint appointment of the sixty-seven year old Lord Roberts with Lord Kitchener, who was in his prime.[8] The appointment of the two generals caught the imagination of an alarmed public, and subsequently the combination worked well.

There was no disguising the fact that, quite apart from his bereavement, Salisbury was aging. On top of increasingly frequent bouts of 'flu, his eyesight was failing. His wife's death and his immediate illness inevitably raised again the possibility of his resignation. Salisbury did not offer to resign; the will to power was still there. But the remarkable fact in December 1899, in contrast to the spring of 1898, was the general desire, amounting in some cases to a plea, that Salisbury remain at the helm of state. There was enough uneasiness about the war's justice to rule out his obvious replacement, Chamberlain, no matter how effectively Chamberlain could arouse the patriotic passions of the nation nor how great his reputation as a vigorous administrator. Parliament and the public tended to draw a not fully warranted[9] distinction between the two men's responsibility for the pre-war negotiations. Chamberlain was held accountable for what was aggressive in the conduct of the negotiations, while Salisbury's adherence to their outcome was interpreted as the best guarantee of their justice. If Salisbury had resigned at any point before the war's end, no matter how he explained his action, it would have released doubts about the original justification for the war or about the wisdom of pressing it to a victorious conclusion. His retention of office dispelled those doubts among most Unionists, and kept them to manageable proportions among Liberals. His concern for bipartisan support, the same concern which had weakened his hold on the Foreign Office in 1898, riveted him to the office of prime minister once the Boer War began. Ironically, his contribution in July 1899 to the failure of the pre-war negotiations only confirmed his hold upon the highest office. If Britain's record in the negotiations had not been disturbing, the country might have entered the war unanimously convinced of its necessity, and in that case the suspicions which prevented Chamberlain from replacing Salisbury would not have been so powerful. As it was, Salisbury was held in office as the keeper of the nation's imperial conscience.

The deficiencies of the Cecilian temper for wartime leadership were conspicuously revealed in January 1900. Because Black Week had occurred just before the customary holiday over Christmas and New Year, no leader of the Government spoke to the nation until nearly the middle of January when Balfour addressed his constituents in Manchester. The public looked to the Ministry for an inspiring lead and for evidence of resolve. Balfour and, three weeks later at the opening of

Parliament, Salisbury, disappointed these hopes. Both men discoursed with seeming detachment on the impediments which the popular, civilian character of British government put in the way of prompt, effective military action. Balfour tried to explain how the need to carry the public with the Government in the spring and summer of 1899 had prevented it from strengthening its armed forces in South Africa in preparation for the possibility of war; and his explanation angered far more people than it satisfied. Salisbury as well as Balfour reflected passively on the great superiority of the military machines created by the more authoritarian regimes of Continental Europe. Both men admitted, with maddening equanimity, that the Government had gravely under-estimated the Boers' military capacity.

Of the two speeches Salisbury's was worse. In order to minimize the Government's misjudgement about the quantity of Boer armaments, he exaggerated the Government's ignorance. The Government had, in fact, received quite a variety of reports on the Boer military build-up, some of them fairly accurate. Conscious of the weakness of his case, Salisbury went too far, and made the Government's pre-war ignorance seem childishly naive and helpless. 'How on earth', he asked, could the Government have known about the artillery and munitions of war that the Boer republics were introducing?

> I believe, as a matter of fact—though I do not give this as official—that the guns were generally introduced in boilers and locomotives, and the munitions of war were introduced in pianos.[10]

Lord Rosebery, who had been cultivating an image of lofty reserve, came to the Lords to hear Salisbury's speech with no intention of speaking himself. Exasperated at what he heard, he intervened in the debate in order to insist that the country 'will have to be inspired by a loftier tone and by a truer patriotism than we have heard from the Prime Minister to-night.'[11] Rosebery voiced the common reaction. 'Chilling' was the word one Conservative M.P. used for the effect of his leader's statement. Another usually sympathetic commentator thought that 'Lord Salisbury never made so inept a speech on a great occasion.'[12] Balfour had regularly failed to gauge popular expectations, but Salisbury had rarely done so. Though seldom accused of playing to the gallery, he had usually possessed a robust, sober, well-informed appreciation of the electorate's requirements. That appreciation was indeed one of the foundation stones of his authority. But age, grief, and the resurgence of his pre-marital gloom[13] made his natural insulation hard to penetrate. They also reduced his ability to adjust his thinking to the changes which the war was creating or accelerating in the Parliamentary and popular cast of mind.

Dissatisfaction with the lead that Balfour and Salisbury provided gave the Unionist whips in the Commons a few weeks of anxiety. Sullen abstentions and the absence of soldier-M.P.s at the front nibbled at the edges of the Government's usually huge voting majorities in the Commons. Chamberlain tried but did not entirely succeed in performing his usual feat of rousing the backbenchers. It took a speech by a junior Minister, George Wyndham, to do so. The life of the Government was never in serious jeopardy, however, because of the divisions within the Opposition. The Liberals tried to divert attention from their disagreements about the justice and wisdom of the war by concentrating their attack upon the way it was being conducted. Their attempt fooled no one, least of all each other. The Boer War made Liberal Imperialists and Little Englanders more convinced than ever of the validity of their rival creeds, and more impatient than ever with each other. Therefore, no matter how acute their criticisms of the Government, the official Liberal leaders could not present themselves as a credible alternative war Ministry; and the Government did not need what little additional support a coalition with the Liberal Imperialists could bring.

The fortunes of war and the popular estimate of the Government ebbed and flowed together. Lord Roberts' defeat of General Cronje at Paardenberg in mid-February eased the gloom at Westminster. There were still bad moments in store, particularly when despatches about 'the sickening fiasco'[14] at Spion Kop were published. Publication of these despatches revealed General Buller's incapacity even in a subordinate command, and also raised questions about the Government's wisdom in sanctioning the publication. Furthermore, a dispute between Salisbury and Lansdowne as to whether the Cabinet had actually agreed to the publication illustrated, to the few who knew of it, the executive deficiencies of the Government. But the blackness of the winter defeats made the victories of spring brighter. Jubilation reached frantic proportions in May when Mafeking was relieved. Roberts' capture of Pretoria, one of the twin Boer capitals, in June made England blissfully sure of speedy total victory. The last pitched battle of the war took place on 27 August, just before the electorate went to the polls and returned the Government to office with a majority in the Commons almost as large as the majority it had won in 1895.

The electoral returns were barely complete when the war entered a new, guerrilla phase. Guerrillas are always excruciatingly difficult to suppress; and the Boers' guerrilla activities were to persist for another seventeen months, much longer than the conventional phase of the war. In the first phase, even in the dark days of December, the war had drawn together more than it had divided Britain. The electoral results of 1900 implied that public willingness to bear the costs of imperialism had increased substantially since the late 1870s. The Government's imperial mandate remained intact. The guerrilla phase of the war corroded that mandate. The continued, increasing cost of the war in men and money discouraged the public. But the critical cost of the guerrilla war was moral. The Boers' refusal to capitulate when their armies were defeated in the field, and the support of civilian Boers, which enabled the guerrillas to launch their attacks and then disappear, proved that the war was a conflict of peoples. Furthermore, the 'methods of barbarism' to which the British authorities felt obliged to resort in order to crush the guerrillas undermined belief that empire was a civilizing mission. The imperial conscience, of which Salisbury was keeper, seemed to be no conscience at all.

The guerrilla war brought out a hard streak in Salisbury's makeup, previously seen in his persecution of Parnell. Salisbury responded to determined defiance with unflinching repression. He suggested branding as a way to identify captured Boer soldiers who took an oath of neutrality and then managed to escape, only to violate their oath by taking up arms again.[15] He evinced no qualms about farm burning, as a way to deprive guerrillas of their base of supply: 'You will not conquer these people', he told his new Secretary for War in the first months of the guerrilla campaign, 'until you have starved them out.'[16] Farm burning added hosts of homeless wives and children to the concentration camps which the British opened for Boer civilians. The unfamiliarity of the Boers, as rural people, with the requirements of urban public health aggravated the problem of overcrowding beyond the ability or determination of the camp administrators to ensure basic hygiene. The death rate among the occupants soared. Salisbury clenched his teeth. 'War is a terrible thing', he told a scandalized humanitarian:[17] 'The Boers should have thought of its horrible significance when they invaded the Queen's dominions without a cause.' After defending farm burning as a military necessity and concentration camps as its inevitable corollary, he did not hesitate to go on:

> The huddling together of so many human beings, especially women and children, could not but cause a great mortality; particularly among a people so dirty as the Boers.

Still, repelled by the slightest appearance of sentimentality, Salisbury had gone out of his way to shock his correspondent's sensibilities. At almost the same time that he penned these words, he was injecting humanitarian considerations into Cabinet discussion, arguing that punishments should be inflicted more carefully and sparingly 'in view of the present state of opinion here–& the probable effect later on the memories of Boers of unwise measures.'[18]

In addition to its demoralizing effects, the guerrilla war revived and intensified charges of governmental and military ineptitude. Some of the charges were groundless. Critics focused attention on the permission granted to Lord Roberts to return home just as the guerrilla campaign was about to become serious. Roberts, however, was sixty-eight. Salisbury, far from fooling himself that the war was over, wanted Roberts back home in order to free Kitchener for more energetic measures.[19] Still, the guerrilla war demonstrated that Britain's military and civilian authorities had again underestimated the enemy's determination and skill. The lack of a well informed, forward looking general staff for the army continued to be exposed. Revelations of tension and disagreement within the military and civilian agencies supervising the war, particularly between the Treasury and the War Office, drew attention to the need for much better coordination at a still higher level. The continuing need for fresh supplies of soldiers, not only for South Africa but for home defence, strained the traditional British devices for recruitment, and revealed the poor physical condition common in working-class volunteers.

In short, the conflict in South Africa demonstrated that Britain was not ready for war, 'the great test of institutions' as Salisbury had once put it.[20] Where the Boer War did not breed disenchantment with imperialism, it bred impatience with the traditional practices and civilian restraints of British military administration. This second reaction, though the less popular of the two and confined largely to practising or would-be politicians with an appetite for administration, eroded support for the Government as surely as the first; and the implications of the two reactions were equally far-reaching. The criticism of the second group[21] was not confined to the ideologically neutral ground of administrative machinery. Underneath the specific points of criticism lay a Bismarckian fear that civilian, Parliamentary, partisan government produced nerveless leadership and was not likely to make the most efficient use of the nation's resources. Though they rarely attacked Salisbury personally, the advocates of 'national efficiency' poured scorn on the administrative consequences of his manner of government and questioned some of its basic assumptions.

Salisbury responded to charges of governmental ineptitude by drawing attention to the limitations within which British government, unlike its Continental counterparts, had to work: to the Treasury's tradition of minute scrutiny over expenditure; to the tradition of civilian, Parliamentary supremacy which prevented the creation of an autonomous, supreme army council composed of professional soldiers; and to the rooted British aversion to conscription. But he did not suggest overriding these restrictions. On the contrary, while he equivocated about Treasury control, he insisted upon respecting the other two.[22] His inability to conduct the most enterprising wartime administration compatible even with these limitations betrayed his advancing age, depression and fatigue. But exhaustion did not account for his acceptance of the limitations. He regarded them as necessary and, still more, as desirable. Salisbury hated war, a hatred which deepened with age,[23] because he loved the institutions, the constitutional limitations and restraints which war always subjected to a searching test. What he loved inhibited his imagination in responding to what he loathed. Characteristically, the arguments with which he attempted to preserve acceptance of time-honoured limitations upon the country's military conduct were for the most part pragmatic. He presented the restraints as imposed either by the historic, unchanged will of the country,[24] or by 'our constitutional system'. 'It may be good or bad', he told Brodrick, '—but we have got to make it work.'[25] He warned Parliament of the danger of resorting, under the duress of war, to novel experiments: if they failed, they would create panic at home and 'sinister pleasure and anticipation on the part of our enemies abroad.'[26] As the war dragged on and attempts were launched to bring the public to a less inhibited frame of mind, he occasionally argued the case for the old values explicitly, without pragmatic camouflage. The case against an autonomous military high command and conscription boiled down to a defence of individual freedom. Freedom for the individual held the highest rank in Salisbury's hierarchy of values, both for its intrinsic worth and for its practical utility. He told the House of Lords in the spring of 1901 that,

> the success of your military system, the victories you are to win, the results of all your efforts, are not obtained by any machine, however theoretically just, however carefully polished, but will be attained, and have been attained in every age of history, simply by the strength and brilliancy and vigour of the men you employ.[27]

The limitations which Salisbury defended were inextricably related to the constitutional restraints which he had sought to invigorate from his earliest days as party leader. Both served to impede the mobilization of power, which he feared, not of course because he loved administrative inefficiency and military ineptitude, but because of the use to which those who would pander to the demands of the popular electorate could put it. As a lifelong defender of the rights of propertied and educated minorities, the idea of conscription made him as uneasy as any Liberal Little Englander. The fear that had made him suspicious of tightening the House of Commons' procedural rules[28] had not abated. That problem had come up in the early 1880s, and he had surmounted it. Now, however, age deprived him of the time and energy to devise safeguards for or to accommodate himself to the demands of the disciples of national efficiency.

However wise or foolish his defence of Britain's traditional military policy may have been, one proposal which he made for remedying its deficiencies reflected a mind shaped by and unable to move beyond the experience of the 1880s. He suggested that the local habitations of the Primrose League, which had served the Empire so well in the fight against Home Rule, should rise to the current challenge by fostering the creation of rifle clubs in each parish. He made his proposal nothing short of ridiculous by describing it as an attempt to revive 'the skill and the fame of [our] ancestors many centuries ago, who by their practice in archery, first raised this country to its high level of military glory.'[29] Rosebery used temperate language when he described this response to what was going on in South Africa as 'extraordinarily inadequate'.[30]

There was a final twist to the moral tale of Salisbury and the Boer War. Just as his retention of the highest office calmed doubts about the initial justice of the war, so his continuance in office was needed to reduce doubts about the justice of keeping up the war until the Boers capitulated on Britain's terms. In his explanation of Britain's intentions at the outset of the war, he had pleased the doubtful with a ringing assertion that, 'we seek no goldfields'.[31] What he meant to dispel was the suspicion that Britain's object was the gold and diamond mines of the Transvaal. The remark, however, could also be interpreted to indicate that Britain would be satisfied with something less than complete annexation of the Boer republics. Salisbury meant no such thing, believing that if Britain settled for anything less than complete annexation, the old trouble in South Africa would begin all over again. A stiff policy was popular during the war's conventional phase, for the military might which the Boers threw into this warfare proved that they had taken advantage of their previous freedom from close British scrutiny to make vast preparations. The guerrilla war revived interest in a negotiated, compromise peace. Salisbury resisted this change of mood every bit as firmly as Chamberlain. But what sounded vindictive in Chamberlain's mouth sounded just in Salisbury's. As Alfred Austin put it, blind to the underlying cynicism:

> The whole world credits you with a love of Peace, with a repugnance rather than an inclination to the extension of Empire, & with a dislike and distrust of extreme courses. Proceeding from you, therefore, any declaration of Policy towards the two Rebel States would mean something of the inevitableness & the justice of Moral Law; &, if accompanied by a touching allusion to the sacrifices & the anxiety inflicted on the nation & the Empire, would, I am convinced, greatly strengthen the Executive, & create a sense of tranquil certainty well calculated to baffle Faction at home, & to overawe unfriendliness abroad.[32]

Salisbury did not deliberately deceive the public either over the pre-war negotiations or over the terms for peace. His public statements about the conditions upon which Britain would end the war were chillingly explicit. In the spring of 1902, when the Boers were finally coming round and the scent of peace was strong, he relayed to Chamberlain the anxiety of Hicks Beach and Edward VII that British intransigence might spoil the prospect, but he went on to indicate that he did not share their feeling himself.[33] Nonetheless, the credit which Salisbury had accumulated before the war continued to blind most Englishmen to the persistent severity of his South African policy and to convince many that it was temperate and just. He used up his moral savings to uphold the imperial interest resolutely in South Africa, yet he insisted upon constitutional and political inhibitions in the armed enforcement of that policy. This tension bedevilled his Government's conduct over the Boer War from the pre-war negotiations to the final peace.

## ii. The Sour Taste of Electoral Success

If the Boer War strained the bonds of imperial confidence between Salisbury and the British body politic, it also shook Salisbury's short-lived confidence in the sobriety of the electorate. Few Governments since the first Reform Act had survived general elections. Since the second Reform Act, general elections had defeated incumbant parties and installed their opponents with the regularity of clockwork. Until the spring of 1899 it looked very much as if the third Salisbury Ministry would fall victim to this pattern. The tide of by-elections flowed, though with fluctuating strength, against the Government. Salisbury intimated publicly in the summer of 1898 that he expected the results of the next general election to be like those of 1892.[34] A year later, before the war broke out, the expected magnitude of the Unionists' prospective defeat expanded alarmingly,[35] but by the end of the year the expected dimensions had shrunk again to 1892 proportions.[36]

Far from disturbing Salisbury, this prospect actually pleased him. Overwhelming defeat had no attractions. But defeat on the scale of 1892 had many. Without giving the Liberals a powerful popular mandate, it would allow the Unionist leaders time to recoup their strength. It would help redress the balance of power between the two Houses of Parliament as had happened between 1892 and '95, though Salisbury would undoubtedly himself retire. A brief reminder to the public of what Liberalism was like in practice would be salutary; or, as Salisbury put it wistfully in 1900 after electoral victory had been heaped upon him, 'A spell of Opposition is so good for bracing up the Conservative fibre of our country.'[37]

The military victories in the spring of 1900 had turned the expectations of electoral defeat for the Unionists into an increasingly bright promise of victory. Chamberlain responded to the change eagerly, as did Middleton and the Conservative whips and they carried with them the sympathies of all the Cabinet Ministers in the Commons.[38] Early in June, as soon as Pretoria fell to the British, Chamberlain pressed for a

general election in July, when the prospects for success would be at their
best. From June until the end of August, Salisbury resisted the pressure,
whether it came from Chamberlain or Middleton or Balfour.[39] As he
explained to a high spirited member of the family:

> You are like Joe, who again is like Randolph. You don't care the least for *character*.
> We could not dissolve with our work unfinished without loss of character.[40]

Salisbury recoiled from exploiting the popular exhilarations of war, not
simply because the war was unfinished, but also from fear of popular
passion of any sort.

But the Boers' defeat in their last stand in open field against the
British, followed by Lord Roberts' annexation of the Transvaal at the
end of August undercut Salisbury's resistance. Early in September, he
agreed to call a general election for the next month. For the Government
could not complete its work now without an election. The Government
was subsequently blamed for calling an election before the war was
really over and the Boer leaders had sued for peace. But there was good
reason to believe that, in hope of better terms from a Liberal than from a
Unionist Government, the Boers would not contemplate surrender until
Britain had gone to the polls. In other words, re-election of the Unionist
Government, preferably with a commanding majority, was deemed
necessary to drive the Boers to the peace table.

Even so, Salisbury did nothing in the ensuing campaign to increase
the ardour of the electorate. For the first time in his career as leader he
did not make a single public speech after the Government's intention of
dissolving Parliament was announced. He did not even want to issue a
printed manifesto. When the Duke of Devonshire told him that he ought
to do so he replied, to Devonshire's vast amusement, that 'he had
nothing to say'.[41] When he was finally prevailed upon to issue a
manifesto, it turned out to be deflating. After identifying military reform
as one of the most urgent tasks which Britain would have to tackle after
the election, he went on:

> Some may think, though I should not agree with them, that the task might be as
> effectively performed by our opponents, if they possessed an adequate majority,
> and a party organization capable of sustaining the burden of government. But it
> certainly could not be discharged by a nearly divided House of Commons and a
> Ministry depending upon a broken party.[42]

Little wonder that Chamberlain described the manifesto as 'most
depressing'.[43] Chamberlain did most of the campaigning as far as the
Unionist leadership was concerned. His rhetoric was as inflated as
Salisbury's was depressing, and reached the strident climax that, 'Every
seat lost to the Government is a seat gained to the Boers'. Salisbury

looked with cool disdain on the performance. In congratulating Balfour on his main campaign swing through Lancashire and Glasgow, he commented:

> It was very opportune, for the political world was running the danger of being divided into pro-Boer and pro-Joe: which I think is not an exhaustive statement of the sentiments of Her Majesty's subjects.[44]

The results of the election equalled the most optimistic forecasts of Conservative party headquarters. The Unionists piled up a majority in the House of Commons of 134 seats, just 18 short of its accomplishment in 1895, and, with that one exception, the largest majority won by either party since 1832. The Unionist percentage of the total popular vote in 1900 was 51.1, even higher than in 1895.

As Salisbury viewed it, the electoral pendulum had gone right back to the position from which it should naturally have swung. Until the results came in, while he may not have truly 'indulged the hope that we should be beaten',[45] he had certainly refused to make arrangements which assumed reelection.[46] The electoral returns puzzled and disturbed him. Shortly before the election, he had worried publicly about the unhealthy consequences of the Liberals' disarray.[47] The Liberal party entered the election gloomy about its prospects, still acutely divided, unsure of its stance on almost every issue including the war. Liberals failed to run candidates in 143 constituencies, 34 more than in 1895, and found candidates for some other constituencies at the last moment, too late to stand a chance of winning. Furthermore, if Salisbury had examined the final vote totals for the general election of 1900 as acutely as he had done for previous elections, he would have discovered unmistakeable sign of voter apathy. The total electoral vote was down from the figure in 1895 by more than a million, and though that fact could be discounted by referring to the greater number of uncontested constituencies, the turnout in most contested constituencies was also down. Finally, as a recent analyst of the general election of 1900 has pointed out, 'most Conservatives did not fight a 'Khaki' election. They tended to point out, quite reasonably, that a disunited Liberal Party could not be trusted to carry out an effective settlement in South Africa.'[48] In other words, the tone of the campaign struck by most Conservatives was much closer to Salisbury's manifesto than to the rhetoric of Chamberlain.

Salisbury, however, as gloomy in his own way as the Liberal leaders, succumbed to the widespread assumption that the sweeping Conservative and Unionist victory of 1900 was produced by chauvinistic exhilaration. Far from pleasing him as evidence of popular commitment to the Empire, this exhilaration disturbed him as further evidence that the electorate was still, perhaps irredeemably, passionate.

The appetites which the events of 1898 in China and along the Nile aroused in the country had made him wonder whether he had interpreted popular response to the Queen's Jubilee in 1897 too optimistically.[49] The character of the election of 1900 undermined the confidence which he had derived from the electorate's behaviour in 1895 and reactivated his earlier fears. He hoped that the mood which Chamberlain had captured was an 'accidental and temporary' phenomenon. 'But it may mean', he told Cranbrook,[50]

> that the Reform Bills, digging down deeper and deeper into the population, have come upon a layer of pure combativeness. If that is the case I am afraid the country has evil times before it.

There had always been a layer of combativeness in Salisbury too, beneath the gloomy observer. Instead of resignedly adjusting himself to Chamberlain's seeming electoral power, he dealt with the task of reconstructing his Government in a way intended to take the khaki out of the khaki election. He took the work of reconstruction into his own hands. He had constructed his third Ministry in continuous consultation with Devonshire, Chamberlain and Balfour; his second with Churchill; his first in almost open session of the council of Conservative leaders. He constructed his fourth, by contrast, almost without reference to Chamberlain, who had carried the heat and burden of the electoral day and had become the focus of attack and defence on every platform. Salisbury consulted a little more with the Duke of Devonshire as official leader of the Liberal Unionist party, but largely in relation to one man, Lord James of Hereford. Even Balfour was left in the dark.[51] Balfour's influence on the work of reconstruction, in fact, never exceeded that of a commentator. He was not allowed, as some supposed, to reshape to his liking the Ministry over which he was likely sooner or later to preside.

Most of the marks of Salisbury's intentions were faint. Extensive reconstruction was next to impossible because the Cabinet of 1895 had survived virtually intact. Of its members, only Goschen at the Admiralty now tendered a firm resignation. Most others clung to their posts. Apart from the Admiralty, therefore, the only way to open offices up was to move or remove their occupants. Furthermore, Salisbury always preferred safe, experienced men whom he knew, to lively young men whom he did not; and the imperialistic ardour shown back of the Treasury bench since 1895 hardened this prejudice into policy. In making new appointments Salisbury looked to competent administrators such as St. John Brodrick, Balfour of Burleigh, and Ritchie, or to members of his family circle such as Selborne who, whatever his loyalty to Chamberlain and Milner, was a dedicated churchman whose fundamental instincts Salisbury felt he could trust. He could not avow, he scarcely even hinted at, the intention behind the changes he made.

The two men he sacked, Chaplin as President of the Local Government Board and Ridley as Home Secretary, were administrative incompetents, and they were dismissed on those grounds. Still, Chamberlain did not fail to observe that they were also men who had sympathized with domestic as well as imperial policies which he had advocated in Cabinet. Ridley had agreed with Chamberlain on elementary education, Chaplin on old age pensions, and both were to become ardent tariff reformers. Salisbury's point was clearer in his handling of the succession to Chaplin. Londonderry, who led the opposition to Chamberlain's Workmen's Compensation Bill in 1897 and had entered the Ministry (but not the Cabinet) in 1900 as Postmaster General, was offered the choice between his existing post and Chaplin's. Though he declined to be transferred, he was given Cabinet rank in order, as Salisbury told the Queen, 'to reassure [the] Tory Party some of whom are frightened of Mr Chamberlain'.[52]

Whatever his symbolic value Londonderry would be no match for Chamberlain in the Cabinet. The action of Salisbury which most strongly indicated his concerns had to do with Hicks Beach and the Chancellorship of the Exchequer. A sturdy upswing in the economy and the new revenue from Harcourt's death duties had enabled Hicks Beach to pay the soaring imperial, military and, to a lesser extent, domestic bills with which colleagues confronted him. Until 1898, he did so without increasing taxation or tinkering with the national debt. But expenditure—whether on the Uganda railway, on economic cultivation of colonies and protectorates, on the armed services, for local government, postal service, or education—was increasing faster than revenue, and in 1899, even before the Boer War broke out, it passed the limit which the death duties allowed.[53] Hicks Beach had already seen the danger signals, and he had irritated the heads of the major spending departments, especially the service chiefs and Chamberlain, with his nagging critique and diminution of their demands. His dismay at the ever-rising financial demand of his colleagues deepened in 1899 to a critical level. On the eve of hostilities in South Africa, he offered his resignation in protest against spending to increase mail service, as the Cabinet wished, between Capetown, Natal, Delagoa Bay and Beira. In his letter to Salisbury,[54] he broadened the grounds of divergence between himself and a majority of his colleagues to include old age pensions: he regarded old age pensions as financially impossible, while they treated old age pensions as politically indispensable.

In the privacy of Cabinet negotiation, Hicks Beach was a difficult man. 'It is rare to get a letter from Beach without a "No, I will not" on the first page', Salisbury observed.[55] The roughness of Hicks Beach's tongue in private jarred colleagues like Chamberlain who pressed their views upon the Cabinet with civility. In public, however, the two men reversed their speaking styles. Chamberlain became abrasive, while Hicks Beach conveyed an impression of 'virile commonsense and moderation'.[56] In the final analysis, Hicks Beach's behaviour within the Cabinet was in keeping with his public rather than his private style of speech. After expressing himself with all the vigour at his command, he sought 'to prove his willingness, so far as possible, to meet differences of opinion'.[57] Unlike Churchill he was a good Cabinet man. Though neither Salisbury nor the Cabinet came round to his opinion on South African mail service, he allowed Salisbury to persuade him to stay on for fear of breaking up the Queen's Government at the beginning of a war. A similar concern for political cohesion, this time in Parliament, led Hicks Beach to keep his first estimates of the expenditure which the Boer War would require low. Just as Salisbury had been concerned about Liberal opinion on foreign policy, so Hicks Beach was concerned about the reaction of Liberals, above all of Harcourt, to his financial provisions. His first set of wartime requests to Parliament, far from quickening doubts about the wisdom of the war, met with almost universal approval.[58]

Hicks Beach could not expect decisive support in Cabinet controversy from the prime minister. Salisbury had begun his political career as critical of the Manchester School's financial as of its foreign policy. 'National ignominy', he had declared, 'is the logical consequence of Manchester finance'.[59] This was the issue on which he had parted company with Hicks Beach's friend Churchill. Salisbury's aversion to the Gladstonian traditions and supervisory pretensions of the Treasury deepened with experience. His attack at the beginning of 1900 upon the Treasury brought it under an invidious spotlight, and produced a bristling defence from Hicks Beach, whom Salisbury had then to exempt from his strictures. He sympathized with the Chancellor of the Exchequer's uneasiness about the expense which old age pensions would involve. But the only ground upon which Hicks Beach had been able to win any support from Salisbury for reducing the service department's estimates had been the sceptical response which the claims of experts, especially in the Admiralty, regularly aroused in the prime minister.

The Boer War shifted the balance of concerns in Salisbury's mind. Britain's lack of preparedness, and the warning the war provided of what a European conflict would involve, produced a rapid increase in the demands of the experts. Salisbury agreed that everything necessary to win the war in South Africa should be done. But the prospect of a continual rise in military expenditure when that war was over filled him with foreboding. He was not only sceptical of its military necessity. He feared that increases in taxation to meet such expenditure would harm the economy. His deepest fear was political. The rising pretensions of the military experts did not worry him as much as the increased willingness of a majority of his colleagues to satisfy the experts' demands. The Boer War accentuated the generation gap within the Cabinet. It divided the men of the past from the men of the future. The same events which taught the younger or more adventurous Ministers to favour bold, forward looking policies, usually involving new heights of expenditure, drove Salisbury back to mid-Victorian conclusions. Just as the unsettlement of China in 1898 had induced him to point out some wisdom in Cobden's principles of foreign policy, so the Boer War drove him to sympathize with Hicks Beach's defence of Gladstonian finance. The incipient division of the Cabinet over financial policy was aggravated by the behaviour of the electorate. Its seemingly khaki sentiments increased the willingness of the younger Cabinet Ministers to build up the armed forces. When arguing the case for holding down the service estimates, Salisbury sometimes pointed out the risk of provoking a popular reaction against even minimally necessary levels of military expenditures. In more candid moments, he would admit that what he actually feared was popular demand for heightened levels of expenditure on many objects, domestic as well as military. Then the spectre which had haunted him from his youth, of a democratic majority recklessly extravagant at the expense of the propertied minority, would become a reality.

It was in this frame of mind that Salisbury met Hicks Beach after the general election to discuss his place in the Government. Just before the election, Hicks Beach had made Balfour aware that he might not wish to be included within the Ministry when it was reconstructed. Balfour, to say nothing of Chamberlain, responded to this intimation with relief. Balfour canvassed the possibility of retaining Hicks Beach in some other Cabinet post; but the prospect of Hicks Beach holding onto the Exchequer, 'dropping little grains of sand into the wheels of every department',[60] filled Balfour with dismay. He assumed that Salisbury would respond in the same way. The difference between nephew and uncle would have remained latent, hidden from the younger man, if Hicks Beach had been willing to exchange the Exchequer for another office. But the same concerns which made Salisbury anxious to retain Hicks Beach in the Cabinet made Hicks Beach willing to stay in the Government only if he retained his existing post. When the two men met, Hicks Beach warned the prime minister that, 'if we went on as we had done he would have to separate from us, on the Jingo question, and on the Old Age Pensions'.[61] Salisbury responded by persuading Hicks Beach to remain at the Exchequer, assuring him that the Cabinet was far from agreed about pensions and, as Salisbury subsequently took care to tell Balfour, that 'I was much of his way of thinking about the extreme jingo party'. Balfour expressed his regret at the outcome to Salisbury with equal candour.[62]

Salisbury's reserve, which had previously left Balfour ignorant of the shift in his uncle's concerns, continued to block the view of others as well. Salisbury could scarcely avow his intention to impede the expressed desire of the electorate and of a majority of his colleagues. In so far as he had any hope of success, it could only come through point by point, pragmatic discussion within the Cabinet, totally divest of talk about broad objectives. Never did the cloak of courteous detachment in which he wrapped himself serve him better. Chaplin could not believe the prime minister responsible for his dismissal. Lord James of Hereford attributed the firing of Chaplin and Ridley, and the broad hints that he too should retire, to the malign influence of Balfour.[63]

The only feature of the reconstruction where its appearance corresponded with its underlying intent was the age of its members. All but four of the twenty faces round the Cabinet table after reconstruction had been there since 1895. All had been familiar to Parliament since the 1880s. Because of the Cabinet's unwieldy size,[64] an informal inner Cabinet persisted, now broadened beyond the previous triumvirate or quartet to include Lansdowne and Hicks Beach; and three of its members, Devonshire as well as Hicks Beach and Salisbury, had held Cabinet office before 1880. The introduction of more new, young men into the Cabinet would have been popular. The retention of old men was deliberate. It was the old men who, a generation earlier, had imbibed the lessons which Salisbury wished still to apply.

Hicks Beach sensed the deepened affinity between Salisbury and himself. He grew fond of recalling how his ancestor, Sir Michael Hicks, had served as secretary to the great Lord Burleigh and to his son, the first Lord Salisbury. But the understanding between the Chancellor of the Exchequer and the prime minister was largely tacit, and they were still capable of quarrelling along their former lines. When the guerrilla war broke out in earnest toward the end of 1900 and the new Secretary for War called for reinforcements, the Chancellor turned him down, only to be overruled by the prime minister.[65] The Boxer Rebellion in China drew the two men back together, fearful of overextending Britain's resources, financial as well as diplomatic. In the summer of 1901, when the Admiralty presented its first demand for sizeable expenditure on post-war security, specifically for £1 million on coaling facilities at various ports, Salisbury sided with his Chancellor, reacting against the sum as 'very large'. Salisbury had driven Churchill out of the Cabinet fifteen years earlier by supporting a request for an almost identical purpose. He was coming full circle. By majority vote the Cabinet supported the Admiralty against the Treasury. 'This is the type of difference', Salisbury warned the new King,[66] 'which is likely to occur from time to time in the Cabinet, as the financial pressure caused by the demands of the Admiralty and the War Office is felt more acutely: we are only at the beginning of the conflict now.'

In September, before beginning work on the next year's budget, Hicks Beach drew up a long memorandum[67] summarizing the financial situation as he saw it. The prospect on the side of income was discouraging. The ceiling as lifted by the special wartime taxation had been reached. When the next budget was presented in April the South African war would, by all accounts, be either over or reduced to the level of a police action; the special wartime taxes would, therefore, have lost their justification. The hope that the Transvaal, with all its mineral wealth, would be obliged, under the eventual terms of peace, to contribute to the expenses of the war had already dissolved, such were the depredations of the guerrilla warfare. The prosperity at home, which year after year had filled Hicks Beach's coffers to the point of embarrassment, seemed to be ending. On the side of expenditure Hicks Beach's analysis was even more alarming. Expenditure had increased since 1895 by 40% and the war and the service departments were by no means entirely to blame. The estimates for education had risen by £2.5 millions. Grants-in-aid to colonies and protectorates had more than trebled. Hicks Beach's accusing finger pointed to almost all departments. He urged upon them the necessity for economy in preparing their estimates for the coming year, and made concrete suggestions about how they might do so. He concluded by threatening to resign, 'unless some real steps were taken of the kind which I have indicated'.

He circulated the memorandum through all the levels in the Cabinet in order to make sure, once and for all, where its members stood. All but two responded either with indifference or not at all. Chamberlain responded as a respectful antagonist. He outlined the case against returning to pre-war principles of economy,[68] particularly for the armed services. He challenged Hicks Beach's predictions of a popular reaction after the war against perpetuation of the current levels of taxation: Chamberlain argued that popular and Parliamentary opinion was much more likely to side with the experts in 'any serious conflict between the Government and its naval and military advisers on the subject of efficient preparation'. He sprinkled his response, however, with attempts to reduce the disagreement with Hicks Beach to narrow compass.

Only Salisbury responded sympathetically; and his assessment was pessimistic to the point of despair. 'After the beginning of the year', he wrote,[69]

> when I saw how blindly the heads of our defensive departments surrendered themselves to the fatal guidance of their professional advisers, I realised that we were in face of a Jingo hurricane, and were driving before it under bare poles.

He had already lost confidence in the electorate. Now he was losing confidence in some of the instruments, particularly the Cabinet, upon which he had relied to restrain the popular beast. But he could not throw off those same restraints which he had come to accept for himself as the prerequisites for effective leadership within a popular constitution. His nearly twenty-year-old insistence upon cohesive forbearance in the ruling councils of the party had combined with the imperial emergency in South Africa to lock him into a Cabinet of whose strongest leanings he was profoundly suspicious. 'I sympathise deeply with your general view', he told Hicks Beach:

> I believe, however, that whenever any thorough and honest effort is made to turn ,
> it into a practical policy, the Government will go to pieces. I think it is the duty cf
> all of us—I have certainly made it my own—not to do anything which may bring
> about that catastrophe *while the war lasts*. When it has ceased, we shall return to the
> guidance of ordinary rules.

The promise implicit in the last sentence did not deceive Hicks Beach. Both men knew that only the war kept the aging premier in office. Though neither would admit it, both knew that they had already lost their last battle. Still, Hicks Beach agreed to hold his peace. Salisbury, for his part, made a half-hearted effort to induce Brodrick to do whatever could to pare down his estimates. 'It seems to me', Salisbury told Brodrick,[70]

> we ought to do things more economically—but of course I am far too ignorant to
> be able to say how. But Beach's tale is very alarming. I think we shall have a
> Parliamentary explosion before long.

The two old men gained little from their refusal to shake up the Cabinet in wartime. Salisbury delayed for several months a confrontation between Selborne as First Lord of the Admiralty and Hicks Beach over Selborne's wish to increase the rate of British naval building in response to the new German Navy Bill. But in April, neither Salisbury nor Hicks Beach were invited to the meeting of a Cabinet committee convened to resolve the dispute.[71] The moment the war was over, Balfour and Arnold-Forster, Secretary to the Admiralty, publicly accepted commitments for educational and naval expenditure which violated Hicks Beach's requirements, and the Cabinet hummed with rumours of a meeting without Hicks Beach at which they would prepare an ultimatum to him.[72]

## iii. The Change of Command

Throughout Salisbury's career as a leader, he had met unwelcome developments with a mixture of defiance and acquiescence. Both reactions were at work during his fourth Ministry. At the same time that he joined forces with Hicks Beach to resist the advancing tide of governmental expenditure, he gave up his attempt to control British involvement overseas. He had, in reality, lost his control over foreign policy before he gave up the Foreign Office. During the summer of 1900, while Roberts and Kitchener were winning the final formal battles of the Boer War, the Boxer Rebellion broke out in China. A nationalist revolt against all foreign interference, the Boxer Rebellion was not aimed at British influence alone. But by providing a pretext for military intervention by a number of European powers and Japan, the rebellion threatened to accelerate the erosion of British primacy in China. The Boxer Rebellion did not particularly disturb Salisbury, even when rumours that Boxer troops were menacing the foreign legations in Peking thickened. He was slower than anyone else in the Cabinet to admit the gravity of the situation. Until the reality of the danger overwhelmed him, he rejected the pleas of his colleagues for British participation in a joint expedition to relieve the legations.

He had misjudged the facts of the situation, and that error further discredited his judgement in his colleagues' eyes. The most deeply concerned Ministers, rejecting his general critique of alliances, con-cluded that the only way to minimize Britain's losses in China was to form a partnership there with Germany as the least menacing and most congenial of the interlopers. Led on this occasion by Goschen, the proponents of an agreement with Germany won over such hitherto staunch supporters of Salisbury as Lord George Hamilton. Hamilton could only conclude that Salisbury had grown too old for his post.[73] Faced with insistence upon an agreement with Germany not only from Goschen, Chamberlain and Hamilton, but also from Lansdowne, Brodrick and Balfour, Salisbury had to give way. The agreement which Britain extracted from Germany was, even on its face, as valueless as Salisbury had predicted.[74] But the Cabinet's now dominant advocates of British entry into the European alliance system were not discouraged.

When the subject of reconstructing the Ministry arose after the general election, Salisbury hesitated to surrender the Foreign Office. Though he had lost control of foreign policy and was conscious of his diminishing physical resources, he loved the work of the Office. As a result, the Queen found herself the unhappy focus of contrary pressures, which she did not understand, to decide who should have change of the Foreign Office. Salisbury attempted to transfer the decision to her.[75] Lord James, one of the few Ministers still in sympathy with the principles of his foreign policy, used the opportunity of attendance at Balmoral to impress the Queen with the dismay which Salisbury's departure from the Foreign Office might occasion in Europe. Balfour, in response, spoke as a Cecil about the family's concern for his uncle's health under the stress of double office. Torn between her confidence in Salisbury's judgement and her conern for his health, the Queen made sure that the onus for decision went back to Salisbury at Hatfield where it belonged. Akers-Douglas, trusted by the Queen and commissioned by Balfour, accepted and accomplished the 'difficult and unpleasant' task of persuading the old man to propose Lansdowne as Foreign Secretary.

Lansdowne was Salisbury's choice as well as Balfour's. When still uncertain about giving up the Foreign Office, Salisbury selected Lansdowne as the alternative to himself, even though Lansdowne had joined the mutineers over China. Outside commentators assumed that Lansdowne had been weakened by his failure as Secretary for War, and concluded that Salisbury had selected him in order to perpetuate his own control over foreign policy. Their impression seemed to be confirmed by Salisbury's selection of his eldest son, Lord Cranborne, to be Lansdowne's Under-Secretary. But in giving up the Foreign Office, Salisbury gave up his fight on foreign policy. When he promoted Brodrick to the War Office, he added to the Cabinet a solid Anglo-Irish Tory, and an experienced administrator, but, like Lansdowne, a recent recruit to the ranks of those sympathetic to new departures in foreign policy. Henceforth in this sphere, Salisbury would act as a critic, not as the forming mind.

He did not exert his powers even as critic to the full. He managed, by seeking clarification, by raising tactical questions, and by direct criticism, to postpone and hence to kill the proposal to turn the Anglo-German agreement on China into a formal though still limited alliance. He could have done the same on the Anglo-Japanese alliance. There were enough reservations about the alliance in the Cabinet to make its members receptive to his advice. They were, as Lansdowne told him, 'content to leave the settlement of this matter to your decision.'[76] Under the terms of the alliance submitted to the Cabinet, Britain stood to gain much less than Japan, yet Japan left no doubt that it would rather abandon the alliance than significantly modify its terms. In his last lengthy memorandum on foreign policy,[77] Salisbury subjected the treaty to searching criticism. But he concluded by pulling his punches. Rather than recommend rejection of the alliance at least without substantially improved terms, he expressed a bland, uncharacteristic and unfounded hope that the Japanese would allow Britain some discretion in interpreting the existing terms.[78]

Since the change of Foreign Secretary, Salisbury's will to power had been further weakened by the change of monarch. Between Queen Victoria and Salisbury there had been bonds, not merely of long-standing familiarity, but of basic constitutional and broader political agreement, and, still more, of profound respect. Salisbury did not pander to the Queen. Though he treated her with a fittingly deepened version of his natural courtliness, he made no secret of his impatience with court ceremonial or of the repugnance he felt for the dankness of Balmoral. Nonetheless, she reposed a trust in him more complete perhaps than in any of her prime ministers save Lord Melbourne. For his part, discounting the distorting effect of her familial ties with the royal houses of the Continent, Salisbury found the Queen's reactions a frequently reliable indicator of sober middle-class opinion in Britain. It was at least as much from her moral reflexes as from her partisan Conservatism that he derived reassurance and strength.

Correspondingly, the root of his anxiety about Edward VII was moral. The contrast in character between the two men could scarcely have been sharper. Edward was a stickler about uniforms and dress. Salisbury's usual attire was a shapeless, unbrushed coat, baggy trousers and crumpled hat. On one occasion he turned up in the coat of one uniform and the trousers of another. Where Edward cared about appearances, Salisbury cared about character. He knew far more than he wished about Edward's sexual and social conduct as Prince of Wales, and disapproved of all he knew. When once called upon to propose the health of the Prince and Princess of Wales, he devoted his remarks to praise of the Princess.[79] Hatfield was one of the very few houses in the Kingdom which refused to invite the Prince's mistress to accompany him when he came as a weekend guest. The Prince's political behaviour, as Salisbury saw it, was of a piece with his social conduct; he had chosen Dilke and Churchill as principal confidants.[80] Salisbury maintained a practice begun in Gladstone's second Ministry of informing the Prince about important developments particularly in foreign policy, but did not follow Rosebery's later practice of widening the range of that information. Salisbury did not seek, because he did not value, the Prince's judgement. The Prince recognized and resented the snub.

When Queen Victoria died the new King and the old prime minister treated each other with proper respect. But their first disagreement was not long in coming. Edward pressed for a less inhibited effort to delete the anti-Catholic portions of the Royal Declaration than Salisbury, fearful of a Protestant reaction, thought wise. Wishing to protect the King from involvement in the controversy, Salisbury and the other members of the Lords' committee on the Declaration issued their report without consulting him first. Though the King recognized the motive for their action, he did not take it kindly.[81] A more serious disagreement erupted in the spring of 1902 over coronation honours. Edward wished, unexceptionably, to inject a nonpartisan, personal element into this particular set of honours. One of his nonpartisan recommendations, a viscountcy for Sir William Harcourt, Salisbury welcomed.[82] Most of the King's other nominations Salisbury though undistinguished yet tolerable; but he reacted with a dismayed unwillingness to cooperate when Edward proposed peerages for two men who had risen from lowly origins to conspicuous riches.[83] One, Ernest Cassell, a fabulously successful Jewish banker of German birth, had acquired Edward's friendship on the race track, and had given him, before his accession, much needed financial assistance. The other, Thomas Lipton, a Scottish grocer with a penchant for garish but profitable publicity, had heavily subsidized the Princess of Wales' charities. Though Hicks Beach had spoken earlier to Salisbury on Cassell's behalf,[84] peerages for the two men would have fluttered the social dovecotes even of Edwardian England. The collision of the King and prime minister broke through the customary privacy of their discussions. Rumours spread, eventually reaching the proportion among court gossips of an explanation for Salisbury's retirement.[85] The gossip was exaggerated, as even the published list of coronation honours proved. The King gave way, reducing his demands for Cassell to a K.C.V.O. and a privy councillorship, and for Lipton to a baronetcy. Salisbury concurred with relief.

The episode illustrated, nonetheless, a persistent tension which lessened what little congeniality the flagging prime minister still found in his work. He had lost the Foreign Office. The death of the Queen deepened his sense that the days of his generation with its values were almost over. He prepared to make way for the change with foreboding. Since the war which rivetted him to the premiership was grinding toward its end, all that remained for him was to surrender his superintendency over the Government's partisan and domestic policy.

This final transfer took place over the Education Act of 1902. More than any other subject, education was capable of searching the joints of the governing alliance. The subject could reactivate the conflict in religious loyalties which, as much as any other line of division, had distinguished Conservatives from Liberals before the split over Home Rule. Furthermore, the quality of elementary education in Britain and the extension of the state's provision of education to the secondary level had much to do with the industrial competitiveness of the country, and hence were of special concern to the advocates of national efficiency.[86] Two events forced the subject upon the Ministry's attention. The infusion of financial support for denominational schools authorized by Parliament in 1897 had run out by the turn of the century, and they began to collapse at a rate of about sixty a year.[87] Then, in the spring of 1901, a group of prominent churchmen in London[88] secured a judicial decision, the Cockerton judgement, ruling that the London school board's use of revenue from local rates to provide schooling beyond the elementary level was illegal. At the Government's behest, Parliament hurriedly passed an Act permitting London's secondary schools to run for another year. Avowedly a holding measure, this action obliged the Government to devise a more lasting remedy for enactment in 1902.

The obligation descended upon the Government at a vulnerable moment, for it had lost its sense of domestic direction. Even backbenchers realized that the election of 1900 had given the Government nothing more explicit than a mandate to conclude the war; and the unusually meagre diet of legislation which the Government gave the new Parliament when it first met confirmed the impression.[89] Though the Liberal Opposition, in its divided state, did not immediately pick up the scent, all three leaders of the Government, Balfour and Chamberlain as well as Salisbury, smelled their own party's doom. The Cockerton judgement and the plight of the denominational schools confronted them with the first substantial piece of domestic business over which they would have to wrestle with their fate.

The need to draw up an education Bill drove a wedge through the top tier of Ministers at the end of 1901 just as it had at the end of 1896. Once again, it ranged Salisbury and Chamberlain against Balfour who, this time, received strong support from Devonshire. Though the collaboration between Salisbury and Chamberlain had never ceased to be remarkable, and though the strains between them extended from their original religious loyalties through a wide range of domestic and imperial concerns to the current question of national efficiency, the two men knew that their power rested upon respect for the prejudices of each other's popular followings. They had mastered the craft of devising limited resolutions of their supporters' divergent desires, at least in the domestic arena, not least in education—though of course they differed in the way they presented these accomplishments to the public.

The grant of free education in 1891 and the Education Act of 1897 had proven to Salisbury that Nonconformist Unionists could put up with measures designed to provide relief for the financial distress of Anglican schools. The abortive Bill of 1896, on the other hand, had demonstrated to him the danger of attempting to ensure the permanent survival of denominational education by overhauling the entire system of elementary schooling. He had ventured to give a vigorous lead in the Church's interest over that Bill. When his party, including the Church of England's lay spokesmen, failed to cooperate with him, he decided against repeating the attempt. Since that time, he had acquired a deeper appreciation of the contribution which Nonconformists made to the Unionist alliance. Previously he had treated the existence of a Nonconformist Unionist Association with a mixture of gratitude and caution. Subsequently, gratitude gained the upper hand. He selected a meeting of the Association to deliver one of his major addresses on foreign policy, on the Armenian massacres.[90] For the Association provided an audience receptive to his attempt to balance moral concerns with assertion of the national interest. In 1901 Middleton, ever attuned to his Chief, scheduled a dinner for him with the Nonconformist Unionist Association in preference to one with the Newspaper Society.[91]

By that time, the spokesmen for the Church had reached agreement on educational policy. They wanted all that Salisbury had wished for them in 1895/6, and more. The suit which produced the Cockerton judgement illustrated their aggressive assurance. They wanted to

supersede school boards with larger administrative units less sympathetic to Nonconformity. They wanted to override the Cowper-
Temple clause in the Education Act of 1870 which forbade denominational religious instruction in board schools. Above all they
wanted rate aid for their own schools. There was considerable sympathy
for their demands within the Conservative Parliamentary party.[92] But
Salisbury's ardour on their behalf had cooled. 'The demands of the
Church party', he told the King, 'are very high'.[93] He regarded the
demand for aid from the rates as particularly dangerous. Rate aid
unaccompanied by substantial ratepayer control over the voluntary
schools was not likely to prove possible politically, and ratepayer control
would jeopardize the schools' religious integrity.

Salisbury advocated a very modest Bill, limited to relief of the
voluntary schools' financial distress, leaving the decision about rate aid
up to the ratepayers of each locality, and deferring the subject of
secondary education for separate legislative treatment. He was opposed
to doing anything more, either for the quality of education or in the
interests of the Church. His one complaint about the Act of 1897 was
that 'the Inspectors and other experts of the [Education] Office, who
had only a lukewarm appreciation of the value of the Voluntary
Schools, but a keen enthusiasm for theoretic perfection in school
buildings and materials,' had been given a hand in disposing of the
added revenue, with the result that it was prematurely exhausted. 'We
could go on for many years', he told his colleagues,[94]

> without settling the demand for united educational authorities, without abolish-
> ing School Boards, and even without remedying the injustice of the Cowper-
> Temple clause. . . .If we can find a way to finance the impecunious Voluntary
> Schools, the other questions may, for a time at least, be postponed.

This could be dismissed as the advice of a tired, old man. Never was
Salisbury's penchant for destructive criticism of domestic legislative
initiatives, if not of their substance then of their mode of procedure, so
complete and unrelieved by appreciation of their intrinsic worth,[95] as
during his final two years. But on this occasion Chamberlain fervently
seconded Salisbury's counsel. Instinctively, the two politicians attempted to steer clear of the rocks of religious offence.

Balfour and Devonshire saw the rocks too. But the scent of doom in the
air fatalistically weakened their partisan concerns and quickened their
desire to leave a substantial accomplishment behind them when they
fell.[96] Balfour's career was already marked by two characteristics
unusual in a politician: imperviousness to popular opinion, and
fascination with the need to shore up those outworks or departments of
governmental activity where Britain's position seemed to be crumbling.
His position as leader in the Commons had periodically exposed his

political insensitivity without giving him much opportunity to tackle the kind of work which really interested him. He displayed little sense of the distinctive expectations of different audiences, failing, for example, when addressing the Primrose League, to follow his uncle's example of 'stressing the role of the League in awakening imperialistic sentiment, as well as in its practical work for the party'.[97] The counsel and remedial action of Salisbury and Chamberlain had reduced most of Balfour's failings to passing incidents, while his own powers of thought and debate commanded the respect of Parliament. The Unionist Government's collective achievement did not, however, satisfy him. He had assumed the direction of the Government's educational policy in 1897 as a congenial subject, but Unionist dissension and Liberal obstruction in Parliament had reduced what he was able to accomplish to less than modest proportions.

Devonshire, as the Minister formally responsible for education, shared with Balfour the task of framing the new Bill. He also had come to share Balfour's combination of administrative ambition and partisan unconcern. This combination had not been manifest during Devonshire's career as a Unionist thus far. On the contrary, his languour and his passionless pragmatism had given Salisbury congenial reinforcement. But beneath the languour lay dedication to the service of the state, and beneath the pragmatism lay an aversion to religious prejudices. At regular intervals since 1895, Devonshire had done battle against Salisbury's efforts to protect the Church of England's educ- ational endowments; and Salisbury's ability to win commanding majorities against him in the House of Lords[98] had bred mounting impatience. In 1900 over a lesser education Bill, the two men conducted a dress rehearsal for their conflict a year later. Devonshire argued against denominational religious instruction, and, in the accents of national efficiency, stated that 'unless Secondary Schools receive some assistance [from the rates], I am afraid that we shall remain per- manently behind other countries'.[99]

Balfour and Devonshire drew strength for the coming controversy within the Cabinet from their responsibility for the new Bill's drafting. They were also favoured by the terms in which the Cabinet conducted its debate. Because the Unionist leadership was divided by religious affinities and ultimate objectives, the Cabinet from ingrained habit eschewed mention of these concerns in discussing all subjects, even when these concerns were really at stake. Instead, they thrashed out their disagreements by talking about the prejudices of their followers or about administrative practicalities. Salisbury was a master of this art of indirect debate. But, for once, this language favoured the administrative reformers. Anglican loyalties and fear of foreign competition gave them strong support on the back benches. These sentiments muffled what

Salisbury could say, but not Chamberlain. He warned about the reaction of his Nonconformist supporters in Birmingham. What wore Chamberlain down were the administrative practicalities. Robert Morant, the chief civil servant behind the Bill, visited Chamberlain in Birmingham. With remorseless logic, referring for example to the impossibility of further aid for education from the Exchequer because of the costs of the war, Morant drove Chamberlain toward the conclusion that at least optional rate aid was indispensable. Later Chamberlain proposed to protect Nonconformist susceptibilities by allowing ratepayers to allocate their rates to schools of their choice. The proposal was defeated by the existence of vast numbers of compound householders who would be unable to exercise this choice because they paid their rates indirectly through their rent.[100] Still, from December of 1901 until the following July, the balance of political weight between the two pairs produced a bearable compromise. Salisbury conceded a big Bill, embracing secondary as well as elementary education; Chamberlain conceded the supersession of school boards by county authorities; and both men conceded rate aid. Balfour and Devonshire, having won most of their points, gave the county authorities the power to decide whether or not to give aid from the rates to denominational schools.

The balance collapsed as soon as Salisbury decided to retire. Chamberlain happened to be disabled at the time as a result of an accident in a hansom cab. On the 9th of July, while Salisbury was arranging with the King for his retirement, Balfour allowed the Commons a free vote on the clause which left the imposition of rate aid to the discretion of the county authorities. Without the clause, rate aid for denominational schools would be compulsory. Balfour knew that the Anglican loyalties of the Conservative majority in the Commons made rejection of the clause on a free vote likely, and he argued against the clause himself. Austen Chamberlain, representing his father's position, voted to retain the clause; but it was thrown out by a large majority. Immediately, militant Nonconformists raised the cry of 'Rome on the rates'. Already the Bill had restored sorely needed unity to the Liberal Opposition, and the amendment added passion to the Liberals' cohesion. Just as quickly the Unionist alliance began to disintegrate. Chamberlain moaned unforgivingly in September to Devonshire: 'Our best friends are leaving us by scores and hundreds, and they will not come back.'[101]

The damaging chain reaction was not yet finished. Rejection of the optional clause on rate aid distorted the Bill's tenuous religious balance in favour of the Church of England. Ratepayers would now be obliged to support Anglican schools over whose religious curriculum they had no compensating control. The unfairness of this situation disturbed Balfour, though not the Anglican backbenchers whose votes had enabled him to make the rate aid compulsory. In order to restore the balance, he inspired another amendment, the Kenyon-Slaney clause, which transferred control of religious instruction in denominational schools from their foundation managers, largely clergy, to the whole body of managers which would include a substantial elective element. The clause, presented to the Commons as a way to curb the excesses of ritualistic clergymen, secured enough support to pass. Still, to the dismay of dedicated churchmen of many shades,[102] the clause bore out the old fear that rate aid would involve ratepayer control and hence the loss of the denominational schools' religious integrity. Salisbury observed the sequence of events from Hatfield. Retirement excused him from any obligation to go up to London and cast his vote on the Bill when it reached the Lords. But he did not scruple to reveal his dismay to enquirers,[103] and, after the Bill became law, he told the Duke of Rutland that he was 'still puzzled to understand why it was thought expedient to administer a gratuitous affront to the clergy'.[104]

The change of command from Salisbury to Balfour had taken place, with all the inconspicuousness that the old man so valued, while the Bill was in committee. Anxious to take no step which could create an impression of disunity within the Cabinet over the Boer War, Salisbury had stayed in office until peace was concluded in Vereeniging at the end of May 1902. Physically, he had held up remarkably well. But no longer able to regulate his need for sleep, he found himself dropping off in the midst of a despatch or a Cabinet meeting, and knew that he could not go on. When he rose to announce the terms of peace to a jubilant House of Lords on the 2 June, he spoke with difficulty. He meant to resign right after the King's coronation, set for 26 June. Almost on the eve of the coronation, the King was stricken with acute appendicitis; and Salisbury had to postpone his resignation. By the beginning of July, the King was out of danger, and his doctors ordered him to leave for further convalescence on his yacht. Salisbury might have stayed on for another few weeks until the delayed coronation took place. But his secretary, Schomberg McDonnell, was so disturbed by the state of Salisbury's health that he induced Salisbury and the King to use the opportunity between the King's recovery and departure from London to transact the business of the prime minister's retirement.[105]

Salisbury thus became the first prime minister in more than a century to bring his career to an end voluntarily. Though his colleagues were aware of his fatigue, they had displayed no desire to hurry his departure, and were surprised by the speed of his exit. But he knew, as he told Lord Curzon, that

> we are near some great change in public affairs—in which the forces which contend for the mastery among us will be differently ranged and balanced. If so, it

is certainly expedient that younger men should be employed to shape the policy which will no longer depend upon the judgements formed by the experience of past times.[106]

He went on in this letter to discuss the menacing 'aggregation of human force' which lay around the Empire. He also recognized the divisive threat which this and other purely domestic forces posed to the political combination which he had nursed for eighteen years in order to discipline popular government in Britain. But, never blessed with Gladstone's sanguine self-confidence, he could not be entirely sure of the worth of his own 'judgements formed by the experience of past times'. As a result, though he looked ahead with foreboding, he lacked the will, as well as the physical strength, to overcome his colleagues' doubts about his prescriptions.

He did not 'slope away' with quite the 'insouciance'[107] that observers believed. Resignation in itself was simple, but it carried with it the more delicate matter of selecting a successor. The power of appointment lay with the King, but if he asked for the retiring prime minister's nomination, that advice was binding. Neither man doubted who would be chosen. Early in the spring, *The Times* and the *National Review* had advanced the claims of Chamberlain. But Chamberlain had at least as many distrustful critics as ardent supporters within the Unionist alliance. The King was among the distrustful, and by March he had intimated to Salisbury his intention of appointing Balfour whenever Salisbury chose to retire.[108]

The first, unnoticed, indication of Salisbury's impending retirement came at the beginning of July with the appointment of his long-time private secretary, Schomberg McDonnell, to be secretary of the Office of Works, a position which involved close contact with the royal household.[109] Thus advantageously placed, McDonnell tried to arrange Salisbury's retirement to the old man's satisfaction. McDonnell saved him from announcing his intention at a final Cabinet. That, Salisbury commented, 'would be embarrassing. . . . The outcry would have been formidable'.[110] But the absence of fanfare with which he wished to retire, and the haste with which McDonnell had to act as a result of the early date set for the King's departure, affected the formal selection of Salisbury's successor. That made him uneasy. To the very end, he was concerned for concord in the party and the alliance, and was sceptical about his personal influence upon them.

> Remember [he told McDonnell] that I have a bad character for nepotism, & that any steps taken to control the succession to my office will be judged in the light of that reputation. . . .I have no doubt that if left to themselves [the party] will prefer Arthur: but that is quite a different thing to having him forced upon them in such a fashion that they will have no time either to resist or to discuss. Add to this, (the outside circle will say) that a time has been selected when the other

candidate, Mr. Chamberlain, is *hors de combat* for a week : & when the King is not able to attend to business. I fear the arrangement will be denounced as an intrigue—& in very vigorous language.[111]

Salisbury proposed to solve the dilemma by having Edward VII ask for his retirement, thus taking responsibility both for the retirement and for the appointment of a successor.

Salisbury's fears proved as exaggerated as his advice was extraordinary. The King would not do as he suggested. Salisbury therefore wrote on Thursday 10 July, to tell Devonshire, Chamberlain and Hicks Beach of his intention to resign next morning. After surrendering his seals to the King, he took his leave of his other colleagues by letter. With similar quietness, the King offered Balfour the post of prime minister on Friday ; and, after assuring himself of Chamberlain's support, on Saturday Balfour accepted. The public knew nothing of these events until Monday. But they aroused the barest modicum of carping comment. Chamberlain had prepared himself and his supporters for cordial acceptance of Balfour's elevation. The only person who felt aggrieved was Devonshire, and his resentment focused, not on Salisbury, but on Balfour and the King for failing even formally to consult him beforehand as the titular leader of the Liberal Unionist party and as one who had declined the premiership on three previous occasions.[112]

Salisbury's letters to his colleagues announcing his resignation, and their responses to him, were models of courtesy. They took the news quietly ; yet they knew that it would disturb the old balance. Almost all, even those like Lord Halsbury who were uneasy about the prospect, stayed on. But Hicks Beach knew, in spite of blandishments by Balfour, that without Salisbury's support he could not sustain his battle against soaring estimates,[113] and he accompanied Salisbury into retirement. So, at Balfour's behest, did Lord James of Hereford, another indication that the old balance was gone. For though Lord James had added little weight to the Cabinet for some years, and though Salisbury had wished to replace him in 1900, since that time James had sided with the departing leader over taxation and education. More than once before his own retirement, Salisbury commented to McDonnell, 'Things will be in a very fluid state after my disappearance'.[114]

## iv. The Crumbling Forces of Discipline

The electoral forces of Unionism began to fall away from the moment Salisbury left office. The Government had fared remarkable well since 1900 in by-elections. It had retained nine seats, gained one from the Liberals in a three-way contest created by the intervention of a Labour candidate, and sustained only one loss, which could be accounted for by

the recent conversion of the Governmental candidate to Unionism.[115]
Two weeks after the change of prime minister, the Government lost
North Leeds, since 1885 a Unionist stronghold. A month later, the
Unionist majority in Sevenoaks was slashed from nearly 5,000 to under
1,000. The alienation of Nonconformists who had formerly voted for the
Government was unmistakable, and Chamberlain warned Balfour that
he could no longer rely upon constituencies containing a substantial
Nonconformist element as safe.[116]

The contentious provisions which Balfour introduced into the
Education Bill were not the only rocks of offence over which previously
Unionist electors stumbled. Middleton was more alarmed about the
impact of the registration duty on imported corn which Hicks Beach had
introduced in his last budget to help defray the accumulated costs of the
war. The euphoria of victory over the Boers wore off quickly, eroded by a
succession of damning reports by commissions of enquiry into the
conduct of the war and the provision of wartime supplies. The electoral
enchantment with imperialism was rapidly dispelled. Was a war which
required nearly half a million British and colonial troops to subdue a
Boer population which totalled barely one hundred thousand, including
women and children, worth the effort? When Milner authorized the
immigration of indentured Oriental workers to man the Rand mines,
even some Conservatives who had ardently upheld the war effort were
sickened.[117]

Opposition to Home Rule, the original common cause of Unionism,
also began to lose its cohesive power. By the turn of the century, there
was fresh evidence that the Unionist prescription of firm maintenance of
order combined with economic amelioration could not settle the Irish
question. A new awareness of the cultural genius of Ireland manifested
itself through the Gaelic League founded in 1893. William O'Brien
revived agrarian unrest after 1898 through his United Irish League. In
1900 the Irish Parliamentary party overcame its disunion. And in 1902
the Government felt obliged to reactivate the Coercion law over much of
Ireland. The new Irish Secretary, George Wyndham, true to the spirit of
Balfour's policy in the '80s, responded to the unrest with the final and
most ambitious of the Land Acts, the 'Wyndham' Act of 1903. It
completed the transfer of the ownership of the land from great
landowners to tenants, to widespread satisfaction. A conference in
Dublin between some of the great Unionist landowners and Nationalist
representatives of the tenants preceded and worked out the terms for the
Act. This success emboldened the Unionist conferees, led by Lord
Dunraven, to tamper with the Ark of the Union. Assisted by
Wyndham's Under-Secretary, they drew up a proposal for financial and
legislative councils for Ireland, not quite Home Rule but unmis-
takably a step in that direction. When word of the proposal reached

Wyndham, he quickly and publicly repudiated it. But most Irish landlords, still sore about Gerald Balfour's legislation of the late '90s, and the fierce Unionists of Ulster were not convinced by Wyndham's denials. Their angry suspicions eventually induced him to resign.

Sins of omission as well as commission by the Government came home to roost. If Balfour and Devonshire bore responsibility for the contentious features of the Education Act, Salisbury bore responsibility for the absence of any other legislative initiatives, particularly in the social sphere. Old Tory Democrats, preeminently Sir John Gorst, grew restive at the Government's domestic sterility. The impatience of organized labour was turned into active hostility by the Taff Vale decision of 1900 which declared unions financially liable for offences against property committed by their members during the course of industrial action. The decision deprived union funds of the protection which Disraeli's legislation of the 1870s, to the credit of his party, had seemed to give them. The Government led by his successors refused to pass legislation restoring those rights.

Thus, while disillusionment about the Empire and uncertainty about Ireland weakened the sentiments which had nourished Unionism, the domestic record of the Government aroused religious and class antagonisms which divided its supporters and sent new life surging through the Liberal party. The Middleton machine, even in its sharpest fighting trim, could cope only with a passive or potentially friendly electorate, not with one aroused by hostile emotions. And, by the turn of the century, the Conservative party's electoral organization had passed its prime. The victory of 1895 had not immediately relaxed Middleton and his men. They agreed with Salisbury that,

> New difficulties will arise, new dangers will be apparent, and the present preponderance will not enable us to meet them, unless we maintain our political effort in the spirit which has hitherto distinguished the Conservative and Unionist Association . . . . [118]

But the persistent inability of the Liberals in the late '90s to mount a serious attack seemed to belie this fear. Year after year, the National Union's Council reported that, 'There has been no great movement in the political circles in the country'. Quietly, the machine slipped into a lower gear. In 1897, the agents' journal *The Tory*, ceased publication. Middleton, no longer fully stimulated by the work of electoral organization, lifted his eyes to legislative policy, and then accepted an outside business appointment. Akers-Douglas rose from tending Parliamentary fences to facilitating transfers of office among members of the Cabinet. The National Union came under fire from *The Times* in 1901 for failing to transmit the uneasiness in the party at large about military organization and imperial defence to the party's leaders.

Middleton's career as Principal Agent coincided closely with Salisbury's as prime minister. The two men's physical resources declined together. Middleton fell seriously ill early in 1901 but, to Salisbury's relief, recovered. In the spirit of his Chief he returned to his post 'until absolutely unable to bear the strain longer'.[119] He resigned one year almost to the day after Salisbury left office. As soon as Middleton departed, the tight electoral organization which he had created began to break up. At the meeting of the National Union Central Council that received Middleton's resignation, quarrelling over tariff reform broke out for the first time.[120] The National Union displayed impatience about remaining in the leading strings of the Central Office; and the new Principal Agent did not take the office of Honorary Secretary through which Middleton had controlled the National Union.

The blight that afflicted Unionism at the ballot box afflicted the Parliamentary party in a somewhat different but equally acute form. Like the Middleton machine, the Parliamentary party was suffering by the turn of the century from lassitude. William Walrond, the Whip in the Commons, proved an indifferent successor to Akers-Douglas,[121] and was replaced, when Salisbury retired, by a stronger man. But by then the rot had set in too deeply to the cured by good whipping. The break-up of the Parliamentary party began with Balfour's violation of the original compact between Conservatives and Liberal Unionists over the Education Act. By allowing the Commons a free vote over compulsory rate aid for denominational schools, he had observed the forms of the compact: the forms but not the spirit. Because the issue divided Devonshire from Chamberlain as well as Balfour from Salisbury, the violation of the compact was not obvious, but it was nonetheless effective. It allowed Chamberlain to demand for himself similar freedom of initiative. The use that he made of his freedom overshadowed Balfour's initial violation. When Chamberlain unfurled the flag of Empire-binding preferential tariffs at Birmingham on 15 May 1903, he blew the shell of Unionist discipline to pieces. The Cabinet and the Parliamentary party broke in three. Tariff reform infused many of the drooping spirits on the Government's back benches with an invigorating sense of purpose. But this purpose, and the intolerant ardour with which it was propagated, turned a small but talented minority of Unionists into equally passionate, equally dogmatic devotees of free trade. The furious dispute between the two groups turned a third, led by Balfour, into anxious advocates of party unity as the overriding consideration. But Balfour had compromised his credentials for pursuing this objective over the Education Act. He attempted to restore party unity over tariff reform through rarefied disquisitions on a middle course which the Government might pursue over tariffs, but his efforts did not convey a sense of his own conviction, let alone carry conviction among the rank and file. He could not reinforce his appeals with the transparent strength of what Salisbury had called 'character'.

'In an Oriental court', Salisbury once told Lord Curzon, 'call no man successful until he has retired'.[122] If this maxim were true of Occidental government Salisbury was a failure. The edifice which he had constructed and tended for twenty years collapsed in three. He lived just long enough to observe, with powerless fury, the beginning of the splits over tariff reform within the party and alliance for whose cohesion he had subordinated so many of his own predilections. He lived to see Chamberlain reveal himself, for the first time since 1885, as an untamed activist who, still worse, might prove able to turn the Unionist army into a force for change. Two and a half years after Salisbury's death, the Liberals, riding upon a surge of popular feeling such as he had sought to limit and control if not prevent, swept all before them in a general election. The results of the election of 1906 indicated that the electoral base of Unionism was shallow, that the Unionist successes of the previous twenty years owed much less to acceptance of Unionist objectives than to electoral passivity.[123] Certainly the curse of abstentions and defections, which Home Rule and other quarrels had inflicted upon Liberals since 1885, passed from them to the Unionists. And potential electors who had never before voted or indicated a preference for either party turned up now in their thousands to vote Liberal. For some years thereafter it was Liberal politicians, particularly Asquith, rather than the Conservatives who displayed a Salisburian appreciation of the need to combine determination with restraint. The Conservative party had learned from Salisbury how to stand up, but not when; they had acquired his spine but not his suppleness. As a result they spent almost a decade in the political wilderness, and brought the country to the verge of civil war. Both the country and the party were rescued only by a greater war on the Continent; and that war destroyed much of the old world and discredited many of the values which Salisbury had sought to maintain.

Salisbury did not, however, insist upon an Oriental scale to measure Occidental achievement. In his days as a Conservative rebel, he had laid down the maxim that, 'delay was life'.[124] When he succeeded Disraeli in the party leadership, the cardinal reality which confronted him was the advent of popular government. The third Reform Bill was widely expected to inaugurate a further leap into the Radical dark. Instead, it had been followed by twenty years of predominantly Conservative government. Admittedly, in order to restrain the impulses of popular government, Salisbury had accepted the necessity of disciplining his own impulses. He had accepted the sovereignty of the electorate, and even stressed its implications in the conduct of foreign relations. He had deferred between elections to the supremacy of the House of Commons, at least when it had a Unionist majority. His thirteen and a half years as prime minister, a record unmatched since the Great Reform Act, owed more to his acceptance of these disciplines than to popular acceptance of his purpose of disciplining democracy. The base of electoral support on which he relied was thin and artificially cultivated.

Still, he had held back the popular tide for twenty years. As *The Times*, in its final comment upon him put it:[125]

> Lord Salisbury, perhaps in some degree by virtue of that half-cynical superiority with which he looked on popular movements, was able to lay a strong hand upon them. He measured them, gauged, to some extent, their natures and their force, checked their extremes, appreciated something of their worth and their capacity, and held them more or less in hand.

The worth of delay followed by a deluge was questionable. The smashing defeat of 1906 left Salisbury's achievement much more doubtful than the narrow defeat he had hoped for in 1900 would have done. Even so, Britain's subsequent course in the twentieth century was to supply evidence that the twenty-year delay which Salisbury had earned served part of its intended function. It dissipated the 'dangerous' enthusiasms which attended the coming of democracy. Salisbury helped to divest democracy's arrival in Britain of the expectations which Andrew Jackson associated with it in the United States, of the moral exhaltation which Gladstone would have given it, and of the constructive energy with which an unfettered Chamberlain would have infused it.

Furthermore, Salisbury bore very limited responsibility for the deluge of 1906. He had restricted the output of social legislation from his Governments, especially after 1895, to an imprudently low level. Otherwise, his chief failing was his inability to instil his successors with the wisdom he had acquired in the 1880s. Salisbury had learned by the end of his first decade as leader of the Conservative party that effective Conservatism was not a matter of public policy but of political craft. He spent his youthful years in Parliament in an angry effort to preserve the propertied, educated electorate created by the 1832 Reform Act. But by the end of his second Ministry, however much he would have preferred the old electorate, he had discovered that he could defend the interests and the institutions he had at heart almost as well by shaping and managing an enlarged electorate, by utilizing some of its prejudices, and, above all, by devising prosaic adjustments among the varied forces within the Conservative party and the Unionist alliance, adjustments in which he gave full weight to the wishes of his least progressive supporters. It was a quiet, inglorious craft. It failed to capture anyone's imagination and to produce disciples. His colleagues began to violate it even before his retirement, and forgot it quickly thereafter, but to their heavy cost.

Salisbury survived for little more than a year after he retired. The immediate impact of release from office was to buoy him up. Within ten days, he threw a garden party at Hatfield, the first in three years, and he betrayed his enjoyment of his new freedom by emerging in a grey slouch hat to greet his guests. The prospect of attending the King's coronation, on the other hand, physically depressed him, and he secured permission on medical grounds to stay away. His recovery after his resignation was, in fact, brief. In September, while on holiday in Switzerland, he was confined to his room with a chill and a mild attack of gout. Convalescing on the Continent he resorted for exercise, as he had for some years, to a tricycle, from which he fell and bruised his leg.[126] An ulcer developed and failed to heal. Back at Hatfield he had a fainting fit. From then on he slept in a chair because, with his great weight, he had difficulty in breathing when he lay down. One night early in August he fell from his chair. The fall brought on a heart attack, from which he did not rally well, and blood poisoning set in from his ulcerated leg. He lapsed into unconsciousness, sank slowly, and died on August 22 at sunset.

### NOTES

1. Salisbury to the Queen, 27 June 1890, Royal Archives E65/44.
2. Lady Gwendolen Cecil, *Life of Salisbury*, IV, p. 189.
3. See John Ehrman, *Cabinet Government and War, 1890–1940* (Cambridge, 1958), N. H. Gibbs, *The Origins of Imperial Defence* (Oxford, 1952), and F. A. Johnson, *Defence by Committee* (London, 1960).
4. T. J. Spinner, Jr., *George Joachim Goschen* (Cambridge, 1973), pp. 190–7.
5. F. A. Johnson, *Defence by Committe* (London, 1960), p. 41.
6. The Earl of Midleton, *Records & Reactions, 1856–1939* (New York, 1939), p.123.
7. McDonnell to Curzon, 1 December 1899, Curzon papers.
8. The Earl of Midleton, *Records & Reactions, 1856–1939* (New York, 1939), pp. 214–5. Mainly because of Salisbury's illness, no one secured the approval of the Queen or the Commander-in-Chief before these appointments were made.
9. *Supra*, p. 284.
10. *Hansard*, 4th ser., LXXVIII, 27 (30 January 1900).
11. *Hansard*, 4th ser., LXXVIII, 39 (30 January 1900).
12. A. A. Baumann, *Personalities* (London, 1936), p. 154; H. R. Whates, *The Third Salisbury Administration, 1895–1900* (London, 1900), p. 343.
13. In a letter responding to a request from his son-in-law, Lord Selborne, for advice about whether to accept the Governorship of the Cape Colony, Salisbury's gloom broke through his usual reserve: 'your principal duty will be persuading Dutchmen. If you can imagine yourself sitting for a constituency of which Schreiner and Rhodes are the principal types of electors, I fancy you can represent the life you will lead with tolerable fidelity. But you ought to know more about it than I do—and I am afraid of going on; for pessimism gets hold of my pen and controls it.' Salisbury to Selborne, 24 September 1900, Selborne papers, Bodleian Library I MSS Selb.
14. Chamberlain's expression: J. L. Garvin, *Life of Chamberlain*, III, p. 540.
15. Salisbury to Brodrick, 2 July (?) 1901, Midleton papers.

16. Salisbury to Brodrick, 19 December 1900, Midleton papers.
17. Salisbury to Canon MacColl, 18 November 1901, in Malcolm MacColl, *Memoirs and Correspondence* (London, 1914), pp. 230–1.
18. Salisbury to Brodrick, 28 November (?) 1901, Midleton papers.
19. *The Letters of Queen Victoria*, 3rd ser., III, p. 618.
20. Quoted in Paul Smith, ed., *Lord Salisbury on Politics* (Cambridge, 1972), p. 98.
21. See G. R. Searle, *The Quest for National Efficiency* (Oxford, 1971).
22. This insistence did not prevent him from giving serious thought to the possibility of appointing a general as Secretary of State for War. Salisbury to Balfour, 9 October 1900, Balfour papers (Whittinghame).
23. 'X' (Lord Robert Cecil), 'Lord Salisbury', *Monthly Review* (October 1903), p. 4.
24. *Hansard*, 4th ser., LXXIX, 47 (15 February 1900).
25. Salisbury to Brodrick, (?) 6 January 1901, Midleton papers.
26. *Hansard*, 4th ser., LXXIX, 550 (20 February 1900).
27. *Hansard*, 4th ser., XC, 547 (5 March 1901). Cf. LXXIX, 49 (15 February 1900).
28. *Supra*, pp. 118–9.
29. Salisbury to the Primrose League, *The Times*, 10 May 1900, 4d.
30. *Hansard*, 4th ser., LXXXVI, 1469 (27 July 1900).
31. Salisbury at the Guildhall, *The Times*, 10 November 1899, 7c.
32. Austin to Salisbury, 11 March 1900, Salisbury papers.
33. Salisbury to Chamberlain, 29 March 1902, in Julian Amery, *Life of Chamberlain*, IV, pp. 55–6.
34. Salisbury to the United Club, *The Times*, 30 June 1898, 10b.
35. M. E. Y. Enstam, 'The "Khaki" election of 1900 in the United Kingdom', Duke University Ph.D. dissertation, 1967, p. 43.
36. Kenneth Young, *Arthur James Balfour* (London, 1963), p. 190.
37. Salisbury to Lord Granby, 6 October 1890, Rutland papers.
38. J. L. Garvin, *Life of Chamberlain*, III, p. 584.
39. Balfour to Salisbury, 5 July 1900, Salisbury papers.
40. Lady Frances Balfour, *Ne Obliviscaris* (London, 1930), II, p. 335.
41. J. S. Sandars to Balfour, 20 September 1900, Balfour papers, B. L. Add. MSS. 49760.
42. *The Times*, 24 September 1900, 8a.
43. J. L. Garvin, *Life of Chamberlain*, III, p. 595.
44. Salisbury to Balfour, 9 October 1900, Balfour papers (Whittinghame).
45. Salisbury to Lord Granby, 6 October 1900, Rutland papers.
46. Lord Newton, *Lord Lansdowne* (London, 1929), pp. 186–7.
47. Salisbury to the Primrose League, *The Times*, 10 May 1900, 4c-d.
48. Richard Price, *An Imperial War and the British Working Class* (London, 1972), p. 105.
49. A. E. Gathorne-Hardy, *Gathorne Hardy, first Earl of Cranbrook* (London, 1910), II, p. 369.
50. Salisbury to Cranbrook, 19 October 1900, in A. E. Gathorne-Hardy, *op. cit.*, II, p.374.
51. Bigge to the Queen, 4 October 1900, in *Letters of Queen Victoria*, 3rd ser., III, p. 599; and the Queen to Bigge, 6 October 1900, *op. cit.*, p. 603.
52. Londonderry to Salisbury, 6 November 1900, Salisbury papers; Salisbury to the Queen, 8 November 1900, Royal Archives A76/74.
53. Bernard Mallet, *British Budgets, 1887–88 to 1912–13* (London, 1913), pp. 133–44.
54. In Lady Victoria Hicks-Beach, *Life of Sir Michael Hicks-Beach (Earl St. Aldwyn)* (London, 1932), II, pp. 109–10.
55. Lady Gwendolen Cecil, *Life of Salisbury*, III, pp. 177–8.
56. Lord George Hamilton, *Parliamentary Reminiscences and Reflections*, II, (London,

1922), p. 29. 'Beach and Hartington possessed to a marked degree the faculty of expressing in better language than he could command the ideas of the man in the street'.

57. Lady Victoria Hicks-Beach, *op. cit.*, II, pp. 111.
58. *Ibid.*, p. 113.
59. In Paul Smith, ed., *op. cit.*, p. 132.
60. Balfour to Salisbury, 20 October 1900, Salisbury papers.
61. Salisbury to Balfour, 19 October 1900, Balfour papers (Whittinghame).
62. Balfour to Salisbury, 20 October 1900, *loc. cit.*,
63. Lord Askwith, *Lord James of Hereford* (London, 1930), p. 259.
64. Increased from the 19 of 1895 to 20.
65. The Earl of Midleton, *op. cit.*, 124–5.
66. Salisbury to the King, 6 July 1901, P. R. O. CAB 41/26.
67. Hicks Beach to Salisbury, 13 September 1901, Salisbury papers; and printed memorandum for the Cabinet, October 1901, St. Aldwyn papers.
68. Chamberlain to Hicks Beach, 30 September 1901, in Lady Victoria Hicks-Beach, *op. cit.*, II, pp. 154–6.
69. Salisbury to Hicks Beach, 14 September 1901, In Lady Victoria Hicks-Beach, *op. cit.*, II, p. 153.
70. Salisbury to Brodrick, 17 September 1901, Midleton papers.
71. Selborne to Balfour, 4 April 1902, Balfour papers, B. L. Add. MSS. 49707.
72. Lady Victoria Hicks-Beach, *op. cit.*, II, p. 171; Devonshire to Balfour, 19 June 1902, Balfour papers, B. L. Add. MSS. 49769.
73. J. A. S. Grenville, *Lord Salisbury and Foreign Policy* (London, 1970), pp. 309 and 322–323. Here as elsewhere, my discussion of foreign policy relies heavily on Grenville's work. I am also indebted to George Monger's *The End of Isolation* (London, 1963).
74. For a somewhat different interpretation of Salisbury's acceptance of this argument, see L. K. Young, *British Policy in China, 1895–1902* (Oxford, 1970), p. 207.
75. Viscount Chilston, *Chief Whip* (London, 1961), pp. 286–92.
76. Quoted in George Monger, *The End of Isolation* (London, 1963), p. 60.
77. Dated 7 January 1902, P. R. O. CAB 37/60.
78. But see also the argument of L. K. Young, *op. cit.*, pp. 295 ff., that Salisbury desired the alliance. Cf. I. H. Nish, *The Anglo-Japanese Alliance* (London, 1966), p. 370.
79. Salisbury at the United Club, *The Times*, 16 July 1891, 10a.
80. Philip Magnus, *King Edward the Seventh* (London, 1964), p. 195.
81. Sidney Lee, *King Edward VII*, II (New York, 1927), pp. 23–4.
82. A. G. Gardiner, *The Life of Sir William Harcourt* (London, 1923), II, pp. 542–3.
83. McDonnell to Salisbury, 15 February 1902, and attached note by Salisbury, Salisbury papers, with Edward VII's letters to Salisbury.
84. Hicks Beach to Salisbury, 22 July 1901, Salisbury papers.
85. Edward Legge, *King George and the Royal Family* (London, 1918), I, pp. 50–1.
86. See G. R. Searle, *The Quest for National Efficiency* (Oxford, 1971), pp. 207–16.
87. Marjorie Cruickshank, *Church and State in English Education, 1870 to the Present Day* (London, 1963), p. 70.
88. Led by Salisbury's son, Lord Robert Cecil.
89. A. S. T. Griffith-Boscawen, *Fourteen Years in Parliament* (London, 1907), pp. 165 and 182.
90. I am grateful to David Bebbington for this information.
91. Middleton to McDonnell, 4 January 1901, Salisbury papers.
92. Almeric Fitzroy, *Memoirs* (New York, n.d.), I, p. 72.
93. Salisbury to the King, 31 January 1902, P. R. O. CAB 41/27.

94. Memorandum for the Cabinet, 17 December 1901, P. R. O. CAB 37/59.
95. Working-class housing still constituted an outstanding exception. See Salisbury to the annual conference of the National Union, *The Times*, 19 December 1900, 12a.
96. Almeric Fitzroy, *op. cit.*, pp. 69 and 73–4.
97. J. H. Robb, *The Primrose League, 1883–1906* (New York, 1942), pp. 66–7.
98. *Supra*, p. 287, n. 49.
99. Devonshire to Salisbury, 21 April 1900, Salisbury papers.
100. Marjorie Cruickshank, *op. cit.*, pp. 76 and 78.
101. Bernard Holland, *The Life of Spencer Compton Eighth Duke of Devonshire* (London, 1911), II, p. 284.
102. A. S. T. Griffith-Boscawen, *op. cit.*, p. 246.
103. Salisbury to the Duke of Rutland, 6 December 1902, Rutland papers; Salisbury to Canon MacColl, 7 December 1902, in Malcolm MacColl, *op. cit.*, p. 229.
104. Salisbury to Rutland, 12 February 1903, Rutland papers.
105. Salisbury to McDonnell, 10 July 1902, marked 'Secret', McDonnell papers, and McDonnell to Curzon, 2 October 1903, Curzon papers.
106. Salisbury to Curzon, 9 August, 1902 in J. A. S. Grenville, *Lord Salisbury and Foreign Policy* (London, 2nd ed., 1970), p. 439.
107. J. W. Mackail and Guy Wyndham, *Life and Letters of George Wyndham* (London, 1925), II, p. 447.
108. McDonnell to Lord Curzon, 14 March 1902, Curzon papers.
109. See McDonnell to Lord Curzon, 3 July 1902, Curzon papers.
110. Salisbury to McDonnell, 10 July 1902, McDonnell papers.
111. Salisbury to McDonnell, 10 July 1902, marked 'Secret', *loc. cit.*,
112. Lord James's diary, typed copy, ff. pp. 106–8, James of Hereford papers.
113. Lady Victoria Hicks-Beach, *op. cit.*, II, p. 174.
114. McDonnell to Curzon, 2 October 1903, Curzon papers.
115. Neal Blewett, *The Peers, the Parties and the People: The General Elections of 1910* (Toronto, 1972), p. 24.
116. *Ibid.*, pp. 27–8.
117. See J. A. Bridges, *Reminiscences of a Country Politician* (London, 1906), pp. 214–5.
118. Salisbury to the Agent of the Lancaster Division of the Conservative and Unionist Association, *The Tory*, XLIX (March 1897), pp. 17–18.
119. *The Times'* obituary of Middleton, 28 February 1905.
120. National Union Central Council Minutes, 12 June 1903.
121. McDonnell to Lord Curzon, 3 September 1902, Curzon papers.
122. Quoted in Kenneth Rose, *Superior Person* (London, 1969), p. 321.
123. Neal Blewett, *op. cit.*, pp. 21–3 and 36–7; Richard Price, *An Imperial War and the British Working Class* (London, 1972), chap. 3.
124. Quoted in Robert Blake, *The Conservative Party from Peel to Churchill* (London, 1970), p. 88.
125. *The Times*, 24 August 1903, 7b.
126. McDonnell to Curzon, 2 October 1903, *loc. cit.*

# LIST OF SOURCES

## Collections of Private Papers, MSS., Memoranda and Minutes

Ashbourne [1st Baron] papers (House of Lords Record Office)
Alfred Austin papers (University of Bristol)
Balfour [1st Earl] papers (British Library)
Balfour [1st Earl] papers (Whittinghame)
Balfour of Burleigh [6th Baron] papers (National Register of Archives, Scotland)
Barrington [7th Viscount] MSS. (Duke University Library)
Beaconsfield papers (Hughenden Manor)
Archbishop Benson papers (Lambeth Palace)
Cabinet Letters [reports to the monarch on Cabinet councils], 1885–1902 (Royal
    Archives: copies in the Public Record Office)
Cabinet papers, 1880–1902 (Public Record Office)
Cadogan [5th Earl] papers (House of Lords Record Office)
Cairns [1st Earl] papers (Public Record Office)
Carnarvon [4th Earl] papers (Public Record Office)
Joseph Chamberlain papers (Birmingham University Library)
Chilston [1st Viscount] papers (Kent Archives Office U564)
Lord Randolph Churchill papers (Churchill College, Cambridge)
Cranbrook [1st Earl] papers (Ipswich and East Suffolk Record Office)
Cross [1st Viscount] papers (British Library)
Curzon [Marquess] papers (India Office Library)
Derby [15th Earl] papers (Brown, Picton and Hornby Libraries, Liverpool)
Devonshire [8th Duke] papers (Chatsworth, 2nd series)
Sir Charles Dilke papers (British Library)
T. H. S. Escott papers (British Library)
Goodwood [6th Duke of Richmond] MSS. (County Record Office, Chichester)
Goschen [1st Viscount] papers (Bodleian Library)
Hambleden [W. H. Smith] MSS. (W. H. Smith and Son Ltd, Strand House, New
    Fetter Lane, London)
Halsbury [1st Earl] papers (British Library)
Sir Edward Hamilton diaries (British Library)
Edward Hardcastle MSS. (Duke University Library)
Harrowby [3rd Earl] papers (Sandon Hall)
Hobbs [16th Earl of Derby] papers (Corpus Christi College, Cambridge)
Iddesleigh [1st Earl] papers (British Library)
James of Hereford [Baron] papers (Hereford County Record Office M 45)
London County Council, Minutes of Proceedings, 1895–9
Londonderry [6th Marquess] papers (Durham Record Office)
Sir Schomberg McDonnell papers (Glenarm Castle)
Midleton [1st Earl] papers (Public Record Office)
National Society of Conservative Agents Minutes Book, 1895–1903 and The Secretary's
    Letterbook, 1891–1894 (Westminster City Library, Buckingham Palace Rd.)
National Union of Conservative and Constitutional Associations, Annual Conference
    Minutes, 1880–1903; Central Council Annual Reports, 1880–1905; Central Council

Minutes, 1899–1903; and Executive Committee Minutes 1897–1903 (Conservative Central Office)
Onslow [4th Earl] papers (Guildford Muniment Room)
Revesby Abbey [Edward Stanhope] papers (Lincolnshire Archives Committee)
Ridley [1st Viscount] MSS. (Northumberland Record Office)
Royal Archives (Windsor Castle)
Rutland [7th Duke and Duchess, and 8th Duke] papers (Belvoir Castle)
St. Aldwyn [1st Earl] papers (Glouchestershire Records Office D2455)
Salisbury [3rd Marquis] papers (Hatfield House)
Selborne [2nd Earl] papers (Bodleian Library)
Archbishop Temple papers (Lambeth Palace)

## Conservative Party Literature

Association of Conservative Clubs, *Monthly Circular*, Apr. 1895–December 1897, continued as *Conservative Clubs Gazette*, January 1898–December 1903

British Conservative Party Scrapbook, ca. 1880-ca. 1920, 70 volumes on microfilm, University of North Carolina at Chapel Hill

*The Campaign Guide*: An election handbook for Unionist speakers, prepared by a Committee of the Council of the National Union of Conservative Associations for Scotland (Edinburgh, 1892)

*The Campaign Guide* (Edinburgh, 5th ed., 1894)

*The Campaign Guide* (Edinburgh, 6th ed., 1895)

*The Campaign Guide* (Edinburgh, 8th ed., 1900)

*Campaign Notes*, 1885 (London, Conservative Central Office, 1885)

*The Conservative Agents' Journal*, 1902–3

*The Conservative Clubs Gazette*, 1898–1903

*The Constitutional Yearbook*, 1885–1904

"*Ten Years Work*": A review of the legislation and administration of the Conservative and Unionist Government, 1895–1905 (London, Conservative Central Office, 1905)

*The Tory*, 1892–7

*The Unionist Record, 1895–1900* (London: National Union of Conservative and Constitutional Associations, n.d.)

*The Unionist Record, 1895–1905*: A fighting brief for Unionist candidates and speakers (London: 2nd ed., National Union of Conservatives and Constitutional Associations, n.d.)

## Biographies, Autobiographies, Memoirs, Diaries, and Published Correspondence

Agg-Gardner, J. T., *Some Parliamentary Recollections* (London, 1927)

Alverstone, Lord, *Recollections of Bar and Bench* (London, 1914)

Amery, Julian, *The Life of Joseph Chamberlain*, IV: 1901–1903 (London, 1951)

Argyll, Dowager Duchess of, ed., *George Douglas Eighth Duke of Argyll, K.G., K.T. (1823–1900)*: Autobiography and memoirs, 2 vols. (London, 1906)

Askwith, Lord, *Lord James of Hereford* (London, 1930)

Austin, Alfred, *The Autobiography of*, 2 vols. (London, 1911)

Bahlman, D. W. R., ed., *The Diary of Sir Edward Walter Hamilton*, 2 vols. (Oxford, 1972)

Balfour, A. J., *Chapters of Autobiography*, ed. Mrs. Edgar Dugdale (London, 1930)

Balfour, Lady Frances, *A Memoir of Lord Balfour of Burleigh* (London, 1925)

Balfour, Lady Frances, *Ne Obliviscaris*: Dinna Forget, 2 vols. (London [1930])

Baumann, A.A., *Personalities* (London, 1936)

Bell, G. K. A., *Randall Davidson, Archbishop of Canterbury*, 2 vols. (New York, 1935)

Benson, A. C., *The Life of Edward White Benson, Sometime Archbishop of Canterbury*, 2 vols. (London, 1899–1900)

Bridges, J. A., *Reminiscences of a Country Politician* (London, 1906)

Blunt, W. S., *My Diaries*, foreward by Lady Gregory, 2 vols. (New York, 1922)

Bryce, James, *Studies in Contemporary Biography* (London, 1904)

Buckle, G. E., ed., *The Letters of Queen Victoria*, 2nd series, 1862–1885, vol. 3 (London, 1928) and 3rd series, 1886–1901, 3 vols. (London, 1930–1932)

Buckle, G. E., *The Life of Benjamin Disraeli, Earl of Beaconsfield*,vol. VI (New York, 1920)

Cartwright, Julia, ed., *The Journals of Lady Knightley of Fawsley, 1856–1884* (London, 1916)

Cecil, Lady Gwendolen, *Biographical Studies of the Life and Political Character of Robert Third Marquis of Salisbury* (London, n.d.)

Cecil, Lady Gwendolen, *Life of Robert, Marquis of Salisbury*, 4 vols. (London, 1921–32)

Cecil, Lord Hugh, '*The Life of Gladstone*', *Nineteenth Century and After*, LIX, 349 (March., 1906), 360–370

Cecil, Lord Hugh, 'Lord Rosebery's *Randolph Churchill*', *Dublin Review*, CXL, 280 (January 1907), 139–149

Cecil of Chelwood, Viscount, *All the Way*(London, 1949)

'X' [Lord Robert Cecil], 'Lord Salisbury', *Monthly Review* (October 1903), 1–10

Chamberlain, Austen, *Down the Years* (London, 1935)

Chamberlain, Joseph, *A Political Memoir, 1880–92*, ed. C. H. D. Howard (London, 1953)

Chilston, Viscount, *Chief Whip* (London, 1961)

Chilston, Viscount, *W. H. Smith* (London, 1965)

Churchill, R. S., *Winston S. Churchill*, vol. I and II (London, 1966–7)

Churchill, W. S., *Lord Randolph Churchill*, 2 vols. (London, 1906)

Churchill, W. S., *My Early Life* (London, 1947)

Clarke, Sir Edw., *The Story of My Life* (London, 1918)

Clarke, Sir Ernest, *Charles Henry Gordon-Lennox, Sixth Duke of Richmond and Gordon* (London, 1904)

Cooke, A. B., and A. P. W. Malcolmson, comp., *The Ashbourne Papers, 1869–1913* (Belfast, 1974)

Cooke, A. B. and J. R. Vincent, 'Select Documents: XXVII, Ireland and party politics, 1885–7: an unpublished Conservative memoir', *Irish Historical Studies*, XVI, 62 (September 1968), 154–172; 63 (March 1969), 321–338; 64 (September 1969), 446–471

Cooke, C. W. R., *Four Years in Parliament with Hard Labour* (London, 1890)

Dugdale, B. E. C, *Arthur James Balfour*, 2 vols. (London, 1936)

Dunraven, Earl of, *Past Times and Pastimes*, 2 vols. (London, [1922])

Durnford, Walter, ed., *Memoirs of Colonel the Right Hon. William Kenyon-Slaney, M.P.* (London, 1909)

Elliot, A. R. D.., *The Life of George Joachim Goschen, First Viscount Goschen, 1831–1907*, 2 vols. (London, 1911)

Evelyn, Helen, *The History of the Evelyn Family*, (London, 1915)

Feaver, George, *From Status to Contract*: A biography of Sir Henry Maine, 1822–1888 (London, 1969)

Fitzmaurice, Lord Edmund, *The Life of Granville George Leveson Gower, Second Earl Granville*, 2 vols. (London, 1905)

Fitzroy, Almeric, *Memoirs*, 2 vols. (New York, n.d.)

Flynn, J. S. , *Sir Robert N. Fowler, Bart., M.P.* (London, 1893)

Fox, A. W., *The Earl of Halsbury, Lord High Chancellor (1823–1921)* (London, 1929)

Fraser, Peter, *Joseph Chamberlain*: Radicalism and empire, 1868–1914 (London, 1966)

Gardiner, A. G., *The Life of Sir William Harcourt*, 2 vols. (London, 1923)

Garvin, J. L., *The Life of Joseph Chamberlain*, 3 vols. (London, 1932–4)

Gathorne-Hardy, A. E., *Gathorne Hardy, First Earl of Cranbrook*: A memoir, 2 vols. (London, 1910)

Gooch, G. P., *Life of Lord Courtney* (London, 1920)

Griffith-Boscawen, A. S. T., *Fourteen Years in Parliament* (London, 1907)

Griffith-Boscawen, A. S. T., *Memoirs* (London, 1925)

Gwynn, Stephen and Tuckwell, G. M., *The Life of the Rt. Hon. Sir Charles W. Dilke*, 2 vols. (London, 1917)

Hamilton, Lord George, *Parliamentary Reminiscences and Reflections*, 1868 to 1906, 2 vols. (London, 1917–22)

Hardinge, Arthur, *The Life of Henry Howard Molyneux Herbert, Fourth Earl of Carnarvon, 1831–1890*, 3 vols. (London, 1925)

Hicks-Beach, Lady Victoria, *Life of Sir Michael Hicks-Beach (Earl St. Aldwyn)*, 2 vols. (London, 1932)

Holland, Bernard, *The Life of Spencer Compton Eight Duke of Devonshire*, 2 vols. (London, 1911)

Jeyes, S. H. and F. D. How, *The Life of Sir Howard Vincent* (London, 1912)

Kennedy, A. L., *Salisbury, 1830–1903*: Portrait of a Statesman (London, 1953)

Lang, Andrew, *Life, Letters, and Diaries of Sir Stafford Northcote, First Earl of Iddesleigh*, 2 vols. (London, 1890)

Lecky, Mrs. W. E. H., *A Memoir of the Right Hon. William Edward Hartpole Lecky* (London, 1909)

Lee, Sidney, *King Edward VII*: A Biography, 2 vols. (New York, 1925–7)

Legge, Edw., *King George and the Royal Family*, 2 vols. (London, 1918)

Londonderry, Marchioness of, *Henry Chaplin*: A memoir (London, 1926)

Long of Wraxall, Viscount, *Memoirs* (London, 1923)

Lucas, Reginald, *Colonel Saunderson, M.P.*: A memoir (London, 1908)

Lucas, Reginald, *Lord Glenesk and the 'Morning Post'* (London, 1910)

Lyttelton, Edith, *Alfred Lyttelton*: An account of his life (London, 1917)

McCarthy, Justin, *British Political Leaders* (London, 1903)

MacColl, Malcolm, *Memoirs and Correspondence*, ed. G. W. E. Russell (London, 1914)

Mackail, J. W. and Guy Wyndham, *Life and letters of George Wyndham*, 2 vols. (London, 1925)

Mackay, Thomas, ed., *The Reminiscences of Albert Pell, Sometime M.P. for South Leicestershire* (London, 1908)

Maclean, J. M., *Recollections of Westminster and India* (Manchester, 1902)

Magnus, Philip, *King Edward the Seventh* (London, 1964)

Magnus, Philip, *Kitchener* (New York, 1968)

Malcolm, Ian, *Vacant Thrones* (London, 1931)

Mallet, Bernard, *Thomas George Earl of Northbrook* (London, 1908)

Mallock, W. H., *Memoirs of Life and Literature* (London, 1920)

Majoribanks, Edward, *Carson the Advocate* (New York, 1932)

[Marsh, C.M.], *Brief Memoirs of Hugh McCalmont, First Earl Cairns* (London, 1885)

Maxwell, Herbert, *Evening Memories* (London, 1932)

Maxwell, Herbert, *Life and Times of the Right Honourable William Henry Smith*, 2 vols. (Edinburgh, 1893)

Midleton, Earl of, *Records & Reactions, 1856–1939* (New York, 1939)

Milner, Viscountess, *My Picture Gallery, 1886–1901* (London, 1951)

Morley, John, *The Life of William Ewart Gladstone*, 3 vols. (New York, 1903)

Mowbray, John, *Seventy Years at Westminster*, ed. his daughter (London, 1900)

Naylor, L. E., *The Irresponsible Victorian*: the story of Thomas Gibson Bowles (London, 1965)

Nevill, Lady Dorothy, *The Reminiscences of*, ed. Ralph Nevill (London, 1906)

Newton, John, *W. S. Caine, M.P.* (London, 1907)

Newton, Lord, *Lord Lansdowne* (London, 1929)

Palmer, Roundell, First Earl of Selborne, *Memorials*: Part II: Personal and political, 1865–1895, 2 vols. (London, 1898)

Petrie, C. A., *The Life and Letters of the Right Hon. Sir Austen Chamberlain*, 2 vols. (London, 1939)

Petrie, C. A., *Walter Long and His Times* (London, 1936)

Porter, Rose, *The Life and Letters of Sir John Henniker Heaton Bt.* (London, 1916)

Raikes, H. St. J., *The Life and Letters of Henry Cecil Raikes* (London, 1898)

Ramm, Agatha, ed., *The Political Correspondence of Mr. Gladstone and Lord Granville, 1876–1886*, 2 vols. (Oxford, 1972)

Rentoul, J. A., *Stray Thoughts and Memories* London, 1921)

Rose, Kenneth, *The Later Cecils* (London, 1975)

Rose, Kenneth, *Superior Person*: A portrait of Curzon and his circle in late Victorian England (London, 1969)

Rosebery, Lord, *Lord Randolph Churchill* (London, 1906)

Rosebery, Lord, 'Lord Salisbury', in his *Miscellanies Literary and Historical*, I (London, 1921), 264–74

Ross, John, *The Years of My Pilgrimage* (London, 1924)

Rowse, A. L., *The Later Churchills* (London, 1958)

St. Helier, Lady, *Memoirs of Fifty Years* (London, 1909)

[Sandars, J. S.], 'A Privy Councillor', *Studies of Yesterday* (London, 1928)

Shane Leslie, J. R., et. al., 'Henry Matthews, Lord Llandaff', *Dublin Review*, CLXVIII (1921), 1–22

Spinner, T. J., Jr., *George Joachim Goschen*: The transformation of a Victorian Liberal (Cambridge, 1973)

Stephenson, Lady Gwendolen, *Edward Stuart Talbot, 1844–1934* (London, 1936)

Taylor, A. J. P., 'Lord Salisbury', in *From Napoleon to Stalin*: Comments on European History (London, 1950)

Taylor, Robert, *Lord Salisbury* (New York, 1975)

Temple, Richard, *The Story of My Life*, 2 vols. (London, 1896)

Thornton, P. M., *Some Things We Have Remembered* (London, 1912)

Trevelyan, G. M., *The Life of John Bright* (New York, 1913)

Ullswater, Viscount, *A Speaker's Commentaries*, 2 vols. (London, 1925)

Walker-Smith, Derek and Edw. Clarke, *The Life of Sir Edward Clarke* (London, 1939)

Whibley, Charles, *Lord John Manners and His Friends*, 2 vols. (Edinburgh, 1925)

Wilson, John,*C. B.*: A life of Sir Henry Campbell-Bannerman (New York, 1973)

Wilson-Fox, A., *The Earl of Halsbury* (London, 1926)

Wolff, Henry Drummond, *Rambling Recollections*, 2 vols. (London, 1908)

Wright, Thomas, *The Life of Colonel Fred Burnaby* (London, 1908)

Young, Kenneth, *Arthur James Balfour* (London, 1963)

Zebel, S. H., *Balfour* (Cambridge, 1973)

Zetland, Marquis of,*Lord Cromer* (London, 1932)

## Useful Secondary Works

Allyn, Emily, *Lords versus Commons* (New York, 1931)

Barker, Michael, *Gladstone and Radicalism*: The reconstruction of Liberal policy in Britain, 1885–94 (New York, 1975)

Berrington, Hugh, 'Partisanship and dissidence in the nineteenth-century House of Commons', *Parliamentary Affairs*, XXI, 4 (Autumn 1968), 338–74

Blake, Robert, *The Conservative Party from Peel to Churchill* (London, 1970)

Blewett, Neal, 'The franchise in the United Kingdom, 1885–1918', *Past & Present*, XXXII (Dec. 1965), 27–56

Blewett, Neal, *The Peers, the Parties and the People*: the general elections of 1910 (Toronto, 1972)

Block, G. D. A., *A Source Book of Conservatism* (London, 1964)

Bristow, Edward, 'The Liberty and Property Defence League and Individualism', *Historical Journal*, XVIII, 4 (December 1975), 761–789

Brown, B. H., *The Tariff Reform Movement in Great Britain, 1881–1895* (New York, 1943)

Cecil, Lord David, *The Cecils of Hatfield House*: An English ruling family (Boston, 1973)

Chadwick, M. E. J., 'The role of redistribution in the making of the third Reform Act', *Historical Journal*, XIX, 3 (September 1976), 665–683

Chadwick, Owen, *The Victorian Church*, pt. II (London, 1970)

Chapman, S. D., ed., *The History of Working-Class Housing*: A Symposium (Totowa, N. J., 1971)

Chilston, Viscount, 'Lord Salisbury as party leader (1881–1902)'. *Parliamentary Affairs*, XIII, 3 (Summer 1960), 304–317

Clarke, P. F., 'Electoral sociology of modern Britain' *History*, LVII, 189 (February 1972), 31–55

Clarke, P. F., *Lancashire and the New Liberalism* (Cambridge, 1971)

Clarke, P. F., 'The progressive movement in England', *Transactions of the Royal Historical Society*, 5th ser., XXIV (1974), 159–181

Cohen, Percy, *Disraeli's Child*: A History of the Conservative and Unionist party organization, 2 vols. (typescript in possession of the Conservative Research Department, 1964)

Comfort, G. O., *Professional Politicians: a Study of the British Party Agents* (Washington, 1958)

Cooke, A. B., and J. R. Vincent, *The Governing Passion*: Cabinet government and party politics in Britain, 1885–86 (Brighton, 1974)

Cornford, J. P., 'The adoption of mass organization by the British Conservative party', in Erik Allardt and Yuigo Litturen, ed., *Cleavages, Ideologies and Party Systems*: Contributions to a comparative political sociology, Transactions of the Westermark Society (Helsinki, 1964)

Cornford, J. P., 'The Parliamentary foundations of the Hotel Cecil', in Robert Robson, ed., *Ideas and Institutions of Victorian Britain* (London, 1967), 268–311

Cornford, J. P., 'The transformation of Conservatism in the late nineteenth century', *Victorian Studies*, VII, I (September 1963), 35–66

Cruikshank, Marjorie, *Church and State in English Education, 1870 to the present day* (London, 1963)

Curzon, Lord, *Modern Parliamentary Eloquence* (London, 1913)

Curtis, L. P., Jr., *Coercion and Conciliation in Ireland, 1880–1892*: A study in Conservative Unionism (Princeton, 1963)

Davis, Peter, 'The Liberal Unionist party and the Irish policy of Lord Salisbury's Government, 1886–1892', *Historical Journal*, XVIII, I (March 1975), 85–104

Dunbabin, J. P. D., 'Expectations of the new County Councils, and their realization', *Historical Journal*, VIII, 3 (1965), 353–79

Dunbabin, J. P. D., 'Parliamentary elections in Great Britain, 1868–1900: A pse-phological note', *English Historical Review*, LXXXI. 318 (January 1966), 82–99

Dunbabin, J. P. D., 'The politics of the establishment of County Councils', *Historical Journal*, VI, 2 (1963), 226–252

Ehrman, John, *Cabinet Government and War, 1890–1940* (Cambridge, 1958)

Enstam, M. E. Y., 'The "Khaki" election of 1900 in the United Kingdom', Duke University Ph.D. dissertation, 1967

Fair, J. D., 'Royal mediation in 1884: A reassessment', *English Historical Review*, LXXXVIII, 346 (January 1973), 100–113

Feuchtwanger, E. J., *Disraeli, Democracy and the Tory Party*: Conservative leadership and organization after the second Reform Bill (Oxford, 1968)

Fraser, Peter, 'The Liberal Unionist Alliance: Chamberlain, Hartington, and the Conservatives; 1886–1904', *English Historical Review*, LXXVII, 302 (January 1962), 53–78

Gauldie, Enid, *Cruel Habitations*: A history of working-class housing, 1780–1918 (London, 1974)

Gibbs, N. H., *The Origins of Imperial Defence* (Oxford, 1952)

Greaves, R. L., *Persia and the Defence of India, 1884–1892*: A study in the foreign policy of the third marquis of Salisbury (London, 1959)

Granville, J. A. S., *Lord Salisbury and Foreign Policy* (London, corrected ed., 1970)

Gulley, E. E., *Joseph Chamberlain and English Social Politics*, Studies in History, Economics and Public Law, Columbia University, CXXIII, 1, (New York, 1926)

Halliley, Elton, 'A Short History of the National Society of Conservative and Unionist Agents', *Conservative Agents Journal*, December 1947

Hamer, D. A., *Liberal Politics in the Age of Gladstone and Rosebery* (Oxford, 1972)

Hammond, J. L., *Gladstone and the Irish Nation* (London, 1938)

Hanes, D. G., *The First British Workmen's Compensation Act, 1897* (New Haven, 1968)

Hanham, H. J., 'The creation of the Scottish Office, 1881–87', *Juridical Review*, X n.s., 205–244

Hanham, H. J., *Elections and Party Management*: Politics in the time of Disraeli and Gladstone (London, 1959)

Hanham, H. J., 'Opposition techniques in British politics (1867–1914)', *Government and Opposition*, II, 1 (November 1966), 35–48

Hanham, H. J. 'Political patronage at the Treasury, 1870–1912', *Historical Journal*, III, 1 (1960), 75–84

Hanham, H. J., 'Politics and community life in Victorian and Edwardian Britain', *Folk Life*, 4 (1966), 5–14

Hanham, H. J., *The Reformed Electoral System in Great Britain, 1832–1914*. Historical Association pamphlet G. 69 (London, 1968)

Hanham, H. J., 'The sale of honours in late Victorian England', *Victorian Studies*, III, 3 (March 1960), 277–89

Hardie, Frank, *The Political Influnce of Queen Victoria, 1861–1901* (London: 2nd ed., 1938)

Hayes, W. A., 'The background and passage of the third Reform Act', University of Toronto Ph.D. dissertation, 1972

Herrick, F. H., 'Lord Randolph Churchill and the popular reorganization of the Conservative Party', *Pacific Historical Review*, XV, 2 (June 1946), 178–191

Hindle, W. H., *The Morning Post, 1772–1937* (London, 1937)

Holt, Edgar, *The Boer War* (London, 1958)

Howard, C. H. D., 'The Parnell manifesto of 21 November, 1885, and the schools question', *English Historical Review*, LXII, 242 (January 1947), 42–51

Howard, Christopher, *Splendid Isolation*: A study of ideas concerning Britain's international position and foreign policy during the later years of the third Marquis of Salisbury (London, 1967)

Howarth, Janet, 'The Liberal revival in Northamptonshire, 1880–1895: A case study in late nineteenth century elections', *Historical Journal*, XII, 1 (1969), 78–118

Hurst, M. C., *Joseph Chamberlain and West Midland Politics, 1886–1895*, Dugdale Society Occasional Papers, No. 15 (Oxford, 1962)

Hurst, M. C., 'Joseph Chamberlain, the Conservatives and the succession to John Bright, 1886–9', *Historical Journal*, VII, 1 (1964), 64–93

Iremonger, Lucille, *The Fiery Chariot* (London, 1970)

James, R. Rhodes, *The British Revolution*, vol. I: British Politics, 1880–1914 (London, 1976)

James, R. Rhodes, *Lord Randolph Churchill* (New York, 1960)

James, R. Rhodes, *Rosebery* (New York, 1963)

Johnson, F. A., *Defence by Committee*: The British Committee of Imperial Defence, 1885–1959 (London 1960)

Jones, Andrew, *The Politics of Reform, 1884* (Cambridge , 1972)

Jones, G. A., 'Further Thoughts on the Franchise, 1885–1918', *Past & Present*, XXXIV (July 1966), 134–8

Jones, G. S., *Outcast London*: A study in the relationship between classes in Victorian society (Oxford, 1971)

Kedourie, Elie, 'Tory ideologue: Salisbury as a Conservative intellectual', *Encounter* (June 1972), 45–53

Kellas, J. G., 'The Liberal party in Scotland, 1876–1895', *Scottish Historical Review*, XLIV, 137 (April 1965), 1–16

Kinnear, Michael, *The British Voter*: An atlas and survey since 1885 (Ithaca, 1968)

Kunze, Neil, 'Lord Salisbury's ideas on housing reform, 1883–1885', *Canadian Journal of History*, VIII, 3 (December 1973), 247–66

Laski, H. J., *The British Cabinet, a Study of its Personnel, 1801–1924*, Fabian Tract No. 223 (London, 1928)

Lindsay, J. L., 'The Liberal Unionist party until December 1887', University of Edinburgh Ph.D. dissertation, 1955

Lippincott, B. E., *The Victorian Critics of Democracy*: Carlyle, Ruskin, Arnold, Stephen, Maine, Lecky (Minneapolis, 1938)

Lloyd, Trevor, *The General Election of 1880* (London, 1968)

Lloyd, Trevor, 'Uncontested seats in British general elections, 1852–1910', *Historical Journal*, VIII, 2 (1965), 260–5

Lyons, F. S. L., 'John Dillon the Plan of Campaign, 1886–90', *Irish Historical Studies*, XIV, 56 (September 1956), 313–47

McDowell, R. B., *British Conservatism, 1832–1914* (London, 1959)

McGill, Barry, 'Francis Schnadhorst and Liberal party organization', *Journal of Modern History*, XXXIV, 1 (March 1962), 19–39

Mackenzie, Robert, *British Political Parties* (New York, 2nd ed., 1964)

Mallalieu, W. C., 'Joseph Chamberlain and workmen's compensation', *Journal of Economic History*, X, 1 (May 1950), 45–57

Mallet, Bernard, *British Budgets, 1887–88 to 1912–13* (London, 1913)

Marder, A. J., *The Anatomy of British Sea Power*: A history of British naval power in the pre-Dreadnought era, 1880–1905 (Hamden, Conn., 1964)

Monger, George, *The End of Isolation*: British Foreign Policy, 1900–1907 (London, 1963)

Moody, T. W., '*The Times* versus Parnell and Co., 1887–90', *Historical Studies VI* (London, 1968), 147–175

Nish, I. H., *The Anglo-Japanese Alliance*: The diplomacy of two island empires, 1894–1907 (London, 1966)

O'Brien, C. C., *Parnell and his party, 1880–90* (Oxford, 2nd ed., 1964)

Pelling, Henry, *Popular Politics and Society in Late Victorian Britain* (London, 1968)

Pelling, Henry, *Social Geography of British Elections, 1885–1910* (New York, 1967)

Penson, Lillian, *Foreign Affairs under the Third Marquis of Salisbury* (London, 1962)

Pilling, N., 'The Conservatism of Sir Henry Maine', *Political Studies*, XVIII, 1 (March 1970), 107–120

Pinto-Duschinsky, Michael, *The Political Thought of Lord Salisbury* (London, 1967)

Porter, Andrew, 'Lord Salisbury, Mr. Chamberlain and South Africa, 1895–9', *Journal of Imperial and Commonwealth History*, I, 1 (October 1972), 3–26

Price, Richard, *An Imperial War and the British Working Class*: Working-class attitudes and reactions to the Boer War, 1899–1902 (London, 1972)

Pumphrey, R. E., 'The creation of peerages in England, 1837–1911', Yale University Ph.D dissertation, 1934

Pumphrey, R. E., 'The introduction of industrialists into the British peerage: A study in adaptation of a social institution', *American Historical Review*, LXV, 1 (October 1959), 1–16

Rempel, R. A., *Unionists Divided*: Arthur Balfour, Joseph Chamberlain and the Unionist Free Traders (Newton Abbot, 1972)

Robb, J. H., *The Primrose League, 1883–1906* (New York, 1942)

Robinson, Ronald and John Gallagher, *Africa and the Victorians* (London, 1961)

Roseveare, Henry, *The Treasury*: The evolution of a British Institution (New York, 1969)

Savage, D. C., 'The General Election of 1886 in Great Britain and Ireland', University of London Ph.D. thesis, 1958

Savage, D. C., 'The origins of the Ulster Unionist party, 1885–6', *Irish Historical Studies*, XII, 47 (March 1961), 185–208

Savage, D. C., 'Scottish politics, 1885–6', *Scottish Historical Review*, XL, 130 (October 1961), 118–35

Searle, G. R., *The Quest for National Efficiency* (Oxford, 1971)

Semmel, Bernard, *Imperialism & Social Reform*: English social-imperial thought, 1895–1914 (Garden City, 1968)

Simon, Alan, 'Church disestablishment as a factor in the general election of 1885', *Historical Journal*, XVIII, 4 (December 1975), 791–820

Smith, Paul, *Disraelian Conservatism and Social Reform* (London, 1967)

Smith, Paul, ed., *Lord Salisbury on Politics*: A Selection from his articles in the *Quarterly Review*, 1860–1883 (Cambridge, 1972)

Soldon, N., 'Laissez-faire as dogma: The Liberty and Property Defence League, 1882–1914', in Kenneth D. Brown, ed., *Essays in Anti-Labour History* (Hamden, Conn., 1974), 208–233

Stansky, Peter, *Ambitions and Strategies*: The struggle for the leadership of the Liberal party in the 1890s (Oxford, 1964)

Stephen, J. F., *Liberty, Equality, Fraternity*, 2nd ed., 1874, ed. R. J. White (Cambridge, 1967)

Sutherland, Gillian, *Policy-Making in Elementary Education, 1870–1895* (Oxford, 1973)

Thompson, F. M. L., *English Landed Society in the Nineteenth Century* (London, 1963)

Tuchman, B. W., *The Proud Tower*: A potrait of the world before the war, 1890–1914 (New York, 1967)

Tucker, A. V., 'W. H. Mallock and Late Victorian Conservatism', *University of Toronto Quarterly*, XXXI, 2 (January 1962), 223–41

Urwin, D. K., 'The development of the Conservative party organization in Scotland until 1912', *Scottish Historical Review*, XLIV, 138 (October 1965), 89–111

Weston, C. C., 'The Royal mediation in 1884', *English Historical Review*, LXXXII, 323 (April 1967), 296–322

Wilkinson, W. J., *Tory Democracy*, Studies in History, Economics and Public Law, Columbia University, CXV, 2 (New York, 1925)

Wohl, A. S., ed., *The Bitter Cry of Outcast London*, by Andrew Mearns, with leading articles from the *Pall Mall Gazette* of October 1883 and articles by Lord Salisbury, Joseph Chamberlain and Forster Crozier (New York, 1970)

Wohl, A. S., 'The Bitter Cry of outcast London', *International Review of Social History*, XIII, pt. 2 (1968), 189–245

Wollaston, E. P. M., *The 'Flowing Tide', 1886–92*: A study in 'Political Meteorology' (Gladstone Prize essay. London School of Economics, 1959)

Young, L. K., *British Policy in China, 1895–1902* (Oxford, 1970)

# INDEX